T0373499

The Translator

Acclaimed for her best-selling translations of Cervantes, Gabriel Garcia Márquez, and Mario Vargas Llosa, EDITH GROSSMAN has received many awards, including the PEN/ Ralph Manheim Medal for Translation.

The Editor

ANNA MORE is Professor of Hispanic Literatures and Literary Theory at the University of Brasília, specializing in colonial Latin American literature and critical theory. She is the author of *Baroque Sovereignty: Carlos de Sigüenza y Góngora and the Creole Archive of Colonial Mexico.* She is translator, with Ilan Stavans, of the Norton Critical Edition of Mariano Azuela's *The Underdogs.*

Norton Critical Editions
Renaissance

For a complete list of Norton Critical Editions, visit
wwnorton.com/nortoncriticals

A NORTON CRITICAL EDITION

Sor Juana Inés de la Cruz
SELECTED WORKS

A NEW TRANSLATION
CONTEXTS
CRITICAL TRADITIONS

Translated by
EDITH GROSSMAN

Edited by
ANNA MORE
UNIVERSITY OF BRASÍLIA

W · W · NORTON & COMPANY · *New York* · *London*

W. W. Norton & Company has been independent since its founding in 1923, when William Warder Norton and Mary D. Herter Norton first published lectures delivered at the People's Institute, the adult education division of New York City's Cooper Union. The firm soon expanded its program beyond the Institute, publishing books by celebrated academics from America and abroad. By midcentury, the two major pillars of Norton's publishing program—trade books and college texts—were firmly established. In the 1950s, the Norton family transferred control of the company to its employees, and today—with a staff of four hundred and a comparable number of trade, college, and professional titles published each year—W. W. Norton & Company stands as the largest and oldest publishing house owned wholly by its employees.

Library of Congress Cataloging-in-Publication Data

Names: Juana Inés de la Cruz, Sister, 1651–1695, author. | Grossman, Edith, 1936– translator. | More, Anna Herron, editor.
Title: Selected works : a new translation, contexts, critical traditions / translated by Edith Grossman ; edited by Anna More.
Description: First edition. | New York : W. W. Norton & Company, 2016. | Series: A Norton critical edition | Includes bibliographical references.
Identifiers: LCCN 2015039764 | ISBN 9780393920161 (pbk.)
Classification: LCC PQ7296.J6 A6 2016 | DDC 861/.3—dc23 LC record available at http://lccn.loc.gov/2015039764

W. W. Norton & Company, Inc., 500 Fifth Avenue, New York, NY 10110
        wwnorton.com

W. W. Norton & Company Ltd., Castle House, 75/76 Wells Street, London
WIT 3QT

1 2 3 4 5 6 7 8 9 0

For Clarice and Olivia

Contents

Contexts

Critical Traditions

Introduction

The Mexican poet and nun Sor Juana Inés de la Cruz is one of the most compelling authors of the seventeenth-century Hispanic world: a religious woman who forged a unique path as a writer based largely on her convictions rather than on models or precedents. From her lifetime until the present, readers, historians, and literary critics have been fascinated by her strident resistance to attempts to limit her studies and her writing. Her works are superb examples of courtly conventions that reveal glimpses of their author as she plays with or even openly flouts these generic expectations. At their best, Sor Juana's writings translate the challenges of her life into stunning poetic concepts and philosophical language.

Nonetheless, there are still many mysteries about her life, which contained both early affronts to the religious hierarchy over her right to study and write and, at the end of her life, acts of contrition and acceptance of the limitations placed on religious women during the period. Without a clear road map for understanding her writings, readers must stake out a middle ground between cautious skepticism and interpretive hubris, remaining aware of historical lacunae while attentive to the subtle ways in which Sor Juana's writings surpassed her historical context. The following wide selection of her works in a new translation by Edith Grossman, accompanied by a variety of contextualizing documents, intends to provide the key elements necessary to appreciate the innovation of Sor Juana's verse and prose in light of her historical context and reception in the present.

Early Life

Sor Juana Inés de la Cruz was born Juana Ramírez de Asbaje, most likely in 1648, in the small town of San Miguel Nepantla at the outskirts of Mexico City, capital of the viceroyalty of New Spain.[1] A precocious child, she reputedly learned to read and write by age

---

1. While Sor Juana's first biographer gave a birthdate of 1651, most scholars now believe that she was born in 1648 following an entry in a baptismal record for the jurisdiction of Nepantla, which reads "Inés, daughter of the Church" and cites Sor Juana's uncle and aunt as godparents. "Of the Church" was a phrase referring to an illegitimate birth

three and was versed in Latin by age nine. Juana's relatives in Mexico City were able to introduce her into the viceregal court, where, at the age of sixteen, she became a lady-in-waiting. It was there that her prodigious talents were discovered by a wider public and cultivated by admiring patrons. She became particularly close to several viceroys and their vicereines who sponsored much of Sor Juana's theater and poetry. At age nineteen, she entered a cloistered convent of the Discalced Carmelites, but, finding its rigid discipline disagreeable, soon left. She chose instead the more relaxed convent of Saint Jerome, becoming a Hieronymite novice in 1669. She herself declared that the decision was made by a combination of faith and pragmatics, both out of repugnance at marriage and a desire to pursue her studies.[2] Inside the convent she amassed an impressive library, collected scientific instruments, and continued to write poetry and plays on secular subjects. She also wrote on religious topics and published *villancicos* (carols) for the Metropolitan Church of Mexico City.

The success of these carols garnered the admiration of the council of the Metropolitan Church, which in 1680 selected Sor Juana to design one of the two triumphal arches that would be erected along the festive route to receive the incoming viceroy, the Marquis of Laguna, an honor doubly significant given her youth and gender. Following this public event, Sor Juana's fame grew. In 1682 she participated under a pseudonym in the poetic competition at the Royal University of Mexico, winning two prizes for her poems. Sometime during this period she also engaged in the first documented affront to the church patriarchy by writing a letter to her then confessor, the Jesuit Antonio Núñez de Miranda. In this, she complained about his attempts to rein in her studies, claiming, among other things, that he had called her behavior a "public scandal." She ended the letter apparently by dismissing him as her confessor.[3]

If Sor Juana was able to confront the Church hierarchy so directly it was because, in a world structured around patrimonial relations, she counted on the protection of the highest members of the New Spanish elite. As time went on, her work gained more prominence and became the further target of both praise and attack. Upon returning to Spain, the Countess of Paredes, a vicereine who had become a close friend and supporter of Sor Juana, was instrumental

and Juana's mother's testament confirms that she was conceived out of wedlock. Octavio Paz, *Sor Juana: Her Life and Her World*, trans. Margaret Sayers Peden (London: Faber & Faber, 1988), 65. For a contrasting position, that defends 1651 as the correct birth date, see Georgina Sabat de Rivers, "Introducción biográfica y crítica," in *Inundación castálida* (Madrid: Castalia, 1982). The viceroyalty of New Spain covered the entire territory of what is now Mexico, as well as the Philippines and parts of Central America.
2. See "Response" on p. 97.
3. See "Letter by Mother Juana Inés de la Cruz" on p. 152.

in publishing the first anthology of her works, *Inundación castálida* (Castalian inundation) (1689).[4] Another compendium was published during her lifetime, *Segundo volumen* (Second volume) (1692), and a last was published soon after her death, *Fama y obras posthumas* (Fame and posthumous works) (1700).[5] The villancicos, the mystery play *The Divine Narcissus,* and her famous critique of the Maundy Thursday sermon by António Vieira were among the few of her works published in Mexico during her lifetime. Her fame was transatlantic and transhemispheric: as her works circulated in print she received letters and accolades from throughout the Hispanic world. The title pages and encomia in her publications praised her as an exception to her sex, the "Tenth Muse" and the "Mexican Phoenix."[6]

Verse

The dearth of historical documents about Sor Juana's life stands in contrast to the range and extent of her writings, which included poetry in a variety of meters, secular and religious plays, and prose works. Sor Juana showed particular talent for verse. A reflection of courtly culture, poetry served as examples of wit, philosophical reflection, and political alliance. Much of what Sor Juana wrote may be categorized under occasional poetry, playful or laudatory verse written at the behest of courtly patrons who continued to solicit works even after Sor Juana entered the convent. Even in highly conventional poems, however, Sor Juana displays the witty ingenuity for which she was known.

In all her writings, Sor Juana is heir to the Spanish literature that flourished in the sixteenth and seventeenth centuries. One finds in her verse resonances of the great poets of this period: Garcilaso de la Vega, San Juan de la Cruz, Luis de Góngora, Lope de Vega, and Francisco de Quevedo. Her plays are at times explicitly modeled on the masterful works of Pedro Calderón de la Barca. She also knew, whether firsthand or through the numerous compendia of her period, works of the Greek and Roman classics. She was inspired by emblem literature,[7] by theological works, and by the Bible

---

4. The title refers to the Castalian springs, located near the Greek oracle of Delphi and said to be the source of inspiration for poets.
5. In the absence of manuscripts, these are the main sources for Sor Juana's work; all of them went through several editions, with revisions or slight differences among them.
6. That is, an extraordinary person. "Tenth Muse": adds Sor Juana to the nine classical muses. The first term was used on the title page to the *Second Volume* (1692) and the second appeared on the title page of *Fame and Posthumous Works* (1700), but both also appeared in others' writings in praise of Sor Juana.
7. A popular genre in the early modern period, emblems were complex visual icons, usually depicting themes drawn from classical myths and accompanied by adages. Taken together, the visual and linguistic enigmas formed keys to a moral lesson.

and patristic writings. She was interested in natural philosophy and scholastic logic. Following the precept of imitation that still held sway in her period, Sor Juana's works sought innovation within a tradition rather than originality: with the great exception of "First Dream," Sor Juana's works looked backward rather than forward.

Sor Juana's innovation within the constraints of convention reflects the ambition and eclecticism of an autodidact who treated Western knowledge as a toolbox for experimentation. One prominent example is the voice of her lyric. Her poems were often penned to women, especially to the two vicereines with whom she had close relations: Leonor Carreto, Marquisa de Mancera, and María Luisa de Gonzaga, the Countess of Paredes. There is no way to know definitively, although there is much speculation, whether her verse indicates amorous relations with María Luisa. Critics have often noted that Sor Juana's poems to María Luisa, whom she calls Lisi in her verse, push the limits of courtly love.[8] The poems written at the death of Leonor Carreto are some of the most painfully heartfelt in Sor Juana's corpus and evidence of a passionate and intimate friendship between the two women. In other poems, Sor Juana plays with the convention of male desire for a female subject, employing a female voice and a male object of desire, or a neuter voice with a female object of desire.[9]

Of all her verse, however, "First Dream" (ca. 1691) stands out for its originality and ambition. Sor Juana herself acknowledged the importance of "First Dream" when in her "Response of the Poet" she singles it out: "I do not recall having written for my own pleasure except for a trifle they call *The Dream*." Recounting the journey of the soul in search of absolute knowledge during the sleep of the body, the 975-verse poem weaves mythology, Neoplatonism, and scholasticism through its narrative.[1] The ultimate decision as to whether the poem is a critique or celebration of human knowledge depends in great part on the interpretation of its final verses: "the world illuminated with more / certain light, and I, awake." Whereas for some, Sor Juana's poem ends disillusioned with the possibility of human access to divine knowledge, for others the poem asserts a secular impulse that breaks with the pessimistic failures represented during the dream.[2] These lines also provide the only indication of the gender of the speaker in the feminine adjective for awake

8. See Bergmann on pp. 282–83.
9. See Sabat de Rivers on p. 265.
1. Although originally 975 verses, the English translation by Edith Grossman used in this edition is a more efficient 815.
2. Alejandro Soriano Vallès and Octavio Paz, respectively, represent some of the clearest positions on either end of this spectrum.

(*despierta*), a fact that has fueled numerous feminist readings of the poem. The poem is a cipher for Sor Juana's erudition, and as it continues to prompt critical studies, its depths will surely be further sounded.

Controversies

The most decisive event in Sor Juana's life, and the one for which she is best remembered, occurred just as her fame was at its zenith. In 1690, separated by a grille from the receiving hall of her convent where an audience was gathered to hear her, Sor Juana pronounced an oral critique of a sermon by the great Portuguese Jesuit António Vieira (1609–1697). A member of the public requested the critique in writing, and soon afterward it appeared in print with the title *Carta atenagórica* (Athenagoric letter).[3] The Bishop Manuel Fernández de Santa Cruz, who was responsible for the publication, also wrote a prologue in which, under the pseudonym of Sor Filotea, he admonished Sor Juana to turn her studies and writings to sacred rather than secular subjects.[4]

The bishop's prologue prompted one of the most important pieces of writing in Hispanic literature, known now by the title under which it was printed in the posthumous publication of Sor Juana's works, "Response of the Poet to the Very Eminent Sor Filotea de la Cruz." In a stunning march of rhetorical pirouettes, patristic and biblical citations, and argumentative wit Sor Juana defended herself against the bishop's accusation that her writing challenged the ideal "state of obedience" for women religious. Her argument revolves around four main positions: first, that she is compelled to write and study by a divine impulse; second, that theology can be approached only by those already learned in secular subjects; third, that examples in Church and secular history confirm the historical acceptance of women who study and write; and fourth, that the minds of women and men have a common origin in the divine and thus, implicitly, share a right to study, critique, and write.

While notable, it is not entirely surprising that the "Response" would be written at the end of the seventeenth century in Mexico City. A colonial city literally built on top of the Mexica capital Tenochtitlan, by the mid-sixteenth century Mexico City already claimed a university, printing presses, and a book trade. At the end of the seventeenth century its geographically peripheral position

---

3. Although the title has often been translated "Letter Worthy of Athena," it more likely refers to Athenagoras, the author of an *Apologia* (177 C.E.) defending Christianity against pagan accusations.
4. See "A Letter from Sor Filotea" on p. 86.

allowed for substantial innovation within the generally repressive culture of Counter-Reformation Spain. Sor Juana's voracious appetite for learning, her eclectic and perhaps even heterodox influences, and her prodigious wit were allowed to develop within this setting. What has been harder to explain is the stark contrast of the final years of her life. Beginning in 1693 and until her death in 1695, Sor Juana signed a number of declarations renouncing her studies and renewing the vows she took upon entering the convent.[5] In 1695 she died in her convent, victim of an epidemic that was sweeping the city.

It has been impossible to give a definitive reading of what are generally termed the "final years" of Sor Juana's life. What prompted the sudden renunciation of her studies and writings after she had confronted the Church hierarchy in writing several times to defend herself? Was it the result of an interior battle or a more forced and violent decision? Scholars have been polarized between these two possible narratives. At stake are contrasting interpretations of Sor Juana: either as an embattled precursor of women's rights or as an example of the complex decisions wrought by the gulf between faith and secularism.[6] It is, of course, quite possible that Sor Juana had both motives. Without further documents, however, all narratives must be treated as speculative.

Historical Reception

Sor Juana was widely celebrated both in her lifetime and directly after her death, during which time her works were republished in several editions. By the mid-eighteenth century the shift in Hispanic letters to a neoclassical style and new philosophical forms of argument meant that her verse was increasingly disregarded, although she continued to attract attention as a historical figure. Sor Juana was brought back into scholarly view in the late nineteenth century, in philologically inspired literary histories, and received even more attention following the revival of Baroque style in the twentieth century. Increasingly, Mexican scholarship undertook philological projects of her works and proclaimed Sor Juana a national treasure, while a handful of international Hispanists from the United States, France, and Italy provided new historical documentation and theoretical approaches.

---

5. See "Petition and Documents" on p. 153.
6. Despite many criticisms of Octavio Paz, most feminist readings follow his narrative of an embattled and solitary Sor Juana. An example of the second interpretation may be found in the recent work of Alejandro Soriano Vallès, who in turn follows the lead of Alfonso Méndez Plancarte, responsible for the standard edition of Sor Juana's writings.

The Mexican poet and scholar Octavio Paz's monumental 1982 biography and study of Sor Juana's works was a watershed publication that brought much of the previous scholarship to an international audience. In the wake of this publication and its translation into English, studies of Sor Juana proliferated. Paz was particularly responsible for promoting the historical narrative of Sor Juana's struggles with the ecclesiastical patriarchy that has led to numerous artistic representations of her as a lone and prescient figure in a repressive era. While many Mexican authors draw subtle inspiration from Sor Juana's works, much of the artistic reworking of her figure has been visual and performative. In works such as the Argentine filmmaker María Luisa Bemberg's[7] cinematic interpretation of Sor Juana's works and life or the provocative installations by the Chicana activist and artist Amalia Mesa-Bains,[8] Sor Juana takes on an iconographic status as a feminist precursor. Often, these works have made use of the striking posthumous portraits of Sor Juana[9] in which she is depicted in her library, standing or writing. Aside from regular performances of Sor Juana's plays in Mexico, the latest artistic interpretations of Sor Juana's life and works have also included an opera, two novels, and a theatrical recitation of "First Dream" by the Mexican performance artist Jesusa Rodríguez.[1]

Throughout the reception of Sor Juana's works, beginning even in her lifetime, it has been impossible to separate her figure from her writing. Sor Juana herself made her fame a theme for reflection in verse and her "Response." As she writes in a poem discovered after her death:

> as though a stranger to myself,
> among your quills I wander,
> not as I am, but as you see
> and what you wished to imagine.[2]

Despite the fact that false modesty was a well-worn trope, her humility and her consternation over her embattled reputation seem genuine. Verse and theater appeared for Sor Juana to be media for thought, debate, and critical intervention at a time when autonomy was not an option. Indeed, the force of Sor Juana's writings appears to rest on the fundamental paradox that permeates her work: in a period defined by constraint, she created forms of freedom, most especially

---

7. See Bergmann on p. 281.
8. See Villaseñor Black on p. 297.
9. See Villaseñor Black on pp. 213 and 297.
1. The Dallas-Forth Worth opera performed Daniel Crozier's and Peter M. Krask's *With Blood, with Ink* (2014), an opera based on Sor Juana's life. The novels are Alicia Gaspar de Alba's *Second Dream* (1999) and Paul Anderson's *Hunger's Brides* (2004). On Jesusa Rodríguez's performance, see "'First Dream' Performed" on p. 304.
2. Ballad 51 on p. 156.

through art. The attraction for most readers has been to understand these forms of freedom as critique, whether or not they are understood as ultimately supporting or breaking away from the real institutional, rhetorical, and sexual norms of her time. It is this freedom within a context of constraint that provides the most compelling link between Sor Juana's time and ours.

A Note on Translations
and Editions

This Norton Critical Edition is based on a new translation by Edith
Grossman of selected works by Sor Juana Inés de la Cruz. In trans-
lating Sor Juana's works, the challenge is to reveal her voice amid
the poetic conventions of her period. Grossman has firmly decided
in favor of poetic voice and readability. She does not attempt to
reproduce the more archaic aspects of Sor Juana's language or
syntax; in translating verse she stays true to meter but does not
imitate the original rhyme. Avoiding the more convoluted elements
of seventeenth-century verse permits a stronger emphasis on the
poetic images, conceits, and well-wrought turns of phrase that mark
the originality of Sor Juana's writing. Grossman and I were in con-
tact as she translated, and she graciously accepted suggestions that
maintained the translation as close as possible to the original. The
result is a luminous version of Sor Juana that reflects both the tight
precision of her works and the unusually strident voice that marked
all of her writings, from the most generic commissioned pieces to
the most strikingly personal.

None of the manuscripts of Sor Juana's works has survived and
thus all modern editions are based on seventeenth- and early-
eighteenth-century printed editions. It is impossible to know to what
extent the editors of these various publications amended Sor Juana's
originals. It is probable that the subtitles to her poems, for instance,
are not her own, but without concrete indications, most modern
editions do include these. The standard modern edition of Sor Juana's
works are the four volumes edited by Alfonso Méndez Plancarte and
published in 1951–57 by Fondo de Cultura Económica. Méndez
Plancarte established an order for the poems based on their meter
and made several editorial decisions to correct what he viewed
were typographical or other errors in the *princeps* publications.
Several recent editions, including the second edition of Méndez
Plancarte's first volume as edited by Antonio Alatorre, dispute
many of these corrections. This Norton translation reflects these

editorial amendments and thus the reader may note divergences with previous translations that followed Méndez Plancarte.

To facilitate the cross-referencing of other editions, this edition has followed the standard ordering of the poems, as established by Méndez Plancarte, including the numbers he assigned them. In annotating, I have also consulted several other editions of specific works of Sor Juana, including Amanda Powell and Electa Arenal's edition of the "Response"; Vincent Martin and Electa Arenal's edition of *Allegorical Neptune*; Nina Scott's translation of "The Letter to Father Antonio Núñez"; and Jeremy Lawrance's unpublished editions and translations of the "Letter from Sor Filotea" and the "Response." I thank Lawrance for his generosity in providing me with his superb edition.

In the "Selected Works" section, notes are by the translator unless otherwise indicated. Unless noted otherwise, all biblical citations in "Selected Works" are to the Douay–Rheims Bible (based on the Vulgate and published in 1582); all in "Contexts" and "Critical Traditions" are to the King James Version (published 1611).

Acknowledgments

Carol Bemis invited me to edit this Norton Critical Edition, and her wisdom has accompanied it from start to finish. It was a joy to work with her. I am also indebted to Edith Grossman, who has given us such a captivating new translation of the verse and prose of Sor Juana. It was thrilling to discuss the translations as she completed them, and I am grateful to her for considering all the scholarly details that came up along the way. Isabel Gómez translated all the critical materials from Spanish, including a number of very challenging additional works by Sor Juana. Her talents as a translator are manifest, but her contributions went well beyond that to include substantial commentary, advice, revision, and notes. She is a brilliant scholar and a generous collaborator.

My deepest thanks go to those from whom I have learned so much about the work and life of Sor Juana: Emilie Bergmann, Margo Glantz, Yolanda Martínez-San Miguel, Marie-Cécile Bénassy-Berling, Christopher Johnson and Stephanie Kirk. A special thanks goes to Charlene Villaseñor Black, who contributed two pieces and numerous images to this edition. At Norton, Rivka Genesen, Thea Goodrich, and Rachel Goodman also assisted in a great many ways.

As always, my family has served as my ideal audience. My parents, John and Livezey More, read and commented on sections of the manuscript and Bene, Clarice, and Olivia constantly remind me of all the reasons for bringing the seventeenth century into the twenty-first. I hope that this edition contributes to their and others' appreciation for a woman whose unique perspective on her period still challenges us in ours.

Selected Works of
SOR JUANA INÉS DE LA CRUZ

Ballads[1]

Ballad 1[†]

Prologue to the reader from the author, who composed and sent it with the same haste used for those already copied, obeying the supreme command of her extraordinary patron, Her Excellency the Countess of Paredes,[2] that they be made public: this Sor Juana had denied her verses which, like the poet herself, were in the safekeeping of the countess, for the poet barely had a single draft in her possession

These verses, my dearest reader,
dedicated to your delight,
have but one virtue in them:
I know how imperfect they are,

5   I do not wish to discuss them
or even commend them to you,
for that would mean wishing to pay
them attention unmerited.

I do not seek your gratitude
10   for, if truth be told, you should not
esteem something I never deemed
worthy of being in your hands.

I grant and cede you liberty
if you should wish to censure them;
15   after all, to conclude, you are
free, and I have concluded too.

---

1. Ballads, called *romances* in Spanish, are composed of an indefinite number of stanzas of generally octosyllabic lines, the odd lines unrhymed, the even lines using assonant rhyme.
† First published in the revised edition of the first volume of Sor Juana's poems: *Poemas de la única poetisa americana* (Poems of the singular American poetess) (Madrid, 1690) [*Editor*].
2. María Luisa, Countess of Paredes, was the wife of Tomás de la Cerda, third Marquis de la Laguna, Viceroy of New Spain from 1680 to 1686.

Nothing enjoys greater freedom
than the human understanding;
if God does not violate mind
20   then why would I even try?

Say all that you wish about them,
for the more merciless you are
in finding fault, the greater your
obligation will be to me,

25   for then you will owe to my Muse
that most flavorsome of dishes[3]
—speaking ill of another—as
an old adage of the court says.

I am always at your service,
30   whether I please you or do not:
if I please you, you are amused;
if not, you can speak ill of me.

I could easily say to you
as an excuse, that I did not
35   have the time to revise them,
they were copied so rapidly;

they are written by diverse hands,
and some, being the hands of boys,
kill the sense in such a way that
40   the word is no more than a corpse;

when I have written them myself,
it has been in the brief space
of leisure that can be bought from
the exigencies of my state;

45   for my health is poor and I am
so often interrupted that
even as I say this my pen
races along at breakneck speed.

But none of this is to the point,
50   for you will think I am boasting

3. The metaphor plays on the idea of finding fault, in the previous stanza, which is to "bite" in Spanish.

that perhaps they might have been good
if I had composed them slowly;

I do not wish you to think that,
no, but only that I brought them
55 to light in order to comply,
to obey another's command.

True, believe it or not, this is
not a question of life or death
to me, and to conclude, you will
60 do whatever occurs to you.

And farewell, for this merely shows
you a small sample of the cloth:
but if the piece does not please you,
then do not unroll the whole bolt.

Ballad 2[†]

*She acknowledges the excesses of a good deal of erudition, which
she fears is useless even to learning and injurious to living*

Let us pretend I am happy,
melancholy Thought, for a while;
perhaps you can persuade me, though
I know the contrary is true:

5   for since on mere apprehension
they say all suffering depends,
if you imagine good fortune
you will not be so downcast.

Let my understanding at times
10 allow me to rest a while,
and let my wits not always be
opposed to my own advantage.

All people have opinions and
judgments so multitudinous,
15 that when one states this is black,
the other proves it is white.

† First published in *Castalian Inundation* (1689) [*Editor*].

Some find attractive precisely
what others deem an annoyance;
an alleviation for one
20 is bothersome for another.

One who is sad criticizes
the happy man as frivolous;
and one who is happy derides
the sad man and his suffering.

25 The two philosophers of Greece[1]
offered perfect proofs of this truth:
for what caused laughter in one man
occasioned tears in the other.

The contradiction has been famed
30 for centuries beyond number,
yet which of the two was correct
has so far not been determined;

instead, into their two factions
all people have been recruited,
35 temperament dictating which
band each person will adhere to.

One says that the inconstant world
is worthy only of laughter;
another, that its misfortunes
40 are only to be lamented.

A proof is found for everything,
a reason on which to base it;
and nothing has a good reason
since there is reason for so much.

45 All people are equal judges;
being both equal and varied,
there is no one who can decide
which argument is true and right.

Since no one can adjudicate,
50 why do you think, mistakenly,

---

1. Heraclitus of Ephesus (ca. 540–ca. 480 b.c.e.) and Democritus of Abdera (ca. 460–370 b.c.e.), pre-Socratic philosophers who claimed that life was a cause, respectively, for weeping or for laughter.

that God entrusted you alone
with the decision in this case?

Oh why, inhuman and severe,
and acting against yourself, in
55   the choice between bitter and sweet
do you wish to choose the bitter?

If my understanding is my
own, why must I always find it
so slow and dull about relief,
60   so sharp and keen about distress?

discursive reason is a sword
quite effective at both ends:
with the point of the blade it kills;
the pommel on the hilt protects.

65   If you, aware of the danger,
wish to wield the point of the sword,
how can the steel blade be to blame
for the evil acts of your hand?

Knowing how to create subtle,
70   specious reasons is not knowledge;
true knowledge consists only in
choosing salutary virtue.

Scrutinizing all misfortunes
and examining bad omens
75   achieves nothing but the growth of
the bad through anticipation.

In future deliberations
our attention, grown more subtle,
will imagine threatened attacks
80   as more alarming than the risks.

How blithesome is the ignorance
of one who, unlearned but wise,
deems his affliction, his nescience
all he does not know, as sacred!

85   The most daring flights of genius
do not always soar assured when

they seek a throne in the fire
and find a grave in copious tears.[2]

For knowledge is also a vice:
90   if it is not constantly curbed,
and if this is not acknowledged,
the greater the havoc it wreaks;

and if the flight is not brought down,
fed and fattened on subtleties
95   it will forget the essential
for the sake of the rare and strange.

If a skilled hand does not prevent
the growth of a thickly leafed tree,
its proliferating branches
100   will steal the substance of the fruit.

If the bulk of ballast does not
impede the speed of a swift ship,
that flight creates the headlong fall
from a most precipitous height.

105   It is futile amenity:
what does the flowering field care
if Autumn finds no fruit as long
as May can display its blossoms?

What benefit to intellect
110   to gestate so many offspring,
if that multitude is followed
by ill-fated miscarriages?

And perforce this great misfortune
must be followed by mischance:
115   the one who gestates will be left
if not dead, then gravely injured.

Our intellect is like fire:
deeply ungrateful to matter,
flame consumes more matter the
120   brighter the fire appears.

2. An allusion to Phaethon. The son of Helios, the sun god, Phaethon drove his father's
chariot through the air, losing control of the horses and plunging to his death. On
Phaethon in Sor Juana's verse see Paz on p. 255 [*revised by Editor*].

So rebellious a vassal to
its own legitimate Lord,
that fire transforms the weapons of
its defense into offenses.

125   This appalling, daunting practice,
this harsh and onerous toil
God gave to the children of men
for the sake of their discipline.

What mad ambition carries us,
130   having forgotten who we are?
If we live for so short a time,
why do we wish to know so much?

Oh, if there were only a school
or seminary where they taught
135   classes in how not to know
as they teach classes in knowing.

How happily the man would live
who with languid circumspection
would simply laugh at the menace
140   of the influence of the stars!

Let us learn about not knowing,
O Thought, for we then discover
that for all I add to discourse
I usurp as much from my years.

Ballad 24[†]

*The Vicereine having already baptized her child,[1] the poet offers
congratulations on his birth*

I have not wanted, dear Lysi,[2]
to send my felicitations

---

† First published in *Castalian Inundation* (1689) [*Editor*].

1. José María Francisco Omnium Sanctorum, born July 5 and baptized on July 14, 1683. The vicereine of New Spain (1680–86) was María Luisa Manrique de Lara y Gónzaga (1649–1725), the Countess of Paredes [*Editor*].

2. Pseudonym in Sor Juana's poetry for her friend and patronness, the Countess of Paredes [*Editor*].

for the child God has given you
until you returned him to God:[3]

5   in your religion, señora,
though your beauty engenders him,
you would not want to call him yours
if he does not belong to God.

It speaks well of your piety
10   that you wish to call your son,
His Excellency, *child of the
Church*,[4] although born legitimate;

and having been born in the light,
until there dawns above him
15   the light of Grace, you do not prize
unduly the light of Nature.[5]

In grace you enjoy him, aeons
of such great Christian purity
that Grace received increases
20   and Grace acquired is not lost.

You see, in his behavior, the
piety and greatness, as did
Olympias in Alexander,[6]
and Helena in Constantine.[7]

25   Entwine in heroic mingling
of arms and letters,[8] the laurels
of warlike Mars[9] with the olives
of the learned Minerva.[1]

May he be the glory of his
30   land,[2] the envy of all others;

3. That is, until the child was baptized and therefore "returned" to God.
4. Offspring born out of wedlock were called "children of the Church."
5. A reference to baptism, which brings the "light of Grace" to redeem "Nature," or original sin.
6. Alexander the Great, the Greek king who conquered North Africa and Asia. Olympias (ca. 375–316 B.C.E.) was his mother [*Editor*].
7. Roman Emperor Constantine the Great. Saint Helena (ca. 250–ca. 330 C.E.) was his mother [*Editor*].
8. The two ideal attributes of a Renaissance courtesan, signifying military and poetic abilities [*Editor*].
9. In Roman mythology, the god of war [*Editor*].
1. In Roman mythology, the goddess of wisdom [*Editor*].
2. Having been born in Mexico, the child José María is American [*Editor*].

and America, with his gifts,
will vanquish those of all others.

May he bring his high lineage
in a propitious moment to
35 the Occident; Europe closely
mingles so many royal bloodlines.

Let a proud America raise
high the head that wears a crown,[3]
and let the Mexican Eagle
40 spread its great imperial wings,[4]

for now in its royal palace
where all the grandeur of pagan
Moctezumas[5] lies, Catholic
Cerda[6] scions are being born.

45 Let this generous Cupid blossom,
and grow in valor and beauty;
he is born of Mars and Venus,[7]
may he favor Mars and Venus.

May Bellona[8] give him weapons,
50 and Eros[9] offer his arrows,
Alcides[1] turn over his club,
Apollo[2] offer his knowledge.

Let this new Alexander[3] grow,
this pious Aeneas[4] live long,
55 this greater Pompilius[5] endure,
this heroic Maecenas[6] excel.

---

3. A reference to José María's nobility [Editor].
4. A reference to the foundation myth of the Mexicas in which an eagle devouring a snake while poised on a nopal cactus would signal the place where they should build their city, Tenochtitlan [Editor].
5. Moctezuma II (1466–1520), the Mexica tlatoani, or leader, who ruled the Mexica empire at the beginning of the Spanish conquest of Tenochtitlan [Editor].
6. The viceroy of New Spain from 1680 to 1686, and the father of the child celebrated in this poem, was Tomás de la Cerda, third Marquis de la Laguna.
7. Roman goddess of love [Editor].
8. Roman goddess of war [Editor].
9. Greek god of love [Editor].
1. Another name for Hercules [Editor].
2. Greek god of music, art, and poetry [Editor].
3. Alexander the Great [Editor].
4. Trojan hero and legendary founder of Rome [Editor].
5. Numa Pompilius (753–673 B.C.E.), second king of Rome [Editor].
6. Gaius Cilnius Maecenas (68–8 B.C.E.), adviser to the Roman emperor Caesar Augustus [Editor].

His birth in the month of July
was not by chance: necessity
ruled that, being so great a Prince,
60   he be born a Julius Caesar.[7]

Now I imagine I see him
in the years of early childhood,
learning to read in the primer
until he resembles Cato,[8]

65   and since that age was deemed by the
Romans as full grown and mature,
they traded medals and pretext[9]
for the toga[1] of true manhood.

Here his valor and eloquence
70   will surely be seen in him,
the Campaigns that will astonish,
the Schools in which he will excel;

here the world will surely see in
his right hand a confusion of
75   the flourishes of a pen and
the violent strokes of a sword;[2]

here the contrary professions
will surely call and summon him,
Peace on account of his prudence,
80   War on account of his valor;

here the better Julius in
erudition and prudence will
surely be his own chronicler
and write of his deeds and prowess;[3]

---

7. The wordplay in Spanish is based on *Julio* being the word for both July and Julius.
8. Another example of wordplay: a reading primer is a *catón*, which is also the Spanish word for Cato.
9. Medals were worn by children in Rome to protect them from spells.
1. The *praetexta* was the garb of boys, while the toga was worn by men.
2. A reference to the courtly values of arms and letters [*Editor*].
3. The reference here is to Julius Caesar's *Gallic Wars*, in which the author was also the protagonist.

85 here there will surely be seen
a new, unheard-of miracle:
the addition of more to more
is what the Mexican grows on.

Here if I live long enough,
90 even if I walk with crutches,
my Muse surely intends to add
quill pens and language to his Fame.

And here I cease writing to you,
and let this long argument end
95 with the Boy living eternities
and you being there to see it.

Ballad 44[†]

*To the same most excellent lady,[1] sending her an embroidered
shoe, in the Mexican style, and a gift of chocolate*

Throwing down a glove, señora,
is a signal of defiance;
so that throwing down a shoe
must be a sign of submission.

5 The wish to take another's hand
indicates a certain boldness;
but humbling oneself at her feet
demonstrates one's submission.

Yet it is true that in your feet
10 this principle is proven false,
for they increase in their substance
and decrease in the sound they make.

Rising to the soles of your feet
is so haughty an intention,
15 that on high one does not possess
knowledge of the danger involved.

---

† First published in *Second Volume* (1692) [*Editor*].
1. The Countess of Galve was the vicereine and wife of the Count of Galve, viceroy of New
Spain (1688–96) [*Editor*].

      Not the one who recklessly dared
      to circle round the whirling blue,[2]
      nor one who tried to defy the
20   burning orb with feathers and wax,[3]

      could give the warning learned from their
      experience of the downfall;
      for a lesser plunge cannot serve
      as a precautionary tale.

25   But I fly too high, and to where?
      It seems now that I follow them,
      for the path, twisting and turning,
      takes me so far from my intent.

      I mean, señora, that the day
30   of that most holy of Bishops[4]
      when miracles were no such thing
      because they arose constantly,

      is celebrated with liquor
      and this gift, while not very blessed,[5]
35   in a show of its origin,
      carries the message: *pulvis es*,[6]

      and sends you a true affection,
      and seeing you are a wonder
      of beauty, presumes that by a
40   miracle the Saint fashioned you.

      This gift, being insufficient,
      bears a likeness to its owner;
      for an ancient proverb blesses
      the one who resembles her own.[7]

2. A reference to Phaethon, son of Helios, god of the sun, who attempted to drive the sun's chariot across the sky and came so close to Earth that the planet almost caught fire. Zeus killed him with a thunderbolt. For Phaethon's importance in Sor Juana's verse see Paz on p. 255 [*revised by Editor*].

3. A reference to Icarus, son of Daedalus, whose father made him a pair of wings. Ignoring instructions, Icarus flew too close to the sun; the wax holding the feathers together melted, and he fell into the sea. Like Phaethon, Icarus was also a figure in "First Dream." See p. 55 [*revised by Editor*].

4. The bishop has been tentatively identified as either Saint Gregory of Nazianzus (329–389 C.E.) or Saint Nicholas of Bari (270–343 C.E.).

5. Drinking occurs on a feast day, but in contrast, the gift of chocolate is in powdered form, used for preparing a beverage.

6. *Pulvis es* (Thou art dust) is said on Ash Wednesday by the priest as he draws a cross on the forehead of each worshiper.

7. The proverb states, "Honor to those who resemble their families."

45   This is the reason, señora,
       it comes so fearful and submissive
       that I think that Amor himself
       hid it away, fully concealed.

       Until this gift is duly assessed,
50   it remains so mute and noiseless
       that even the wheels of the hand
       mill[8] keep and maintain the secret.

       Because the one who it is wants
       you to know there is a Cupid,[9]
55   making Amor a true calling,
       for you are as fair as Psyche,[1]

       but not to know who he may be:
       for it would be a foolish whim,
       when snubbed for insufficiency,
60   to boast of how splendid he is.[2]

       I must serve you, and so I know
       in serving I do not oblige,
       nor make a present of a debt
       nor find service in repayment.

65   Since you do not know who I am,
       I am inclined to brevity,
       for a face loses character
       when the mouth is firmly closed.

       That is how I plan to keep it;
70   because I only reduce the
       vanity of adoring you
       in the glory of serving you.

8. The reference is to the hand mill in which the chocolate was ground to powder.
9. Roman god of erotic love and desire [*Editor*].
1. Goddess of the soul or breath and Cupid's lover [*Editor*].
2. The owner of the gift and the gift itself are definitively identified, though Sor Juana insists on the anonymity of the giver—that is, Galve. It is assumed that the ballad was written at the beginning of the Galve viceregency.

Redondillas[1]

Redondilla 87[†]

*Paints the eyes' perception of beauty as a symmetrical harmony,
as if another musical one*

My wish, Feliciana, is to
sing your celebrated beauty;
and since it is to be sung,
you will be the instrument.

5 About your ornamented head
my love says, with no misgiving,
that the high notes of your tresses
are in a harmony so fair

that with some audacity
10 love proclaims in a gentle voice
that he knows how to arrange them,
and his touch alone will strum them.

You must allow love to attempt
to configure the clefs and notes
15 from the expanse of your forehead
to the ruling lines of your brows.

At the music stand that occupies
your countenance, your eyes sing
re, mi, fa, sol to the rhythmic
20 tempo and measure of your nose.

The harmonious carnation
on your face is not discordant,
because along with the lily
it tempers and tunes your fair hue.

---

1. The *redondilla* is a stanza of four octosyllabic lines, usually rhymed ABAB.
† First published in *Castalian Inundation* (1689). Subtitle translated by the editor [*Editor*].

25 Your miraculous discretion
    harmonizes with your beauty,
    but the wisest, most prudent word
    stammers if it touches your lip.

    Your throat is the part that provides
30 the singing with inventions,
    because of the diatonic
    sequences that it crowds in.

    You conquer the hearts of all
    with your own sovereign command
35 for in your hand you sustain
    the signs and the inclinations.

    I shall not play the slenderness
    of your fine, exquisite torso
    for the bend of your waist is as
40 troubling as a trill in the song.

    Upon your foot my hope places
    all its pleasures and delights,
    for since it does not go higher
    it never makes a mutation.

45 And although it does not dare
    to rise in plainsong, on pitch,
    when counterpoint is adjoined
    it emblazons the whole note.

    Your body, its rhythm framed
50 from proportion to persistence,
    creates a divine harmony,
    it is so finely composed.

    I shall be silent, for my love
    does not interpret you well
55 in crude songs; to your perfections
    you alone know the notation.

Redondilla 91[†]

*Begging pardon for her silence, on the occasion of breaking a
precept to maintain it*

I wish to beg your forgiveness,
señora, for my silence, if what
was intended as courtesy
makes it seem ill-bred instead.

5 And you cannot reprehend me
if my behavior until now
has been so concerned with loving
that it forgot to explain.

For in my amorous passion
10 it was not neglect or waning
to take from my tongue its speech
and give it instead to my heart.

Nor did I cease to invoke you;
because, as this passion of mine
15 could see you here in my soul,
here in my soul it spoke to you.

And in this notable idea
it lived felicitous, content,
for I could feign and pretend
20 that you looked on me with favor.

With so bizarre a design
did my useless hope survive;
for thinking of you as divine,
it could make you human again.

25 Oh how mad I saw myself
in the ecstasy of your love,
when even pretended your favors
could make me mad with delight!

Oh how, in your beautiful sun,
30 my ardent love set ablaze,

---

† First published in *Second Volume* (1692) [*Editor*].

enflamed and fed by your brilliance,
it forgot about the dangers.

Forgive me if it was boldness
to dare approach your pure ardor,
35 for there is no holy place safe
from blameworthy lapses of thought.

It was in this manner that my
crazed hope deceived and deluded,
and deep inside me I had
40 all the good I did desire.

But now my mute silence breaks
your precept, severe and stern,
for it alone could be the key
to my adoration and praise.

45 And although loving your beauty
is a crime without a pardon,
let me be punished for the fault
rather than for indifference.

Do not, then, rigorous lady,
50 wish the one who declared her love
to be in truth unfortunate
when she had been joyful in jest.

If you condemn my irreverence,
condemn your power as well,
55 for if my obedience is wrong,
your command was not a just one.

If my intent is culpable,
my affection is ever damned,
because loving you is a crime
60 for which I shall never atone.

I find this in my affections,
and more I cannot explain;
but you, from what I did not say
will infer what I do not say.

Redondilla 92†

*She proves the inconsistency in the pleasure and censure of men
who accuse women of what they themselves cause*

O foolish men who accuse
women with so little cause,
not seeing you are the reason
for the very thing you blame:

5   for if with unequaled longing
you solicit their disdain,
why wish them to behave well
when you urge them on to evil?

You contend with their resistance,
10   then say gravely that the conquest
arose from their licentiousness
and not your extreme diligence.

The audacity of your mad
belief resembles that of the
15   child who devises a monster
and then afterward fears it.

With foolish presumption you wish
to find the woman you seek,
for your mistress, a Thais,¹
20   and Lucretia² for your wife.

Whose caprice can be stranger than
the man who ignores good counsel,
clouds the looking glass himself,
then complains it is not clear.

25   You occupy the same place
whether favored or disdained,

---

† First published in *Castalian Inundation* (1689) [*Editor*].
1. Saint Thais, a fourth-century courtesan who lived in Alexandria, Egypt, and converted
   to Christianity [*Editor*].
2. Wife of a Roman nobleman (6th century B.C.E.) who killed herself after being raped by
   the son of the Roman king. Nearly the exact same antithesis is also found in Martial,
   Epigrammata, 1.11.104, with the substitution of Laida for Thais: *Si te delectat gravitas,
   Lucretia toto / sis licet usque die: Laida nocte volo* (If seriousness pleases you, you may
   be a Lucretia throughout the day: Lais I wish for at night) [*Editor*].

complaining if women are cruel
and mocking them if they love.

You think highly of no woman,
30 no matter how modest: if she
rejects you she is ungrateful,
and if she accepts, unchaste.

Always foolish in your actions,
with a measure that is uneven
35 you condemn one for being cruel,
another for being easy.

Then how can the woman you woo
be temperate toward your courting?
Ungrateful, she offends you,
40 and if easy, she angers.

But between anger and sorrow
the object of your caprice,
may be one who does not love you,
and then you may truly complain.

45 To their sorrow your lovers give
wings to restraints; they fly away,
and after you make them sinful
you wish they were filled with virtue.

Who carries the greater guilt
50 in a passion gone astray:
the woman, beseeched, who falls,
or the man who begged her to yield?

Or which one merits more blame
although both deserve our censure:
55 the woman who sins for pay,
or the man who pays to sin?

But why are you so alarmed
by the guilt you plainly deserve?
Love them for what you make them
60 or make them what you can love.

Cease your incessant entreaties,
and then, with justification,

you can accuse the affection
of the one who solicits you.

65　　But I conclude your audacity
　　　does battle with countless weapons,
　　　for in promises and pleading
　　　you join world, and flesh, and devil.

Epigrams[1]

Epigram 93

A satirical lesson for one who is vain about her beauty

You say, Leonor, for beauty
you should be given the palm;
the one for virgin is better,
and this your face guarantees.
5   Do not boast with such insolence
that you steal the heart of each man:
if you have been given the palm,
it is, Leonor, for bogeyman.[2]

Epigram 94

*In which she discovers the honorable lineage of a
highborn drunkard*

So that your blood may be known
you tell everyone, Alfeo,
you come from kings; I believe
you are of very fine stock,
5   and that you anger all you meet
with your talk about those kings,
who, more than the kings of swords,
must have been the kings of cups.[1]

---

1. Epigrams are short, often satirical, statements in verse. Greek and Latin epigrams were popular in Renaissance Europe and spawned examples in Neo-Latin and vernacular languages. In emblems such as those Sor Juana created for *Allegorical Neptune* (p. 136), they complemented the visual iconography with a riddle. The following epigrams were all published in *Second Volume* (1692) [*Editor*].
2. The pun is based on dual meanings for *palma* and *coco*. The first is both a palm tree and the equivalent of victory laurels; the second is both a coconut and a bogeyman used to frighten children.
1. Swords and cups are two of the suits in the Spanish deck of cards (*baraja*), which is similar to the tarot deck.

Epigram 95

Which provides a proud man with the eyewash[1] he deserves

Not having an upright father
would be a defect, in my eyes,
if I had chosen him, as I
received my being from him.
5   Your mother was more merciful,
for she made you heir of many,
so that among them all, you can
take the one who suits you best.[2]

Epigram 96

Some moral advice to a modern captain

Don Juan is a captain now:
but my mind would much prefer
for him to be more reformed[1]
and a little less the captain.
5   For truly it perturbs me,
in so venturesome an action,
to see him not govern the bridle,
and dare to use the short stirrup.[2]

Epigram 97

Which reveals to a sergeant the conditions he does not possess

A certain sergeant armed himself
with a victorious halberd;[1]
but then he and she ended up

---

1. Eyewash, or collyrium, a traditional treatment for diseases of the eye. The implication is that the man needs to be cured of the ailment that allows him to see other people's defects, but not his own.
2. Sor Juana was born out of wedlock. The epigram seems to be a response to someone who criticized her for her birth.
1. The pun is based on the dual meanings of *reformado*: "cashiered," in the military sense, and "reformed," in the moral sense.
2. The shortened stirrup, in Spanish *a la jineta,* was considered a more difficult manner of riding [*Editor*].
1. A halberd is a medieval weapon consisting of an ax blade at the top of a long pole.

as what I shall tell you now:
5   an "a" disappears from her,
and she becomes a packsaddle;
his "sar" turns into the mange,
and the silver does not appear.[2]

2. In Spanish the halberd is *alabarda*; if an "a" is removed, it becomes *albarda*, or pack-saddle. Sergeant in Spanish is *sargento*, *sarna* is mange, and *argento* is silver.

Décimas[1]

Décima 102[†]

Which accompanied a portrait sent to a certain person

She who is my original[2]
has forwarded me to you,
and although you see her drawn,
you will never see her withdrawn;
5   completely transformed in me,
she hands you the conquest: her love;
do not wonder at the calm
and silence you find in me:
my original, for your sake,
10   I believe has lost her soul.

Envious of my arrival,
and seeing in my good fortune
how she feels woe and sadness
and I, not feeling, have great luck.
15   I am doubtless attended by
a far more advantageous sign,
a far more favorable star;
for I was born of a paintbrush,
and had less life in my being
20   than she, but much more good fortune.

If by chance my lot were to change
and you wounded me, in order
not to see you do not love me
I would wish to be without life.
25   For the fact of being unloved
would be an event so dire,

---

1. A *décima* is a stanza of ten octosyllabic lines. Rhyme schemes can vary, but the rhyme itself is usually consonant.
† First published in *Second Volume* (1692) [Editor].
2. The portrait speaks in first person [Editor].

the strength of that anguish would force
me, although painted, to feel:
for pain knows how to instill
30 souls in order to have feeling.

And if it is inopportune
for you that I lack a soul,
in me you can instill one
of the many you have captured:
35 for since I gave her soul to you,
and my being names itself yours,
although you are amazed to see
me in such insentient calm,
you are the soul of this body,
40 and the body of this shadow.

Décima 103†

She depicts her respectful love; she speaks to the portrait and is
not silent as it is twice her master

Divine copy[1] in which I see
the paintbrush presume, arrogant
when it sees that it has gone
where my desire could not go;
5 a high, sovereign use and mastery
of a more than human talent
free of impertinent boldness,
for your incredible beauty,
since it goes past what is possible,
10 cannot be reached even by thought.

What paintbrush was so supreme
that it sufficed to copy you?
What muse inspired and moved its mind?
What virtue guided its hand?
15 Let the futile art that shaped you
so perfectly not boast of this;
to form your beauty, a portent,
it was agreed and all concurred

---

† First published in *Castalian Inundation* (1689) [*Editor*].
1. A painted portrait.

that the instrument was human,
20   but the prompting impulse, divine.

I so wonder at you as spirit,
believe in you as deity,
that I find your unseen soul
and doubt the body I see:
25   I abrogate all my reason,
filled with wonder at your beauty
displayed with such reality,
and leaving the judgment serene
that even the soul is copied,
30   and the deity is seen.

Seeing the height of perfection
that I look upon in you,
then I scarcely can believe
that any can equal you;
35   and if there were no original
whose rare, unwonted perfection
had found its copy in you,
then I, a second Pygmalion,[2]
and lost in fondness of you,
40   would implore that you come to life.

I touch you to see whether a
hidden life appears in you;
can it possibly be lacking
in what steals away my judgment?
45   Can you possibly not feel
this hand that caresses you
and incites you to attend
to my devoted, humble spoils?
Can there be no light in those eyes,
50   can there be no voice in that mouth?

I well can voice my complaint
when you calmly leave me alone
that you steal away my soul
yet still do not come to life;
55   and when, pitiless, you trample

2. In Ovid's *Metamorphoses* (Book 10), a legendary sculptor who fell in love with the statue he created [*Editor*].

my humility so proudly,
thereby purifying my pain,
your mercy moves so far away
that I lose my poor complaint
60   and torment is all that remains.

At times I think that, merciful,
you respond to my devotion;
and at others my heart fears
that, disdainful, you refrain.
65   Now joyful, my bosom takes heart,
now downcast at harshness, it dies,
but either way it acquires
the good fortune of possession,
for in the end, in my power,
70   you will be whatever I wish.

Although, faithful, you display the
harshness of your original,
the paintbrush has granted to me
what love cannot and never could.
75   I live, blissful in the favor
that a cold bronze offers to me,
for although you show indifference
and, at your worst, may say
you are unfeeling, never can
80   you declare, that you are not mine.

Décima 106†

She points out the lucid profundity of an eminent orator

Spanish Cicero: my pen can
barely laud on seeing you,
for wishing to praise you means
presuming to understand you,
5   although one who gives ear to you
comes to know your discernment is
so vast it can cause dismay;
and so in your great subtlety
one knows there is lofty grandeur
10   but cannot measure the amount.

† First published in *Castalian Inundation* (1689) [*Editor*].

You are a sea that everyone
can contemplate but not fathom,
can marvel at when they see it,
but no one can ever sound;
15 when one comes to admire it,
from its great expanse one only
can infer its immensity:
for if by what can be seen
of the surface one is amazed,
20 what is the effect of the depths?

And although what I can see
fills me with vast admiration,
I know full well its perfection
cannot be fully encompassed
25 but, since I cannot understand
so much greatness, or encompass
the very thing I am hearing,
boldly I venture to praise it:
what I can grasp, with my reason;
30 what I cannot, with my faith.

Décima 107[†]

*She comments in verse on the excuses of one who refused
to speak in prose*

The offense of being silent
you have attempted to excuse,
and you are much more convincing
in the things that you have said:
5 I have weighed and judged the offense
by your own clear declaration,
for one who speaks with this kind
of discretion quite clearly shows
that being silent was merely
10 a desire, not necessity.

When you excuse with discretion
the reason you remained silent,
you remind me of the loss
of all that you failed to say:

† First published in *Castalian Inundation* (1689) [*Editor*].

15 you increase for me the sorrow
    I felt on the day I saw you
    because then I could not hear you;
    for proceeding with that silence,
    I could neither weigh nor judge
20 the very thing I had lost.

Décima 109[†]

To a discerning and valiant captain

Your plumes, I infer, are a sign
of bravery and discernment
but I cannot decide whether
for your helmet or your inkwell.[1]
5 In your crest is clearly displayed
a well-armed discernment joined
to a well-lettered bravery,
and to summarize I say
your blade cut and sharpened your quill,
10 your quill measures and scans your blade.

Décima 125[‡]

For herself she refuses the liberty she begs of the Vicereine[1]
for an Englishman

Today I bow at your feet
with the requisite deference,
I worship you as a god
and entreat you as a god.
5 Do not say I deny you
your rite, seeking the benefit
of your favor and protection,
for to the principal god,
invoking her favor and grace
10 is the most pleasing sacrifice.

---

† First published in *Second Volume* (1692) [*Editor*].
1. The plumes in the crest on the helmet of an officer could indicate his status as a soldier
   or as a writer.
‡ First published in *Castalian Inundation* (1689) [*Editor*].
1. Most likely, María Luisa, Countess of Paredes, married to the Marquis de la Laguna,
   viceroy from 1680 to 1686 [*revised by Editor*].

Samuel[2] appeals to your mercy,
pleading in various ways,
for he seeks to find his freedom
where everyone loses theirs.
15   Release him from his slavery,
señora, the reasons are just
and clement toward such ill fortune,
and at some time emancipate
all of those you have made captive.

20   In conflict my will here strives
for two contrary desires:
for the Englishman, liberty,
and for myself, to be your slave,
although I was born unworthy
25   of your giving me that name,
surely you will resist in vain
the marker of my slavery,
for I am bound to be yours
although you do not accept me.

30   The two petitions are contrary
if you peruse them with care,
for one aspires to liberty
and I yearn to be confined;
but your discernment, keen-sighted,
35   never impeded by doubt,
can, if it gauges intentions,
bring joy to us both today
by acceding to what I bring
and conceding to what he begs.

2. An unidentified Englishman [Editor].

Sonnets[1]

Sonnet 145[†]

In which she attempts to refute the praises of a portrait of the poet, signed by truth, which she calls passion

This thing you see, a bright-colored deceit,
displaying all the many charms of art,
with false syllogisms of tint and hue
is a cunning deception of the eye;

5 this thing in which sheer flattery has tried
to evade the stark horrors of the years
and, vanquishing the cruelties of time,
to triumph over age and oblivion,

is vanity, contrivance, artifice,
10 a delicate blossom stranded in the wind,
a failed defense against our common fate;

a fruitless enterprise, a great mistake,
a decrepit frenzy, and rightly viewed,
a corpse, some dust, a shadow, mere nothingness.[2]

---

1. Sonnets are composed of fourteen verses of hendecasyllables, or iambic pentameters. They are organized as two quatrains and two tercets, commonly with a rhyme scheme of ABBA in the quatrains and variable in the tercets. Often, the quatrains introduce an argument or problem that is ingeniously solved by the tercets. Imported to the Spanish court from Italy in the sixteenth century, they became the preeminent form for courtly love and moral reflection, with examples from all the great poets of the sixteenth and seventeenth centuries [*Editor*].
† First published in *Castalian Inundation* (1689).
2. A direct reference to the final verse of *carpe diem* sonnet CLXVI by Luis de Góngora: "*en tierra, en humo, en polvo, en sombra, en nada*" (in earth, in smoke, in dust, in shadow, in nothing) [*Editor*].

Sonnet 146[†]

*She complains of her adverse fortune, suggests her aversion
to vice, and justifies her diversion with the Muses*

O World, why do you wish to persecute me?
How do I offend you, when I intend
only to fix beauty in my intellect,
and never my intellect fix on beauty?

5   I do not set store by treasures or riches;
and therefore it always brings me more joy
only to fix riches in my intellect,
and never my intellect fix on riches.

I do not set store by a lovely face that,
10   vanquished, is civil plunder of the ages,
and perfidious wealth has never pleased me,

for I deem it best, as one of my truths,
to deplete the vanities of this life
and never this life to deplete in vanities.

Sonnet 147[‡]

*In which she morally censures a rose, and thereby all that
resemble it*

O rose divine, in gentle cultivation
you are, with all your fragrant subtlety,
tuition, purple-hued, to loveliness,
snow-white instruction to the beautiful;

5   intimation of a human structure,
example of gentility in vain,
in whose one being nature has united
the joyful cradle and the mournful grave;

how haughty in your pomp, presumptuous one,
10   how proud when you disdain the threat of death,
then, in a swoon and shriveling, you give

† First published in *Castalian Inundation* (1689) [*Editor*].
‡ First published in *Second Volume* (1692) [*Editor*].

a withered vision of a failing self;
and so, with your wise death and foolish life,
in living you deceive, dying you teach!

Sonnet 148[†]

She prefers to die rather than expose herself to the indignities
of old age

Celia[1] looked at a rose that in the meadow
so happily displayed vain pomp and show,
and with creams of scarlet and crimson paint
gaily drenched and daubed her lovely face;

5   and Celia said: "Enjoy with no fear of fate
the too brief course of this your flowering youth,
for never can the death that comes tomorrow
take away from you the joy of today;

and even though death hurries and hastens near
10   and fragrant life leaves and abandons you,
do not lament your dying so fair and young:

remember—the wisdom of the world will say
you were fortunate to die while beautiful
and not endure the indignity of age."

Sonnet 149[‡]

She earnestly recommends the choice of a condition
that lasts until death

If one considered the dangers of the sea,
one would never set sail; if the hazard were
clearly seen, no one would dare to provoke
the attack of a brave, undaunted bull;

5   if the prudent rider pondered the bolting
fury of a spirited galloping beast,

---

† First published in *Castalian Inundation* (1689) [*Editor*].
1. Celia is a frequent name in the pastoral tradition.
‡ First published in *Castalian Inundation* (1689) [*Editor*].

never would anyone bring it to a halt
with an able hand controlling the reins.

But if there were someone valiant enough
10   that, despite the danger, he would attempt
to drive with daring hand the swift chariot

bathed in light of great Apollo himself,[1]
he might do all this but never enter
a state that must last the rest of his life.

Sonnet 152[†]

Green[1] rapture and delight of human life,
crazed Hope, in delirious gilded frenzy,
the intricate sleep of those who are awake,
as bereft of treasures as it is of dreams;

5   soul of the world, exuberant old age,
and then decrepit verdancy imagined;
of the favored the long awaited today,
and of the less fortunate, the tomorrow:

let those with green lenses before their eyes,
10   seeing all things painted to their desire,
follow your shadow, in search of your day;

for I, wiser, more prudent in my fortune,
hold in both of my hands both of my eyes,
and see no more than those things I can touch.

Sonnet 164[‡]

*In which she responds to jealous suspicion with the rhetoric
of weeping*

This afternoon, my love, when I spoke to you,
I could see in your face, in what you did,

---

1. A reference to Phaethon, who convinced his father, Helios (at times identified with Apollo), to let him drive the sun chariot; he lost control and fell to his death [*Editor*].
† Not published, but painted on the 1713 posthumous portrait of Sor Juana by Juan de Miranda [*Editor*].
1. Traditionally the color of hope. Today we would speak of rose-colored glasses.
‡ First published in *Second Volume* (1692) [*Editor*].

that you were not persuaded by mere words,
and I wished you could see into my heart;

5 and Love,[1] assisting me in my attempt,
overcame the seeming impossible,
for among the tears that my sorrow shed
was my breaking heart, liquid and distilled.

Enough of anger now, my love, enough;
10 do not let tyrant jealousy torment you,
nor base suspicion roil your serenity

with foolish specters and deceptive clues;
in liquid humor[2] you have seen and touched
my broken heart and held it in your hands.

Sonnet 165[†]

Which restrains a fantasy by making it content with decent love

Halt, O faint shade of my elusive love,
image of the enchantment I love best,
fair illusion for whom I gladly die,
sweet fiction for whose sake I live in pain.

5 If th'attraction, the magnet of your charms
draws my heart as if it were made of steel,
why woo and win me over with flattery
if then you will deceive me, turn and flee?

But, satisfied and proud, you cannot boast
10 that your tyranny triumphs over me:
for though you escape and slip through the tight cords

that bind your imagined form in fantasy,
it matters not if you elude my arms,
my dear, when thought alone can imprison you.

1. The reference is to the classical god of love.
2. Humor here refers to a bodily fluid.
† First published in *Second Volume* (1692) [*Editor*].

Sonnet 173[†]

The very distressing effects of love, but no matter how great,
they do not equal the qualities of the one who causes them

Do you see me, Alcino,[1] here am I caught
in the chains of love, shackled in its irons,
a wretched slave despairing of her freedom,
and so far, so distant from consolation?

5   Do you see my soul filled with pain and anguish,
wounded by torments so savage, so fierce,
burned in the midst of living flames and judging
herself unworthy of her castigation?

Do you see me without a soul, pursuing
10 a folly I myself condemn as strange?
Do you see me bleeding along the way

as I follow the trail of an illusion?
Are you very surprised? See then, Alcino:
the cause of harm to me deserves much more.

Sonnet 177[‡]

She reflects upon her inevitable weeping in view of the
one she loves

You command me, Anarda,[1] to come without
weeping before your eyes, and I suspect
that not knowing the cause is what has made you
wish me to undertake so great a triumph.

5   Love, my lady, finds in me no resistance,
for my exhausted heart he sets ablaze,
causing the blood in my bosom to flee
and vaporize in my sight as ardency.

And then my eyes seek and search for your presence,
10 which they judge the object of their sweet charm,
and when my attention pays homage to you,

---

† First published in *Castalian Inundation* (1689) [*Editor*].
1. A standard name used in pastoral poetry in the early modern period [*revised by Editor*].
‡ First published in *Castalian Inundation* (1689) [*Editor*].
1. A standard name used in early modern pastoral poetry [*revised by Editor*].

the rays from my eyes, during all that time,
finding in you the resistance of snow,
transmute what left as vapor into tears.

Sonnet 179[†]

Which explains the most sublime quality of love

I adore Lisi[1] but do not pretend
that Lisi will return my token of love,
for if I deem her beauty within reach,
I offend both her honor and my mind.

5   To intend nothing is all my intention;
for I know that to merit so much grandeur
no merit can suffice, and it is foolish
to act contrary to my understanding.

I conceive her great beauty as something so
10 sacred that audacity does not wish
to give the slightest opening to hope:

for yielding my great happiness to hers,
in order not to see it badly used,
I think I would regret seeing her mine.

Sonnet 186[‡]

Convalescing from a serious illness, she addresses the Vicereine,
Señora Marquisa de Mancera, attributing to her great love her
improvement even in dying

In this life of mine that ever was yours,
O divine Laura, and ever will be,
the savage Fate, determined to pursue me,
wanted to claim my mortal foot in triumph.

---

† First published in *Second Volume* (1692) [*Editor*].
1. A standard name used in early modern pastoral poetry. It is unclear whether the Lisi of
this poem is a pseudonym for the Countess of Paredes, as it is in others [*revised by
Editor*].
‡ Sonnets 186–189 were first published in *Castalian Inundation* (1689). The vicereine
Marquisa de Mancera, Leonor Carreto (1616–1674), was a patronness and friend of Sor
Juana. She died in 1674 on her journey back to Spain while still in New Spain. In
poems in her honor, Sor Juana addresses Leonor as "Laura" [*Editor*].

5   I was astounded by her rash daring,
    for if great power lies 'neath her domain,
    she no longer can wield any in mine:
    you allowed me to free myself from her.

    I saw the mortal, fearsome scissors open
10 to cut through the thread she never had spun;
    oh savage, terrible Fate! I said then,

    know that no one but Laura commands here;
    and she, abashed, departed and sped away,
    leaving me to die for you, no one but you.

Sonnet 187

On the death of the most excellent Señora Marquisa de Mancera

    The heavens, enamored of the comeliness
    of Laura, stole her away, took her on high,
    for it did not seem correct to illumine
    these unhappy valleys in that pure light;

5   or because mere mortals, deceived, misguided
    by the beauteous structure of her body,
    astonished at the sight of extreme beauty,
    did not consider themselves as fortunate.

    She was born where the east draws a scarlet veil
10 at the rising of the rubicund star,
    and she died where, with burning, ardent desire,

    the depths of the sea swallows that red light;[1]
    for it was needed for her divine flight
    that like the sun she travel around the world.

Sonnet 188

On the same subject

    A beautiful merging severed in Laura,
    O immortal soul, O glorious spirit,

---

1. That is, she was born in the east, in Spain, and died in the west, in New Spain [*Editor*].

why did you leave a body so beauteous
and why to that soul have you bid farewell?

5 But now it has penetrated my reason
that you endure so rigorous a divorce
so that on the last day you can with joy
once again become eternally joined.

Begin your rapid flight, O fortunate soul,
10 and released now from your beauteous prison,
leaving its rosy hue turned into ice,

rise up to be crowned by luminous stars:
for all of boundless heaven is required
so that you will not miss your beauteous home.

Sonnet 189

She laments with others the death of Señora Marquisa
de Mancera

Because you have died, Laura, let affections
die too that yearn, desiring you in vain,
along with these eyes you deprive of the sight
of the beautiful light you once bestowed.

5 And let my forlorn lyre die, where you inspired
echoes that mournfully cry out for you,
and let even these ill-favored strokes become
the black tears of my melancholy pen.

Then let Death herself be moved to take pity,
10 who was compelled and could not pardon you;
and let Love lament his own bitter fate,

for if at one time, he longed to enjoy you
and wished to have eyes so that he could see you,
now they will serve him only to weep for you.

Sonnet 205[†]

She applauds the astronomical science of Father Eusebio
Francisco Quino, of the Society of Jesus,[1] who wrote
of the comet that appeared in the year 1680, declaring
it free of portents

Although the pure light of heaven is bright,
and bright is the moon and the stars are bright,
and bright the ephemeral lightning streaks
that the air raises and fire consumes;

5　although the thunderbolt is bright, whose harsh
production costs the wind a thousand disputes,
and the lightning flash that made of its tracks
a fearsome light in the ebony dark;

all of our human knowledge, dim and slow,
10　lay in darkness without our mortal feathers
able to be, in proud and boastful flight,

another Icarus[2] of reasoned discourse,
until you, O sovereign Eusebio,
shed light upon the very lights of heaven.

---

† First published in *Castalian Inundation* (1689) [*Editor*].
1. That is, the Jesuit order. Eusebio Kino (1645–1711) was an Austrian Jesuit who stopped over in Mexico City on his way to the mission in Sonora in 1680. While in Mexico City, he entered into a debate with Carlos de Sigüenza y Góngora (1645–1700), Mexican polymath and mathematician, over the significance of the 1680 comet. While Kino supported the view that the comet was an ill omen, Sigüenza y Góngora argued that God's designs could not be scrutinized and that comets were merely astronomical phenomena. Sor Juana's implicit support for Kino is notable, given her apparently friendly rapport with Sigüenza y Góngora. This may be due to Kino's close relationship with the Portuguese Duchess Aveiro, whom in the "Response" (p. 112) Sor Juana lists among contemporary female intellects and who was a friend of the Countess of Paredes [*revised by Editor*].
2. In Greek mythology, the son of Daedalus, the master craftsman, who requested wings of wax from his father. After he flew too close to the sun, Icarus's wings melted and he fell to the sea where he drowned. Icarus is often associated with hubris [*Editor*].

First Dream

The poem "First Dream" is widely considered to be Sor Juana's masterpiece. The seventeenth-century editions of the poem, which are the basis for modern editions, title it "First Dream" and add the subtitle: "as titled and composed by Mother Juana Inés de la Cruz, in imitation of Góngora." In her "Response of the Poet to the Very Eminent Sor Filotea" (p. 90), however, Sor Juana herself refers to the poem as "a trifle they call *The Dream*" and there is no way to know whether it was she or her publisher who added "First" to the title or what meaning the epithet had for the poem.

The subtitle's reference to the verse of the Spanish poet Luis de Góngora may also have been introduced by the publisher, although it was a logical comparison. Undoubtedly the poem has many resonances with Góngora's difficult style. What became known as "gongorism" or *culteranismo* was marked by recondite mythological allusions, Latinisms, and extreme syntactical rearrangements or *hyperbaton*. The meter of "First Dream" is a *silva*, a flexible verse form of randomly interspersed hendecasyllables (11 syllables) and heptasyllables (7 syllables), made famous by Góngora's poem *Soledades* (The solitudes, 1613). While formally the poem follows *The Solitudes*, its images and verse echo his exquisite *Fábula de Polifemo y Galatea* (Fable of Polyphemus and Galetea, 1613). Also like Góngora and other contemporary Hispanic poets, Sor Juana is heavily influenced by classical myths, many drawn from Ovid's *Metamorphoses*.

The topic of Sor Juana's *silva* is unique in the literature of her time, however. Its narrative is relatively simple: after night falls, the body sleeps and the soul is reduced to its intellective form. As if dreaming, the soul embarks on a search for absolute knowledge, following two distinct but equally unsucessful routes. First, the soul attempts a mystical, Neoplatonic knowledge, but is unable to contain the infinite in its finite form. Recovering, it then attempts understanding by employing techniques of scholastic method. In this case, the obstacle is time itself, as the soul's task is ultimately interrupted by the break of day. The body awakens and, in one last series of metaphors, the poem recounts the retreat of the night and the arrival of the sun, ending, famously, "the world illuminated with more / certain light, and I, awake."

43

While the poetic dream had literary precedents and the search for
absolute knowledge was the object of mystical practices common in
seventeenth-century Spain and Spanish America, the confluence
of these two tropes was unusual. Sor Juana's treatment of the topic of
absolute knowledge, moreover, is decidedly not mystical. Instead,
through mythological references and poetic tropes, Sor Juana explores
the gray area between human morality and the psychological drive to
knowledge, understood in the terms of her time. Her physiological
description of the body and the mind is neo-scholastic, inspired by
Luis de Granada's *Introducción del símbolo de la fe* (Introduction of
the symbol of faith, 1584). The language and accuracy of her descrip-
tion of the body and mind suggest more than a superficial knowledge
of the works of Thomas Aquinas, the foundation of Catholic theology,
and perhaps even familiarity with late scholastics who followed him.
Her poetic images, however, are often drawn from Neoplatonic
sources, especially the works of the Jesuit polymath Athanasius
Kircher (1602–1680), whose natural philosophy provided a Catholic
alternative to the seventeenth-century New Science. Finally, Sor
Juana appears to have culled the poem's many classical references
from Jorge de Bustamante's 1545 Spanish translation of Ovid's *Meta-
morphoses,* although she may have read the Latin original as well. She
also surely consulted the Renaissance compendia of symbols and
emblems referenced in her other works.[1]

As impressive as the breadth of this knowledge is Sor Juana's ability
to weave these sources together in a narrative exploration of episte-
mology and the human mind. Strikingly, "First Dream" resists assign-
ing the soul a gender, employing very few markers in the first person
until the last lines. The arrival of daylight at the very end of the poem
parallels the revelation of the gender of the speaker in the final term
despierta, which, as an adjective, is marked as feminine in Spanish.
Sor Juana's posthumous biographer, Diego Calleja, interprets the
poem as a personal journey and, in the "Response," the poet mentions
how much she discovers while asleep.[2] The insistence throughout the
poem on a neuter soul, however, also accords with Sor Juana's argu-
ment in the "Response" that the mind has no gender.[3] The poem thus
represents its terms as personal and universally applicable. Often
considered one of the most difficult poems in Hispanic literature,
"First Dream" is a physiologically and theologically sophisticated
account of the human desire for knowledge.

1. For proof that Sor Juana consulted the 1545 translation of Ovid's *Metamorphoses,* see
   note 8 on p. 47. On Sor Juana's references to compendia of symbols and emblems, see
   Allegorical Neptune and corresponding notes on p. 136.
2. See "Response" on p. 110. For Calleja's citation of Sor Juana's description of "First
   Dream" see Calleja on p. 193.
3. See "Response" on p. 119.

A note on the translation: Grossman's translation has stayed loyal to the original sense of the poem but has softened if not eliminated one of the hallmarks of its difficulty—extreme hyperbaton or syntactical interruption. Slight divergences from the original, including places where English cannot reproduce Spanish specificity, have been noted.

First Dream[†]

*As titled and composed by Mother Juana Inés de la Cruz,
in imitation of Góngora*

Pyramidal, funereal, a shadow
born of earth, aspiring to highest heaven,
the haughty tip of its great obelisks
striving in vain to climb up to the stars,
5   and yet their resplendent light
(sparkling always, always unassailable)
from their great height scoffed at and
mocked the gloom of the war
waged on them with black vapors
10   by fearsome, ephemeral
shadows, whose dark glower could not reach even
the outer convexity of the sphere
of the thrice comely goddess
who shows us a trio of fair visages;[1]
15   could master no more than mere
air that misted in the rush
of thick dense breath exhaled by that grim shadow;
and in the contained stillness of the soundless empire
only muffled voices of nocturnal birds
20   were countenanced and approved,
so obscure, so serious,
their calls did not unsettle the quietude.
Sluggish of flight, with a song
irksome to the ear, more so to the spirit,
25   a shamed Nyctymene[2] lurks at
chinks and cracks in sacred doors

---

† First published in *Second Volume* (1692) the poem was composed before 1691, as Sor Juana refers to in her "Response of the Poet to the Very Eminent Sor Filotea" on p. 121 [*Editor*].

1. Some scholars understand this as a reference to Selene, who in classical mythology had three faces: Luna or the moon in the sky, Diana or Artemis on earth, and Persephone or Hecate in the underworld. Others understand it as a reference to three phases of the moon [*revised by Editor*].

2. After having been raped by her father, Epopeus, King of Lesbos, she was changed by Minerva into an owl [*Editor*].

    or the most propitious gaps in high lunettes
    which may offer a breach to her intention
    to reach, in sacrilege, the
30 bright sacred lamps of the eternal flame
    and extinguish them, unless she defames them
    first, consuming the dense oil
    found in the cloudless liquid
    that the fruit of the famed tree of Minerva[3]
35 gave up in anguished drops when cruelly pressed.
    And those three maidens[4] who saw
    their house turned to wasteland, their cloth to weeds,
    for having disobeyed the divine Bacchus,
    no longer recounting a mélange of tales,
40 they too have been turned into odious shapes,
    forming a second haze,
    fearing to be seen even in the shadows,
    birds with wings but no feathers:
    those three diligent maidens,
45 sisters, I say, too daring,
    received the dire punishment
    of bare drab membranes for wings,
    so ill disposed the most hideous birds do
    mock them: they, with one who once
50 served as the long-tongued minister to Pluto
    but now is superstitious sign to augurs,[5]
    alone composed the fearsome
    tuneless choir, intoning black maximas
    and longas,[6] more with long pauses than voices,
55 waiting perhaps for greater proportion from
    this dull, slow-moving measure
    than from the phlegmatic motion of the wind,
    whose rhythm was so dilatory, so slack,
    it may have slept between strokes.
60 This, then, melancholy, intercadent sound
    from the fearsome, shadowed crowd
    attracted attention less
    than it moved one to slumber;
    but first, so laggardly, its

3. The reference is to the olive tree.
4. The Minyades, three daughters of the Thebian Minyas, who stayed home weaving and telling one another stories instead of worshiping Dionysus (Bacchus in Roman mythology), the god of wine and the harvest; as punishment they were turned into bats [*revised by Editor*].
5. Ascalaphus, guardian of the orchard in the underworld who told Pluto, the god of the underworld, that Persephone had eaten part of a pomegranate, thereby obliging her to spend half the year in the underworld. As punishment she turned him into a horned owl [*revised by Editor*].
6. Terms used in mensural notation, the system of musical notation common in Europe from the thirteenth to the seventeenth centuries.

65 consonance sluggish and dull
induced one to quiet rest
and invited all one's limbs to calm repose;
suggesting utter silence to the living,
silent dark Harpocrates,[7] the night, seals
70 lips, one after the other
with an indicant finger,
to whose imperious, but not harsh, precept
each deferred, obedient.
Serene the wind now, the dog quiet in sleep,
75 one lies still, the other hushed;
not even atoms moving,
fearing the faint murmurous sound might make a
noise, sacrilegious though slight,
to violate the silent tranquility.
80 The sea, no longer perturbed,
did not even rock the unstable cradle,
cerulean blue, where the sun sinks to sleep;
and the fish, forever mute, slumbering deep
in the muddied beds of their
85 lightless, cavernous grottoes
were rendered now doubly mute;
and among them the deceitful enchantress
Almone,[8] who once had changed
simple lovers into fish,
90 here changed as well, now revenged.
In the hidden concave hollows of the high
mountains, those rough and cragged peaks
guarded less by ruggedness
than by their obscurity,
95 in whose dark, somber dwelling
deepest night reigns at midday,
and unknown still to the sure,
steady, tracking foot of the expert hunter,
forgotten the fierceness of
100 some, the terror of others,
the lowly animals slept,
paying to Nature the same
universal tribute imposed by her might;

7. In Greek mythology, the god of silence; a transformation of the Egyptian god Horus, mother of Isis [*Editor*].
8. A naiad in Ovid's *Metamorphoses*. For many years, it was thought that the name Almone was an error and modern editions corrected it to Alcione or Halcyon; until now, all English translations have followed this editorial correction. However, in his 1595 Spanish translation of Ovid's *Metamorphoses* Jorge de Bustamanete assigned the name Almone to a naiad. Thus, recent editors have respected the *princeps* Almone. From reference, it appears that Sor Juana read Bustamante's translation and not the Latin original of Ovid [*revised by Editor*].

and their king,[9] affecting vigilance, even
105   with open eyes kept no watch.
      A powerful monarch once,
      torn to pieces by his own fierce hunting dogs
      but now a timorous hart[1]
      with hearing most attentive
110   to the least perceptible tremor that may
      disturb the atoms, first one
      then the other of his sharp ears responds, moves
      and quivers and hears the sound
      even in his deep slumber.
115   And in the serene quietude of their nests,
      hammocks formed of offshoots
      in the densest, most opaque parts of the trees,
      the buoyant throng gathers together and sleeps,
      the wind resting in the cessation of the
120   constant cutting of their wings.
      The noble bird of Jupiter,[2] highborn queen,
      does not give herself to rest
      entirely, deeming sleep in excess vice,
      and takes care to avert faults
125   of omission caused by lack of vigilance,
      resting her entire weight on just one foot
      and clutching in the other a tiny stone,
      an alarm calculated to waken her[3]
      in the event she drowses:
130   for if a light sleep proves beyond her control
      it would not last but be interrupted first
      by regal or rather pastoral care.
      Oh heavy burden and cost of majesty,
      which does not forgive the least neglect or slip!
135   The reason, perhaps, that the crown is circular,
      a mysterious gold circle that denotes
      a no less unbroken zeal.
      In short, all was possessed by sleep; all, in short,
      was occupied by silence:
140   even the thief lay sleeping,
      and even the watchful lover closed his eyes.
      Dead of night had almost passed, the darkness half
      concluded, when wearied by their daily tasks,
      (and oppressed not only by

9. The lion, king of the animals.
1. Actaeon saw Artemis, the goddess of the hunt, and her nymphs bathing and was turned
   into a stag that was then torn to pieces by his hunting dogs [*revised by Editor*].
2. The eagle.
3. The original text uses the term *cálculo*, a reference to a small stone used by Romans for
   calculation [*Editor*].

145 grueling physical labor but tired too
     of delight, since any constant incidence,
     no matter how delightful,
     also exhausts the senses:
     for nature always alternates,
150 moves between first one, then the other scale,
     allotting actions to leisure and labor
     in the alternation, faithful unfaithful,[4]
     with which she guides the great machine of the world);
     the limbs, then, occupied by sweet, profound sleep,
155 the senses, if not deprived
     of their usual pursuit (work after all,
     yet work well loved if
     toil's ever lovable)
     then suspended for a time,
160 and ceding to the image contrary to
     life that, slowly armed, cowardly charges and then
     lazily conquers all with drowsing weapons,
     from the lowly staff to the haughty scepter,
     no distinction made between
165 coarse wool and the purple royal:
     for the leveler of sleep, all powerful,
     grants privilege to none, not
     the one whose sovereign tiara is formed
     by three crowns,[5] nor the one who
170 dwells in a hovel of straw;
     not the one whose golden hue
     comes from the surging Danube,[6]
     nor one who with humble reed builds his poor hut;
     with an ever equal rod
175 Morpheus[7] (that powerful image of death)
     measures the roughest cloth, the finest brocade.
     The soul, then, unburdened of
     external rule that holds sway when, occupied
     by material concerns, for good or ill
180 she[8] spends the day, remote now
     but not completely apart,
     only confers wages of vegetative
     warmth[9] to languid limbs and tranquil bones oppressed

---

4. The scale [*Editor*].
5. The pope.
6. The Holy Roman emperor.
7. Roman god of dreams who appears in Ovid's *Metamorphoses* (Book 11) [*Editor*].
8. *Alma* (soul) is feminine in Spanish [*Editor*].
9. The Aristotelian tripartite soul assigned distinct tasks to the vegetative, the sensitive, and the intellectual souls. In this case, the vegetative warmth reflects the action of the vegetative soul, held in common by all living things [*Editor*].

   by that passing death, for the body serene
185 is like a corpse with a soul,
   dead to life, alive to death,
   the vital balance wheel of the human clock[1]
   proffers scant signs of living,
   if not with hands then arterial concord,
190 a few small proofs beating a measured display
   of its well-ordered movement.
   This member, then, the king and living center
   of the vital spirits, with
   its companion, a breathing
195 bellows (the lung that like a magnet attracts
   air in never uneven movements, either
   constricting or expanding
   the conduit, muscular yet clear and soft,
   making it breathe in the cool surrounding air
200 that it exhales when heated,
   and the air avenges its expulsion by
   committing small thefts of our natural warmth
   at some time wept for but never recovered,
   and if not felt now, call no
205 theft small when oft repeated):
   these then, I say, exceptions, each a truthful
   witness, safeguarded that life,
   while with muted voices, silent, the senses
   impugned their testimony,
210 no reply their only proof,
   as did the tongue, slowed and dull,
   refuting them as it could no longer speak.
   And that most able scientific workshop[2]
   a skilled and provident dispenser of heat
215 to other members never
   a miser, ever active, not preferring
   the nearer part or forgetting the removed,
   and on a just, natural quadrant making
   note of the portion each member should receive
220 of the chyle,[3] that constant heat distilled from food
   which, merciful mediator, interposed
   its innocent substance between that heat and
   the radical moisture, paying full price

1. The heart. Sor Juana most likely drew the physiological descriptions that follow from Friar Luis de Granada's *Introducción del símbolo de la fe* (Introduction of the symbol of faith, 1584), which uses most of the same imagery [*revised by Editor*].
2. The stomach.
3. In galenic medicine, a fluid formed in the small intestine during digestion [*revised by Editor*].

for the compassion, perhaps the arrogance,
225   the inane foolhardiness
that exposed it to a voracious rival,
a punishment deserved, even if excused
for one who intervenes in
the dispute of another:
230   this, if no forge of Vulcan,[4]
then a temperate fire of human heat
that transmitted to the brain
the damp but most clear vapors[5]
of the four tempered humors[6]
235   that not only did not cloud the semblances
the intellect gave to imagination
which, for safer keeping and in purer form,
presented them to diligent memory[7]
that etched them, tenacious, and guards them with care,
240   but permitted fantasy
to form diverse images. And just as on
the untroubled surface, crystalline portent
of Pharos,[8] that uncommon refuge and port,
in the quicksilver mirror
245   at vast distances one sees clearly almost
all the realm of Neptune,[9] despite the expanse,
and the far-off ships that furrowed it, the size,
number, and fortune of bold vessels risked on
a shifting, transparent field,
250   while their light sails and weighty keels divided
waters and blustering winds:
so did serene fantasy[1]
copy images of all things, the unseen
brush shaping, without light, bright mental colors,
255   the figures not only of all sublunar
creatures but also of those
clear hues that are intellectual stars

4. Roman god of fire [Editor].
5. According to Aristotelian physiology, sleep was produced by vapors that emanated from the stomach after digestion. They are clear because although they impede external senses, they do not impede the internal senses [Editor].
6. A balance among the four humors (blood, phlegm, black bile, and yellow bile) was considered necessary for good health [revised by Editor].
7. In Aristotelian physiology and psychology, the imagination is the same as the fantasy. During the night, images that are stored in memory become available to the imagination, which transmits them to the intellect [Editor].
8. A legendary lighthouse on the island of Pharos in the harbor of Alexandria, Egypt [Editor].
9. Roman god of the oceans [Editor].
1. In Aristotelian psychology, responsible for images that were internal rather than external [Editor].

and in the manner that the invisible
can be conceived, ingeniously represents
260   and displays them to the Soul.
She, meanwhile, transformed into
immaterial being and beautiful
essence, contemplated that
spark shared with highest Being and cherished it
265   deep inside, in His image;
and deeming herself almost separated
from the coarse corporeal chain² that keeps her
ever bound, hinders the flight of intellect
that measures the immensity of the sphere,
270   or ponders the predictable orbits of
diverse heavenly bodies,
the study of astrology, however,
a serious fault, the deserved punishment,
(severe contortion of tranquility)
275   of a uselessly judicial study³
then placed, it seemed to her, upon the highest
peak of a mountain that Atlas,⁴
the giant presiding over all others,
deferred to as if a dwarf
280   and Olympus,⁵ that never
permitted an agitated soft breeze to
violate the serenity of its brow,
could not be called its foothill;
for the clouds, an opaque crown
285   on the highest mass of stone,
the haughtiest volcano,
which like a giant reaches up from the earth,
declares war on the sky,
are hardly a dense part of
290   its proud height, and on its vast
waist they are a mere rough cord that, badly tied,
is undone by the surly wind
or drained by the heat of the proximate sun.
The first region of its loft
295   (the lowest part, I mean to say, dividing
its fearsome sheer height in three)

2. The body that confines the soul. As the soul does not separate, Sor Juana maintains the
   orthodox Aristotelian position of the substantive soul [revised by Editor].
3. Judicial astrology, or the prediction of future events, was condemned by the Church in
   the Middle Ages and Renaissance.
4. In Greek mythology, the titan who held up the universe. Also associated with a moun-
   tain range [Editor].
5. The highest peak in Greece and home to the gods [Editor].

the swift flight of the eagle could not attain
(challenging the heavens and drinking the rays
of the sun, wishing to nest in that splendor),
300   now striving more than ever with all its strength,
now beating its two feathered sails, now raking
the air with its talons, struggling to break that
impunity with two wings,
weaving steps out of atoms.
305   The two pyramids (blazons
of vain Memphis,[6] if not now flags fixed, unwaving,
a masterwork hard-wrought of architecture),
whose summit crowned with barbaric trophies, tomb
and banner to the Ptolemies,[7] proclaimed to
310   the wind, to the clouds (if not heaven itself)
Egyptian glories, the great deeds of Memphis,
their proud, ever triumphant
city, called Cairo today,
for fame, struck dumb by the number, did not sing
315   that glory, those deeds, but they are imprinted
even in the wind, the sky;
these, whose height in graded symmetry rose
with so much tapering art
(as it mounted to the sky)
320   that the eye, no matter how keen, beheld it
vanish in the winds, unable to see the
subtle tip that appears to touch the first sphere[8]
until, wearied by wonder,
it[9] did not descend but plunged,
325   found itself at the foot of the ample base,
scarcely recovered from vertigo, the harsh
retribution for winged, visual daring,
whose opaque bodies[1] not opposed to the sun
but reconciled with its light, and if not
330   confederated (as, in effect, adjoined),
so completely bathed in its brilliance, so bright,
that to scorched travelers they
ne'er offered a small cover, a vestige of shade
for wearied breath or for weakening feet;
335   these, whether they be glories

6. The original name for Cairo [*Editor*].
7. Pharoahs. Sor Juana appears to be following the attribution of the pyramids in Luis de
Góngora's *The Solitudes* (1613), verses 956–57 [*Editor*].
8. The sphere of the moon.
9. That is, the eye [*Editor*].
1. That is, of the pyramids [*Editor*].

of Egypt or profane pomp,
barbarous hieroglyphs of blind error,
according to the sweet Greek poet,[2] also
blind (because he writes the heroic feats of
340   Achilles,[3] or the martial
subtleties of Ulysses,[4] the learned guild
of historians does not admit him, or
accepts him when it counts him in its records
to swell these more by glory than by number),
345   it would be easier to take the blazing
bolt of lightning from the dreaded Thunderer[5]
or the heavy studded club from Alcides[6]
than a single hemistich
from the countless series of sweet verses a
350   well-disposed Apollo[7] dictated to him:
Following the maxim,[8] I say, of Homer,
pyramids were mere material models,
are the intentional species[9] of the soul,
as the ambitious flame burns upward in a
355   pyramidal tip toward heaven, so does the
human mind, miming that form,
ever aspire to the First Cause,[1]
the center toward which all straight lines extend, if
not the circumference that holds,
360   infinite, all essences.
Then these two spurious mounts
(be they marvel, be they miracles)
and even that blasphemous haughty tower,[2]
its mournful remains today
365   not stones but discordant tongues
because voracious time does not consume them,
diverse idioms that render difficult
amicable conversation among peoples
(making those created as one by nature
370   seem different because their languages are strange),
if all of these were compared

2. Homer. The Homeric reference to the pyramids has not been found.
3. In Homer's *Iliad* [*Editor*].
4. In Homer's *Odyssey* [*Editor*].
5. Jupiter.
6. Hercules [*Editor*].
7. Roman god of sun, light, and truth [*Editor*].
8. This maxim has not been identified [*Editor*].
9. A scholastic term for mental or internal images (species) that translate the external images for the intellect [*Editor*].
1. In scholasticism, following Aristotelian terminology, God [*revised by Editor*].
2. The Tower of Babel.

to the sublime mental pyramid where the
soul was placed and saw herself, not knowing
how, they would be so diminished one would judge
375   the tip of that pyramid one of the spheres;
for the ambitious longing of the soul rose
higher than her own flight, placed part of her mind
on a soaring pinnacle,
so far above herself that she believed she
380   had left herself behind for a new region.
At that great, almost immeasurable height,
joyful but perplexed, perplexed
but resolute, amazed although resolute,
the queen, supreme sovereign[3] of the sublunar
385   world, freely cast the keen gaze
of her beautiful eyes of intellect, no
spyglass[4] before them (without fear of distance,
or mistrust of obstacle,
or concealing object interposed), over
390   all creation, whose immense entirety,
incomprehensible accumulation,
appeared clear and possible
to the eye but not the understanding, which
(stunned by a glut of objects,
395   its power far exceeded by their grandeur)
retroceded, a coward.
And so a repentant eye revoked the goal,
so rash, to vainly boast of
a contest with an object whose excellence
400   exceeds the visual lines,
against the Sun, I say, the brilliant body
whose rays are fiery punishment, unequal
forces scorning they chastise,
ray by ray, the arrogant
405   challenge, presumptuous first, then lamented
(a foolish experiment
that proved so costly to Icarus[5] whose own
tears, compassionate, drowned him),

3. The human soul.
4. Most editors have assumed that *antojo* was an archaic version of *anteojo* or spyglass. The term also signified judgment without fundament, however, and this may have been the meaning Sor Juana intended. For the latter argument, see Alberto Pérez-Amador Adam, *El precipicio de Faetón: Edición y comento de* Primero sueño *de Sor Juana Inés de la Cruz* (Frankfurt am Main/Mexico: Iberoamericana/Vervuert/Universidad Autónoma Metropolitana, 2015), pp. 327–28 [*Editor*].
5. In Greek mythology, the son of the master craftsman Daedalus who builds him wings of wax. When Icarus flies too close to the sun the wings melt and he falls to his death in the ocean below [*revised by Editor*].

as the understanding, here
410 vanquished as much by the immense multitude
      (the weighty apparatus
      of so many species comprised in a sphere)
      as by the qualities of each, surrendered:
      so awe-stricken that (placed in such profusion
415 and therefore impoverished by indifference
      in a sea of marvels, its choices confused),
      it was lost and almost foundered in the waves;
      and looking at everything, nothing it saw,
      and could not even discern
420 (the intellective faculty repelled by
      so many diverse species,
      so extensive, so incomprehensible,
      which it gazed upon, from the axis, where the
      whirling mechanism of the world rested,
425 to the antipodal pole)
      the parts, now not only those
      that all the universe deems
      not trappings but perfections of ornament
      but even the integrant,
430 proportionally able
      parts of its massive body.
      But like one for whom prolonged obscurity
      has usurped colors from visible objects,
      if struck by sudden brilliance
435 is left more blind by the excess of the light
      (for excess has the opposite effect on
      a dulled, unaccustomed faculty that then
      cannot bear light of the sun)
      and against these offenses of the light,
440 one summons the darkness, once the gloomy
      impediment to one's sight,
      over and again, a hand
      keeping vacillant rays from weak dazzled eyes,
      shade, pious arbiter, now the instrument
445 of their recovery by
      stages so that after they
      perform more steadfastly their operation
      a natural recourse, an innate knowledge
      confirmed by experience,
450 mute teacher, perhaps, but worthy oratory
      could persuade other Galens,[6]

6. Aelius Galenus (129–ca. 200 C.E.), or Galen, was a prominent Greek physician and philosopher. Here, represents any doctor [*revised by Editor*].

that from a fatal toxin, occult noxious
qualities might be measured in scrupulous
proportioned doses, whether for abundant
455   excess of heat or cold, or to affect the
unknown sympathies or antipathies by
which natural causes make their progress
course (displaying to astounded wonderment a
certain effect from an unknown cause, with
460   fecund sleeplessness and careful
empirical attention
examining brutes first to lessen danger),
the beneficial concoction was prepared,
highest goal of the Apollonian science,[7]
465   an amazing antidote,
and so perhaps from evil can come great good:
in no other way did the soul, awestruck
at the sight of so vast an
object summon her attention that, scattered
470   by so much diversity
still could not recover from the portentous
awe that had calmed her discourse,[8]
allowing only the formless embryo
of a confused concept which, so misshapen,
475   depicted in disordered chaos all the
blur of species it embraced,
come together with no order, come apart
with none, and the more they attempt to combine
the more they dissolve apart,
480   too filled with their difference,
encircling with violence the diffuseness
of so many objects in a container
so small, scant even for the least and lowest.
And so, sails furled, entrusted unwittingly
485   to a traitorous sea, disquieting wind
(seeking fidelity in a heedless sea
and constancy in the wind),
she anchored unwillingly
on the mental shore, chastened,
490   rudder destroyed, mast broken,
the ship-kissing sands of the beach with splinters,
where, now recovered, prudent
reflection usurped repairs, and circumspect

7. Medicine [*Editor*].
8. Reason [*Editor*].

judgment replaced lack of thought:
495   and curbed in her actions she deemed it best to
reduce to a single theme,
or separately to examine
what can be reduced to the
two times five and ingenious categories:[9]
500   metaphysical reduction that teaches
(conceiving of general entities in
a few mental images
in which reason, abstracted, disdains matter)
how to form knowledge from universals,
505   correcting with forewarned art
the inability to grasp in only
one intuitive act all of creation,
but scaling a ladder, ascends, step by step,
from one concept to the next
510   and that of comprehending a relative
order, following, of necessity, the
limited vigor of the understanding
that bases its gains on successive discourse;
doctrine strengthens, with learned nourishment, her
515   feeble forces, and the lengthy, if clement,
continuing current of the discipline
instills a robust spirit so that boldly
she aspires to the glorious laurel
of the most arduous striving, and ascends
520   the high rungs, devoting herself first to one
then another faculty,
until immaterially she looks upon
the honorable summit,
the sweet conclusion of her arduous zeal
525   (bitterly sown, a fruit pleasing to the taste,
even her long fatigue a small price to pay)
and with valiant foot she trods
the soaring pinnacle of that lofty brow.
My[1] understanding desired to follow
530   the method of this series,
that is, to pass from the lowest degree of
inanimate being (least favored if not
most unprotected of all produced by the

---

9. These are the ten Aristotelian categories indicating what can be predicated about something in a proposition. They are substance, quantity, quality, relation, place, time, posture, having, action, and affection.
1. One of the few times the poem employs a personal pronoun [*Editor*].

second cause[2]), to the nobler ranking that in
535 vegetal life is first born, although crude, of
Themis[3] (the first who at her
fertile maternal breasts with
attractive virtue expressed
the sweet springs of terrestrial humor that
540 as natural sustenance is the sweetest food),
a ranking adorned by four
diverse, quite contrary acts,
which attracts, then diligently segregates
what it deems unsuitable,
545 expels the superfluous, and makes the most
useful substances its own;[4]
and (once investigated)
probes a more beautiful form
(adorned with senses and more
550 than senses apprehensive
imaginative power),
that with reason can give rise to a dispute,
when not an insult to the inanimate
star that gleams and shines most bright
555 with haughty splendor, for the
lowest creature, the most humble can provoke
envy, possess advantage;[5]
and making of this bodily knowledge the
foundation, however meager, moves on to
560 the supreme, the marvelous, the tripartite
composite ordered of three harmonious
lines and of all lower forms
a mysterious recapitulation:[6]
the decisive joining of pure nature raised
565 to the heights, enthroned, and the
least noble, the most contemptible creature:
adorned not only with the five faculties
of sense but ennobled by
the three directing internal ones,[7] the gift,
570 and not in vain, of a wise, powerful hand,

2. In scholasticism, nature, created by God, the First Cause [*revised by Editor*].
3. The Greek titaness, daughter of heaven and earth. Mentioned in Ovid's *Metamorphoses* (Book 1). Some scholars assume this was an error in the *princeps* and have corrected to Tethys, the sea goddess. Many previous translations follow this editorial intervention [*Editor*].
4. This passage describes the four operations of vegetative life, according to Aristotle.
5. These are the attributes of animals in the Aristotelian tradition [*revised by Editor*].
6. This passage describes human beings, "tripartite" because they incorporate vegetative, sensitive, and rational elements [*revised by Editor*].
7. The three aspects of the soul: intellect, memory, and will.

to be mistress of the rest:
the zenith of His works, the circle that joins
the sphere and earth, ultimate perfection of
creation and ultimate
575 delight of the Eternal Creator, and
in whom, satisfied, His vast magnificence
came to rest, portentous origination:
no matter how haughtily it reaches for
heaven, dust closes its mouth,
580 its mysterious image
might be the sacred vision that the Eagle
of the Evangels[8] saw in Patmos, which walked
among the stars and on earth with equal steps,
or the huge statue[9] whose rich high head of the
585 most precious metal was made,
its base of the most scorned and weakest substance,
shattered at the least motion:
man, I say, in short, the greatest wonder that
human understanding can devise, absolute
590 compendium that resembles the angels,
the plants, the brutes; whose exalted lowliness
partakes of all of nature.
Why? Perhaps because more fortunate than the
rest, it is elevated
595 by the grace of a loving union.[1] And oh,
grace, though repeated, never well enough known
as it seems to be ignored
so little valued and so unrequited!
These, then, were the steps I[2] wished at times to take,
600 but at others I forswore
that wish, judging it excessive boldness
in one who failed to comprehend the smallest,
the most simple part of natural effects
nearest at hand, to attempt
605 to apprehend everything;
one who could not grasp the secret, obscure way
the pleasant fountain[3] led its crystalline course,

8. The reference is to Saint John the Divine, who wrote the Book of Revelation.
9. Described in Daniel 2:31–33, the image dreamed by Nebuchadnezzar and interpreted by Daniel.
1. The Incarnation by which God became man in Jesus Christ [revised by Editor].
2. The original uses only a conjugated verb, quería, with no marked pronoun. The subject could be either first or third person singular and therefore might be "my understanding" from v. 530, rather than "I," a pronoun not often used in the poem [Editor].
3. The fountain of the nymph Arethusa became a river that ran underground, through Hades and the Elysian Fields. She reported to Ceres (the "golden goddess") the whereabouts of her daughter Persephone (the "triform wife").

lingering, detained, in slow meanders, through
the fearsome bosom of Pluto,[4] dire caverns
610 of the dreadful abyss, bright
tracker searching the smiling meadows, lovely
Elysian Fields,[5] the nuptial
chamber of a triform wife
(useful curiosity, though wearisome,
615 for she gave a true account
of the beautiful daughter, unrecovered,
to the golden goddess[6] who troubled mountains,
forests, questioned meadows, woods,
seeking her life but losing it in sorrow);
620 one who did not know why an ivory cast
circles the frail beauty of a brief flower:
why a mingling of colors, scarlet blending
with the whiteness of dawn, is
its fragrant finery, or
625 why it exhales the scent of amber, unfolds
to the wind its raiment, beauteous because
delicate, which multiplies
into countless new daughters,[7] forming a frilled
display fringed with gold tracings
630 and, the white bud seal broken,
boastfully flaunts the plunder,
the sweet wound of the goddess of Cyprus[8] and,
if that which colors it did
not usurp the whiteness from dawn, the purple
635 from the break of day, blending
them into a purpled white,
a snowy russet: iridescent blossom
inciting the same applause from the meadow
that it solicits, perhaps
640 a tutor in vanities if not profane
exemplar of feminine skill that makes the
most active poison two times more venomous
in the veil of appearance
of one who feigns a radiant complexion.

4. God of the underworld [Editor].
5. Afterlife reserved for heroes in Greek myth [Editor].
6. Ceres, goddess of harvest [Editor].
7. Modern editors have debated whether the original *hija*, or daughter, is an errata and one has suggested that *hoja*, or leaf, makes more sense in the context. For the latter argument, see Cruz, *Obras completas*, 2nd ed., vol. 1, pp. 527, n. 739–40 [Editor].
8. Venus. Poets commonly attributed the color of the rose to the wound Venus received to her heel while running amid roses in search of Adonis. Cruz, *Obras completas*, vol. 1, 2nd ed., 528, n. 743 [revised by Editor].

645   Then—my[9] timid thought repeated—if before
      a single object knowledge flees, and reason,
      a coward, turns away; if before a lone
      species deemed independent of the rest and
      free of affiliation, understanding
650   turns its back and a frightened reason withdraws
      from the difficult contest it refuses
      to enter valiantly, for,
      a coward, it fears it will understand it
      badly, or never, or late,
655   how could it reflect on so fearsome and vast
      a mechanism, its weight
      terrible, unbearable if it did not
      rest on its very center, enough to crush
      the back of Atlas,[1] even exceed the strength
660   of Alcides;[2] would the one with sufficient
      counterweight to the sphere judge the immense mass
      less weighty, less ponderous
      than the intent to investigate nature?
      Other times, more fearless, it denounced as
665   too cowardly ceding the laurel even
      before entering into harsh combat, and
      turned to the bold example
      of that illustrious youth,[3]
      proud charioteer of the fiery coach,
670   his gallant if luckless high impulse firing
      the spirit to the place where valor finds more
      open paths of daring than fear encounters
      examples of chastisement,
      for once traveled, no punishment threatened
675   can halt a second attempt,
      (second ambition, I say).
      Neither deep mausoleum,
      cerulean tomb for his unhappy ashes,
      nor vengeful fulminating thunderbolt moves
680   despite its warning, an arrogant valor
      that, despising life, resolves
      to make his name eternal
      in his own ruination.

9. The original, which reads "*el pensamiento,*" or "the thought," could be interpreted with
   or without a personal pronoun "my" in English [*Editor*].
1. The titan who supported the universe on his shoulders [*Editor*].
2. Hercules [*Editor*].
3. Phaethon, the son of Helios, the Sun. The "cerulean tomb" (line 678) refers to the Po
   River, where his body fell. The "thunderbolt" (line 679) was used by Jupiter to kill him.

Rather it is a model: a pernicious
685 example that engenders the wings for a
repeated flight of the ambitious spirit
that flatters terror itself
to compliment bravery,
spells glories among the letters of havoc.
690 Would that the punishment never be made known
so that the crime would never be attempted:
politic silence instead
as a circumspect ruler
might destroy the records of the case, either
695 simulating with feigned ignorance, or with
secret penalties punishing insolent
excess, not suggesting to popular view
a noxious example: word of the evil
of a great crime is its threat,
700 knowledge inciting extensive contagion;
for repeating a merely single crime would
be more remote among the ignorant than
among those who were cautioned.
But while choice foundered, confused, among the reefs,
705 touching sandbars of courses impossible
to follow each time it tried,
heat, finding nothing on which to feed, for its
temperate flame (a flame after all even
if temperate, for in its active mode it
710 consumes and well may inflame)
could not avoid transforming
its sustenance, turning the foreign matter
into its own substance: and the boisterous
boiling produced by the union of moisture
715 and heat in the wondrous natural vessel[4]
had ceased (lacking more fuel), and so the vapors
rising from it, damp, soporific hampered
the throne of reason (and from there sweet torpor
poured on the limbs) consumed by the mild ardor
720 of heat, unlocking the chains
of sleep: and the extended limbs feeling want
of food, weary of rest, not fully awake
nor asleep, signal desire for movement
with indolent stretches, slowly extending
725 benumbed nerves, and tired bones
(still without the entire will of their master)

4. The stomach [*revised by Editor*].

returning to the other
side, senses (so sweetly hindered by natural
henbane[5]) began to recover their powers
730 eyes opening and closing.
And from the mind, now idle,
the phantoms[6] fled and, as if of lightest
vapor, their form changed to evanescent smoke
and wind. As a magic lantern[7] represents
735 diverse feigned and painted figures on a white
wall, assisted no less by shadow than by
light: maintaining in tremulous reflections
the distance mandated by
a learned perspective, the measurements
740 verified in countless trials,
the fugitive shadow that vanishes in
splendor itself, feigns the form
of a body, adorned by all dimensions,
when it does not deserve to
745 be deemed even a surface.
Meanwhile the fiery father of light knew
the fixed time had come to near the orient,
and he bade farewell to the opposite pole,
setting behind the mountains:
750 for the same point where his light in tremulous
swoons, meets their occident it
luminously adorns our orient.
But before that the beautiful, gentle star
of Venus[8] cast the first light
755 with the beauteous wife of old Tithonus[9]
(an Amazon[1] clad in a thousand lights and
armed against the night, beautiful though bold, brave
though shedding copious tears)
who showed her beautiful brow
760 crowned with morning glow, tender
and yet spirited prelude to the blazing
planet recruiting novice glimmerings as
troops, reserving more robust veteran lights

5. A natural soporific.
6. Phantasms, or images, formed during sleep [revised by Editor].
7. An image projector, which was a forerunner of the cinematographic camera, described by the Jesuit polymath Atanasius Kircher (1602–1680) in his Ars Magna Lucis et Umbrae (Great art of light and shadow, 1671) [Editor].
8. The last "star" seen at dawn [revised by Editor].
9. In Greek mythology, the lover of Eos, the titaness of the dawn. Known in Roman mythology as Aurora [revised by Editor].
1. Mythical woman warrior. While classical in origin, amazons became symbols of the Americas after the reputed existence of women warriors there [revised by Editor].

for the rearguard against the
765 tyrannous usurper of
the empire of day, girdled in black laurel
of a thousand shadows made,
and with a fearsome nocturnal scepter she
governed the shadows that frightened even her.
770 But barely had the fair precursor, standard-
bearer to the Sun, raised her banner in the
orient than sweet yet martial clarions
of the birds sounded the call to arms (deft but
artless resounding trumpets),
775 when (like a cowardly tyrant, and hampered
by fearsome misgivings she tried to display
her forces, opposing brief repairs of her
gloomy cloak to the slashes
of light she received as wounds, though her courage,
780 badly satisfied, was an ill-formed pretext
for her fear, knowing her resistance was weak),
trusting in flight more than force
to save her, she sounded her raucous cornet
to gather in the black squadrons and retreat
785 in order, just as she was attacked by a
nearer plenitude of gleamings that dawned on
the highest peak of the ramparts of the world.
The Sun, in short, arrived, closing the golden
ring it engraved on a sapphire blue heaven:
790 a thousand times thousand points,
a thousand golden flows (lines,
I say, of brilliant light) shone
from a luminous circumference, scoring
the cerulean page of the heavens, and
795 forming troops they charged the erstwhile ebony
tyrant of their empire, who in disorder hastily fled
stumbling on her own horrors,
treading on her own shadow,
attempting to reach the occident with her
800 now routed, disordered army of shadows,
pursued by the light following close behind.
At last her fugitive step came within view
of the occident, and (recovered from her
defeat, regaining her valor in ruins),
805 in the half of the world undefended by
the Sun, the second time a
rebel, determines to be crowned once again,
while the fair golden mane of the Sun lit our

hemisphere, with just light and distributive
810   order, gave all things visible their colors,
restoring to the external senses their
function, the world illuminated with more
certain light, and I, awake.[2]

Loa to the Mystery Play *The Divine Narcissus*: An Allegory[†]

Mystery plays, called *autos sacramentales* in Spanish, were a genre of religious theater that used allegorical narratives to explain theological concepts. With roots in street performances by itinerant theater troupes in the medieval period, mystery plays eventually became important fixtures of courtly theater. While the topics (the Eucharist, the Trinity, or Final Judgment) were constant, the allegories could vary greatly depending on the audience. Mystery plays were often preceded by *loas*: theatrical prologues that introduced the main theme of the mystery play. These, although tied to the mystery play, were entirely separate allegories and may be read as stand-alone pieces.

The *loa* to Sor Juana's 1690 mystery play *El divino narciso* (The divine Narcissus) is her most famous and one of three to employ American themes. Through an allegorical representation of the Spanish conquest of Mexico, it explains the mystery of the Eucharist while representing arguments of early Christian missionaries, some of whom claimed that pre-Columbian religions contained veiled prefigurations of Christian theology and ritual. Through pairs of male and female figures, representing Mexica and Spanish sides of the Conquest, Sor Juana revives the defense of conquest by religious conversion rather than by war, a position most forcefully articulated by the Dominican crusader Bartolomé de las Casas (c. 1484–1566) as opposed to such legal institutions as ritual readings of the "The Requirement" (1514).[1] Sor Juana, like Las Casas, defends only the parts of pre-Columbian worship believed to prefigure Christianity, considering everything else to be diabolic deviation and confusion.

The play ends with the successful persuasion of the Mexica to listen to Christian doctrine in the mystery play that follows. This complex three-act play employs the classical myth of Narcissus to represent the identification of Christ with his flock, or the Church. Because of its unusual theme and verse that poignantly evokes the great early sixteenth-century Spanish poetry of Garcilaso de la Vega and San Juan de la Cruz, the play itself is considered one of Sor Juana's masterpieces. The *loa* and the play were first published

2. As adjectives mark gender in Spanish, the original *despierta* ("awake") is the only self-reference in the poem that also establishes a feminine subject.
† Headnote by the editor. All notes are by the translator unless otherwise noted [*Editor*].
1. See "The Requirement" on p. 171 [*Editor*].

separately in 1690 and then republished in the 1691 revision of Sor
Juana's first volume of works, *Castalian Inundation,* and again in
her *Second Volume* (1692). Although the end of the *loa* suggests
that the play was to be performed in the Madrid court, there is no
evidence that this ever occurred.

DRAMATIS PERSONAE

OCCIDENT
AMERICA
ZEAL
RELIGION
MUSIC
SOLDIERS

Scene I

[*Enter* OCCIDENT,[2] *an elegant Indian wearing a crown, and*
AMERICA *at his side, an Indian noblewoman in the richly
embroidered cloth and headdress worn when singing the*
tocotín.[3] *They sit on two chairs; around them dance Indian men
and women, holding the feathers and shells ordinarily used in
this dance; as they dance,* MUSIC *sings.*]

MUSIC   Mexicans[4] most noble,
    whose ancient lineage
    has its genesis in
    the bright rays of the sun:[5]
    this is the blessed day,   5
    the day in all the year
    when we pay homage to
    our highest deity;[6]
    then come now, come adorned
    with your emblems of rank,   10
    join to your piety
    your joy, let them be one;

2. From the perspective of Europe, the Americas were "Occidental" or Western [*Editor*].
3. A Mexica dance with its accompanying music.
4. In the sixteenth and seventeenth centuries, the term "Mexican" was used almost exclusively to refer to the native Americans of central Mexico, now referred to as "Mexica." "Aztec" is a term invented in the nineteenth century [*Editor*].
5. The sun god Tonatiuh was one of the most important of the Mexica pantheon and cosmogony [*Editor*].
6. Huitzilopochtli, the war god, was one of the most important gods of the Mexica pantheon and recipient of human sacrifices. Half of the *Templo Mayor* (Major Temple) in the center of Tenochtitlan, the Mexica capital that later became Mexico City, was dedicated to his cult. The other half was dedicated to Tlaloc, the rain god [*Editor*].

in festive pageantry
come worship and revere the great God of Seeds![7]

And since prosperity   15
in all our provinces
is owed to him who brings
abundance, pious ones,
make offerings to him
for they are owed to him   20
of the first fruits, bounty
of the year's rich harvest.
Let the finest blood flow
from your veins, blend the blood,[8]
so it may serve his cult;   25
in festive pageantry
come worship and revere the great God of Seeds!

> [OCCIDENT *and* AMERICA *take their seats, and* MUSIC *falls silent.*]

OCCIDENT   For among all the most high gods
   solemnly adored in my rites,
   so many deities that in   30
   this famed, illustrious city
   they number more than two thousand,
   to him we offer in savage
   unrelenting sacrifice hot
   human blood spilled, entrails throbbing,   35
   heart pulsating still, oh most cruel;[9]
   and though they number so many
   (I say this again) my greatest
   devotion is fixed upon him,
   the highest of all the high gods,   40
   exalted, the great God of Seeds.

AMERICA   And with reason, for this great god
   alone upholds our beloved
   realm, supporting our monarchy,

---

7. The God of Seeds refers to the practice of venerating Huitzilopochtli in a figure formed of amaranth seeds. In Spanish depictions, such as that of the Spanish conquistador Hernán Cortés in his *Second Letter,* the seeds are held together with blood of the sacrificed [*Editor*].
8. The Mexica forms of sacrifice included bloodletting through piercing one's tongue or cutting and spilling the blood [*Editor*].
9. Human sacrifice was part of Mexica ritual; it was often seen by the Spanish as proof of native American barbarism [*Editor*].

sustaining our kingdom with his 45
lush abundance of succulent
fruits; this benefit is supreme,
containing all other boons, since
it preserves the life that it makes
possible, and for this alone 50
we deem it most precious of gifts;
knowing this truth, why would we care
that our mines, a bounty of gold,
make rich America richer,
if the miasma from those mines 55
turns fields barren, the fertile land
sown with seeds that once bloomed into
fruit, made desolate, a wasteland?
Then too, his divine protection
provides more than corporeal 60
food for us to eat. Afterward,
in precious viands sanctified,
formed from his own flesh (but purged first
of all bodily corruption)
he cleanses our souls of their stains.[1] 65
And so, devoted to his cult,
let all of you repeat with me:

OCCIDENT, AMERICA, *and* MUSIC   In festive pageantry,
    come worship and revere the great God of Seeds!

Scene II

[*They exit, dancing; enter the Christian* RELIGION, *a Spanish
lady, and* ZEAL, *an armed captain general, and behind them,
Spanish* SOLDIERS.]

RELIGION   You are Zeal, and being Zeal, how
    can your Christian fury bear to
    see idolatry, false and blind,
    celebrate with superstitious
    cults an idol, a vile affront 5
    to me, the Christian Religion?

ZEAL   Religion: please do not complain
    so quickly of my omission,

1. The reference is to the ritual *teocualo*, by which worshipers ingest part of the Huitzilo-
pochtli statue formed of seeds. The idea of cleansing one's sins is a distinctly Chris-
tianized version of the ritual [*Editor*].

or lament my poor blandishments;
for my right arm now is upraised   10
and brandishing my sword, and I
shall avenge these wrongs, for your sake.
Withdraw, my lady, to one side
while I claim your rightful vengeance.

[*Enter* ᴏᴄᴄɪᴅᴇɴᴛ *and* ᴀᴍᴇʀɪᴄᴀ, *dancing, and from the
other side* ᴍᴜꜱɪᴄ *and accompaniment.*]

ᴍᴜꜱɪᴄ   In festive pageantry   15
come worship and revere the great God of Seeds!

ᴢᴇᴀʟ   They have come out; I shall approach.

ʀᴇʟɪɢɪᴏɴ   I shall go too; pity moves me
to draw near (before your anger
charges them, enraged, for my sake)   20
and invite them, in peace and love,
to receive the truth of my cult.

ᴢᴇᴀʟ   Then let us hurry, for now they
have begun their indecent rite.

ᴍᴜꜱɪᴄ   In festive pageantry   25
come worship and revere the great God of Seeds!

[ᴢᴇᴀʟ *and* ʀᴇʟɪɢɪᴏɴ *approach.*]

ʀᴇʟɪɢɪᴏɴ   Oh, most powerful Occident,
beautiful, rich America,
who live impoverished amid
these prodigal bounties of wealth: 30
put aside this blasphemous cult
incited by Satan himself.
Open your eyes! And now follow
my true belief, the one true faith,
persuaded by my Christian love.   35

ᴏᴄᴄɪᴅᴇɴᴛ   Who are they, what strangers are these
I see before me? Oh heavens,
why do they wish to impede the
course of my joys and happiness?

AMERICA   What nations unheard of and strange   40
   wish to counter the primacy
   of my most ancient rule and sway?

OCCIDENT   Oh you, strange and foreign beauty,
   oh you, a lovely rare pilgrim!
   Tell me who you are who comes now   45
   to trouble my great jubilance.

RELIGION   I am the Christian Religion,
   and I shall endeavor to turn[2]
   your provinces to my worship.

OCCIDENT   A fine avowal you demand!   50

AMERICA   A fine lunacy you intend!

OCCIDENT   What you contrive, impossible!

AMERICA   No doubt she is mad; just leave her,
   and let our worship continue!

OCCIDENT, AMERICA, *and* MUSIC   And in festive pageantry,   55
   come worship and revere the great God of Seeds!

ZEAL   How, most barbarous Occident,
   and how, most blind idolatry,
   can you disdain sweet Religion,
   my dearly loved and gentle wife?   60
   For you have already drained dry
   the cup of your iniquities,
   and our Lord God will not allow
   you to continue your sinning,
   and has sent me to punish you.   65

OCCIDENT   Who are you? The mere sight of your
   face can strike fear deep in my heart.

ZEAL   I am Zeal. Why are you surprised?
   When all your excesses rebuff
   Religion, my beloved spouse,   70
   Zeal will appear to avenge her

---

2. The original uses *reducir* (literally, to reduce), a term that served as a euphemism for civilizing what Spanish policy often portrayed as indigenous barbarism [*Editor*].

by chastising your insolence.
A Minister of God am I,
and seeing that your tyrannies
have already gone so far, and   75
weary of seeing you live for
so many years in deep error,
He has sent me to punish you.
And therefore these mighty armed hosts,
vibrating thunderbolts of steel,[3]   80
the ministers are of His wrath
and the instruments of His ire.

OCCIDENT   What God, what error, what offense,
    what punishment do you proclaim?
    I do not understand your words,   85
    have no idea of your meaning,
    or who you are that you dare to
    interfere with the great task of
    my people as they gather here
    to recite as our cult demands: 90

MUSIC   And in festive pageantry,
    come worship and revere the great God of Seeds!

AMERICA   Barbarian,[4] madman, blindly
    with words none understands you wish
    to perturb the serenity   95
    that we enjoy in tranquil calm
    and peace: and cease in your efforts
    or you will be reduced to ash,
    and not even the winds will bear
    news that you once lived! And you, spouse,   100

        [*To* OCCIDENT.]
    and your vassals, be deaf and blind
    to his words, ignore, do not heed
    his fantasies; proceed with your
    righteous worship, do not allow
    upstart foreign nations in their   105
    insolence to interrupt you.

3. A reference to Spanish harquebuses, precursors to muskets. It was a common idea that
   Native Americans confused the firing of Spanish firearms for lightning [*Editor*].
4. Although in its original use, "barbarian" signified any foreigner, the term came to be
   used by the Spanish to describe Native Americans with what they viewed as perverse
   cultural traits. The reversal imitates Bartolomé de las Casas's polemical relativism (see
   p. 171) [*Editor*].

MUSIC   And in festive pageantry
   come worship and revere the great God of Seeds!

ZEAL   Since the first proposal of peace
   you have so haughtily turned down,   110
   then the second, for war, you must
   accept despite your arrogance.[5]
   Sound the call! To arms! This is war!

    [*Drums and bugles sound.*]

OCCIDENT   What monstrosities has heaven sent
   against me? What weapons are these,   115
   such arms my eyes have never seen?
   Ah, my guards! And you, my soldiers:
   those arrows you always prepare,
   now is the time to let them fly!

AMERICA   What lightning bolts does heaven hurl   120
   against me? What terrible orbs
   of burning lead[6] rain down like hail?
   What monsters, hideous centaurs[7]
   do battle against my people?

    [*Offstage voices:*]
To arms, to arms! A war, a war!   125

    [*Instruments play.*]
Long live Spain! And long live her king!

    [*The battle is joined, the* INDIANS *enter through one door
    and go out the other, the* SPANIARDS *in pursuit; behind them,*
    OCCIDENT *retreats before* RELIGION, *and* AMERICA *before*
    ZEAL.]

Scene III

RELIGION   Surrender, haughty Occident!

OCCIDENT   Now your valor must conquer me
   for I stand firm against mere words.

---

5. Zeal here represents a defense of war epitomized by the Spanish juridical document,
   "The Requirement," on p. 171 [*Editor*].
6. Cannonballs [*Editor*].
7. Horses and their riders. It was a common idea that Native Americans, unaccustomed to
   horses, thought that the horse and rider were one being [*Editor*].

ZEAL   Die, insolent America!

RELIGION   Wait, Zeal, wait, oh do not kill her,   5
    for I need her to be alive!

ZEAL   But how is it you defend her
    when you are the one offended?

RELIGION   There can be no doubt: her conquest
    fell to your valor, your prowess,   10
    but what falls to me is mercy
    and the pity to spare her life;
    your charge, to conquer her by force,
    but mine to vanquish her with words,
    with the persuasive gentleness   15
    of mild, invincible reason.[8]

ZEAL   You have seen the perversity
    in their blind abomination
    of your faith; is it not better
    that all die?

RELIGION   Oh cease your justice,   20
    Zeal: you must not, cannot kill them:
    for I am by nature benign
    and I do not want them to die
    but to convert, and then to live.

AMERICA   If your request that I not die   25
    and this show of your compassion
    are because, oh arrogant one,
    you expect to conquer me first
    with bodily weapons and then
    with the arms of intellect, you   30
    are mistaken, you are deceived;
    for although I, a captive, weep
    for my liberty, my free will
    with even greater liberty
    still will worship my deities![9]   35

OCCIDENT   I have already said that force
    obliges me to cede to you;

---

8. A position resonant with that of Bartolomé de las Casas. See p. 171 [*Editor*].
9. Catholic dogma was strongly tied to free will over predestination, espoused by Protestants [*Editor*].

this is true, but hear me: clearly
there is no force, no violence
that can hinder my will, keep it   40
from acting with total freedom;
and so, as your captive I moan,
but you cannot stop me, here, deep
in my heart, from proclaiming that
I worship and revere the great God of Seeds!   45

Scene IV

RELIGION   But wait, what I tender to you
is not force but a mild caress.
Which God is the one you revere?

OCCIDENT   He is a God who makes fertile
the fields that produce our harvests;   5
before whom the heavens bow down,
and whom even the rains obey;
the same God who washes away
our sins, no matter how vile, then
becomes the food he offers us.[1]   10
Tell me if there can ever be
from the most loving deity
more benefits for humankind
than these I describe for you now.

RELIGION [*Aside*]   Lord save me! What crafty designs   15
and devices, what mimicries
do these falsehoods intend toward our
holiest, our most sacred truths?
Oh wiliest of serpents, most
venomous of snakes! Oh hydra[2]   20
spewing out of your seven mouths
all the deadly hemlock of that
most noxious poison, lethal brew!
How far will this malice of yours
imitate and feign the holy   25
miracles of our one true God?[3]
But with your own lies and deceit,
if God grants this skill to my tongue,
I shall most surely convince you.

1. This description is a Christianized version of two Mexica ("Aztec") deities and their functions: Huitzilopochtli and Tlaloc, the rain god [*Editor*].
2. Hydra, snake, and serpent all refer to Satan.
3. Christian missionaries often argued that similarities between Christianity and Native American cults were signs of diabolic intervention and perversion [*Editor*].

AMERICA   Oh, silent one, what is it you   30
    envision? Do you not see? No
    other God can confirm his works
    and his wonders with benefits.

RELIGION   I must reason with the doctrine
    of Paul, for when he preached to the   35
    people of Athens he knew of
    their law that mandated death for
    any seeking to introduce
    new gods to the city; he was
    aware as well of the altar   40
    dedicated "to an unknown
    God," and declared these words to them:
    "This is not a new deity,
    no, this God I tell you about
    is the unknown God you worship   45
    and adore here at this altar."⁴
    I shall do the same . . . Occident,
    listen; blind idolatry, hear;
    for all your good fortune lies in
    heeding my words! Listen and hear.   50
    Those miracles you tell about,
    those prodigies you have revealed,
    those glimmers and rare features glimpsed
    behind the veils of false belief,
    the curtains of superstition;   55
    those portents that you misconstrue,
    attributing wondrous effects,
    to your gods of mendacity,
    are works of the only true God
    and of His infinite wisdom.   60
    For if the flowering meadow
    is fertile, if fields are fruitful,
    and if the fruit proliferates,
    and if the sown fields grow and bloom,
    and if the clouds distill the rain,   65
    all is the work of His right hand;
    neither the arm that cultivates,
    nor the rain that fecundates,
    nor the warmth that animates, none
    of these could make the plants flourish   70

---

4. Acts 17:22–23. The exact citation that Sor Juana attributes to Saint Paul does not appear
    in the passage [revised by Editor].

and grow without the presence of
His productive Providence that
gives the plants their vegetative
soul.[5]

AMERICA   If all that you say is true,
  tell me: is this deity so   75
  benign that he will allow me
  to touch him with my own hands like
  the idol that my hands create,
  using the seeds and the rivers
  of innocent blood that is shed here,   80
  spilled here, caught for this one cause here,
  and for this sole effect alone?

RELIGION   Even though His essence divine
  is invisible and immense,
  it is already deeply joined   85
  to our mundane, earthly nature,
  and draws near us so humanly
  that it allows the unworthy
  hands of priests, but no others, to
  approach the godhead and touch it.   90

AMERICA   In this, then, you and I agree,
  because as for my God, no one
  at all is sanctioned or allowed
  to touch him save those who serve him
  as priests; and not only may they   95
  not touch him, but the common folk,
  the laity, may not even
  enter his sanctified chapel.

ZEAL   Oh what reverence, more worthy
  to be paid to our one true God!   100

OCCIDENT   Tell me this, although you tell me
  other things too: is this God made
  of matter as fine and as rare
  as the red blood shed and offered
  in sacrifice, as the seed that   105
  is our sustenance and support?

---

5. In scholastic Aristotelianism, the soul was tripartite, divided into vegetative, sensitive,
and intellectual [*revised by Editor*].

RELIGION I said this before: His divine
 majesty is infinite, not
 material; but His blessed
 humanity, bloodless in the   110
 holy sacrifice of the Mass,
 makes chance use of pure white wheat seeds
 that then are transformed into His
 very flesh, His very blood;
 and His most precious blood, when caught 115
 in the chalice, is the blood, pure
 and innocent and pristine that,
 offered on the altar of the
 Holy Cross, is the salvation
 and the redemption of the world.[6]   120

AMERICA Since you wish me to believe these
 things that are unheard-of and strange,
 can the deity you describe
 be as loving as our God, the
 one whom I adore, and offer   125
 Himself to us as sustenance?

RELIGION Yes, and all His divine wisdom,
 for that aim and purpose alone,
 dwells on earth among humankind.

AMERICA And shall my eyes not see this God, 130
 so that I may be persuaded,

OCCIDENT and so that finally, at last,
 my obstinacy will leave me?

RELIGION Yes, you will see when you are washed
 in the clear, crystalline fountain 135
 of Baptism.[7]

OCCIDENT Oh yes, I know
 that before I sit at the rich
 table I must carefully wash,
 for that is my ancient custom.[8]

6. A reference to the sacrifice of Jesus Christ, enacted in the Christian ritual of the Eucharist, in which his flesh and blood are consumed in the communion bread and wine [Editor].
7. Only baptized Christians could receive communion in the Eucharist [Editor].
8. Ritual baths of Mesoamerican rites [Editor].

ZEAL   That is not the kind of washing   140
    demanded by the stains[9] you bear.

OCCIDENT   What kind is it?

RELIGION   A sacrament
    that like the living waters can
    wash away and cleanse all your sins.

AMERICA   The brevity of the great news   145
    you bring confounds me, and I would
    like to hear this in detail once
    more, for divine inspiration
    moves me to want to fathom it.

OCCIDENT   And me; and to know of the life   150
    and death of that resplendent God
    who, you tell us, is in the bread.

RELIGION   All right, let us begin. First you
    must know it is a metaphor,
    an idea dressed in the colors   155
    of rhetoric and visible
    therefore to your eyes, as I shall
    reveal to you; for I well know
    you are more inclined to favor
    objects that can be seen over   160
    the words that faith can tell you;
    and so, my friends, instead of ears
    you need to use your eyes to learn
    the teaching that faith will show you.[1]

OCCIDENT   True: I would rather see it   165
    than have you recount it to me.

Scene V

RELIGION   Let us begin.

ZEAL   Religion, please
    tell me how you determine the
    form to represent mysteries.

9. Christian sin [*Editor*].
1. A justification of presenting Christian dogma in a dramatic allegory. This is a preparation for the mystery play, *The Divine Narcissus*, that will follow [*Editor*].

RELIGION   In an allegorical play
   I wish to make them visible
   so that she[2] and the entire
   occident will be instructed
   in all that they have desired
   to know.   5

ZEAL   And what will you call the
   play that you allegorize here?   10

RELIGION   *The Divine Narcissus*, because if
   that most unhappy one[3] had
   an idol she truly worshiped,
   whose strange signs and traits the Demon
   attempted to twist into a   15
   feigned high mystery of our faith
   —the Holy Eucharist—know too
   that there have been among other
   Gentile peoples other signs and
   traces of so high a marvel.   20

ZEAL   And where will your play be performed?

RELIGION   In the crowned city of Madrid,
   the royal center of our faith,
   and the most regal seat and throne
   of their Catholic Majesties   25
   to whom the Indies[4] owe the holy
   lights of our most Christian Scripture
   shining bright in the occident.

ZEAL   Do you see impropriety
   in writing it in Mexico   30
   and performing it in Madrid?

RELIGION   Do you mean you have never seen
   a thing created in one place
   that is of use in another?
   Moreover, writing it was not   35
   only a whim or mere caprice
   but an act of due obedience

---

2. America [*Editor*].
3. America [*Editor*].
4. A Spanish term for the Americas [*Editor*].

striving for the impossible.
And so the work, perhaps rustic
and rough, perhaps needing polish,   40
is the result of obedience,
not the child of audacity.

ZEAL   Well then, tell me, Religion, now
        that you have brought forth this play, how
        do you avoid the complaint   45
        that you introduce the Indies,
        then wish to take them to Madrid?[5]

RELIGION   Since the play intends only to
            celebrate this high mystery,
            and those who have been introduced   50
            are simply no more than a few
            abstractions that embody and
            make visible what the play means,
            nothing must be denied or changed
            although I take them to Madrid: 55
            for concepts of the intellect
            no distances are a hindrance
            and no oceans an obstacle.

ZEAL   This being so, let us kneel before
        the royal feet[6] where two worlds meet   60
        and most humbly beg for pardon;

RELIGION   and their bright, illustrious queen,

AMERICA   whose majestic, sovereign feet
           the Indies do most humbly kiss;

ZEAL   and her supreme noble councils;   65

RELIGION   her ladies who illuminate
            their hemisphere;

AMERICA   and her wise men,
           whom my poor wisdom humbly prays
           to pardon and forgive its wish

---

5. See the headnote on p. 67 [*Editor*].
6. In 1690 the king of Spain was Charles II (1661–1700) and the queen was Maria Anna
   of Neuburg (1667–1740), his second wife [*Editor*].

to summon a great mystery   70
with these rough and clumsy verses.

OCCIDENT   Let us begin, for my longing
   aches to see what the God is like
   who will be served to me as food,

        [AMERICA, OCCIDENT, *and* ZEAL *all sing.*]

   saying that only now   75
   do the Indies perceive
   who the true God of Seeds
   really is! And so we
   say that with tender tears
   distilled by our great joy,   80
   let all gaily repeat
   and raise rejoicing voices:

ALL   Oh let us bless the day
   when we came to know the great true God of Seeds!
              [*Exit dancing and singing.*]

A Letter from Sor Filotea to Sor Juana Inés de la Cruz *and* Response of the Poet to the Very Eminent Sor Filotea de la Cruz

Even as a cloistered nun, Sor Juana received gifts of books, continued to write, maintained a robust epistolary correspondence, and circulated her manuscripts. She also met with visitors in the *locutorio*, a small receiving room that permitted nuns to converse from behind an iron grille while remaining cloistered. Sor Juana's years in the viceregal court had connected her to the highest spheres of New Spanish society and, according to Father Calleja's posthumous biography, while in the convent she received visits from the political and intellectual elite of Mexico City.[1]

During one of these visits Sor Juana expounded a critique of the Maundy Thursday Sermon preached in 1650 in the Royal Chapel of the Jesuit College in Lisbon by the famous Portuguese Jesuit António Vieira (1608–1697). Vieira's sermon took the story of Christ's washing of his disciples' feet at the Last Supper as a pretext for a reflection on which of Christ's qualities (*finezas*) was the greatest, considering first the opinions of three Church Doctors (Saint Augustine, Saint Ambrose, and Saint John Chrysostom). Sor Juana appears to have read Vieira's Maundy Thursday sermon in the 1678 Spanish translation, which Vieira had dedicated to the Jesuit Francisco de Aguiar y Seijas, the archbishop of New Spain. Because of the personal connection between the two Jesuits, it is probable that this edition circulated widely among the Mexican elite.

While Sor Juana's critique of Vieira's sermon is not often read now, it was considered impressive because of its tight scholastic logic, which included a consideration of the three doctors in Vieira's sermon and a pronouncement of her own conclusion on the matter of Christ's greatest quality. After Sor Juana first delivered her critique orally in the *locutorio* of the convent, a now unknown person asked for a version in writing. Apparently Sor Juana complied, as shortly afterward it was published in Puebla, the second largest city in colonial Mexico. The

---

1. See Calleja on p. 191.

printed version was titled *Carta Athenagórica* (Athenagoric letter),[2] although a separately published version in the 1692 *Second Volume* of Sor Juana's works titled it "Crisis de un sermón" (Critique of a sermon) and this may be the title Sor Juana herself preferred. The Puebla publication also contained a short prologue signed by another nun, Sor Filotea de la Cruz (see p. 86), praising Sor Juana's talents but reprimanding her for dedicating so much time to studying and writing on secular rather than sacred subjects.

Sor Filotea, or "Lover of God," was not a nun but a pseudonym that permitted the true author of the prologue, the bishop of Puebla, Manuel Fernández de Santa Cruz (1637–1699), to communicate his reprimand as sisterly advice from one nun to another. Sor Juana knew exactly who had written the prologue but followed the ruse. After a period of silence, she penned a lengthy epistle, now known as "Response of the Poet to the Very Eminent Sor Filotea de la Cruz," following the title given when it was printed in 1700 in the posthumous volume of her works. In an exquisite rhetorical architecture, Sor Juana employs a variety of strategies to dismantle the criticism she had received from the bishop, honing arguments that she had already employed ten years earlier in response to similar criticism from her then confessor, the influential Jesuit Antonio Núñez de Miranda (see p. 144). The "Response," however, is a tighter and lengthier argument that employs strategies from forensic oratory to unravel step by step the bishop's accusation and to build an alternative case.

The center of Sor Juana's letter is a defense against the bishop's main charge that "God does not want letters that give rise to presumption in woman." Sor Juana counters this charge that writing on secular subjects leads to vanity and disobedience with four main arguments: (1) "except for a trifle they call *The Dream*," she had never written anything according to her own will but rather to satisfy the requests of others; (2) from the time she was born she has shown a natural inclination toward study and writing and that this inclination was a "divine impulse" that human mandates, including her own, had not been able to stifle; (3) the Church itself has numerous examples of learned women, all of whom are celebrated rather than maligned; and (4) as the intellect of men and women has a common origin in the divine, they should be treated equally.

The rhetorical labyrinth in which Sor Juana couched this argument was as important as its essence.[3] The irony, even sarcasm, of the letter is especially evident in the opening superlatives and exaggerated rhetoric of humility, the most acceptable stance for religious women in her period.[4] Irony also marks her expression of gratitude toward the bishop

---

2. Although the title has often been translated "Letter Worthy of Athena," it more likely refers to Athenagoras, the author of an *Apologia* (177 C.E.) defending Christianity against pagan accusations.
3. Rosa Perelmuter Pérez has shown that the "Response" follows the rhetorical structure of forensic argument, including an exordium, narration, proof, and conclusion as well as other essential strategies suggested by Cicero and Quintillian, such as the opening *captatio benevolentiae* that flatters the recipient. Rosa Perelmuter Pérez, "La estructura retórica de la *Respuesta a Sor Filotea*," *Hispanic Review* 51. 2 (1983): 152–53.
4. See the selection from Saint Teresa's *The Life*, on p. 174.

for publishing her letter, even as he warned her against the vanity that such recognition could cause. While not strictly an autobiography, Sor Juana's recounting of her prodigious abilities as a girl and her experience in the convent community, including when a mother superior prohibited her from studying, are some of the few sources for information on her life. It is often forgotten that these occur within a greater argument that she is naturally "inclined" to study and write. In essence, Sor Juana trumps the Church hierarchy by claiming that her natural abilities are God-given. Yet her short-circuiting of the Church as an institution holds none of the rhetoric of mysticism, nor does it depend on the rhetoric of holy ignorance adopted by the models she cites in her list of learned women: Saint Teresa and Sor María de Ágreda. Sor Juana does not gain knowledge through mystical abnegation but through natural impulse and laborious study.

Sor Juana's arguments that girls be allowed to study or her exegesis of the main biblical source for suppressing women's learning, the Pauline dictum *mulieres in ecclesiis taceant* (let women in the church be silent), are more directly reasoned. Her conclusions, that if men are problematic teachers, the solution is to train more women to teach, or that Paul intended his dictum to address women's public speech rather than private study, are ingeniously argued. Yet Sor Juana also constantly authorizes her conclusions by a range of patristic sources, by biblical examples, and even by the little-known Mexican theologian Dr. Arce.[5] At other times, her biting wit cuts the counterargument to the quick, as in when she writes that her arguments should be heeded also by men, "who for the simple fact of being men think they are wise." Such statements go so far as to imply that by attacking her, the Church hierarchy, including even the bishop himself, is allied with ignorance, vanity, or simply nonsensical reasoning.

Yet perhaps the most important argument in the "Response" rests on the idea that the intellect has no gender, expressed near the end of the letter when she notes that her intellect and Vieira's share a common origin, and should have the same freedom to critique authorities. This does not mean that Sor Juana adopts an implicitly male point of view. In fact, she continually evokes a gendered perspective, citing girls' love of long hair or sweets or arguing in favor of studying in the kitchen, and concluding that "if Aristotle had cooked, he would have written a great deal more." Implicitly, by unleashing her abilities in the "Response" she both gives lie to the notion that women are incapable intellects and supports her statement that to speak or not to speak, to reason or not to reason is not a matter of her free will but a necessity. Sor Juana constantly asserts that she is impelled by an interior and natural truth.

Critics have debated to what extent the "Response" is the culmination of a lifelong battle between Sor Juana and the Church hierarchy. Often at stake is the sincerity of her statements, a sincerity almost impossible to judge given the rhetorical cloaking of her arguments. Third party writings, such as the Calleja biography that prefaced her final, posthumous volume of works, imply that Sor Juana was indeed

5. See p. 112.

attacked, especially after the publication of the "Athenagoric Letter." But others were drawn to her "scholastic reasoning," and the battle, carried out in manuscripts or in encomiastic poems, appears to have been evenly balanced between supporters and attackers.[6] Because only two years later she renounced her secular studies, sold her books, and retook her vows, it remains unclear exactly what place the "Response" holds in the interior and exterior battles surrounding Sor Juana's lifelong impulse to study and write.

This edition retains section breaks added by Edith Grossman in her translation. They did not appear in the original letter.

A Letter from Sor Filotea to Sor Juana Inés de la Cruz[†]

Señora:

I have seen the letter from Your Grace in which you challenge the qualities of Christ which Reverend Father Antonio de Vieira described in his Maundy Thursday Sermon[1] with so much subtlety that it has seemed to the most erudite men that, like another Eagle of the Apocalypse, this singular talent had soared beyond itself, following in the footsteps of the most Eminent César Meneses,[2] one of the finest minds in Portugal; but in my judgment, whoever reads Your Grace's apologia[3] cannot deny that your pen was cut finer than either of theirs, and they can take pride in finding themselves challenged by a woman who is the glory of her sex.

I, at least, have admired the acuteness of your concepts, the sagacity of your proofs, and the forceful clarity, inseparable companion of learning, with which you argue the matter, for the first word the Deity said was *light*,[4] because without clarity there is no word for learning. Even Christ, when He spoke of the highest mysteries behind the veil of parables, was not admired

---

6. Several of these manuscripts, discovered in Peru by José Antonio Rodríguez Garrido, give key details about the chronology of Sor Juana's critique and the extent of the scandal that followed it. José Antonio Rodríguez Garrido, *La Carta atenagórica de Sor Juana: textos inéditos de una polémica* (Mexico: UNAM, 2004).

† The actual author was the bishop of Puebla, don Manuel Fernández de Santa Cruz. The pseudonym "Filotea" (literally, "lover of God") may reflect its use by the influential archbishop of Mexico Juan de Palafox y Mendoza in his *Peregrinación de Filotea al Santo templo y monte de la Cruz* (The pilgrimage of Filotea to the holy temple and Mount of the Cross, 1659) [*revised by Editor*].

1. Several sermons by the Portuguese Jesuit António Vieira (1608–1697) carry the title of Maundy Thursday, preached on the Thursday of Easter week. The one that Sor Juana critiqued was preached in 1650 in the Royal Chapel of the Jesuit College in Lisbon. The mass recalls Christ's washing of his disciples' feet at the Last Supper (John 13:3–20) [*Editor*].

2. Sebastião César de Meneses (d. 1671) was an archbishop of Lisbon and author of theological works that inspired Vieira [*Editor*].

3. In rhetoric, a self-defense [*Editor*].

4. God's commandment "let there be light" (*fiat lux*) in Genesis 1:3 [*Editor*].

in the world; only when He spoke clearly was He acclaimed for knowing everything. This is one of the many benefits Your Grace owes to God, because clarity is not acquired through effort and industry: it is a gift that is infused[5] with the soul.

I have had your letter printed so that Your Grace may be seen in better form and may recognize the treasures God has placed in your soul and, having more understanding, may be more grateful: for gratitude and understanding were always born at the same time. And if, as Your Grace says in your letter, whoever has received more from God has a greater obligation to repay, I fear Your Grace may be deeply in debt, for few creatures owe the Lord greater natural talents; therefore express your gratitude so that if until now you have used those talents well (which I believe of anyone who has entered your order), from now on you will use them better.

My judgment is not so austere a censor that it takes exception to your verses—for which Your Grace has been so celebrated—since Saint Teresa and Gregory of Nazianzus[6] and other saints canonized this ability with their poems, but I should like you to imitate them in the choice of subjects as well as in technique.

I do not condone the vulgarity of those who reprove the practice of letters in women, for many applied themselves to this study, and not without the praise of Saint Jerome.[7] True, Saint Paul says that women should not teach, but he does not direct women not to study in order to learn, because he wished only to avoid the danger of presumption in our sex, always so inclined to vanity.[8] Divine Wisdom removed a letter from the name Sarai and added one to the name Abram, not because the man has to have more letters than the woman, as many believe, but because "i" added to the name Sara indicated pride and authority. *My lady* is translated as *Sarai*, and it was not proper for one who worked as a servant in the house of Abraham to be a lady.[9]

---

5. The verb *infundir*, a theological term for the process of receiving knowledge through divine grace. Mysticism was known as an "infused knowledge" (*ciencia infusa*) [*Editor*].

6. Saint Gregory of Nazianzus, also called Gregory Nanzianzen (540–604 C.E.), Doctor of the Church and archbishop of Constantinople. Saint Teresa, also called Teresa de Jesús and Teresa of Ávila (1515–1582), a prominent Spanish mystic and writer who was canonized in 1622 (see p. 174). Each wrote small bodies of verse [*Editor*].

7. A Doctor of the Church (347–410 C.E.) known for his erudition and founder of the Hieronymite order to which Sor Juana's Convent of Saint Paula pertained [*Editor*].

8. The dictate is found in 1 Corinthians 14:34–35: "Let your women keep silence in the churches: for it is not permitted unto them to speak; but they are commanded to be under obedience as also saith the law. And if they will learn any thing, let them ask their husbands at home: for it is a shame for women to speak in the church." It was one of the major fundaments for delineating women's participation in the Church [*Editor*].

9. The reference is to the Old Testament story of Sarah, who gave her servant Hagar to her husband Abraham to bear them a child. In Genesis 17:15 God removes the letter "i" from Sarai, making her Sarah in Hebrew. Both mean "mistress" or "princess," and thus underscored Sarah's authority in the household. Santa Cruz appears to confuse Hagar, who was the servant, for Sarah, the mistress [*Editor*].

God does not want letters that give rise to presumption in woman, but the Apostle[1] does not censure letters unless they remove woman from a state of obedience. It is well known that study and learning have kept Your Grace in a subordinate state and helped you perfect the graces of obedience; for if other religious women sacrifice their will to obedience, Your Grace has ceded your understanding, which is the most arduous and pleasing offering that can be made in the name of a religious calling.

By giving this advice, it is not my intention that Your Grace alter your nature by renouncing books but improve it by reading the book of Jesus Christ from time to time. None of the Evangelists called the genealogy of Christ a book except Saint Matthew, because in his conversion he wished not to change his inclinations but to improve them, so that if once, as a tax collector,[2] he spent his time on books that dealt with contracts and interest, as an Apostle he devoted himself to improving his nature by exchanging the books of his perdition for the book of Jesus Christ. Your Grace has spent a good deal of time studying philosophers and poets; now is the proper moment for you to perfect your pursuits and improve the books you read.

Was there ever a nation more erudite than Egypt? The first letters in the world originated there, and their hieroglyphics were a cause for astonishment. Extolling the wisdom of Joseph, Holy Scripture calls him unmatched in his knowledge of Egyptian erudition.[3] And yet the Holy Spirit states openly that the Egyptian nation is barbaric, for all their learning merely penetrated the movements of the stars and the heavens but could not rein in the disorder of their passions; all their knowledge was devoted to perfecting man in his political life but did not enlighten him on how to attain the life eternal. And knowledge that does not light the way to salvation is deemed foolishness by God, Who knows all things.

This was the opinion of Justus Lipsius[4] (a wonder of erudition) when he was close to death and the final reckoning, a time when our understanding is most enlightened: as his friends consoled him, recalling the many erudite books he had written, he said, pointing to a crucifix: *Knowledge that does not come from the Crucified God is foolishness and mere vanity.*[5]

1. Saint Paul, according to the dictate mentioned in n. 8, p. 87 [*Editor*].
2. Or bookkeeper; see Matthew 9:9 [*Editor*].
3. Santa Cruz's references are vague. In Acts 7:10–22 Joseph is called wise, but "Egyptian wisdom" is attributed to Moses. Lawrance, n. 172. Neoplatonists were responsible for the common Renaissance idea that Egypt was the oldest source of human knowledge and that hieroglyphs were an Adamic script [*Editor*].
4. A prominent Flemish humanist (1547–1606) whose influential works espoused a Christian Neostoicism [*Editor*].
5. The source is unknown [*Editor*].

I do not condemn the reading of these authors for this reason, but I repeat to Your Grace what Gerson[6] advised: Lend yourself to these studies, do not let them betray you or rob you. Human letters are slaves to divine letters and tend to make use of them, but should be condemned when they steal from Divine Wisdom its possession of human understanding and transform those destined for servitude into fine ladies. They are commendable when the reason for curiosity, which is a vice,[7] becomes studiousness, which is a virtue.

The angels whipped Saint Jerome because he read Cicero,[8] seduced rather than as a free man, as he preferred the delight of his eloquence to the solidity of Holy Scripture; yet it is to be commended that the Holy Doctor made use of the facts and profane erudition obtained from such authors.

The time Your Grace has spent on fields of knowledge that arouse curiosity is not negligible; now, like the great Boethius,[9] turn your attention to fields that are more profitable, joining to the subtleties of natural knowledge the usefulness of moral philosophy.

It is a pity when so great an understanding becomes so immersed in base earthly matters that it does not wish to penetrate what occurs in Heaven; and since you humble yourself to the earth, sink no lower but consider what happens in Hell. And if on occasion you desire sweet and tender tidings, turn your understanding to Mount Calvary,[1] where, observing the loving kindness of the Redeemer and the ingratitude of the redeemed, you will find ample scope for pondering the abundance of infinite love and marshaling a defense, not without tears, against utmost ingratitude. Or, on other occasions, most usefully launch the magnificent galleon of Your Grace's intelligence onto the high seas of divine perfections. I have no doubt that you will have the same experience as Apelles,[2] who painted the portrait of Campaspe, and with each stroke of his brush on the canvas, the arrow of love left a wound in his heart, so that the painter was at once perfecting the portrait while his love for the original inflicted mortal wounds to his heart.

---

6. Jean Gerson (1363–1429), a Parisian theologian responsible for numerous spiritual treatises [Editor].
7. Curiosity was commonly held to be a vice, as it led to vain knowledge [Editor].
8. In his Letter to Eustochium on Virginity, Epistula 22.30, Saint Jerome recalls a dream in which he is whipped by angels for reading the pagan Cicero [Editor].
9. Anicius Manlius Severinus Boethius (ca. 480–524), a Roman philosopher who wrote On the Consolation of Philosophy, widely read in Christian Europe as a treatise on death and fortune, while awaiting execution. He was incorrectly presumed to be a Christian [Editor].
1. The site immediately outside of Jerusalem's walls where Christ, the "Redeemer" in Santa Cruz's statement, was said to have been crucified for the sake of humanity, the "redeemed" [Editor].
2. He painted a portrait of Campaspe, the mistress of Alexander the Great, and subsequently fell in love with her [Editor].

I am very certain that if Your Grace, with the keen rationality of your understanding, were to form and depict an idea of divine perfections (whatever the dark shadows of faith allow), at the same time you would find your soul illuminated by light and your will blazing with and sweetly wounded by love of God, so that Our Lord, who has so abundantly showered Your Grace's nature with positive benefits, will not find Himself obliged to grant only negative benefits to your spirit; for no matter how Your Grace's intelligence may call them kindnesses, I deem them punishments, because it is a benefit only when God prepares the human heart with His Grace so that we may respond with gratitude, making use of a recognized benefit so that Divine Generosity is not held back but makes those benefits even greater.

This is the wish for Your Grace of one who, ever since she kissed your hand many years ago,[3] has lived enamored of your soul with a love that neither distance nor time has cooled; for spiritual love does not suffer periods of mutability, and love that is pure does not acknowledge mutability unless it leads to growth. May Our Lord hear my prayers and make Your Grace very holy and keep you well.

From the Convent of the Holy Trinity, in Puebla de los Ángeles, 25 November 1690.

I kiss Your Grace's hand and am your affectionate servant,

Filotea de la Cruz

Response of the Poet to the Very Eminent Sor Filotea de la Cruz[†]

Very eminent lady, my señora:
Neither my will nor scant health nor reasonable apprehension has delayed my response for so many days. Is it any surprise that my dull pen stumbled over two impossibilities at its first step? The first (and for me the more severe) is how to respond to your most learned, most prudent, most saintly, and most loving letter.[1] For if the Angelic Doctor of the Schools, Saint Thomas, when questioned regarding his silence in the presence of Albertus

---

3. This statement has been seen as proof that the bishop was not the one who requested the *Athenagoric Letter* in writing, as it would seem that he was not present when she first spoke her critique [*Editor*].

† Sor Juana responds to the "Letter from Sor Filotea" (p. 86). Sor Juana knew that the bishop of Puebla, Manuel Fernández de Santa Cruz, was the actual author of the letter but accepts the pretense of the pseudonym, addressing her own response to Sor Filotea and referring throughout to its recipient as "Señora" and a nun [*Editor*].

1. In the original, these superlatives are marked by the suffix *-ísimo* and are clearly ironic [*Editor*].

Magnus,[2] his teacher, replied that he was silent because he could find nothing to say worthy of Albertus, with how much more reason should I be silent, not, like the saint, out of humility, but because in reality, I know nothing worthy of you. The second impossibility is how to thank you for the favor, as unwarranted as it was unexpected, of having my rough scribblings printed; a good turn so immeasurable that it surpasses the most ambitious hope and most fantastic desire, which could find no place, even as a rational concept,[3] in my thoughts; in short, it is of such magnitude that it not only cannot be reduced to the limits of words but exceeds the capacity of gratitude, as much for its dimensions as for how unforeseen it was, for as Quintilian said: *Hopes give rise to the lesser glory, benefits to the greater.*[4] So much so that they silence the beneficiary.

When the happily barren, only to be made miraculously fruitful, mother of the Baptist saw so magnificent a visitor as the Mother of the Word in her house, her understanding became clouded and her speech failed, and so instead of thanks she burst into doubts and questions: *Et unde hoc mihi?* From whence comes such a thing to me?[5] The same occurred to Saul when he found himself elected and anointed king of Israel: *Am I not a son of Jemini of the least tribe of Israel, and my kindred the last among all the families of the tribe of Benjamin? Wherefore then hast thou spoken this word to me?*[6] And so say I: from whence, illustrious señora, from whence comes so great a favor to me? Am I by chance anything more than a poor nun, the most insignificant creature in the world and the least worthy of your attention? *Wherefore then speakest thou so to me? From whence comes such a thing to me?*

To the first impossibility I can respond only that I am unworthy of your eyes, and to the second I cannot respond with anything other than exclamations, not thanks, saying that I am

---

2. Albertus Magnus (ca. 1200–1280) was Saint Thomas's teacher at the University of Paris. "The Angelic Doctor": a common epithet for Saint Thomas Aquinas (ca. 1225–1274), author of the *Summa Theologica* and other works that adapted Aristotelian metaphysics to Christian theology and dogma. The Thomist corpus was considered the foundation for scholastic theology, or the "Schools" [*Editor*].

3. Sor Juana uses the Spanish translation of the scholastic term *ens rationis*, or an abstract object of understanding with no real presence outside of the mind [*Editor*].

4. Marcus Fabius Quintilianus (35–ca. 96 c.e.), a Roman rhetorician and author of the influential *Institutio oratoria* (ca. 95 c.e.) outlining the principles of rhetoric. Sor Juana's phrase, *minorem spei, maiorem benefacti gloriam pariunt,* misquotes his *Institutio oratoria* III 7.13: "*quo minores opes fuerunt maiorem bene factis gloriam parit*" (where wealth is less, [panegyric] gets more glory from good deeds). Throughout, Latin phrases in the text will be translated and italicized [*Editor*].

5. Luke 1:43. The phrase was uttered by Elizabeth, cousin of the Virgin Mary and mother of John the Baptist, a birth considered a miracle because of Elizabeth's advanced age. In an event known as the Visitation, her pregnancy was announced when the Virgin Mary visited her cousin and the child leapt in Elizabeth's womb [*Editor*].

6. 1 Samuel 9:21. The response of Saul to Samuel's prophecy that he will be the first king of Israel [*revised by Editor*].

not capable of offering you even the smallest portion of the gratitude I owe you. It is not false modesty, señora, but the candid truth of all my soul, that when the letter your eminence called *Athenagoric*[7] reached me, I burst (although this does not come easily to me) into tears of confusion, because it seemed that your favor was nothing more than a reproach from God for how poorly I meet His expectations; while He corrects others with punishments, He wants to reduce me by means of benefits. A special favor, for which I know I am in His debt, as I am for other infinite benefits from His immense kindness, but also a special mode of shaming and confusing me: for it is a more exquisite method of punishment to have me, with my knowledge, serve as the judge who sentences and condemns my own ingratitude. When I ponder this, here in solitude, I often say: *Lord may You be blessed, for You not only did not wish any other creature to judge me, and did not give me that responsibility either, but kept it for Yourself and freed me from me and the sentence I would have given myself—which, compelled by my own knowledge, could not be less than condemnation—and reserved that for Your mercy, because You love me more that I can love myself.*

Señora, forgive the digression that the power of truth demanded of me, and if I must confess the whole truth, this is also a search for havens to escape the difficulty of responding, and I almost decided to leave everything in silence, but since this is negative, although it explains a great deal with the emphasis on not explaining, it is necessary to add a brief explanation so that what one wishes the silence to say is understood; if not, the silence will say nothing, because that is its proper occupation: saying nothing. The sacred chosen vessel was carried away to the third heaven, and having seen the arcane secrets of God, the text says: *He . . . heard secret words, which it is not granted to man to utter.*[8] It does not say what he saw but says that he cannot say; and so it is necessary at least to say that those things that cannot be said cannot be said, so it is understood that being silent does not mean having nothing to say, but that the great deal there is to say cannot be said in words. Saint John says that if all the miracles performed by Our Redeemer were to be written down, the entire world could not hold the books;[9]

---

7. When the Bishop Manuel Fernández de Santa Cruz published Sor Juana's critique in 1690, he titled it *Athenagoric Letter*. While for many years it was assumed that "Athenagoric" referred to "Athena," rendering the translation "Letter Worthy of Athena," it likely refers to Athenagoras, the author of an *Apologia* (177 C.E.) defending Christianity against pagan accusations [*revised by Editor*].

8. 2 Corinthians 12:4. Sor Juana mistakenly attributes the vision to the "sacred chosen vessel" or Paul himself (Acts 9:15), when Paul's anecdote refers to another man [*revised by Editor*].

9. John 21:25.

and Vieira states that the Evangelist says more in just this passage than in everything else he wrote; the Lusitanian Phoenix, speaks very well (but when does he not speak well, even when he does not speak well?),[1] because here Saint John says everything he did not say and expressed what he did not express. And I, señora, will respond only that I do not know how to respond, will only give thanks, saying I am not capable of giving thanks to you, and will say, as a brief explanation of what I leave to silence, that only with the confidence of a favored woman and the benefits of an honored one can I dare speak to your excellency. If this is foolishness, forgive it, for it is a jewel of good fortune, and in it I will provide more material for your kindness, and you will give greater form to my gratitude.

Because he stammered, Moses did not think he was worthy to speak to the Pharaoh, and afterward, finding himself so favored by God fills him with so much courage that he not only speaks to God Himself but dares ask Him for impossibilities: *Shew me thy face.*[2] And I too, señora, no longer think impossible what I wrote at the beginning, in view of how you favor me; because the person who had the letter printed without my knowledge, who gave it a title and paid for it, who honored it so greatly (since it is entirely unworthy both for its own sake and the sake of its author), what will she not do, what will she not pardon, what will she cease doing, and what will she cease pardoning? And so, under the assumption that I speak with the safe-conduct of your favors and under the protection of your kindness, and your having, like another Ahasuerus, given me the tip of the golden scepter of your affection to kiss as a sign of granting me benevolent license to speak[3] and propound in your illustrious presence, I say that I receive in my soul your most saintly admonition to turn my studies to sacred books, which although this comes in the guise of advice will have for me the substance of a precept, with the not insignificant consolation that even earlier it seems my obedience foresaw your pastoral suggestion, as well as your guidance, inferred from the subject and proofs of the same letter. I know very well that your most sage warning is not directed at it[4] but at how much

1. António Vieira; "Lusitanian" is Portuguese, and a "phoenix" is a remarkable person. Sor Juana herself was called the "Mexican Phoenix." The citation is from his "Sermon of Our Lady of Peñafrancia" preached in 1652: "*Pergunto agora: Em que disse mais S. João: em estas duas ultimas regras ou em todo seu Evangelho?*" (I ask now: In which did Saint John say more: in these last two lines or in his entire gospel?) [Editor].
2. Found in the Song of Solomon 2:14. Lawrance notes that Sor Juana combines various biblical passages to come to this conclusion. Moses's stutter is mentioned in Exodus 4:10. In Exodus 33:18, Moses says "shew me thy glory." Lawrance, n. 14 [revised by Editor].
3. Esther 5:2. The Persian King Ahasuerus gave Esther permission to speak by holding out his golden scepter for her to touch [revised by Editor].
4. That is, the bishop's reprimand does not refer to the contents of the *Athenagoric Letter*, which are theological [Editor].

you have seen of my writings on human affairs; and so what I
have said is only to satisfy you with regard to the lack of applica-
tion you have inferred (and rightly so) from other writings of
mine. And speaking more specifically I confess, with the candor
that is owed you and with the truth and clarity that in me are
always natural and customary, that my not having written a
great deal about sacred matters has been due not to defiance or
lack of application but to an abundance of the fear and rever-
ence owed to those sacred letters, for whose comprehension I
know myself highly incapable and for whose handling I am
highly unworthy; resounding always in my ears, with no small
horror, is the Lord's warning and prohibition to sinners like
me: *Why dost thou declare my justices, and take my covenant in
thy mouth?*[5] My great father Saint Jerome confirms this ques-
tion, and that even learned men are forbidden to read the
Song of Solomon and even Genesis before the age of thirty
(the latter because of its obscurity, the former so that imprudent
youth will not use the sweetness of those nuptial songs as an
excuse to alter their meaning to carnal love), by ordering that it
be the last book studied, for the same reason: *At the end one
may read, without danger, the Song of Songs; for if it is read at
the beginning, when one does not understand the epithalamium
to the spiritual marriage beneath the carnal words, one may
suffer harm;*[6] and Seneca says: *In the early years, faith is not
bright.*[7] Then how would I dare hold it in my unworthy hands,
when it is in conflict with my sex, my age, and especially, my
customs? And so I confess that often this fear has removed the
pen from my hand and made subjects withdraw into the same
understanding from which they wished to emerge; this diffi-
culty was not encountered in profane subjects, for a heresy
against art is punished not by the Holy Office[8] but by the pru-
dent with laughter and the critics with condemnation; and
this, *just or unjust, there is no reason to fear it,*[9] for one can still
take Communion and hear Mass and therefore it concerns me
very little or not at all; because according to the same opinion
of those who cast aspersions, I have no obligation to know and
no aptitude for being correct; therefore, if I err there is no blame
and no discredit. There is no blame because I have no obliga-
tion; there is no discredit because I have no possibility of being

---

5. Psalm 50:16 [*revised by Editor*].
6. Saint Jerome, *To Laeta, Upon the Education of Her Daughter* (written ca. 403 C.E.).
7. The 1700 edition of the "Response" incorrectly attributes this to *De beneficiis* (On
Kindness) by Lucius Annaeus Seneca (ca. 4 B.C.E.–65 C.E.). It is from *Octavia* 1.538, a
play most likely incorrectly attributed to Seneca, and the wording differs slightly from
Sor Juana's original. Lawrance, n. 18 [*Editor*].
8. The Spanish Inquisition.
9. A citation from the *Decretum*, a collection of rules and regulations of the Church, compiled
in 1140 by the Benedictine monk Gratian, C.11.3.1. Lawrance, n. 20 [*Editor*].

correct, and *no one is obliged to undertake impossible things*.[1]
And, truly, I have never written except reluctantly, when I was
forced to, and only to please others; not only with no gratifica-
tion but with positive repugnance, for I have never judged myself
to possess the abundance of letters and intelligence demanded
by the obligation of one who writes; and so my usual reply to
those who urge me to write, especially if the subject is sacred:
"What understanding, what studies, what materials, what
rudimentary knowledge do I possess for this other than some
superficial nonsense? Leave this for someone who understands
it, for I wish no quarrel with the Holy Office, for I am ignorant
and terrified of stating an offensive proposition or twisting the
genuine significance of some passage. I do not study to write,
much less to teach (which would be excessive pride in me), but
only to see whether by studying I will be less ignorant." This is
how I respond and how I feel.

Writing has never been by my own volition but at the behest
of others; for I could truthfully say to them: *Ye have compelled
me*.[2] A truth I will not deny (one, because it is widely known,
and two, because even if used against me, God has favored me
with a great love of the truth) is that ever since the first light of
reason struck me, my inclination toward letters has been so
strong and powerful that neither the reprimands of others—I
have had many—nor my own reflections—I have engaged in
more than a few—have sufficed to make me abandon this nat-
ural impulse that God placed in me: His Majesty knows why
and to what end; and He knows I have asked Him to dim the
light of my understanding, leaving only enough for me to obey
His Law, for anything else is too much in a woman, according
to some; there are even those who say it does harm. Almighty
God knows too that when I did not obtain this, I attempted
to bury my understanding along with my name and sacrifice
it to the One who gave it to me; for no other reason did I enter
a convent, although the spiritual exercises and companionship
of a community were incompatible with the freedom and quiet
my studious intentions demanded; the Lord knows, as does the
only one in the world who had to know, that once in the com-
munity I attempted to hide my name but was not permitted to,
for it was said it was a temptation; and it would have been. If I
could pay you, señora, something of what I owe you, I believe
I could only pay you in full by telling you this, for I have never
spoken of it except to the one who had to hear it.[3] But having

1. One of Boniface VIII's rules of canon law, in his *Regulae iuris* (*Sext.* V. 6). Lawrance,
n. 21 [*Editor*].
2. 2 Corinthians 12:11.
3. This reference and the one above ("as does the only one in the world") are to her con-
fessor, who in 1691 was likely not Antonio Núñez de Miranda (see the chronology on
p. 313) [*Editor*].

opened wide the doors of my heart to you, revealing its deepest secrets, I want you to find my confidence worthy of what I owe to your illustrious person and excessive favors.

I

Continuing the narration of my inclination,[4] about which I want to give you a complete account, I say that before I was three years old my mother sent an older sister of mine to learn to read in one of the primary schools for girls called *Friends*,[5] and, led by affection and mischief, I followed after her; and seeing that she was being taught a lesson, I was so set ablaze by the desire to know how to read that in the belief I was deceiving her, I told the teacher my mother wanted her to give me a lesson too. She did not believe it, because it was not believable, but to go along with the joke, she taught me. I continued to go and she continued to teach me, in earnest now, because with experience she realized the truth; and I learned to read in so short a time that I already knew how when my mother found out, for the teacher hid it from her in order to give her complete gratification and receive her reward at the same time; and I kept silent believing I would be whipped for having done this without her knowledge. The woman who taught me is still alive (may God keep her), and she can testify to this.

I remember at this time, my appetite being what is usual at that age, I abstained from eating cheese because I had heard it made people stupid, and my desire to learn was stronger in me than the desire to eat, despite this being so powerful in children. Later, when I was six or seven years old and already knew how to read and write, along with all the other skills pertaining to sewing and needlework learned by women, I heard there was a university and schools in Mexico City where sciences were studied; as soon as I heard this I began to pester my mother with insistent, inopportune pleas that she send me, dressed as a boy, to the home of some relatives she had in Mexico City, so I could study and attend classes at the university;[6] she refused, and rightly so, but I satisfied my desire by reading many different books owned by my grandfather, and there were not enough punishments and reprimands to stop me, so that when I came to Mexico City, people were surprised not so much by my intelligence as by my memory and the knowledge I possessed at an age when it seemed I had barely had enough time to learn to speak.

---

4. In Thomist teachings, a reference to a natural instinct teleologically oriented toward a divine end. This begins the section in which Sor Juana will describe her natural instinct to study such a divine impulse [*Editor*].
5. Primary schools for girls, called so after the school mistresses [*Editor*].
6. During childhood, Sor Juana lived on the outskirts of Mexico City. The Royal and Pontifical University of Mexico, founded in 1551, was restricted to male students [*Editor*].

I began to learn Latin and believe I had fewer than twenty lessons;[7] my seriousness was so intense that since the natural adornment of hair is so admired in women—especially in the flower of one's youth—I would cut off four to six inches, first measuring how long it was and then imposing on myself the rule that if, when it had grown back, I did not know whatever I had proposed to learn while it was growing, I would cut it again as a punishment for my stupidity. And when it grew back and I did not know what I had determined to learn, because my hair grew quickly and I learned slowly, then in fact I did cut it as punishment for my stupidity, for it did not seem right for my head to be dressed in hair when it was so bare of knowledge, which was a more desirable adornment. I entered the convent although I knew the situation had certain characteristics (I speak of secondary qualities, not formal ones)[8] incompatible with my character, but considering the total antipathy I had toward matrimony, the convent was the least disproportionate and most honorable decision I could make to provide the certainty I desired for my salvation, and the first (and in the end the most important) obstacle to overcome was to relinquish all the minor defects in my character, such as wanting to live alone, and not wanting any obligatory occupation that would limit the freedom of my studies, or the noise of a community that would interfere with the tranquil silence of my books. These made me hesitate somewhat in my determination, until learned persons enlightened me,[9] saying they were a temptation, which I overcame with Divine Grace and entered into the state I so unworthily am in now. I thought I would flee myself, but I, poor wretch, brought myself with me as well as this inclination, my greatest enemy (I cannot determine whether Heaven gave it to me as a gift or a punishment), for when it was dimmed or interfered with by the many spiritual exercises present in the religious life, it exploded in me like gunpowder, proof in my own person that *privation is the cause of appetite.*[1]

I returned to (no, I am wrong, for I never stopped): I mean to say I continued my studious effort (which for me was repose whenever I had time away from my obligations) to read and read some more, to study and study some more, with no teacher other than the books themselves. I learned how difficult it is to study those soulless characters without the living voice and explanations of a teacher; yet I

7. Sor Juana's Latin teacher was Martin de Olivas (see Diego Calleja, "Approval," on p. 187) [*Editor*].
8. Sor Juana is careful to refer to the daily routine rather than to the theological ends of the convent [*Editor*].
9. One of these learned persons was Father Antonio Núñez de Miranda, Sor Juana's confessor (See "Letter by Mother Juana Inés de la Cruz" on p. 144) [*Editor*].
1. The source for the phrase has not been identified, but it is composed of the typically scholastic terms *privatio* and *appetitus* [*Editor*].

gladly endured all this work for the sake of my love of letters. Oh, if it
had only been for the sake of my love of God, which is the correct
love, how meritorious it would have been! I did attempt to elevate it as
much as I could and turn it to His service, because the goal to which
I aspired was the study of theology, for, being Catholic, it seemed a
foolish lack in me not to know everything that can be learned in this
life, by natural means, about the Divine Mysteries; and being a nun
and not a layperson, according to my ecclesiastical state I should pro-
fess vows to letters, and even more so, as a daughter of a Saint Jerome
and a Saint Paula, for it seemed a deterioration if such learned par-
ents produced an idiot child.[2] I proposed this to myself and it seemed
correct, if it was not (and this is most likely) flattery and applause of
my own inclination, its enjoyment being proposed as an obligation.

In this way I proceeded, always directing the steps of my study
to the summit of sacred theology, as I have said; and to reach it, I
thought it necessary to ascend by the steps of human sciences and
arts, because how is one to understand the style of the queen of sci-
ences without knowing that of the handmaidens?[3] How, without
logic, was I to know the general and particular methods used in the
writing of Holy Scripture? How, without rhetoric, would I under-
stand its figures, tropes, and locutions? How, without physics, com-
prehend the many inherent questions concerning the nature of the
animals used for sacrifices, in which so many stated subjects, as well
as many others that are undeclared, are symbolized? How to know
whether Saul healing at the sound of David's harp came from the
virtue and natural power of music or the supernatural ability God
wished to place in David?[4] How, without arithmetic, understand so
many computations of years, days, months, hours, and weeks as mys-
terious as those in Daniel,[5] and others for whose deciphering one
must know the natures, concordances, and properties of numbers?
How, without geometry, can one measure the Holy Ark of the Cov-
enant and the holy city of Jerusalem, whose mysterious measure-
ments form a cube with all its dimensions, a marvelous proportional
distribution of all its parts?[6] How, without architecture, fathom the

2. Sor Juana argues that as a Hieronymite nun she should be additionally bound to study.
   Saint Jerome (ca. 347–420 C.E.), the founder of her order, was one of the four doctors
   of the Church and author of the Vulgate Bible. Saint Paula was Jerome's student and
   co-patron of the Hieronymite convent in Mexico City. "Idiot": a reference to ignorance,
   especially of Latin [revised by Editor].
3. "Queen of sciences": theology (sciences referring to "knowledge"). "Handmaidens": seven
   liberal arts, although Sor Juana adds physics (Aristotelian natural philosophy), archi-
   tecture, and history to the list of grammar, logic, rhetoric, geometry, arithmetic, music,
   and astronomy. Lawrance, n. 35 [Editor].
4. 1 Samuel 16:23 describes how Saul, the first king of Israel, was healed from evil spirits
   by the sound of the harp of David, a young soldier and future king of Israel.
5. Daniel 9:24–27.
6. Exodus 26:15–30 relates the dimensions of the Holy Ark of the Covenant, the chest that
   held the tablets of the Ten Commandments.

great temple of Solomon, where God Himself was the artificer, conceiving the proportion and design, and the wise king merely the overseer who executed it;[7] where there was no base without a mystery, no column without a symbol, no cornice without an allusion, no architrave without a meaning, and so on in all its parts, so that even the smallest fillet was placed not for the service and complement of art alone but to symbolize greater things? How, without great knowledge of the rules and parts that constitute history, can the historical books[8] be understood? Those recapitulations in which what happened earlier often is placed later in the narration and seems to have occurred afterward? How, without great familiarity with both kinds of law, can one apprehend the legal books?[9] How, without great erudition, approach so many matters of profane history mentioned in Holy Scripture, so many Gentile customs, so many rites, so many ways of speaking? How, without many rules and much reading of the Holy Fathers,[1] can one grasp the obscure expression of the prophets? And without being very expert in music, how are we to understand the musical proportions and their beauty found in so many places, especially in the petition of Abraham to God on behalf of the cities,[2] that He spare them if He found fifty righteous men, and from this number he went down to forty-five, which is a *sesquinona,* going from *mi* to *re*; and from here to forty, which is a *sesquioctava,*[3] going from *re* to *ut*;[4] from here to thirty which is a *sesquitertia,* a *diatessaron*; from here to twenty, which is the *sesquialtera* proportion, a *diapente*; from

---

7. 1 Kings 6:2–3 relates the dimensions of the Temple of Solomon, the first temple on Mount Zion [*Editor*].
8. The historical books of the Old Testament (Joshua, Judges, Samuel, Kings, and Chronicles) [*Editor*].
9. The books of the law in the Bible are the first five, or Pentateuch, (Genesis, Exodus, Numbers, Deuteronomy, Leviticus). Law was divided into civil (state) and canon (Church) [*Editor*].
1. Patristic authorities, such as the Apostles, the Apostolic Fathers, and the Doctors of the Church (Ambrose, Augustine, Gregory I, and Jerome), whose interpretations of the Bible were considered authoritative [*Editor*].
2. Sodom and Gomorrah (Genesis 18:24–32) [*Editor*].
3. *Sesquinona*: a minor whole tone or minor second. *Sesquioctava*: a major whole tone or major second.
4. Modern *do*. Sor Juana apparently erred, or the text has been corrupted, when she indicated that the sesquioctava was from *re* to *mi*, the same illustration used for the *sesquinona*. This has been corrected to "from *re* to *ut*." The *sesquinona* and *sesquioctava* are two different types of the interval now known as a whole tone or second. There are no modern equivalents to these two kinds of whole tones. Our thanks to Professor Mario A. Ortiz, Catholic University of America, for his invaluable assistance in clarifying the musical terminology and the Pythagorean concepts presented in this section.
     As indicated by Cecil Adkins, "Monochord," *Grove Music Online, Oxford Music Online,* Oxford University Press: "The Pythagorean concept of division by proportions is based on the relationship of the harmonic and arithmetic means as they are represented by the numbers 6, 8, 9, and 12. The ratio 12:6 produces the octave; 9:6 and 12:8, the fifth; 8:6 and 12:9, the fourth; and 9:8, the major second. Reduced to their lowest terms these ratios are dupla (12:1), sesquialtera (3:2), sesquitertia (4:3) and sesquioctava (9:8)."

here to ten, which is the dupla, a *diapason*;[5] and since there are no other harmonic intervals, he went no further? Well, how could one understand this without music?[6] In the Book of Job, God says: *Shalt thou be able to join together the shining stars the Pleiades, or canst thou stop the turning about of Arcturus?*[7] *Canst thou bring forth the day star in its time and make the evening star to rise upon the children of the earth?*[8] The terms, without knowledge of astronomy, would be impossible to comprehend. And not only these noble sciences, but there is no mechanical art[9] that is not mentioned. In short, it is the book that encompasses all books, and the science that includes all sciences, which are useful for its understanding: even after learning all of them (which clearly is not easy, or even possible), another consideration demands more than all that has been said, and that is constant prayer and purity in one's life, in order to implore God for the purification of spirit and enlightenment of mind necessary for comprehending these lofty matters; if this is lacking, the rest is useless.

The Church says these words regarding the angelic doctor Saint Thomas: *When he read the most difficult passages of Holy Scripture, he combined fasting with prayer. And he would say to his companion, Brother Reginald, that all he knew was not due to study or his own labor, but that he had received it from God.*[1] And I, so distant from virtue and from letters, how was I to have the courage to write? Therefore, having attained a few elementary skills, I continually studied a variety of subjects, not having an inclination toward one in particular but toward all of them in general; as a consequence, having studied some more than others has not been by choice but because, by chance, I had access to more books about those subjects, which created the preference more than any decision of mine. And since I had no special interest that moved me, and no time limit that restricted my continuing to study one subject because of the demands of formal classes, I could study a variety of subjects or abandon some for others, although I did observe a certain order, for some I called study and others diversion, and with these I rested from the first, with the result that I have studied many subjects and know nothing, because some have interfered with my

5. *Diatessaron*: a perfect fourth. *Diapente*: a perfect fifth. *Diapason*: an octave.
6. Sor Juana was known for her musical abilities and claimed to have written a musical treatise, titled "The Shell" (*El caracol*), a manuscript that is now lost [*Editor*].
7. A bright star. "Pleiades": open star cluster in Taurus named after the seven daughters of the titan Atlas [*Editor*].
8. Job 38:31–32. "Day star": Venus. "Evening star": Mercury [*Editor*].
9. Mechanics was considered a commoner's craft whereas the liberal arts were noble [*Editor*].
1. *Roman Breviary*, Office of the Feast of Saint Thomas Aquinas, March 7, Fifth Lesson.

learning others. True, I say this regarding the practical aspect of those subjects that have one, because it is obvious that while one moves a pen, the compass does nothing, and while one plays the harp, the organ is silent, and so on; because since a great deal of physical practice is necessary to acquire a practical skill, the person who is divided among various exercises can never achieve perfection; but the opposite happens in formal and speculative areas, and I would like to persuade everyone with my experience that this not only does not interfere but helps, for one subject illuminates and opens a path in another by means of variations and hidden connections—placed in this universal chain by the wisdom of its Author—so that it seems they correspond and are joined with admirable unity and harmony. It is the chain the ancients imagined issuing from the mouth of Jupiter, where all things hung linked to all other things. Reverend Father Athanasius Kircher[2] demonstrates this in his curious book *On the Magnet.* All things emanate from God, Who is at once the center and circumference from which all created lines emerge and where they end.[3]

As for me, I can state that what I do not understand in an author from one discipline I usually can understand in a different author from another discipline that seems quite distant from the first; and in their explanations, these authors offer metaphorical examples from other arts, as when logicians say that the mean is to the terms as a measurement is to two distant bodies, in order to determine whether they are equal; and that the statement of a logician moves, like a straight line, along the shortest path, while that of a rhetorician follows, like a curve, the longest, but both travel to the same point; and when it is said that expositors are like an open hand and scholastics like a closed fist.[4] This is not an excuse for having studied a diversity of subjects, nor do I offer it as such, for these subjects contribute to one another, but my not having benefited from them has been the fault of my ineptitude and the weakness in my understanding, not of their variety.

2. A Jesuit polymath (1602–1680) based in Rome. Heavily influenced by Neoplatonic sources, he was the author of some forty books covering subjects ranging from Egyptology to volcanoes. "The chain": the image of the golden chain emanating from Jupiter's mouth appears in Homer, *Iliad,* Book VIII [*Editor*].

3. *De Magnete* was the title of William Gilbert's 1600 treatise but Sor Juana appears to refer to Kircher's *Magneticum Naturae Regnum* (Magnetic realm of nature, 1667) as the source of the common Neoplatonic conceit of the "great chain of being." The idea that God is the center and circumference of the universe is derived from the German theologian Nicholas of Cusa (1401–1464) [*Editor*].

4. That is, logicians are scholastic syllogists who reason through a middle term, while rhetoricians are orators, and therefore work through a curved line; expositors are interpreters, and thus work to open a text, while scholastics analyze and thus reduce it to a closed position. Lawrance, n. 50 [*Editor*].

II

What might absolve me is the immense amount of work caused by lacking not only a teacher but other students with whom to confer and practice what I studied, having a mute book for a teacher and an insentient inkwell for a fellow student; and instead of explanation and practice, countless obstacles, not only those of my religious obligations (and we already know what a helpful and profitable use of time these are) but those other things that are inevitable in a community: for instance, when I am reading and in the adjoining cell they take a notion to play their instruments and sing; when I am studying and two maidservants have a quarrel and come to have me judge their dispute; when I am writing and a friend comes to visit, doing me a disservice with nothing but good intentions, and it is necessary not only to accept the intrusion but be grateful for the damage done. And this happens constantly, because since the times I devote to my studies are those not dedicated to the routine duties of the community, those same times are moments of leisure for the other sisters who interrupt me; and only those who have experienced communal life know how true this is, for only the strength of my vocation and the great love that exists among me and my beloved sisters can make my disposition agreeable, and since love is harmony, in it there are no polar opposites.[5]

I do confess that my work has been interminable, which means I cannot say what I enviously hear others say: that they have not had to work for knowledge. How fortunate for them! For me, not the knowing (for I still know nothing) but only the desire to know has been so difficult that I could say with my father Saint Jerome (although not with his achievements): *The labor it has cost me, the difficulties I have endured, the times I have despaired, and the other times I have desisted and begun again, all because of my determination to learn, to what I have suffered my conscience is witness and the conscience of those who have lived with me.*[6] Except for the companions and witnesses (for I have lacked even that solace), I can affirm the truth of the rest. And that my unfortunate inclination has been so great it has overcome everything else!

It used to happen that since a kind, affable temperament is one of the many benefits I owe to God, the other nuns were very fond of me (without noticing, like the good women they are, my faults) and as a consequence they enjoyed my company; knowing this, and moved by the great love I had for them, with more reason than they had for loving me, I enjoyed their company even more; and so, during

5. That is, her love for her convent sisters overcomes their extreme differences [*Editor*].
6. Letter CXXV from Saint Jerome to the monk Rusticus (411 c.e.).

the times all of us had free, I would go to cheer them and take plea-
sure in their conversation. I noticed that during these times I lost
the opportunity to study, and I vowed not to enter any cell unless
obliged to by obedience or charity, because without this severe
restraint, the deterrent of mere intention would be broken by my
love; and this vow (knowing my weakness) I would make for a month
or for two weeks; and when it was fulfilled I would renew it, giving
myself a day or two of respite and using that time not so much for
rest (for not studying has never been restful to me) as for keeping
my dearly loved sisters from thinking me harsh, withdrawn, and
ungrateful for their undeserved affection.

It is clear from this how strong my inclination is. I thank God for
willing that it be turned to letters and not another vice, for it was
practically unconquerable; and it can easily be inferred how my poor
studies have sailed against the current (or rather, how they have
foundered). For I still have not recounted the most arduous of the
difficulties; those I have described so far have been merely obligatory
or accidental obstacles, and therefore indirect. I have not touched
on the direct ones whose intent was to interfere with and prevent
my studies. Who would not think, seeing the widespread acclaim
I have received, that I sailed calm seas with the wind behind me,
surrounded by the applause of general approbation? But God knows
it has not been so, because among the flowers of these same accla-
mations more serpents than I can count of rivalries and persecu-
tions have arisen and awakened, and the most noxious and hurtful
to me have been not those who persecuted me with open hatred
and malice but those who, loving me and desiring my welfare (and
perhaps deserving a great deal from God for their good intentions),
mortified and tormented me more than the others, saying: "Her
studies are not in accord with holy ignorance; she will surely be lost,
and at such heights her own perspicacity and wit are bound to make
her vain." What did it cost me to endure this? A strange kind of mar-
tyrdom, in which I was both the martyr and my own executioner!

As for my ability—doubly unfortunate in me—to compose verses,
even if religious, what sorrows has it not caused me, and causes me
still? In truth, señora, at times I begin to think that the one who
excels—or is made to excel by God, Who alone can effect this—is
received as a common enemy, because it seems to some that this
person usurps the applause they deserve or blocks the admiration
to which they aspire, and so they persecute this person.

That politically barbarous law of Athens, by which whoever
excelled in gifts and virtues was exiled from the republic to keep him
from tyrannizing public liberty with those gifts, still endures and is
still observed in our day, although the motive of the Athenians no
longer exists; but there is another one, no less effective although not

as well founded, for it seems a maxim of the impious Machiavelli, and that is to despise the one who excels because that person discredits others.[7] This occurs, and has always occurred.

If this is not so, what caused the rabid hatred of the Pharisees[8] toward Christ, when there were so many reasons for them to feel otherwise? For if we consider His presence, what gift was more worthy of love than His divine beauty? What gift more powerful in captivating hearts? If human comeliness rules our wills, and with tender and desired force knows how to subject them, what would be the effect of His beauty with its countless prerogatives and sovereign charms? What would that incomprehensible comeliness do, what would it move, what would it not do and not move, when from that beautiful face, as if from polished crystal, the beams of Divinity shone through? What could that countenance not move, when above and beyond incomparable human perfections, it also disclosed illuminations of the divine? If the face of Moses, after only conversing with God, proved unendurable to the fragility of human eyes,[9] what would the humanized face of God Himself be like? And if we turn to His other gifts, what more worthy of love than that celestial modesty, that gentleness and tenderness pouring forth mercy in all His movements, that profound humility and compassion, those words of eternal life and eternal wisdom? How is it possible that all of this did not stir their souls to follow Him, did not elevate them and fill them with love?

My holy mother Saint Teresa[1] says that after she saw the beauty of Christ, she could never again feel an inclination toward any creature because she saw nothing that was not ugly compared to that beauty. How could it have had such contrary effects in men? And even if they were rough and base and had no knowledge of or esteem for His perfections, not even as possibly profitable, how could they not be moved by the advantage and usefulness of all the benefits received from Him: healing the sick, resuscitating the dead, curing those possessed by the devil?[2] How could they not love Him? Oh, God, that was precisely why they did not love Him, that was precisely why they despised Him! They themselves bore witness to that.

7. The works of Niccolò Machiavelli (1469–1527) were on the Spanish Inquisition's index of prohibited books. Sor Juana most likely only knew of the Italian political theorist through his negative reputation among the political theorists of the Spanish monarchy, for whom Machiavelli was synonymous with governance that ignored Christian principles. "Barbarous law": Aristotle, *Athenian Constitution*, Chapter 22, recounts the democratic practice of ostracism, by which a yearly convention exiled those who had become too strong [*Editor*].
8. One of the three major societies of Judaism and responsible, according to Matthew 12:14 and Mark 3:6, for a plot to kill Jesus Christ [*Editor*].
9. Exodus 34:29–30.
1. Saint Teresa of Ávila (1515–1582), a Spanish mystic. Lawrance identifies a possible source for the reference in her autobiography, *The Life*, Chapter 37. Lawrance, n. 63 [*Editor*].
2. Christ's miracles [*Editor*].

They met in their council and said: *What do we? For this man doeth many miracles.*[3] Can this be a motive? If they had said: "This man is a malefactor, a transgressor against the law, an agitator who with deceptions stirs up the people," they would have lied, as they lied when they did say these things; yet there were more coherent reasons for doing what they asked, which was to take His life, but to give as a reason that He performed miracles does not seem worthy of learned men, which the Pharisees were. And so it is that when learned men are overcome by passion, they spew forth these kinds of irrelevancies. Indeed, only for that reason was it determined that Christ should die. Men, if I can call you that when you are so brutish, what was the reason for so cruel a determination? Their only response is *multa signa facit.*[4] Lord have mercy if doing excellent things is a reason to die! This *multa signa facit* evokes *there shall be a root of Jesse, which shall stand for an ensign of the people* and then to *this child . . . [is] a sign which shall be spoken against.*[5] He is a sign? Then He must die! He excels? Then He must suffer, for that is the reward of one who excels!

Figures of the winds and of fame are usually placed at the very top of temples as decoration, and to protect them from birds, they are covered by barbs; this seems a protection yet is nothing but an inevitable attribute: whoever is on high is necessarily pierced by barbs. The animosity of the wind is there, the severity of the elements, the fury of thunderbolts taking their revenge, there is the target of stones and arrows. Oh unhappy heights, exposed to so many risks! Oh excellence, made a target of envy and the object of hostility! Any eminence, whether of dignity, nobility, wealth, beauty, or knowledge, suffers this burden, but the one that suffers most severely is understanding. First, because it is the most defenseless, since wealth and power punish any who attacks them, but not understanding, for the greater it is, the more modest and long-suffering and the less it defends itself. Second, because as Gracián[6] so wisely said, the advantages of understanding are advantages in one's being. For no other reason than greater understanding are angels more than men; and men surpass brutes only in understanding; and since no one wants to be less than another, no man confesses that another understands more, because that is the consequence of being more. A man will suffer and confess that another is more noble than he, wealthier, handsomer, and even more learned; but there is hardly

3. John 11:47.
4. A repetition of the last phrase of John 11:47, from the Vulgate Bible: "[this man] doeth many miracles" or "*signa*" in Latin [*Editor*].
5. "There shall be a root": Isaiah 11:10. "This child": Luke 2:34.
6. Baltasar Gracián (1601–1658), influential Spanish Jesuit moralist. The phrase is found in his *El discreto* (The gentleman, 1646), I: "Nature and Intelligence" [*Editor*].

anyone who will confess that another has more understanding: rare is the man who will concede cleverness.[7] That is why attacks against this gift are so effective.

When the soldiers mocked and jeered and taunted Our Lord Jesus Christ, they brought an old purple cloth and a hollow reed and a crown of thorns to crown Him a derisory king.[8] Now, the reed and the purple cloth were insulting, but not painful; why was only the crown painful? Was it not enough that, like the other emblems, it would be mocking and ignominious, since that was its purpose? No, because the sacred head of Christ and His divine brain were the repository of wisdom; and it is not enough in the world for a wise brain to be ridiculed, it must also be wounded and mistreated; a head that is a treasury of wisdom should not expect any crown other than one of thorns. What garland can human wisdom expect when it sees what divine wisdom received? Roman pride also crowned the various feats of its captains with various crowns: the civic for the man who defended the city, the military for the man who penetrated the enemy camp, the mural for the man who scaled the wall, the obsidional for the man who freed a besieged city or army or field or camp, the naval, the oval, the triumphal for other deeds, as recounted by Pliny and Aulus Gellius;[9] but considering so many different kinds of crowns, I wondered which type was used for the crown of Christ, and I think it was the obsidional, which (as you know, señora) was the most honorable and called obsidional from *obsidio*, which means "siege"; it was not made of gold or silver but of the very grain or grass growing in the field where the feat was accomplished. And since the feat of Christ was to raise the siege of the Prince of Darkness,[1] who had besieged all the world, as it says in the Book of Job: *From going to and fro in the earth, and from walking up and down in it*; and as Saint Peter says: *the devil . . . walketh about, seeking whom he may devour*;[2] and Our Lord came and raised the siege: *now shall the prince of this world be cast out*, and so the soldiers crowned Him not with gold or silver but with the natural fruit produced by the world, which was the battlefield that, after the curse, *thorns and thistles shall it bring forth to thee*,[3] produced nothing but thorns; therefore it was the most suitable crown for the valiant and wise Conqueror, crowned by His mother the Synagogue; and the daughters of Zion came out weeping to see His sorrowful triumph, as they had come rejoicing for

---

7. A paraphrase of Martial (ca. 40–104 C.E.), *Epigrammata*, VIII.xviii.10: *qui velit ingenio cedere, rarus erit* (He who is willing to cede to genius will be rare) [*Editor*].
8. Matthew 27:28–29 [*Editor*].
9. Aulus Gellius (ca. 125–180 C.E.), *Attic Nights*, V.vi. Pliny the Elder (23–79 C.E.), *Natural History*, XXII.iv.6–vi.13 [*Editor*].
1. That is, Satan [*Editor*].
2. "From going to and fro": Job 1:7 (KJV). "The devil": 1 Peter 5:8.
3. "Now shall the prince": John 12:31. "Thorns also": Genesis 3:18.

the other Solomon, because the triumph of the wise is achieved with sorrow and celebrated with weeping,[4] which is how wisdom triumphs; and since Christ, as the King of Wisdom, was the first to wear the crown that was made holy on His temples, other wise men are no longer afraid and understand they cannot aspire to any other honor.

Life Himself wished to give life to the deceased Lazarus;[5] the Disciples were not aware of His intention and replied: *Master, the Jews of late sought to stone thee; and goest thou thither again?* The Redeemer assuaged their fear: *Are there not twelve hours in the day?*[6] Up to this point it seems they were afraid because of the anteced- ent of the people wanting to stone Him when He reproached them, calling them thieves and not shepherds.[7] And so they feared that if He returned to the same place (since no matter how just, rebukes are not often acknowledged as true), He would put His life in dan- ger; but when they knew the truth and realized He was going to give life to Lazarus, what reason could have moved Thomas to say, as did Peter in the garden: *Let us also go, that we may die with him?*[8] What are you saying, Holy Apostle? The Lord is not going to die; what do you fear? For Christ is not going to reprove but to perform an act of mercy, and therefore they cannot do Him harm. The Jews themselves could have reassured you, for when He rebuked them for wanting to stone him: *Many good works have I shewed you from my Father; for which of those works do you stone me?* They replied: *For a good work we stone thee not; but for blasphemy.*[9] For if they say they do not wish to stone him for His good works, and now He is going to perform one as good as giving life to Lazarus, what is it you fear, or why? Would it not be better to say: *Let us go to enjoy the fruits of gratitude for the good work our Master is going to perform; to see Him applauded and thanked for the benefit; to see their wonderment at the miracle? And not to say what appears to be as irrelevant as: Eamus et nos, ut moriamur cum eo.*[1] But oh! The saint feared as an intelli- gent man and spoke as an Apostle.[2] Is Christ not going to perform a miracle? Well, what greater danger? It is less intolerable for pride to hear rebukes than for envy to see miracles. In everything I have said, illustrious señora, I do not wish to say (let no such foolishness find a place in me) that I have been persecuted for knowing, but only for loving knowledge and letters, because I have achieved neither.

---

4. Song of Solomon 3:10–11. "Daughters of Zion": Luke 23:27–29 [*Editor*].
5. See John 11. "Life Himself": Christ [*Editor*].
6. John 11:8–9. That is, there was still time, although Jesus was near death [*revised by Editor*].
7. John 10:1–18 [*Editor*].
8. John 11:16.
9. John 10:32–33.
1. "Let us also go, that we may die with him." John 11:16 as cited above [*Editor*].
2. That is, Saint Thomas, who has spoken the phrase to John [*Editor*].

At one time the Prince of the Apostles[3] found himself so distant from wisdom it was indicated with an emphatic: *But Peter followed afar off*; as far from the praise of the learned man as one known for his lack of intelligence: *Not knowing what he said*; and even questioned regarding his knowledge of wisdom, he himself said he knew nothing of it: *Woman, I know him not. Man, I know not what thou sayest.* And what happens to him? As a result of being known as an ignorant man, he did not have the good fortune of a wise man but only the afflictions. Why? No reason was given other than: *This man was also with him.*[4] He loved wisdom, carried it in his heart, followed after it, valued being a follower and lover of wisdom; and although he was so far off that he did not understand or reach it, it was enough to incur its torments. There was always a foreign soldier to cause him distress, a maidservant to trouble him. I confess I find myself very far from the boundaries of wisdom and have wanted to follow it, although at a distance. Yet this has brought me closer to the fire of persecution, the crucible of torment, to the extent that some have requested that I be forbidden to study.

This once was achieved by a very saintly, very ingenuous mother superior who believed that study was a matter for the Inquisition and ordered me to stop. I obeyed (for the three months her power to command lasted) in that I did not pick up a book, but not studying at all, which is not in my power, I could not do, because although I did not study books, I studied all the things God created, and these were my letters, and my book was the entire mechanism of the universe. I saw nothing without reflecting on it, heard nothing without considering it, even the smallest material things, for there is no creature, no matter how low, in which one does not recognize *God created me*,[5] none that does not astonish the understanding, if one considers it as one should. And so, I repeat, I looked at and admired everything; as a consequence, even the people to whom I spoke, and the things they said to me, gave rise to a thousand considerations: What is the origin of the varieties of intelligence and wit, since we are all one species? What could be the temperaments and hidden qualities that caused them? If I saw a figure, I would combine the proportion of its lines and measure it with my understanding and reduce it to other, different figures. I would walk sometimes in the front part of our dormitory (which is a very spacious room) and observe that while the lines of its two sides were parallel and the ceiling level, the eye made it seem that its lines inclined toward each other and the

3. The Apostle Peter [*Editor*].
4. "And Peter": Luke 22:54. "Not knowing": Luke 9:33. "Woman": Luke 22:57, 60. "This man": Luke 22:56.
5. The source is most likely Saint Augustine, *Sermones*, 68, 6, a meditation on the "book of nature" [*Editor*].

ceiling was lower at a distance than nearby, and from this I inferred that visual lines run straight, not parallel, but form a pyramidal shape instead. And I wondered whether this might be the reason the ancients were obliged to doubt the world was round. Because although it seems so, our sight could deceive us, showing concavities where there might not be any.

I notice everything in this manner and always have and have no control over it; in fact it tends to annoy me, for it wearies my head; I thought this, and composing verses, happened to everyone, until experience showed me the contrary; and this is so much my character or custom that I see nothing without considering it further. Two little girls were playing with a top in my presence, and no sooner did I see the movement and shape than I began, with this madness of mine, to consider the easy motion of the spherical shape and how the already transmitted impulse could last, independent of its cause, for far from the hand of the little girl, which was the motivating cause, the top still danced; not content with this, I had some flour brought in and sifted, so that as the top danced on top of it, I could learn whether the circles described by its movement were perfect or not; and I found that they were merely spiral lines that lost their circular nature as the impulse diminished. Some other girls were playing jackstraws (which is the most frivolous of children's games); I began to contemplate the figures they formed, and seeing that by chance three fell into a triangle, I began to connect one to the other, recalling that some say this was the shape of the mysterious ring of Solomon, which had distant indications and representations of the Holy Trinity, allowing him to perform countless miracles and marvels; and it is said that the harp of David[6] had the same shape, and for that reason Saul was healed at its sound; harps in our day still have almost the same shape.

And what could I tell you, señora, about the natural secrets I have discovered when cooking? Seeing that an egg sets and fries in butter or oil but falls apart in syrup; seeing that for sugar to remain liquid it is enough to add a very small amount of water in which a quince or other bitter fruit has been placed; seeing that the yolk and the white of the same egg are so different that each can be mixed with sugar but together they cannot. I do not mean to tire you with these inconsequentialities, which I mention only to give you a complete view of my nature, and which I believe will cause you to laugh; but, señora, what can we women know but kitchen philosophies? As Lupercio Leonardo[7]

6. See p. 98, n. 4. "Ring of Solomon": inscribed with the secret name of God and shaped as a star of David [Editor].
7. Lupercio Leonardo de Argensola (1559–1613), but the citation's source is actually Luperico's brother Bartolomé Leonardo de Argensola, Satire I.143–44. Lawrance, n. 83 [revised by Editor].

so wisely said, one can philosophize very well and prepare supper. And seeing these minor details, I say that if Aristotle had cooked, he would have written a great deal more. Returning to my continual cogitation, I repeat that this is so constant in me I do not need books; on one occasion, because of a serious stomach ailment, the doctors prohibited my studying; after a few days I suggested to them that it would be less harmful to allow me books, because my cogitations were so strong and vehement that they consumed more energy in a quarter of an hour than studying books did in four days; and so they were persuaded to allow me to read. And further, señora: not even my sleep was free of this continual movement of my imaginative faculty; rather, it tends to operate more freely and unencumbered, examining with greater clarity and tranquility the images of the day, arguing, and composing verses, and I could offer you a large catalogue of them and the arguments and delicate points I have formulated more successfully asleep than awake, but I put those aside in order not to weary you, for what I have said is enough for your intelligence and perspicacity to penetrate and see perfectly my entire nature, as well as the origin, means, and state of my studies.

If these, señora, are merits (I see them celebrated as such in men), they would not be so in me, because I act out of necessity. If they are blameworthy, for the same reason I believe I am not at fault; nonetheless, I am so wary of myself that in this or anything else I do not trust my own judgment; and so I remit the decision to your sovereign talent, submitting to whatever sentence you may impose, without contradiction or opposition, for this has been no more than a simple narration of my inclination toward letters.

III

I confess as well that since this is so true, as I have said, I needed no examples, yet the many I have read, in both divine and human letters, have not failed to help me. For I find Deborah[8] issuing laws, both military and political, and governing a people that had many learned men. I find an exceedingly wise Queen of Sheba,[9] so learned she dares to test with enigmas the wisdom of the greatest of wise men and is not rebuked for that reason; instead, because of it, she becomes judge of the unbelievers. I find numerous illustrious women: some adorned with the gift of prophecy, like Abigail; others, with the gift of persuasion, like Esther; others, with piety, like Rahab; others,

8. Female judge of ancient Israel, named in Judges 4–5.
9. Wealthy queen who visited King Solomon to test his wisdom and bestow gifts, as described in 1 Kings 10.

with perseverance, like Hannah, mother of Samuel, and countless others possessing all kinds of gifts and virtues.[1]

If I turn to the Gentiles, I first encounter the Sibyls,[2] chosen by God to prophesy the principal mysteries of our faith, in verses so learned and elegant they enthrall our admiration. I find a woman like Minerva,[3] daughter of the foremost god Jupiter and mistress of all the knowledge of Athens, worshipped as goddess of the sciences. I find Polla Argentaria,[4] who helped Lucan, her husband, write the great Pharsalia. I find the daughter of the divine Tiresias,[5] more learned than her father. I find Zenobia, queen of the Palmyrenes, as wise as she was valiant. Arete,[6] the most learned daughter of Aristippus. Nicostrata,[7] inventor of Latin characters and extremely erudite in Greek ones. Aspasia of Miletus,[8] who taught philosophy and rhetoric and was the tutor of the philosopher Pericles.[9] Hypatia, who taught astronomy and studied for many years in Alexandria. Leontion,[1] a Greek woman who wrote arguments countering the philosopher Theophrastus, which convinced him. Jucia, Corinna, Cornelia,[2] in short, all the great number of women who deserved fame, whether as Greeks, muses, or pythonesses,[3] for all of them were simply learned women, considered and celebrated and also venerated as such in antiquity. Not to mention countless others who fill the books, for I find the Egyptian Catherine[4] studying and affecting

1. Abigail: Prophet who becomes the wife of King David in 1 Samuel 25. Esther: Jewish queen of Persia (wife of Ahasuerus) who risked her life to save Jewish citizens from slaughter by the vizier Haman, as described in the Book of Esther. Rahab: Prostitute who helped the Israelites take Jericho by hiding spies in her home, as described in Joshua 2. Hannah, mother of Samuel, conceived miraculously at an advanced age, as described in 1 Samuel 1.
2. In ancient Greece, the women oracles who prophesied through a frenzied trance. They were known through the Sibylline books, in Greek hexameter, consulted in Rome at moments of crisis, and as Sor Juana suggests commonly reputed to have prophesied Christianity [Editor].
3. Roman goddess of wisdom, born of the head of Jupiter [Editor].
4. Widow of the poet Lucan and greatly admired by the poet Statius who calls her "patron of the arts" in his Silvae 2.7 [Editor].
5. In Greek mythology, a blind prophet who was transformed into a woman for seven years. His daughter was Manto, as recounted in Ovid, Metamorphoses, 6.7 [revised by Editor].
6. Said to have founded a school of philosophy (4th century B.C.E.). Zenobia: (ca. 240–275 C.E.), queen of the Palmyrene empire in Syria, she conquered Egypt and led a revolt against Rome [revised by Editor].
7. Legendary woman of letters said to have devised the first fifteen letters of the Latin alphabet [Editor].
8. Learned woman (ca. 470–410 B.C.E.) who became the mistress of Pericles [Editor].
9. Hypatia (ca. 370–415 C.E.), Neoplatonist and mathematician in Roman Egypt.
1. Greek Epicurean philosopher (4th–3rd century B.C.E.) who wrote against Theophratus, according to Cicero, De Natura Deorum (On the Nature of the Gods) [revised by Editor].
2. For Jucia, Sor Juana may have meant Julia (Domna), an intellectual Roman empress. Corinna (active 5th century B.C.E.): ancient Greek poet, thought by some to be a contemporary of Pindar. Cornelia (2nd century C.E.): early Catholic saint and martyr.
3. Greek priestesses [Editor].
4. Catherine of Alexandria (active 4th century C.E.), scholar and virgin saint [revised by Editor].

all the wisdom of the wise men of Egypt. I find Gertrude[5] reading, writing, and teaching. And for examples closer to home, I find a most holy mother of mine, Paula,[6] learned in the Hebrew, Greek, and Latin languages and extremely skilled in interpreting Scripture. And none other than the great Saint Jerome scarcely thought himself worthy of being her chronicler, for with the lively thought and energetic exactitude he brings to his explanations, he says: *If all the members of my body were tongues, they would not suffice to publish the wisdom and virtue of Paula.*[7] The widow Blaesilla deserved the same praise, as did the illustrious virgin Eustochium, both daughters of this saint; the second, for her knowledge, was called Prodigy of the World.[8] Fabiola, a Roman woman, was also extremely learned in Holy Scripture.[9] Proba Faltonia, another Roman, wrote an elegant book, a cento of selections from Virgil, on the mysteries of our Holy Faith.[1] It is well known that our queen, Doña Isabel, the wife of Alfonso X,[2] wrote on astronomy. And many others whom I omit in order not to cite what others have said (a vice I have always despised), for in our day the great Christina Alexandra, Queen of Sweden, as learned as she is valiant and magnanimous, and the Most Honorable Ladies the Duchess of Aveiro and the Countess of Villaumbrosa[3] are all flourishing.

The illustrious Doctor Arce[4] (a professor of Scripture, eminent for his virtue and learning), in his *Studioso Bibliorum*, raises this question: *Is it legitimate for women to dedicate themselves to the study of Holy Scripture and its interpretation?* And he offers many judgments of saints that argue against this, in particular the statement of the Apostle: *Let your women keep silence in the churches: for it is not*

5. Saint Gertrude of Helfta (1256–1302), German mystic and Benedictine theologian [*revised by Editor*].
6. Saint Paula (347–404 C.E.): wealthy Roman woman who became a Desert Mother, companion of Saint Jerome, and co-patron of the Hieronymite Order.
7. The first sentence of Saint Jerome's letter to Eustochium (*Letter* 108.1).
8. Blesilla (d. 384) and Eustochium (ca. 368–420 C.E.) were daughters of Saint Paula. Blesilla died young, while Eustochium became a saint and a Desert Mother.
9. Fabiola (d. 399 C.E.): Roman noblewoman who became a follower of Saint Jerome and Saint Paula.
1. Proba Faltonia (ca. 4th century C.E.): Roman Christian poet.
2. Apparently, Sor Juana commits an error. The wife of Alfonso X was Violante of Aragon, who did collaborate on Alfonso's astronomical treatises. Doña Isabel was the wife and queen of Ferdinand V [*Editor*].
3. An Andalusian Dominican nun. Christina Alexandra (1626–1689), Queen of Sweden with an interest in philosophy and science. She was a patroness of René Descartes and others. Duchess of Aveiro (1630–1715), a member of the Portuguese royalty and friend of the Countess of Paredes, vicereine of New Spain. Sor Juana dedicated a poem to her [*revised by Editor*].
4. Doctor Juan Díaz de Arce (1594–1653), professor of theology at the Royal and Pontifical University of Mexico and archbishop of Santo Domingo. Sor Juana refers to his argument in *Quaestionarii expositivi liber quartus de studioso bibliorum* (Expositive inquiries, Book four of concerning a student of books, 1648) [*Editor*].

permitted unto them to speak,[5] et cetera. Then he offers other judgments, including one by the same Apostle in Titus: *The aged women likewise, that they be in behavior as becometh holiness . . . teachers of good things,*[6] with interpretations of the holy fathers; and finally he prudently resolves that giving public lectures from a professor's chair and preaching from a pulpit are not legitimate for women, but that studying, writing, and teaching privately not only are legitimate but very advantageous and useful; it is obvious that this does not apply to all women but only to those whom God has favored with special virtue and prudence, who are mature and erudite and have the necessary talent and requisites for so sacred an occupation. And this is true not only for women, who are considered to be so incompetent, but for men as well, who for the simple fact of being men think they are wise: the interpretation of Scripture should be forbidden unless the men are very learned and virtuous, with tractable, well-inclined natures; I believe that doing otherwise has resulted in countless sectarians and has been at the root of countless heresies, for there are many who study but remain ignorant, especially those whose natures are arrogant, restless, proud, and inclined toward innovations in religion (which turns away from innovations); and so, in order to say what no one else has said, they are not content until they utter a heresy. About them the Holy Spirit declares: *For wisdom will not enter into a malicious soul.*[7] Knowledge does these men more harm than ignorance would. A wise man said that the man who does not know Latin is not a complete fool, but the one who does is qualified to be one. And I would like to add that a fool becomes perfect (if foolishness can reach perfection) by studying his bit of philosophy and theology and having some idea of languages, making him a fool in many sciences and many languages, because a great fool cannot be contained in his mother tongue alone.

These men, I repeat, are harmed by studying because it places a sword in the hands of a madman; being a noble instrument for defense, in his hands it means his death and the death of many others. This is what divine letters became in the hands of the wicked Pelagius and the perverse Arius, the wicked Luther, and the other heresiarchs like our Doctor (he was never ours and never a doctor) Cazalla,[8] all of them harmed by knowledge because, although it is the best nourishment and life of the soul, just as the better the food

5. 1 Corinthians 14:34 (KJV). Sor Juana directly addresses the bishop's argument in "Letter from Sor Filotea" (see p. 87, n. 8).
6. Titus 2:3 (KJV). "Same Apostle": Paul [*revised by Editor*].
7. Wisdom 1:4.
8. Doctor Agustín Cazalla (1510–1559), confessor to Charles V and burned at the stake by the Inquisition for Lutheranism. Pelagius (ca. 354–ca. 430 C.E.), British-Roman ascetic and theologian who oppposed the theory of predestination, instead emphasizing individual free will. Arius (ca. 250–336 C.E.), Alexandrian ascetic and theologian who

in an unbalanced, overheated stomach, the more arid, fermented, and perverse the humors[9] it creates, so it is with these evil men, for the more they study the worse the opinions they engender; their understanding is blocked by the very thing that should have nourished them, for they study a great deal and digest very little, not taking into account the limited vessel of their understanding. Regarding this the Apostle says: *For I say, by the grace that is given me, to all that are among you, not to be more wise than it behoveth to be wise, but to be wise unto sobriety, and according as God hath divided to everyone the measure of faith.*[1] And the truth is that the Apostle did not say this to women but to men; the *taceant*[2] is not only for women but for all those who are not very capable. My wanting to know as much as or more than Aristotle or Saint Augustine, if I do not have the aptitude of Saint Augustine or Aristotle, means that even if I study more than both of them, I not only will not succeed in my ambition, but the lack of proportion in my purpose will weaken and confuse the operation of my weak understanding.

Oh, if all of us—and I before anyone, for I am an ignorant woman—would take the measure of our talent before studying and (what is worse) writing with a voracious desire to equal and even surpass others, how little ambition would we have left and how many errors would we avoid and how many twisted intelligences would we not have in the world! And I place mine in first place, for if I knew as much as I should, I would not be writing this. And I insist I am doing so only to obey you, with so much misgiving that you owe me more for taking up my pen, having this fear, than you would if I had sent you more perfect works. It is good that this will be corrected by you; erase it, tear it up, and reprimand me, for I will value that more than all the vain applause others may offer me: *The just man shall correct me in mercy, and shall reprove me; but let not the oil of the sinner fatten my head.*[3]

And returning to our Arce, I say that he offers as confirmation of his opinion the words of my father Saint Jerome (*To Leta,*[4] *Upon the Education of her Daughter*) where he says: *Accustom her tongue while she is still young to the sweetness of the Psalms. Even the names through which she gradually will become accustomed to form her phrases*

---

opposed the doctrine of the Trinity, instead declaring Christ to be subordinate to God the Father. Martin Luther (1483–1546), German monk and theologian who advocated that salvation is by faith alone, and prompted the Protestant Reformation by challenging the pope's authority [*revised by Editor*].

9. In Hippocratic medicine, the four humors (black bile, yellow bile, blood, and phlegm) must be balanced for health. Imbalance would lead to a choleric (hot and dry) stomach [*Editor*].

1. Romans 12:3. "The Apostle": Paul [*revised by Editor*].

2. "Keep silence" (see p. 87, n. 8).

3. Psalm 141:5 [*Editor*].

4. The daughter-in-law of Saint Paula. Leta's daughter was also named Paula [*Editor*].

should not be chosen by chance but selected and repeated with care;
the prophets must be included, of course, and the Apostles as well, and
all the Patriarchs beginning with Adam down to Matthew and Luke,
so that as she practices other things she will be readying her memory
for the future. Let your daily task be taken from the flower of the Scrip-
tures.[5] If the saint wanted a little girl who had barely begun to speak
to be educated in this way, what would he want in his nuns and spiri-
tual daughters? It is known very well in the above mentioned
Eustochium and Fabiola and in Marcella, her sister Pacatula, and
others whom the saint honors in his letters, exhorting them to this
sacred exercise, as it is known in the cited letter where I noted that
reddat tibi pensum, which affirms and agrees with the *bene docentes*
of Saint Paul, for the *reddat tibi*[6] of my great father makes it plain
that the teacher of the little girl is to be Leta, her mother.

   Oh, how much harm could be averted in our republic if older
women were as learned as Leta and knew how to teach as Saint Paul
and my father Saint Jerome advise! Since they do not, and given the
extreme idleness in which our unfortunate women are left, if some
parents wish to give their daughters more instruction than usual,
necessity and the lack of learned older women obliges them to have
male tutors teach their daughters how to read, write, count, play an
instrument, and other skills, which results in a good amount of
harm, as we see every day in lamentable examples of mismatched
unions, for over time, with close dealings and communication, what
was thought impossible tends to become conceivable. For this rea-
son many parents choose to leave their daughters unlettered[7] and
uneducated rather than expose them to so notable a danger as famil-
iarity with men, which could be avoided if there were learned older
women, as Saint Paul desires, and instruction would be handed
down from one female to another as occurs in the teaching of nee-
dlework and other customary skills.

   For what disadvantage can there be in having an older woman
learned in letters, whose conversation and customs are holy, direct-
ing the education of young girls? The alternative is allowing them
to be lost through lack of instruction, or wishing to teach them by
means as dangerous as male tutors, even when there is no more risk
than the indecency of having a shy girl (who still blushes when her

---

5. Sor Juana combines three separate passages from Saint Jerome's *Letter to Laeta* (Letter
   107.4, 9) [*Editor*].
6. *reddat tibi pensum*: Let your daily task (from Saint Jerome, Letter 107.9; see previous
   note). Marcella (325–410 C.E.), Roman ascetic and saint who housed Saint Jerome
   while he translated the Bible into Latin. Saint Jerome and Saint Paula first met in her
   house. Jerome addresses Pacatula, Marcella's sister, in his letter to her father, Gauden-
   tius. "*Bene docentes*": teachers of good things (from Titus 2:3; see p. 113, n. 6) [*Editor*].
7. Sor Juana's term is *bárbaras,* often used in the colonial context to refer to what the Spanish
   understood as indigenous perversion and savagery, associates civilization with reading
   and writing [*Editor*].

own father looks in her face) sit beside a strange man who will treat her with domestic familiarity and authoritative informality; the modesty required in dealings with men and their conversation is enough reason not to permit this kind of arrangement. I do not find that this form of instruction, when men teach women, can be without danger except in the severe tribunal of a confessional or the decent distance of pulpits or the remote learning from books, but not in immediate proximity. Everyone knows this is true; even so, it is allowed only because of the lack of educated older women; therefore, not having them does great harm. This should be considered by those who, attached to *Mulieres in Ecclesia* [sic] *taceant,* curse the women who learn and teach, as if the Apostle himself had not said: *bene docentes.* Moreover, the prohibition came at a time when, as Eusebius[8] indicates, in the early Church women would teach one another doctrine in the temples, and this sound caused some confusion when the Apostles preached; that is why they were ordered to be silent, as occurs now, when one does not pray aloud while the preacher delivers his sermon.

There is no doubt that to understand many passages of divine letters, one needs to know a good deal about the history, customs, ceremonies, proverbs, and even modes of speech of the times when they were written in order to comprehend the references and allusions of certain locutions. *Rend your heart, and not your garments,*[9] is this not an allusion to the ceremony the Hebrews had of tearing their clothes as a sign of grief, as the evil high priest did when he said that Christ had blasphemed?[1] In many passages the Apostle writes of help for widows, and did they also not refer to the customs of those times?[2] The passage about the strong woman: *Her husband is known in the gates, when he sitteth among the elders of the land,*[3] does it not allude to the custom of holding the tribunal of judges at the gates of the cities? And *give your land to God,*[4] did it not signify making a vow? *Hiemantes,*[5] was this not the name given to public sinners, because they performed their penance in the open air, unlike others who repented in a covered passage? The complaint of Christ to the Pharisee regarding the lack of a kiss and the washing of his feet, was it not based on the custom the Jews had of doing

8. Greek bishop (ca. 260–340 c.e.), who wrote extensively on the early Church [*Editor*].
9. Joel 2:13.
1. Matthew 26:65: "Then the high priests rent his garments, saying: He hath blasphemed."
2. 1 Timothy 5:3–16 [*Editor*].
3. Proverbs 31:23 (KJV).
4. A phrase not found in the Bible. Sor Juana may refer to the act of turning over lands every seven years and forgiving debts in the Jubilee, as recounted in Leviticus 27:21 [*Editor*].
5. Penitents of the early Church, so called ("freezing") because they were required to stand outside, even in the winter [*Editor*].

these things?[6] And countless other passages that one encounters constantly, not only in divine letters but in human letters as well, such as *venerate the purple*, which meant obeying the king; *manumittere eum*,[7] which means to emancipate, alluding to the custom and ceremony of slapping the slave to give him his freedom. And *intonuit coelum*,[8] in Virgil, alluding to the omen of thunder in the west, which was taken as a good sign. And *nunquam leporem edisti*,[9] in Martial, which has not only the charm of ambiguity in *leporem* but the allusion to the property the hare was said to possess. The proverb *Sailing the coast of Malia means forgetting what you have at home*, which alludes to the great danger of the promontory of Laconia.[1] The reply of the chaste matron to the insistent suitor, *the hinges will not be greased on my account, nor will the torches be lit*, meaning she did not wish to marry, alluding to the ceremony of greasing doors with fat and lighting nuptial torches at weddings;[2] as if we were to say today: no dowry will be paid on my account and the priest will give no blessings. There are so many comments of this kind in Virgil and Homer and all the poets and orators. And aside from this, what difficulties are not found in sacred passages, even in matters of grammar, such as using the plural for the singular, or moving from the second to the third person, as in the Song of Songs: *Let him kiss me with the kiss of his mouth, for thy breasts are better than wine?*[3] Or placing adjectives in the genitive instead of the accusative, as in *I will take the chalice of salvation?*[4] Or using the feminine for the masculine, and calling any sin adultery?

All of this demands more instruction than some think who, as simple grammarians or at most with a few terms of formal logic, attempt to interpret Scriptures and seize on *Mulieres in Ecclesiis taceant*, not knowing how it is to be understood. Or *Let the woman learn in silence*,[5] this being a passage more in favor of women than

6. Luke 7:44–45 recalls Christ's complaint to Simon that he has received neither a kiss nor water to wash his feet [*Editor*].

7. That is, "emancipate him." Refers to the commonly held idea that slaves were freed with a slap. In Roman law, referred to the purple robes worn by emperors [*Editor*].

8. Misquotes *intonuit laevum, et de caelo lapsa per umbras* in Virgil, *Aeneid* II.693 ("it thundered on the left and [a star] fell from the skies"). Lawrance notes that it is likely that Sor Juana has culled these phrases from a Renaissance compendium of adages. Lawrance, n. 118 [*Editor*].

9. "You never ate hare" from Martial, *Epigrammata*, v.29: *edisti numquam, Gellia, tu leporem* (You, Gellia, have never eaten hare). It was believed that eating hare heightened a woman's beauty. In Latin, *leporem* was a pun on *hare* and *charm* [*Editor*].

1. Lawrance identifies this as "a well-known Greek proverb" referring to the promontory of Laconia in the Peloponnese and cited in Strabo's *Geography*, VIII.6.20. Lawrance, n. 119 [*Editor*].

2. Anointing doorways and thresholds and burning torches were Roman marriage rituals. It is unclear who the chaste matron is [*Editor*].

3. Song of Songs 1:1.

4. Psalm 116:13.

5. 1 Timothy 2:11. The full citation is: "Let the women learn in silence with all subjection" [*revised by Editor*].

against them, for it commands that they learn, and while they are learning, it is evident they must be silent. And it is also written: *Take heed and hearken, O Israel*,[6] where all men and women are addressed, and all are ordered to be silent, because the person who hears and learns of necessity must also attend and be silent. If this is not so, I should like these interpreters and expounders of Saint Paul to explain to me how they understand the passage *Mulieres in Ecclesia taceant.* Because they must understand it either as physical, the pulpits and cathedras,[7] or formal, the universality of the faithful, which is the Church. If they understand it in the first sense (which is, in my opinion, its true meaning, for we see that, in fact, women are not permitted to read publicly or preach in the Church), why reproach women who study privately? And if they understand it in the second and want the prohibition of the Apostle to be transcendent, so that not even in secret would women be permitted to write or study, why do we find that the Church has permitted Gertrude, Teresa, Birgitta, the Nun of Ágreda,[8] and many other women to write? And if they tell me these women were saints, it is true, but that does not negate my argument; first, because the proposition of Saint Paul is absolute and embraces all women without excepting saints, for in his day there were also Martha and Mary, Marcella, Mary[9] the mother of Jacob, Salome, and many others in the fervor of the early Church, and he does not exempt them; and now we find that the Church permits women who are saints and those who are not saints to write, for the Nun of Ágreda and Sor María de la Antigua are not canonized, and their writings circulate; neither were Saint Teresa[1] and the others when they wrote, which means that the prohibition of Saint Paul was directed only at the public pulpits, for if the Apostle had prohibited writing, the Church would not have permitted it. Now, I do not have the courage to teach—for that would be excessive presumption in me—and writing requires greater talent than mine, and very great deliberation. As Saint Cyprian says: *The things we write demand the most careful consideration.*[2] All that I have wished is to study in order to be ignorant about less: for,

---

6. Not found in the Bible but rather in Saint Jerome, *Letter to Eustochium* (Letter 108.27) [*Editor*].
7. Bishops' official thrones.
8. Sor María de Ágreda (1602–1665), Spanish mystic, nun, and author of *The Mystical City of God*, an autobiography of the Virgin Mary. Saint Birgitta (1303–1373), mystic and the founder of the Bridgettine nuns and monks [*Editor*].
9. The mother of James and Salome and a servant of Christ's who helped bury him in the Sepulchre (Mark 15:40–16:8). The sisters Martha and Mary housed Christ (Luke 10:38–42; John 11:1–6, 12:1–8). Sor Juana might be confusing Jerome's correspondent Marcella in this list [*Editor*].
1. Saint Teresa of Ávila (d. 1582) was not canonized until 1622. Sor María de la Antigua (1566–1617), Spanish mystic and author of *Desengaño de religiosas* (Disillusion of religious women, 1678) [*Editor*].
2. This phrase has not been located in Saint Cyprian's writings [*Editor*].

according to Saint Augustine, one learns some things in order to do them and others only to know them: *Discimus quaedam, ut sciamus; quaedam, ut faciamus.*[3] Then where is my offense if I refrain even from what it is legitimate for women to do, which is to teach by writing, because I know I do not have the disposition to do so, following the advice of Quintilian: *Let each person learn not only from the precepts of others but from his own nature?*[4]

If my crime lies in the *Athenagoric Letter*, did that do more than simply refer to my opinion with all the reverence I owe to our Holy Mother Church? If she, with her most holy authority, does not forbid me to do so, why should others? Expressing an opinion contrary to that of Vieira was insolence in me, and expressing an opinion contrary to that of three Holy Fathers of the Church[5] was not insolence in his paternity? Is not my understanding, such as it is, as free as his, for it comes from the same soil? Is his opinion one of the revealed principles of our Holy Faith, so that we must believe it blindly? Moreover, I did not fail in the deference owed to so great a man, which his defender lacked in addressing me, having forgotten the judgment of Titus Lucius: *Respect is companion to the arts;* nor did I criticize in any way the Society of Jesus; and I wrote only for the judgment of the one who suggested I do so; according to Pliny, *the state of the person who publishes is not the same as that of one who merely speaks.*[6] For if I had thought the letter would be published, it would not have been as carelessly written as it was. If it is, as the censor says, heretical, why does he not denounce it?[7] Then he would be avenged and I content, for I value more, as I should, the name of Catholic and obedient daughter of my Holy Mother Church than all the praise for being learned. If it is brutish—and they do well to say so—then let him laugh, even if it be with feigned laughter, for I do not tell him to praise me, and just as I was free to disagree with the opinion of Vieira, anyone else is free to disagree with mine.

---

3. Saint Augustine, Psalm 118, Sermon 17.3: *Cum itaque alia sint quae ideo discimus ut tantummodo sciamus, alia vero ut etiam faciamus* (Some things we learn so we may know them, and others so we may act upon them) [*Editor*].
4. The passage is a misquotation and misunderstanding of Quintillian, *Institutio Oratoria*, 2.11.1: *qui nihil egere huiusmodi praeceptis eloquentiam putent, sed natura sua et vulgari modo et scholarum exercitatione contenti rideant etiam diligentiam* (For they will urge that eloquence can dispense with rules of this kind and, in smug satisfaction with themselves and the ordinary methods and exercises of the schools) [*revised by Editor*].
5. In his Maundy Thursday Sermon, Vieira argues against Augustine, Thomas Aquinas, and John Chrysostom [*Editor*].
6. The source for this citation from Pliny the Elder has not been identified. There is no author named Titus Lucius; the phrase attributed to him is a misquotation of Quintillian's *Institutio Oratoria*, 9.4.8: *comitetur semper artem decor* (embellishment always accompanies art). "Society of Jesus": Vieira was a member of the Jesuit order, known for their corporate discipline and power in late-seventeenth-century Mexico. Sor Juana underscores that her critique is only of Vieira and does not reflect on the Jesuits as a whole [*Editor*].
7. Sor Juana employs the term "censor" metaphorically to refer to her critics, perhaps alluding to the charge of heresy to which she refers [*revised by Editor*].

But where is this taking me, señora? This does not apply here, and it is not for your ears, but since I am speaking of my accusers, I recalled the phrases of one, which appeared recently, and without being aware of it my pen slipped into an attempt to respond to him in particular, when my intent was to speak in general. And so, returning to our Arce, he says he learned of two nuns in this city: one in the Convent de Regina, who had memorized the breviary so well that she applied its verses, psalms, and the aphorisms and homilies of the saints with great quickness of mind and correctness in her conversation. The other, in the Convent de la Concepción, was so accustomed to reading the epistles of my father Saint Jerome, as well as the saint's words, that Arce says: *I thought I heard Jerome himself, speaking in Spanish*. And about her he says that he learned, after her death, that she had translated the epistles into Spanish; and it pains him that talents like these had not been used in greater studies with philosophical principles, and he does not say the name of either one, although he alludes to them as confirmation of his judgment, which is that not only is it legitimate but very useful and necessary for women to study sacred letters, nuns in particular, which is what you in your wisdom exhort me to do, and with which so many authorities concur.

If I turn to my ability, so often criticized, to make verses—which is so natural in me that I even have to force myself not to write this letter in verse, and I might say: *Everything I wished to say took the form of verse*[8]—seeing it condemned and incriminated so often by so many, I have searched very diligently for what may be the harm in it and have not found it; rather, I find verses in the mouths of the Sybils applauded, and sanctified in the pens of the prophets, especially King David, about whom the great expositor and my beloved father says, explaining the measure of his meters: *In the manner of Horace and Pindar,*[9] *now it races in iambs, now the alcaic resounds, now it rises in sapphic, now it moves forward with broken feet*. Most of the sacred books are in meter, such as the Books of Moses, and Saint Isidore says, in his *Etymologiae*, that the Book of Job is in heroic verse.[1] Solomon wrote the *Song of Songs* in verse, as did Jeremiah the *Lamentations*.[2] For this reason, says Cassiodorus:[3] *All*

---

8. From the Roman poet Ovid (43 B.C.E.–17 C.E.), *Tristia* (Lamentations) 4.10.26 [*Editor*].
9. Greek poet (ca. 522–ca. 443 B.C.E.). King David was the reputed author of many biblical Psalms. The quotation is from Saint Jerome, preface to *Chronicle* (written ca. 380 C.E.). Horace, or Quintus Horatius Flaccus (65–8 B.C.E.), Latin poet, and author of *Odes*; he admired Pindar [*Editor*].
1. Isidore, *Etymologiés*, 6.2.14. The canticle of Moses is found in Exodus 15:1–19 [*Editor*].
2. The biblical book Lamentations is attributed to Jeremiah (ca. 650–ca. 585 B.C.E.), a Hebrew prophet. The Song of Songs is traditionally attributed to Solomon [*Editor*].
3. Flavius Magnus Aurelius Cassiodorus (ca. 485–ca. 585 C.E.), Roman senator and later a monk who founded a monastery at the Vivarium outside Rome. The phrase has not been identified among his writings [*Editor*].

poetic locutions originate in Holy Scripture. Our Catholic Church not only does not scorn verses but uses them in its hymns and recites those of Saint Ambrose, Saint Thomas, Saint Isidore,[4] and others. Saint Bonaventure[5] was so fond of them that there is scarcely a page of his that does not contain verses. It is evident that Saint Paul studied them, for he cites and translates verses of Aratus: *For in him we live, and move, and have our being,*[6] and cites another by Parmenides: *The Cretians are always liars, evil beasts, slothful bellies.*[7] Saint Gregory Nazianzen[8] argues questions of matrimony and virginity in elegant verses. Why should I grow weary? The Queen of Wisdom and Our Lady, with her sacred lips, intoned the Canticle of the Magnificat;[9] and having presented her as an example, it would be an offense to present profane examples, although they may be very serious and learned men, for this is more than enough proof; and seeing that, although Hebrew elegance could not fit into Latin measure, for which reason the holy translator, more attentive to the importance of the meaning, omitted the verse, but even so, the psalms retain the name and divisions of verses; then where is the harm in them? Because the art is not to blame for its evil use but the one who professes evil and debases it, making it a snare of the devil; and this occurs in all the arts and sciences.

If the evil lies in a woman writing verses, it is clear that many have done so in a praiseworthy way; where is the evil in my being a woman? Of course I confess that I am base and despicable, but in my judgment no verse of mine has been called indecent. Moreover, I have never written anything of my own free will but only because others have entreated and ordered me to; I do not recall having written for my own pleasure except for a trifle they call *The Dream*.[1] The letter that you, my lady, so honored was written with more repugnance than anything else, because it dealt with sacred matters for which (as I have said) I have a reverent awe, and because it seemed to impugn, something for which I feel a natural aversion. And I believe that if I could have foreseen the fortunate destiny to

4. The *Te Deum* hymns were attributed to Saint Ambrose. The *Pange Lingua*, to Saint Thomas. The hymns by Isidore have not been identified [*Editor*].
5. A Franciscan friar and scholastic theologian (1221–1274) [*Editor*].
6. Acts 17:28. Aratus (ca. 310–240 B.C.E.): a Greek poet.
7. The citation is credited to the philosopher and poet Epimenides (7th or 6th century B.C.E.), not to the pre-Socratic philosopher Parmenides. Titus 1:12 [*revised by Editor*].
8. Saint Gregory of Nazianzus (329–389 C.E.) was a Greek Father known for his verse. Also cited by the Bishop Santa Cruz in his "Letter from Sor Filotea" on p. 87 [*Editor*].
9. A prayer from Mother Mary's speech at the Visitation (see p. 91, n. 5): "My soul magnifies the Lord," Luke 1:46–55 [*Editor*].
1. Sor Juana's mention of the poem now known as "First Dream" (p. 45) is the only indication that it was written before 1691, when she wrote this "Response." This statement also shows that the poem circulated in manuscript before being published in 1692 in her *Second Volume*. Finally, her statement that "they call" the poem "The Dream" has fueled speculation that the term "First" in the published title was an insertion by the editor [*Editor*].

which it was born—for, like another Moses, I abandoned it in the waters of the Nile of silence, where it was found and treated lovingly by a princess like you[2]—I believe, I repeat, that if I had thought this would happen, I would have drowned it first with the same hands from which it was born, for fear the awkward blunders of my ignorance would be seen in the light of your wisdom. In this the greatness of your kindness is revealed, for your will applauds precisely what your brilliant understanding must reject. But now that its fate has brought it to your door, so abandoned and orphaned that you even had to give it a name, I regret that along with my imperfections, it also bears the defects of haste, not only because of my continuing ill health and the countless duties my obedience imposes, and because I lack someone to help me write and feel the need for everything to be in my own hand, and because writing it went against my nature and all I wanted was to keep my promise to one I could not disobey, I did not have the time to refine it; as a consequence I failed to include entire discourses and many proofs that I had at hand but did not add in order to stop writing; and if I had known it would be printed, I would not have omitted them, if only in order to satisfy certain objections that have been raised, which I could dispatch, but I shall not be so discourteous as to place such indecent objects before the purity of your eyes, for it is enough that I offend them with my ignorance without adding the insolence of others. If they happen to fly to you (for they are so light in weight they may), then I shall do as you command; for if it does not contravene your precepts, I shall never take up the pen in my own defense, because it seems to me that one offense does not require another in response, when one recognizes error in the very place it lies hidden, for as my father Saint Jerome says, *Good discourse does not seek secrets*,[3] and Saint Ambrose: *Concealment is in the nature of a guilty conscience*.[4] Nor do I consider myself refuted, for a precept of the Law says: *An accusation does not endure if not tended by the person who made it.*[5] What certainly is worth pondering is the effort it has required to make copies. A strange madness to put more effort into stripping away approval than acquiring it! I, señora, have not wanted to respond, although others have without my knowledge: it is enough that I have seen some papers,[6] among them one that I send to you because it is learned and because reading it makes up in part for

---

2. The baby Moses was abandoned in a basket by the Nile river but was rescued by Pharaoh's daughter (Exodus 2:1–10), just as the *Athenagoric Letter* was rescued by the "princess," Sor Filotea [*Editor*].
3. Saint Jerome, *Letter to Gaudentius* (413 c.e.) (Letter 128.3) [*revised by Editor*].
4. Saint Ambrose, *On Abraham*, 1.2.4 [*Editor*].
5. This statement has not been found in either civil or canon law [*Editor*].
6. Sor Juana refers to contemporary writings that attacked and defended her *Athenagoric Letter* [*Editor*].

the time you have wasted on what I write. If you, señora, would like me to do the opposite of what I have put forward for your judgment and opinion, at the slightest sign of what you desire my intention will cede, as it ought to; it was, as I have said, to be silent, for although Saint John Chrysostom says: *Slanderers must be refuted, and those who question taught,* I see that Saint Gregory also says: *It is no less a victory to tolerate enemies than to overcome them;*[7] and that patience conquers by tolerating and triumphs by suffering. And if among the Roman Gentiles it was the custom, at the height of the glory of its captains—when they entered in triumph over other nations, dressed in purple and crowned with laurel, their carriages pulled not by animals but by crowned, conquered kings, accompanied by spoils of the riches of the entire world, and the conquering army adorned with the insignias of its feats, hearing the applause of the people in their honorary titles of renown, such as Fathers of the Nation, Columns of Empire, Walls of Rome, Protectors of the Republic, and other glorious names—for a soldier, in this supreme moment of human glory and happiness, to say aloud to the conqueror, with his consent and by order of the Senate: "Remember that you are mortal; remember that you have these defects," not forgetting the most shameful, which is what occurred in the triumph of Caesar, when the lowest soldiers called out in his hearing: "Beware, Romans, we bring you the bald adulterer."[8] This was done so that in the midst of countless honors the conqueror would not become vain, the ballast of these insults would counterbalance the sails of so much praise, and the ship of good judgment would not founder in the winds of acclaim. And I say that if Gentiles did this with only the light of natural law, we who are Catholics, with the precept of loving our enemies, what would we not do to tolerate them? For my part I can assure you that at times calumny has mortified me but never done me harm, because I take for a great fool the person who, having the opportunity to gain merit, endures the great effort and loses the merit, which is like those who do not wish to accept death and in the end die; their resistance does nothing to exempt them from death, but it does take away the merit of resignation and turns what might have been a good death into one that was bad. And so, señora, I believe these things do more good than harm, and consider the effect of praise on human weakness a greater risk,

---

7. According to Lawrance, the citation paraphrases the commentary on 1 Samuel 11:13 by Gregory the Great (ca. 540–604 C.E.), *Commentarii in librum 1 Regum* (commentaries on Book I of Kings) 5.1.13. The first statement is not found in the writings of the Greek Father John Chrysostom (347–407 C.E.) but rather in a text of the twelfth-century Zacharias Chrysopolitanus, *In unem ex quatuor* (In one of four), III. 127. Lawrance, n. 152 [*Editor*].

8. A similar line is recounted in Suetonius, *De vita Caesarum* (About the Life of the Caesars), "Divus Julius," 51 [*Editor*].

for it tends to appropriate what is not ours, and we need to take great care to keep the words of the Apostle etched in our hearts: *And what hast thou that thou didst not receive? Now if thou didst receive it, why dost thou glory, as if thou hadst not received it?*[9] so they can serve as a shield that resists the sharp points of praise, which are like lances that, when not attributed to God, to Whom they belong, take our life and turn us into thieves of the honor of God and usurpers of the talents He gave us and the gifts He lent us, for which we must give a strict accounting. And so, señora, I fear praise more than calumny, because calumny, with only a simple act of patience, is transformed into benefit, while praise requires many acts of reflection and humility and knowledge of oneself to keep it from doing harm. In my case, I know and recognize that knowing this is a special favor of God, allowing me to behave in both instances according to the judgment of Saint Augustine: *One should not believe the friend who praises or the enemy who censures.*[1] Although most of the time, given my nature, I squander what I have been given or combine it with so many defects and imperfections that I debase the good that came from Him. And so, in the little of mine that has been printed, not only my name but consent for the printing has been not of my own choosing but the will of another who does not fall under my control, as in the printing of the *Athenagoric Letter*; this means that only some *Exercises of the Incarnation* and *Offerings of the Sorrows* were printed for public devotion with my approval, but without my name;[2] I am sending copies of these to you, to give (if you agree) to our sisters the nuns of your holy community and others in the city. I am sending only one copy of the *Sorrows* because the others have been distributed and I could find no other. I wrote them years ago, solely for the devotions of my sisters, and afterward they became more widely known; their subjects are so much greater than my mediocrity and ignorance, and the only thing that helped me with them was that they dealt with our great Queen: it is notable that the iciest heart is set ablaze when one alludes to Most Holy Mary. I should like, illustrious señora, to send you works worthy of your virtue and wisdom, but as the poet said:

9. Apostle: Paul. 1 Corinthians 4:7 [*revised by Editor*].
1. Adapted from Saint Augustine, *Contra litteras Petiliani Donastistae* 3.10 (written ca. 400 c.e.): *nam si laudanti amico credendum non est, nec inimico detrahenti* (For, if you should not believe a praising friend, neither should you a detracting enemy) [*Editor*].
2. The original publication dates of the *Exercises of the Incarnation* and *Offerings of the Sorrows* are unknown. Both were published in the posthumous volume of her works, *Fame and Posthumous Works* (1700). These two works are important for Sor Juana's defense, as they fit the bishop's demands that she write on religious subjects. "Printed": the mystery play *The Divine Narcissus* had been published in Mexico in 1690, and a volume of her works, *Castalian Inundation*, had been published in Spain in 1689. Her *Second Volume* would be published the following year, in 1692. Sor Juana's *villancicos* and religious works were commissioned and printed separately, often without authorial attribution (see the chronology on p. 312) [*Editor*].

Although strength may be lacking, the will must be praised.
I think the gods are satisfied with that.[3]

If I write any other trifles, they will always seek out the sanctuary of your feet and the security of your correction, for I have no other jewel with which to pay you, and as Seneca says, whoever begins to offer benefits is obliged to continue them; in this way, your own generosity will repay you, for only in this way can I be freed in an honorable manner from my debt and avoid this warning from the same Seneca: *It is shameful to be surpassed in benefits.*[4] For it is the magnanimity of the generous creditor to give the poor debtor what is needed to satisfy the debt. This is what God gave to the world incapable of repaying Him: He gave his own Son so that He would receive a recompense worthy of Him.[5]

If the style of this letter, illustrious señora, has not been what you deserve, I beg your pardon if in the homely familiarity or lack of respect in my treating you as a veiled nun, one of my sisters, I have forgotten the distance of your most eminent person, for if I had seen you without the veil, this would not have happened; but you, with your wisdom and kindness, will supply or amend the words, and if *vos* seems incongruous, I used it because it seemed that for the reverence I owe you, *Your Reverence*[6] shows very little reverence; change it then to whatever seems honorable and what you deserve, for I have not dared to exceed the limits of your style or go past the boundary of your modesty.

Keep me in your grace and pray for divine grace for me and may the Lord grant you a large portion of it and keep you, which is my plea and my need. From this convent of our father Saint Jerome in Mexico City, on the first day of the month of March in the year 1691. I kiss your hand and am your most favored

Juana Inés de la Cruz

---

3. The poet is Ovid (*Epistulae ex Ponto* 3.4.79–80) [*revised by Editor*].
4. Seneca, *De Beneficiis* (On kindness) 5.2 [*revised by Editor*].
5. That is, he gave the world Jesus Christ [*Editor*].
6. Sor Juana should use "Your Reverence" in speaking to the bishop, as she does when writing to her confessor Reverend Father Antonio Núñez de Miranda in 1681. See "Letter by Mother Juana Inés" on p. 144. "Veiled nun": Sor Juana plays on the double meaning of veil, that is, a nun's veil or a disguise. "*Vos*": Sor Juana uses the familiar form of the second-person singular, reserved for informal and familiar relations [*Editor*].

CONTEXTS

Additional Works

From the *Villancicos* for Saint Peter Nolasco[†]

In the Hispanic tradition, *villancicos* were carols written and performed for festivals. Although their origins were in popular and courtly lyric, by the sixteenth and seventeenth centuries the genre was almost exclusively performed on holy and feast days of the Church calendar. Sung rather than enacted by the church chorale, they nonetheless preserved dramatic dialogues and popular characters, especially in the final *ensaladas* (or "salads," for their mixture of voices). These final verses were jocose compositions of different meters and poetic genres, many times written to imitate the style of speech of a particular social group. By the mid-seventeenth century, *ensaladas* had fallen out of favor in peninsular Spain but remained popular in Spanish America.[1]

Between 1676 and 1691, Sor Juana composed nearly one *villancico* per year, all commissioned by Mexican dioceses and performed during the church liturgy on specific holy days. These were printed separately after the event, many times without authorial attribution. Sor Juana's *villancico* for Saint Peter Nolasco's feast day, January 28, follows the typical tripartite structure of nocturnes,[2] with the first two nocturnes each containing a psalm, a lesson, and a response. The third nocturne, reprinted here, contains a psalm and an *ensalada*. In a reflection of the ethnic diversity of Mexico City at the end of the seventeenth century, the *ensalada* presents voices of an Afro-Mexican, a student, and a native Mexican, all in stereotyped dialects.[3]

Through their dialects, Sor Juana ingeniously links the status of the speaking subjects to the theme of the feast day.[4] Saint Peter Nolasco (1189–1256) was the Catalan founder of the Mercedarians, a congregation dedicated to the redemption of Christian prisoners captured in the ongoing battles with North African and Iberian Muslims over control of the Iberian peninsula. After recounting his story in the first and

---

[†] Translated for this edition by Isabel Gómez. The full title reads: *A villancico sung for the Matins of the Glorious Father Saint Peter Nolasco, founder of the Sacred Family of Redeemers of the Order of Our Lady of Mercy.* Printed on January 31, 1677. Republished in the first volume of Sor Juana's works, *Castalian Inundation* (1689). The notes are the translator's unless otherwise indicated [*Editor*].

1. Martha Lilia Tenorio, *Los villancicos de Sor Juana* (Mexico: El Colegio de México, 1999), 152 [*Editor*].

2. Divisions according to the canonical hour of matins, or nighttime prayers [*Editor*].

3. For the politics of dialects in *villancicos,* see Martínez-San Miguel on p. 275 [*Editor*].

4. See Yolanda Martínez-San Miguel on p. 272 for other examples of this type of intervention in Sor Juana's *villancicos* [*Editor*].

second nocturnes, in the third nocturne Sor Juana uses the theme of
captivity to make Saint Peter relevant to the public of enslaved and free
subjects of late-seventeenth-century New Spain.

Third Nocturne

VILLANCICO VII

Come see a rising Venus star
in him, the Second Redeemer,
who executed here on earth
the just vocation of the First![5]
5 Come see the perfect diligence
of his capacious grace and might!
Run quickly, make haste, you shepherds:
come, you will see in his zeal,
the world has another Redeemer—
10 without the o'ershadowing title—
he gives worldly peace to mankind
and glory to God in Heaven!

VERSES

Because Nolasco gratified
Jesus when he was created,
in his likeness we may perceive
Peter was born in ancient Gaul
5 just as was Christ in Galilee.[6]

Even before he learned to speak,
he already gave away alms—
we would be correct to say:
as soon as our saint was born
10 he already was redeeming.

But the Honeycomb represents
a mystery more sovereign,
exciting more admiration still:
Peter held in his infant hand
15 what graced the Beloved's mouth.[7]

5. That is, Saint Peter, who acts as a redeemer of captives also imitates Christ, the first
redeemer [Editor].
6. The original Spanish plays on the similarity between Gaul (Galia) and Galilea.
7. This verse refers to the swarm of bees that formed a honeycomb in the hand of the baby
Peter asleep in his cradle. Sor Juana connects this episode in the saint's hagiography to
the biblical verse in the Song of Solomon 4:11 "Thy lips, O my spouse, drop as the hon-
eycomb: honey and milk are under thy tongue."

Desiring most his blood to give
with such burning inclination:
what did not flow out from his veins,
in his urge to live the Passion
20   Christlike, his blood transpired.

Even the most reasoned judgment
will not comprehend the fervor
our Saint displayed, for, compassion itself,
he captured the Second Redeemer,
25   himself, to rescue the captive.[8]

That most elevated occupation
of Christ he longed to imitate
in the battle feared above all—
but what could Peter have hoped for
30   when even our God lost his life?

The afflicted would visit him,
their disinterest all on display,
his remedy was what they sought
that as a good Frenchmen he could
35   give them cures for their French malaise.[9]

Of Peter the Apostle and his faith
the signs, they all were there:
even the Cock was seen in him—
just as his namesake heard it crow—
40   our Peter was of this nation.[1]

With the ardor of his charity
he consumed himself with passion
in martyrdom and sacrifice;
Saint Peter wanted more to be
45   a Martyr than a Confessor.

Finally he imitated Christ
and followed in his footsteps—

8. That is, Saint Peter became ("captured") the second redeemer in order to redeem those captured [Editor].
9. Saint Peter was Catalan, most likely from the French side of the Pyrenees mountains. The "mal francés," or the malady of France, is syphilis.
1. This play on words refers to the rooster that crowed after Saint Peter the Apostle denied Christ three times. Peter Nolasco comes from "Gaul," which sounds like "gallo," the Spanish word for rooster.

in his patience he could see,
when all were for themselves, as one,
50   he alone endured for all.

VILLANCICO VIII—*ENSALADILLA*[2]

In laudable celebration
for the founder of their cause,
Nolasco's order of Redeemers[3]
makes him known with just applause.
5   A black man entered the Church
by its grandness was he awed—
to liven up the festival
he sang to the beat of a gourd:

PUERTO RICO[4]—*REFRAIN*

Tumba, la LA la; tumba, la LE le,
Where Pilico[5] go, no slave girl[6] remain!
Tumba, la LA la; tumba, la LE le,
Where Pilico go, no slave girl remain!

5   Ah was sayin in Las Mercedes
tha da Mercedarian Order
gwan have a party for der Father.
Her face asked, Wha party?
She say ta me, Wha Redeemer?
10   thing seem ta entertain her.
Cause ah live in da Oblaje[7]

2. Literally, "little salad," see the headnote (p. 129) [*Editor*].
3. The Mercedarian order, founded by Saint Peter Nolasco [*Editor*].
4. The music sung by the Afro-Mexican. Tenorio, *Los villancicos de Sor Juana*, 156 [*Editor*].
5. A written approximation of *Perico*, an affectionate nickname for Pedro, referring to San Pedro Nolasco. The onomatopoetic patterns Sor Juana uses here to render black speech are similar to what twentieth-century authors such as Nicolas Guillén and Guillermo Cabrera Infante will use. These devices include interchanging *r* and *l* or *t* and *d* sounds and dropping consonants at the ends of words. This convention was common in seventeenth-century Spanish and Spanish-American theater and reflects how outsiders perceived the dialect rather than a linguistically accurate transcription of Afro-Mexican speech. To approximate this stereotyped dialect in English, the translator has drawn on examples from nineteenth- and twentieth-century American works such as those by Mark Twain and Zora Neale Hurston, both of whom created literary versions of African American speech. For the political complexities of Sor Juana's representation of dialects in the *villancicos*, see Martínez-San Miguel on p. 278 [*Translator's note revised by Editor*].
6. In the original, this word appears as *escrava* in Portuguese rather than *esclava*, as a reference to the transatlantic slave trade with the Portuguese and Lusophone African colonies. In this way, the stylistic devices described in note 3 also serve to inflect the Spanish with Portuguese pronunciations of certain shared words. For example, *blanca* in Spanish is *branca* in Portuguese.
7. Refers to the *obraje de paños* or one of the textile factories that used slave labor to produce cotton and other textiles and products for the local market.

an don no Padre come an save me.
      Da other night wit mah conga
ah didn sleep for thinkin
15 dey don wan dark folk like her;
    jus whites are to der likin.
      Dey only save da Spaniard—
mah Gods! look wha duh trick:
tho dey may call us horses,
20 we people tho we black!
      But, wha dam ah sayin? mah God!
Demons musta tricked me
for me da be complainin
against da Redeemin Saint!
25   Ah know Saint Pete'll forgive me,
cause ah was only talkin bold,
cause tho mah body may suffer,
in him is freed mah soul.

THE INTRODUCTION CONTINUES

Then followed quite the student,
an affected young Bachelor's degree,
who would sooner choose to be mute before
in the Castilian tongue would he speak.
5   And thus blossoming with Latin
and bursting to seem scholarly
to the barbarian[8] he found there
he fired off Latinisms such as these:

DIALOGUE

—Today *Nolascus divinus*[9]
In Heaven *est collocatus*.[1]
—But I do like the wine!
Not drink? I'd rather die.
5 —One *Redemptore* passes,
And another *Redemptore natus*.[2]
—Good cream[3] sure I've eaten

8. Sor Juana uses the word *bárbaro*, or "barbarian," to refer to someone who does not speak Latin or who does not understand the language in which he is spoken to. [*Editor*].
9. Divine Nolasco [*Editor*].
1. Is placed [*Editor*].
2. Redeemer is born [*Editor*].
3. In this dialogue, the Student speaks Latin, and his interlocutor responds in Spanish, riffing on homophonic words: the Latin *divinus* becomes "del vino," or "the wine" as the barbarian understands it. Here, the Latin *natus* is taken as *natas*, or "cream."

But then, I've never seen bad.
—For us all was he our *Salvatoris*
10   He is the *perfectior Imago*.[4]
—Magic? Not me, I swear to it,
never in my life have I studied that.
—*Amice*, hold your peace, I *ego
non sermone*[5] in Spanish I'd never.
15   —Why drown yourself in sermons?
Just don't go listen to them.
—*Non* understand what you are saying,
nec quid vis dicere capio.[6]
—He and his soul, they must be fools,
20   for an honorable man am I.

THE INTRODUCTION CONTINUES

To make the peace between them,
an Indio came somersaulting
towards them, taking the measure
of the cathedral with his head.
5   Then, to the dissonant echoes
from the sound of his guitar,
he sang a mestizo *Tocotín*[7]
in Spanish and Mexican tongues.[8]

TOCOTÍN[9]

The blessed Fathers
have uh Redeemer
*I don't believe it,
my God knows better.*
5   Our God's son *Piltzintli*
came down from heaven:
for our sins or *tlatlácol*
he pardoned us all.
But those *Teopixqui*[1]
10   said in their sermon

4. More perfect image [*Editor*].
5. I do not speak [*Editor*].
6. Nor do I understand what you want to say.
7. See note 9 below. "Mestizo": a person of mixed indigenous and Spanish lineage [*Editor*].
8. That is, Nahuatl, the most common indigenous language of central Mexico and native to Mexico City [*Editor*].
9. Mexica dance and lyric. Sor Juana uses this autochthonous Mexican song form and writes her lyrics in a mix of Nahuatl and Spanish. Italicized words appeared in Nahuatl in the original; terms that are defined in the text have not been glossed [*revised by Editor*].
1. Priests [*Editor*].

that this San Nolasco
had bought *everyone*.
I have such devotion
for the Saint that I give
15   the *perfect Xúchil*—[2]
a *flower*—just for him.
Téhuatl,[3] his spokesman,
told us that he stayed
with those Moorish[4] dogs
20   *on one* sad occasion.
God *knows*, if I'd been there,
then I would have killed
four hundred—cen sontle—
with one single blow.
25   Nobody should think
I say this for no reason
though I may be a baker
with quite a reputation.
I might have forgotten
30   I'm not a big talker;
my boss sure knows it,
nor am I a braggart.
One of my comrades
dared to deny it,
35   and with just *one* punch
there was he felled.
Also a *Topil*—the
Governor's deputy—
since I didn't pay tribute[5]
40   was told to arrest me.
But with my *cuáhuitl*[6]
I gave him a blow
on top of his head
I don't know if he died.
45   So I want to buy one
of these Saint Redeemers
like him on the altar
and with it his blessing.

---

2. Flower [*Editor*].
3. You [*Editor*].
4. Pertaining to the Moors, a name Christians assigned to North African Muslims, including those who occupied the Iberian peninsula between 711 and 1492 [*Editor*].
5. One of the major juridical distinctions between indigenous and nonindigenous subjects was that the latter was required to pay tribute or a tax to the Spanish monarchy [*Editor*].
6. Club, or literally, "wood" [*Editor*].

From Allegorical Neptune[†]

In early modern Europe, triumphal arches were used in festivities to mark the entrance of rulers into cities, in imitation of the Roman custom. Unlike Roman counterparts, early modern arches were ephemeral constructions, usually decorated with emblematic iconography paired with adages, as was common in the emblem literature[1] of the period. The symbolic program for the arch was usually an extended allegory meant to reflect on the virtues of the celebrated ruler.

In 1680, Mexico City erected two triumphal arches for the entrance parade to greet the new viceroy to New Spain, Tomás de la Cerda, Count of Paredes. Sor Juana was chosen to create the arch that stood in the central square in front of the cathedral. Carlos de Sigüenza y Góngora (1645–1700) was chosen to create the arch at the Saint Domingo plaza. While distinct in their themes, the arches complemented one another: Sor Juana chose as her theme Neptune, calling the Count of Paredes the new god of the oceans, in an allusion to the lake on which Mexico City was built. Sigüenza y Góngora provocatively chose the lineage of Mexica rulers as his theme, whom he claimed, in a direct reference to Sor Juana's arch, descended from Neptune.

In *Allegorical Neptune* Sor Juana explains and defends the choice of the theme of Neptune to symbolize the incoming viceroy. It is one of the best examples of her ability to write in the encomiastic style common to her period, complete with the numerous citations that show the breadth of her knowledge. From this selection, it is clear that she consulted several of the most popular early modern compendia of classical deities, such as those by Vicenzo Cartari, Natale Conti, and Baltasar de Vitoria. The errors in her text, which follow errors in these sources, indicate that she did not for the most part consult the original sources. Notable in her defense of Neptune as the theme of her arch, and fitting with Neoplatonic interest in Egypt, is her claim that Neptune was the son of Isis, the Egyptian goddess of wisdom. This is one example of how Sor Juana turned common early modern scriptural practices toward feminine subjects.

Allegorical Neptune, an ocean of colors, a political simulacrum: a Triumphal Arch of lucid allegorical concepts erected by the enlightened, sacred, and august Metropolitan Church of Mexico, which deferentially consecrated and lovingly dedicated it at the joyous entrance of the most Excellent Lord Don Tomás Antonio Lorenzo

[†] Translated for this edition by Isabel Gómez. The text was first published separately after the event of the entrance, in 1680. It was republished in the first collection of Sor Juana's works, *Castalian Inundation* (1689). All notes are the editor's unless otherwise indicated.
1. A popular genre in the early modern period, emblems were complex visual icons, usually depicting themes drawn from classical myths and accompanied by adages. Taken together, the visual and linguistic enigmas formed keys to a moral lesson.

Manuel de la Cerda, Manrique de Lara, Enríquez, Afán de Ribera, Portocarrero y Cárdenas de Alcántara, Count of Paredes, Marquis de la Laguna of the Order of the Knights of Alcántara, Commander of Morals, of the Council and Chamber of Commerce of the Indies and War Commissioner, Viceroy, Governor and General Captain of this New Spain and President of the Royal Audience here presiding, etc.[2]

Written by Mother Juana Inés de la Cruz, a nun with the Saint Jerome Convent of Mexico City.

                              *   *   *

Such a dignified invention[3] obliged me to consider all the heroes celebrated in antiquity to discern which feats might best correspond to the illustrious virtues of his Excellency our Lord, the Marquis de la Laguna. I took utmost care to not overlook anyone, from the most notorious to the most hidden—yet nothing I found could even begin to measure up to his incomparable deeds. It was therefore necessary to expand my remarks with fables that cannot be found in historical fact—because it seems Nature lacked sufficient force and dared not put into effect, even in shadows, that which Providence later brought forth shining in the world as a most perfect original.[4] And thus it allowed thought to form an idea of how to depict him: that which cannot fit within natural limits was permitted total latitude in the imagination, whose immense capacity is still too narrow for the glories of such a heroic prince.

   Although custom approves this manner of writing, I cannot neglect to say that divine scripture has its own way of supporting the use of metaphor and parable. For example, in the Book of Judges, Chapter 9, one reads: *The trees went forth to anoint a king over them; and they said unto the olive tree, Reign thou over us*[5]—and so it continues, introducing trees as they debate the governance of their mountain. And in the Second Book of Kings, Chapter 14, it says: *The thistle that was in Lebanon sent to the cedar that was in Lebanon, saying, Give thy daughter to my son to wife: and there passed by a wild beast that was in Lebanon, and trode down the thistle.*[6] Besides, fables are usually founded in real events, and those who the idolaters called gods were in truth great princes to whom they attributed divinity for their rare virtues, or for having been inventors—as

2. Tomás Antonio Manuel Lorenzo de la Cerda y Aragón, also known as the Count of Paredes, was viceroy of New Spain from 1680 to 1686.
3. The arch.
4. That is, the Count of Paredes. "Nature": understood as God.
5. Verse 8.
6. Verse 9.

Pliny says: *Inventors were considered Gods*; and Servius⁷ said that
their virtues had been elevated from those of men to divine great-
ness: *We call them Gods, those who surpass men*. And we see this
power and greatness of virtue in the sacred Psalm: *I have said, Ye
are gods*.⁸

These reasons convinced me to depict some of the unparalleled
virtues of our Prince in the god Neptune—in whom erudite antiq-
uity wished to depict his Excellency so truly. As the concordance of
their exploits will show, their similarities appear less coincidental
than the result of a particular diligence. This heroic prince was son of
Saturn and brother to Jupiter, who became King of Heaven by chance
or birthright, leaving to Neptune the Empire of the Waters, Islands,
and Straights as Natale⁹ states: *Since he was comrade and helpmeet
to Jupiter in the wars, when the die was cast for the dominion over the
world after Saturn was expelled from the kingdom, by chance Neptune
obtained dominion over the sea and all the islands in it.*

His mother was the goddess Ops or Cybele, who is the same as
Isis—both names represent Earth, also called *Magna Mater*,¹ who
was believed to be the mother of all gods, and even of the beasts, as
Laercio calls her:

> *Hence Great Mother of Gods, Mother of Beasts.*²

And Silius Italicus³ in Book 6:

> *Their long-lived mother recognizes the sign of the Gods.*

Isis means the same, according to Natale: *Io was either the name
of the Moon or considered the Earth*, and later on: *Fables tell of Io
transformed into a cow, an animal dedicated to the fertility of the earth
and associated with the cultivation of the fields because it enriches the
very soil.*⁴ In her honor they celebrated circus games (as Plutarch

7. Maurus Servius Honoratus (active 4th and 5th centuries), an Italian grammarian. The
citation is a paraphrase of the original, in his *Commentary on the Aeneid of Virgil* (12,
139). Gaius Plinius Secundus, also known as Pliny the Elder (23–79 C.E.). In his *Natu-
ral History*, Book 7, Chapter 56, he lists 139 inventors and suggests that Ceres came to
be known as a divinity through her invention of bread.
8. Psalm 82:6: "*ego dixi: dii estis*" in the Vulgate.
9. Natale Conti (1520–1582), an Italian humanist whose *Mythologiae* (Mythologies, 1567)
was a main source for the arch. The citation is from the entry on Neptune, 108.
1. Great Mother.
2. Sor Juana is citing Conti in his reference from Lucretius *De rerum natura* (On the nature
of things, 1st century B.C.E.), in *Mythologies*, Book 9, Chapter V. Sor Juana read this
citation in the mythological treatise by Baltasar de Vitoria, *Teatro de los dioses de la
gentilidad* (Theater of the gods of gentility, 1620–23), which spells "Lucrecio" incor-
rectly as "Luercio"; her correction ("Laercio") is also incorrect. Vitoria, *Theater of the
gods*, Vol. I, 36.
3. Tiberius Catius Asconius Silius Italicus (ca. 28–ca.103 C.E.), a Roman consul and epic
poet. The following citation is from his *Punica*, Book 16, 124. It directly follows that of
Lucretius in Vitoria's *Theater of the gods*. Sor Juana repeats Vitoria's incorrect transcrip-
tion of "omina" for *omnia* and citation of Book 6 rather than Book 16.
4. Conti, *Mythologies*, Book 8, Chapter 18.

mentions), which they called *Neptunalia* since they honored Neptune, God of Counsel. Saint Cyprian,[5] Epistle 103: *The circus games were in honor of Neptune as the god of counsel.* His altars were underground, not only to indicate that to be profitable his counsel had to be secret (Servius 8 Aeneid:[6] *Whosoever has a temple in the underground realm makes apparent that counsel must be in secret*[7]) but also to make it known with their hushed caution that they also honored Neptune in the guise of Harpocrates, great god of silence, as Saint Augustine named him in Book 18 Chapter 5 of *City of God*; and Poliziano[8] in Chapter 83 of his *Miscellanea* indicates that the Egyptians used the appellation Harpocrates for the god venerated by the Greeks with the name of Sigalion. Cartari, in *Miner.* p. 250: *Among the principle Numina, the Egyptians venerated the god of silence; they called him Harpocrates whom the Greeks called Sigalion.*[9]

I confess I have not discovered why the ancients venerated Neptune as the god of Silence, at least not in any of those few authors I have perused. But if I may be permitted a conjecture, I would say that, as god of the Waters, his children, the fish, are mute. According to Horace:[1]

> Even to mute fish you could give
> the song of the swan, if you wished.

This is why they depicted Pythagoras, the master of silence, as a fish: among all the animals, only he is mute—and so the ancient proverb: *pisce taciturnior,*[2] applies to those who tend towards quiet. According to Pierio, the Egyptians wore it for a symbol of silence, and

---

5. An early Roman Christian (ca. 200–258 C.E.) and bishop of Carthage. Sor Juana may be following Jules César Boulenger, *De Circo Romano* (On the Roman circus, 1598), Chapter 9. Boulenger cites this as "Epistula 103, *De Spectaculis*" on 36r and notes the *Neptunalia* festivals on 36v.
6. Servius, *Ad Aeneida* (On the Aeneid), 8, 636.
7. In their edition, Vincent Martin and Electa Arenal note that in the text by Servius cited here, the author clarifies that Neptune, conflated with Conso, is the god of *consilium* in the sense of "assembly, tribunal, council" rather than in the sense of "advice, guidance, counsel." Sor Juana, however, uses the Spanish translation of *consejo* meaning "counsel" throughout this text as her chosen meaning, rather choosing *asamblea* meaning "assembly," which is the definition emphasized by the author Servius. Sor Juana Inés de la Cruz, *Neptuno alegórico* (Madrid: Catedra, 2009), 82. n. 53 [*Translator*].
8. Angelo Ambrogini (1454–1494), known as Poliziano, Italian classical scholar and poet, author of *Miscellanea* (Miscellany, 1489). Saint Augustine (354–430 C.E.) was an early Roman Christian and Church father.
9. Vicenzo Cartari's (1520–1570). *Imagines deorum* (Images of the gods, 1581) was the Latin translation of the Italian original (1571). Sor Juana appears to follow Vitoria, *Theater of the gods*, Vol. II, Chapter XIII, on Harpocrates, which cites Saint Augustine and Cartari.
1. Quintus Horatius Flaccus (65–27 B.C.E.), known as Horace, a Roman lyric poet. Ode 4.3.19–20. Cited by Vitoria, *Theater of the gods*, Vol. II, 549.
2. "Quieter than a fish." Pythagoras (ca. 570–ca. 495 B.C.E.), a Greek mathematician whose followers were known for their secrecy. This information is drawn directly from Vitoria, *Theater of the gods*, Vol. II, 549.

Claudian says that Rhadamanthus[3] would transform the loquacious into fish, because their eternal silence would be restitution for sins of speech:

> *Whosoever was accustomed to speak more than was just,*
>   *revealing secrets,*
> *Shall be condemned to the salt waters abundant with fish*
> *So that eternal silence may expiate their excessive words.*

And given that Neptune ruled over such taciturn vassals, with good reason he was worshiped as the god of Silence and Counsel.

But returning to our main purpose, I say that this most celebrated Isis was that queen of Egypt whom Diodorus Siculus.[4] so rightly praised from the first lines of his History, and who was the measure of Egyptian wisdom. Plutarch wrote a whole book about this matter; Piero Valeriano many chapters, Plato[5] many songs of praise, as in Book 2 of his *Laws* discussing Egyptian music, where he wrote: *They say that those songs of the ancients were poems to Isis.* Tiraqueau[6] (Leg. II Connub. n. 30) put her in his learned catalogue of wise women. And she was one to the highest degree, since she invented Egyptian letters—if the ancient verses Petrus Cinitus[7] found in the Septimian Library are credible. One of them reads thus:

> *Isis no less artfully invented Egyptian arts.*

She was also the one who discovered wheat and how to use it for human sustenance, which had only been acorns before; she gave it at the wedding of Iasion son of Corito when he married Tila.[8] She also invented linen, as Ovid[9] makes clear:

> *Now she is a Goddess worshiped by a multitude dressed in linen.*

3. A wise king in Greek mythology, son of Zeus and Europa. Pierio Valeriano Bolzani (1477–1558), born Giampietro Valeriano Bolzani, was an Italian humanist and author of the Renaissance dictionary of symbols *Hieroglyphica* (Hieroglyphics, 1556). Claudius Claudianus (ca. 370–404 C.E.), known as Claudian, was a Roman poet. The following citation is from his *In Rufinum* (Against Rufinus). Sor Juana draws from Vitoria, *Theater of the gods,* Vol. II, 549–550.

4. Greek historian who authored a universal history between 60 and 30 B.C.E. Isis, Egyptian goddess of magic and nature. Also known as Io (see p. 138). Sor Juana follows Vitoria, *Theater of the gods,* Vol. I, 157.

5. Greek philosopher (ca. 428–348 B.C.E.). The following citation is from *De Legibus,* Book 2, CLI. Lucius Mestrius Plutarchus (ca. 46–120 C.E.), or Plutarch, a Greek historian who later became a Roman citizen. His book was *Isis and Osiris.*

6. André Tiraqueau (1488–1558), French jurist and author of *De legibus connubialibus et jure maritali* (Conjual law and rights of marriage, 1513).

7. Pietro Crinitus (1475–1507), Florentine humanist. The following citation is from his *Commentarii de honesta disciplina* (Commentary on proper training, 1504), Book XVII, Chapter 1.

8. Isis was associated with the Roman goddess Demeter, said to have discovered wheat. The anecdote about Iasion's wedding seems incorrect. Demeter and Iasion had an affair at the wedding of Cadmus and Harmonia, prompting Jupiter to kill Iasion.

9. Publius Ovidius Naso (43 B.C.E.–17 C.E.), or Ovid, Roman poet. The following citation is from *Metamorphoses* 1:747. Sor Juana derives her information from Vitoria, *Theater of the gods,* Vol. I, 157.

Finally, not only did she possess all the attributes of the wise, but also wisdom itself, which she signified. Given that Neptune was her son, he clearly had a similar obligation, since being born to wise parents is not so much a merit on its own but rather an obligation to strive for, in order not to degenerate or give the lie to mysterious dogmas of the Platonists.[1] In this sense, Horace wrote in Ode 4, 4:

> . . . and the ferocious eagle
> shall never produce timid doves.[2]

Given that maternal customs commonly serve as norm and example to be followed, not only in the tenderness of infancy but also the robustness of youth, it is unlikely that her offspring will reveal aspects that never adorned her. Juvenal,[3] Satires:

> How can you expect a mother to transmit honest habits,
> different from those she has herself.

But our Neptune was a testament to his origins, with the sublime and sovereign merit of his knowledge, clearly seen through the success of his actions and even in the manner of his sacrifices. They used to sacrifice bulls to Neptune especially. Virgil,[4] Aeneid II:

> Laoconte, designated by chance as priest of Neptune,
> solemnly sacrificed a bull on the customary altar.

And in another part:

> One bull for Neptune and one bull for you, handsome Apollo.

Eustatius:[5]

> A bull was sacrificed to the cerulean king.

Silius Italicus, Book 15:

> . . . altars were erected, a bull felled, honorable victim
> of Neptune.[6]

1. Followers of Plato.
2. Horace, Ode 4, 4, 31–32.
3. Decimus Junius Juvenalis (active 1st and 2nd centuries C.E.), known as Juvenal, a satirical lyric poet. The following citation is from Satires 6, 239–240.
4. Publius Vergilius Maro (70–19 B.C.E.), known as Virgil, Roman poet and author of the epic poem the Aeneid. The following citations are from Aeneid, 2, 201–202 and 3, 119. The citations are both taken from Vitoria, Theater of the gods, Vol. I, 281.
5. Publius Papinius Statius (ca. 45–ca. 96 C.E.), also known as Statius, Roman poet and author of the epic poem the Achilleid, on Achilles. The following citation is from Achilleid, 2, 114. The citation is found in Vitoria, Theater of the gods, Vol. I.
6. From Punica, 15, 252–253. The citation is found in Vitoria, Theater of the gods, Vol. I.

The bull is a known symbol of work, as one can see in Pierio, Book 3. To make their sacrifices, the gentiles would observe attentively which things most pleased each of their gods, and that would be their victim. Therefore they sacrificed bulls to Neptune, perhaps based on the episode when he competed with Vulcan and Minerva over who was best at creating artificial works by hand: he formed a bull. Lucian, in Hermotimus: *Minerva invented a house, Vulcan a man, Neptune fashioned a bull.*[7]

This may well have been the reason, but I discern a very different one. Neptune is the son of wisdom herself—as we have seen—as he is proven to be the son of that errant Goddess named Io who ran around the world and, arriving in Egypt, was adored there in the figure and aspect of a cow, as is elegantly described by Ovid in Epistle 14, *Hypermnestra to Lynceus*:

> *So it is that the resentment of Juno has pursued the human race ever since a human being became a cow, and from that cow came a goddess;*[8]

and Lactantius Firmianus,[9] Book I *De falsa Religione*, Chapter 15: *The Egyptians greatly venerated the cult of Isis.* And this cult even traveled to the Romans, as Lucan[1] writes in *Pharsalia* Book 8, speaking to the Nile:

> *We have accepted into our Roman temples your Isis.*

And [he] says that she was figured as a cow, citing other authors: Natale, Book 6 *Mythologies* Chapter 13; Ovid, Book 3 *Art of Love*:

> *Frequent the altars of the Egyptian cow, smoky with incense.*[2]

---

7. Lucian (ca. 125–180 c.e.), Syrian rhetorician and satirist who wrote in Greek. The following citation is from his philosophical dialogue, *Hermotimus,* 20. The citation is found in Vitoria, *Theater of the gods,* Vol. I. Minerva: Roman goddess of wisdom. Vulcan: Roman god of fire.
8. Ovid's *Heroides,* 14, recounts the plea of Hypermestra to her husband Lynceus. Sor Juana cites, along with his errors, from Vitoria, *Theater of the gods,* Vol. I, 154.
9. Lucius Caecilius Firmianus Lactantius (ca. 250–ca. 325 c.e.) was an adviser to the Christian Roman emperor Constantine I. The citation comes from his *Divinae institutiones* (Divine institutes, ca. 304–11 c.e.). Martin and Arenal note that Sor Juana follows the errors of Ravisius Textor, *Officina* (1520). It is probable that she is continuing to follow Vitoria's erroneous transcription, as he cites Textor on Lactantius in various passages. Cruz, *Neptuno,* 91, n. 81.
1. Marcus Annaeus Lucanus (39–65 c.e.), or Lucan, a Roman poet born in Cordoba, in what is now Spain. The following citation is from the *Pharsalia,* 8, 831. Cited in Vitoria, *Theater of the gods,* Vol. 1, 157, although with a slight error that Sor Juana does not repeat. Martin and Arenal note that Sebastián de Covarrubias, author of an early Castilian dictionary, *Tesoro de la lengua castellana* (Treasure of the Castilian language, 1611), also cites this verse in his definition of "Isis." Cruz, *Neptuno,* 92, n. 83.
2. Ovid's *Ars amatoria* (The art of loving), 3, 393.

So it was that cows were pleasing sacrifices for Isis. Herodotus,[3] in Book 2, wrote: *Among the Egyptians, female cows were frequently consecrated to Isis.* Because Isis is wisdom herself, they could do her no greater honor than to sacrifice to her the symbol of wisdom, a cow, through which they signified her. I infer therefore that this was the image of the Ocean and of Neptune that (as Cartari says) were very similar in their portraits: *Images of Neptune and the Ocean were not very dissimilar from one another.*[4] With good reason: they indicate one and the same thing, although they had various glosses to refer to diverse qualities: to depict Neptune as a sage was the same as to paint him in the semblance of a bull. Euripides,[5] in *Orestes*:

> . . . Ocean god who
> with the head of a bull
> churning wraps his arms around the world.

Since wisdom herself is embodied by a cow, then wise men take the form of a bull.

*   *   *

I could bring in many other supporting arguments to prove the wisdom of Neptune and to make this work more erudite than brief— but this should be enough to legitimize the association. Given that Neptune is so wise, his mother cannot be other than Isis, nor is any other son more like her than Neptune. As the Greek poet Theognis[6] says:

> For the rose never blooms on the allium, nor the hyacinth
> nor can a slave give birth to a son with the qualities of a
>   free man.

And the ancient Athenians were under the tutelage of Neptune and Minerva, whom they revered as gods of Wisdom, engraving their money with the head of Minerva on one side and the trident of Neptune on the other. For example, in *Minerva* p. 259, Cartari mistakes Minerva for Isis, whom the ancients knew by diverse names: Apuleius called her Rhea, Venus, Diana, Bellona, Ceres, Juno, Proserpina, Hecate, and Ramnousia; Diodorus Siculus says that Isis is

---

3. Greek historian (ca. 484–425 B.C.E.), whom Cicero called the Father of History. The citation is from his *Histories*, 2.41. Martin and Arenal note that in his *Mythologies* Conti also cites this passage. Cruz, *Neptuno*, 92, n. 85.
4. Cartari's *Images of the gods*, 174.
5. Greek playwright (ca. 480–406 B.C.E.). The citation is from *Orestes* (408 B.C.E.). Conti cites it in *Mythologies*, VIII, 236, and Vitoria, *Theater of the gods*, Vol. 1, 377–78.
6. Greek lyric poet (6th century B.C.E.). The following citation is found in *Elegy and Iambus*, ed. J. M. Edmonds (Cambridge: Harvard, 1931), 1: 535–38. Sor Juana's source for the Latin translation has not been found.

known as Luna, Juno, and Ceres; Macrobius[7] claims she is no less than Earth herself, or the nature of all things.

Letter by Mother Juana Inés de la Cruz Written to Her Confessor, the Reverend Father Antonio Núñez de Miranda of the Society of Jesus[†]

Sor Juana's relationship to her confessor, the Jesuit Antonio Núñez de Miranda (1618–1695), was marked by tensions, estrangement, and reconciliation. Núñez was a principal figure in New Spain. Author of several treatises on feminine spirituality, he took a special interest in the confession and regulation of nuns, was instrumental in convincing Sor Juana to become a nun, and then served as her confessor.[1] In 1681, Sor Juana wrote a letter to Father Núñez in which she complains that he has criticized her for writing. Although her letter is not clear about the exact charges, Núñez's publications insist on the dangers of intellectual pursuits for nuns, which he sees as potentially contradicting the mandate for feminine humility and obedience.[2] The letter rehearses many of the arguments she will develop in her "Response" (1691) to Bishop Manuel Fernández de Santa Cruz, who similarly charges Sor Juana in his prologue to her *Athenagoric Letter* (1690).[3] The tone of her 1681 letter to Núñez is more strident and caustic than the "Response," likely reflecting Sor Juana's youth and its private nature. Her defiance of Núñez's guidance is sealed at end of the letter when she exercises her right to dismiss him as her confessor. She would reconcile with him only at the very end of her life, in the context of her abjuration and renewal of vows, at which point he once again became her confessor. He acted in this capacity until her death in 1695.

---

7. Macrobius Ambrosius Theodosius (active in 5th century c.e.), or Macrobius, Roman author. The citation is found in his *Saturnalia*, 1.20.18. The source for Sor Juana's Cartari citation has not been found. Lucius Apuleius Madaurensis (ca. 125–ca. 180 c.e.), or Apuleius: Roman prose writer best known for his novel *The Golden Ass*. The citation is from Book 11, when Lucius prays to Isis. Rhea: Greek titaness daughter of Gaia and Uranus. Venus: Roman goddess of fertility and love. Diana: Roman goddess of the hunt, moon, and birth. Bellona: Roman goddess of war. Ceres: Roman goddess of harvest. Juno: Roman goddess and wife of Jupiter. Proserpina: Roman goddess associated with Ceres. Hecate: Greek goddess associated with magic and witchcraft. Ramnousia: Greek goddess of revenge, also known as Nemesis. Siculus's *Histories*, 1.11.4; 1.13.4; 1.13.5.
† From Antonio Alatorre, "La carta de Sor Juana al P. Núñez (1682)," *Nueva Revista de Filología Hispánica* 35.2 (1987). Translated for this edition by Isabel Gómez. Reprinted by permission of Silvia, Gerardo, and Claudia Alatorre. This letter was discovered in 1980 by Monsignor Aureliano Tapia Méndez in an archive in Monterrey, Mexico, and is sometimes called the "Monterrey Letter." The manuscript is not in Sor Juana's hand but rather is an eighteenth-century transcription. All notes are the editor's unless otherwise indicated.
1. Alatorre, "La Carta de Sor Juana," 604–16.
2. Two years before Sor Juana's letter, in his *Platica doctrinal* (Doctrinal guide), Núñez writes: *Por el voto de obediencia, la religiosa renuncia a su propia voluntad y libre albedrío* (Following her vow of obedience, the nun renounces her own desires and free will). Cited in Alatorre, "La carta de Sor Juana," 613.
3. See headnote to "Letter from Sor Filotea" on p. 84.

May the peace of our Lord Jesus Christ be with you.

Various individuals have been telling me for some time now that I am the only one to blame for conversations in which Your Reverence has criticized my actions with bitter statements, saying that they are tantamount to a *public scandal* and other no less horrible epithets. Although my conscience might have moved me to defend myself—since I am not the sole owner of my reputation, tied as it is to my lineage and the community in which I live—nevertheless, I have wished to sacrifice my suffering to the highest veneration and filial affection I have always had for Your Reverence. I prefer that any objection fall on my shoulders rather than appear to have crossed the line of proper respect by arguing with Your Reverence—a sacrifice I sincerely confess deserves nothing from God in return, as it was made out of worldly respect for your person, not Christian patience. In this I am fully aware of the veneration and great esteem that Your Reverence rightly enjoys from all—they listen to you like a divine oracle and respect your words as though dictated by the Holy Spirit—and that the greater your authority, the more diminished my reputation. Even still, I have never wanted to capitulate to suggestions that I respond, made either by reason or self-love (which perhaps sways us all under the cloak of reason). I determined that my silence would best appease Your Reverence— until with time I recognized that my patience only caused irritation, and so I decided to respond to Your Reverence, always preserving, never disputing my enduring love, obligation, and respect.

The crux, then, of the anger displayed by Your Reverence my beloved father and Lord has been only those accursed poems that Heaven inspired in me so against the will of Your Reverence. I have expressly resisted writing them and excused myself as much as possible, not because I found reason for good or evil in them, for I have always judged them to be neutral (as they are). I could say how many saintly and learned men have used them—but I do not wish to intervene in their defense as I would my father or mother: I only say that I would stop writing them to please Your Reverence, without looking for the reasons behind your abhorrence, since love tends to obey blindly. Besides, this would fit with my natural repugnance at writing them, which all who know me can verify—but it was impossible to observe this rigorously without exceptions, such as the two *villancicos*[4] to our Most Holy Virgin. I wrote them only after repeated insistence and an eight year interval between, and with the full permission and license of Your Reverence—which I held in those days as even more necessary than that of the Lord Archbishop Viceroy, my Prelate. I proceeded

4. Dramatic religious carols sung on holy and feast days (see p. 129).

with such modesty that I would not consent to put my name on the first of these compositions; on the second it was printed without my consent or knowledge,[5] and Your Reverence corrected both sets beforehand.

The Arch for the Church came next.[6] This one is my incontrovertible fault—preceded as it was by my rejecting their requests three or four times, until two lay magistrates came to ask me, and only after they had called on my Mother Prioress and commanded me in the name of his Excellency the Lord Archbishop to write it, as the whole council had voted with the approval of his Excellency.

Now I would ask for Your Reverence with your supremely clear judgment to put yourself in my position: how would you have responded to this predicament? Would you simply say you could not? That would have been a lie. That you did not want to? Disobedience. That you did not know how? They asked for no more than my capacity. That they were wrong to vote for me? That would have been such shameless impudence, such crude ingratitude toward those who honored me with the very idea that such an ignorant woman could do what those lucid minds asked of me. Well then, what could I do but obey?

So much for the public works that have so scandalized the world and edified the good: let us turn to the unpublished works. You can barely find this or that little couplet dedicated to a birthday or in praise of some person of my esteem and to whom I owe for aiding me in my necessities (which have been more than a few given that I am poor and have no income): a short play for the birthday of our Lord King commissioned by His Excellency Don Fray Payo, and another panegyric at the request of her Excellency, Lady Countess of Paredes.[7]

At this point, my dear Lord and Father, I beg Your Reverence to put aside for a moment affection for your own judgment (which can sway even the most saintly) and tell me (given that in your opinion it is sinful to write poetry): on which of these occasions has the crime been so serious? If writing is a sin (though I see no reason to call it

5. By 1681, Sor Juana had already written various *villancicos* (see p. 129). Three were dedicated to the Virgin Mary: for the Feast of the Assumption in 1676 and 1679 and for the Feast of the Conception in 1676. All were originally published anonymously but were republished in her 1689 collected works, *Castalian Inundation*. It is unclear to which two specifically Sor Juana refers here.
6. In 1680 Sor Juana was chosen by the Metropolitan Church of Mexico City to create an ephemeral triumphal arch to celebrate the entrance of the new viceroy, the count of Paredes. While the arch does not survive, it is described in *Allegorical Neptune* (1680); see p. 136.
7. María Luisa Manrique de Lara y Gonzaga (1649–1729), Countess of Paredes and wife of the Count of Paredes, viceroy of New Spain (1680–86), became a close friend and patron of Sor Juana, who called her "Lysi" in her poems. Fray Enrique Payo (1622–1684), Augustinian friar and viceroy of New Spain (1673–80).

that), it is forgiven by the very circumstances and occasions in which I have done so against my will. This is clearly proven, for given the facility that everyone knows I have, if this were joined by vain motives (perhaps I am motivated by self-mortification) what greater punishment could Your Reverence want for me than the very applause that hurts me so? What envy fails to target me? Of what ill intention am I not the object? What action may I take without fear? What word may I say without suspicion?

Women resent that I surpass them; men, that I appear their equal. Some wish I knew less, others say I ought to know more to deserve such applause; old women think no one should know more than they do; young women do not like others to look good—and all of them want me to follow their pronouncements, which when taken together impose such a strange martyrdom that I do not believe anyone else has experienced the same.

What more can I say or consider? Even my handwriting has cost me long, difficult persecution for no other reason than that they said it looked like that of a man, which was indecent, so I was required to deform my script on purpose—as witnessed by my whole community—in short, this is not material for a letter but for many copious volumes. Because—what are the facts that damn me? Did I solicit public celebration and applause? All the favors and honors the most Excellent Lords the Marquises[8] bestowed on me by condescension and in their unparalleled humanity—did I go looking for them?

On the contrary—and my witness is the Mother Prioress Juana de San Antonio of this Convent, who would never lie. She was there the first time Their Excellencies honored this house when I asked permission to retire to my cell and not see them or be seen (as though Their Excellencies had done me some harm!) with no other motive than to flee the applause that becomes sharp thorns of persecution— I would have succeeded, had the Mother Prioress not ordered me to do the opposite.

Was it my fault Their Excellencies took a liking to me (although they had no reason to)? Could I deny such royal persons? Should I regret the honor of their visits?

Your Reverence knows full well I should not, as you experienced the same in the times of the Most Excellent Lords Marquises de Mancera,[9] and I heard Your Reverence complain many times about having to neglect your tasks to attend to Their Excellencies without any possibility of refusing—and if the most Excellent Lord Marquis de Mancera entered convents as holy as the Capuchins and the

8. The Count and Countess of Paredes, whose titles were also Marquises de la Laguna.
9. Antonio Sebastián Álvarez de Toledo Molina y Salazar, second Marquis de Mancera (ca. 1625–1710) was viceroy of New Spain between 1664 and 1673. He and his wife, Leonor Carreto, to whom Sor Juana dedicated poems as "Laura," were Sor Juana's patrons.

Teresians[1] as many times as he wished without anyone objecting, how could I deny his Excellency the Lord Marquis de la Laguna entrance into this one? Besides the fact that as I am not the Mother Superior, I am not in charge of regulating the Convent.

Their Excellencies honor me because they wish to, not because I deserve or sought it out from the beginning.

I cannot, nor would I if I could, be so barbarously ungrateful for the favors and care of Their Excellencies, even if so undeserved and poorly returned.

My studies have not harmed or persecuted anyone: for the most part, they have been so extremely private that I have not even availed myself of the guidance of a tutor, but have made do with only my own effort and resources. I know attending school in public is indecent for feminine virtue as this occasions familiarity with men—which is the reason to prohibit public studies. The reason for not challenging such spaces reserved for men may be because women are not considered necessary for the body politic of magistrates (which excludes women for the same reason of modesty), and why should provision be made for those who cannot use it? But who has forbidden women from private and individual study? Do they not have rational souls just as men? Why should they not also enjoy the privilege of enlightenment through letters? Is her soul not as capable of divine grace and glory as his? If it is, why is hers not also capable of receiving learning and knowledge, which are lesser gifts? What divine revelation, what Church policy, what reasonable verdict could have made such a severe law only for women?

Does learning threaten rather than promote salvation? Were not Saint Augustine, Saint Ambrose,[2] and all the other Learned Saints saved? And Your Reverence, weighed down by your knowledge, do you not think that you will be saved?

If your response is that men are ruled by another kind of reason, I say: Did Saint Catherine, Saint Gertrude, and my Mother Saint Paula[3] not study? Did it disturb their contemplation or fatigue their intellects to know Greek? Or learn Hebrew? Was it not my Father Saint Jerome[4] who instructed us to understand and interpret Sacred

---

1. Order founded by Saint Teresa of Ávila, also known as the Discalced Carmelites. The Capuchins are a Franciscan order; one of its female branches is the Poor Clares.
2. Saint Augustine (354–430 C.E.), or Augustine of Hippo, one of the four Doctors of the Church known for many writings, including his *Confessions* and *City of God*. He was influenced by Saint Ambrose Aurelius Ambrosius (ca. 340–397 C.E.), one of the four Doctors of the Church.
3. Wealthy Roman woman (347–404 C.E.) who became companion of Saint Jerome, a Desert Mother, and co-patron of the Hieronymite order to which Sor Juana belonged. Saint Catherine (active 4th century C.E.), Catherine of Alexandria, scholar and virgin saint. Saint Gertrude of Helfta (1256–1302), German mystic and Benedictine theologian.
4. Saint Jerome (ca. 347–420 C.E.), founder of Sor Juana's order, was one of the four Doctors of the Church and author of the Vulgate Bible.

Scripture? Did he not also praise Blesilla[5] daughter of Saint Paula for her learning, even at a young age given that she died at twenty?

How can study be evil in me but good in them? Is my salvation the only one threatened by books?

If I have read the prophets and secular orators (a lapse even the very Saint incurred) I have also read the Sacred Doctors and Holy Scriptures:[6] yet I cannot deny how much I owe the former for innumerable gifts and rules for good living.

What Christian would not flee from rage in light of the genteel patience of Socrates?[7] Who could be ambitious after seeing the modesty of Diogenes[8] the cynic? Who does not praise God in the intelligence of Aristotle?[9] Finally, what Catholic would not be awestruck before the sum of the moral virtues held by all the pagan philosophers?

What can be evil about spending my time studying—when otherwise I would just be gossiping at the cloister grille, murmuring in my cell about whatever takes place outside or inside the convent walls, fighting with another Sister, scolding a poor servant, or just letting my mind wander everywhere?

What's more: when God gave me this inclination, it did not seem to be against his holy law or the obligations of my state—I have this mind, even if it may be evil, it made me what I am; I was born with it and with it I must die.

Your Reverence wants to force on me the salvation of ignorance—but, beloved Father of mine: can I not be saved while learning? In the end, this is the clearest path for me. Why would salvation need to come through the path of ignorance, if that is repugnant to my nature?

Since God is pure goodness, is He not pure wisdom also? Well then, why would He be more accepting of ignorance than of knowledge?

Saint Anthony[1] was saved in his holy ignorance, bless him, while Saint Augustine took the other path—but neither went astray.

Then why is Your Reverence so displeased as to say: "if I had known you were going to write verses I would not have allowed you to enter a religious order but instead have married you off"?

Well, most beloved Father (only by force and with shame do I utter things that I would rather not let slip from my mouth) by what direct

5. Blesilla (d. 384), a daughter of Saint Paula.
6. The Bible. "Saint": that is, Saint Jerome. "Sacred Doctors": authors recognized as particularly important theologians of Christianity, especially the early Doctors of the Church (Saint Jerome, Saint Ambrose, Saint Augustine, and Saint Gregory the Great).
7. Greek philosopher (ca. 470–399 b.c.e.) known through the writings of his student, Plato.
8. Greek philosopher (ca. 412–323 b.c.e.) and founder of the philosophical school of Cynicism.
9. Greek philosopher (384–322 b.c.e.) and a student of Plato's; known as "The Philosopher" in Sor Juana's time for his importance in Catholic dogma, via Thomism.
1. Desert Father (251–356 c.e.) and ascetic from Egypt.

authority did Your Reverence take charge of my person and the free will given to me by God—besides of course the love I have for you and will always have?

When I entered the convent, I had not known Your Reverence for long—and although I am indebted to you for your high hopes and solicitudes for my state, which I will always esteem as I should—when it comes to my dowry, it had been arranged by my godfather the Captain Don Pedro Velásquez de la Cadena[2] long before I met Your Reverence. God provided my remedy only through his setting aside those assets, and there is no basis for any other implication, although I do not deny I owe Your Reverence many other caring gestures and kindnesses for which I am eternally grateful, such as paying for my tutor and more. But why then do these favors not continue, rather than being transformed into vituperations, every conversation including an airing of my faults that provoke the spiritual zeal of Your Reverence for my conversion?

Am I perchance a heretic? And if I were, could force alone make me a saint? If only saintliness could be commanded, then I would have it for sure. I think it must be persuaded more than commanded—if it is to be commanded, I have had Prelates enough who have done so—yet precepts and exterior force will make one prudent if they are moderate, but if the rules are too numerous, they only create desperation. God alone knows how to create saints by His grace and succor.

What, then, is the cause of this anger? Why discredit me? Why hold me up to all as a scandalous woman? Have I offended Your Reverence in some way? Have I asked Your Reverence to help me meet my needs? Or have I bothered Your Reverence in some other spiritual or secular matter?

Does my correction fall under the authority of Your Reverence by obligation, parenthood, upbringing, position, or anything else?

If it is simply out of charity, then let it be charity alone and proceed accordingly, with sympathy—irritating me is not the way to subdue me. I do not have such a servile nature that I can be threatened into doing something I am not persuaded of by reason, nor would I do anything out of respect for man that I would not do for God. To deny myself everything that gives me pleasure, even though it is entirely licit, would be better done as an act of mortification when I wish to do penance—but not the way Your Reverence wishes to obtain it by force of censure—which is not even directed at me in seclusion as befits paternal correction (as Your Reverence has offered to serve as my Father for which I consider myself fortunate), but

2. Secretary of governance and war of New Spain and a rich and powerful figure in the viceregal court.

instead publicly among all, where each reacts accordingly and speaks according to their reaction.

My Father, is it not unavoidable that I should be hurt by this treatment from someone I love and esteem so highly?

If these reprehensions had been provoked by some scandalous communication of mine, I am docile enough that I would distance myself from it and attempt to mend my ways to satisfy you, even against my will—and regardless of the fact that I have never been under the charge of Your Reverence in spiritual or secular matters.

But, if only to contradict the opinion that in essence it matters little whether I write verses or not, and, since I abhor my verses so much that there could be no greater penance for me than to be required to write them, then why such grief?

To contradict your opinion, I could have spoken passionately against Your Reverence on the infinite occasions when Your Reverence has highly displeased me by speaking against me (because opinion on minor matters is as the maxim *alius sic, et alius sic*[3]). Instead, I venerate your opinions and defend them as my own, even those perhaps directed against me, calling them zealous goodness, supreme love, and other titles that my love and reverence invent when I speak with others.

But I cannot refrain from saying to Your Reverence: my heart already overflows with the complaints I have held back for years. If I take up my pen to give them voice, refuting someone I respect so highly, it is because I cannot take any more: I feel it too strongly because I am not as humble as other daughters who may better employ your instruction.

Therefore I beg of Your Reverence, if you no longer wish to favor me, or if you are no longer served by the voluntary boons you have given me, put me out of your mind. Although I will regret the loss, I shall never complain: God created and redeemed me, and He expends so much mercy on me that he will provide a remedy for my soul. I hope that by his will it will not be lost, even without the guidance of Your Reverence. There are many keys to heaven and infinite mansions for diverse natures, which do not follow only one opinion. There are many theologians on earth, and when they are lacking, salvation consists more of desiring than of knowing, and this depends more on me than on my confessor.

What mandate is there that my salvation must be through Your Reverence? Why not another? Is the mercy of God limited and restricted to one man, even one as judicious, learned, and saintly as Your Reverence?

---

3. This maxim could be translated as "one other thus and another thus" or "it is a matter of opinion" [*Translator*].

Surely not, nor have I received up to now any particular inspiration from the Lord who ordered it such—therefore I may govern myself with the general rules of the Holy Mother Church, until the Lord enlightens me otherwise, and I will choose freely the spiritual Father I wish.[4] If my opinion directed my will with the same force with which Our Lord inclined Your Reverence toward me, I would choose no other than Your Reverence, whom I beg to receive this sincerity not as daring or disrespect but rather as the simplicity of my heart which knows not how to say anything but what I feel; rather I have attempted to speak in such a way that cannot leave Your Reverence with any trace of ill will or complaint. Regardless, if there should be a single word in this inventory of my faults that I have misstated—not only willful offense but even insufficient deference to Your Reverence—it was inadvertent. I immediately retract it as badly said and worse written, and I would erase it as soon as I am alerted to it.

I repeat, my intention is only to beg Your Reverence: if you no longer wish to favor me, put me out of your mind, except to commend me to God—given your great charity, I believe you will do so fervently.

May God in his Majesty keep Your Reverence as I wish.

From the Convent of my Father Saint Jerome, in Mexico.

Your

        Juana Inés de la Cruz

---

4. Nuns were permitted great leeway, even under the mandate to obey Church patriarchy. See Lavrin, on p. 209.

Petition in Juridical Form Presented to the Divine Tribunal by Mother Juana Inés de la Cruz, to Beg Pardon for Her Faults†

The years immediately preceding Sor Juana's untimely death in 1695 are the most historically enigmatic of her life. Beginning in 1693, not long after her second volume of works was published in Spain, Sor Juana wrote a series of declarations renewing her vows and renouncing secular pursuits in favor of religious ones. Given her documented battles with the church patriarchy over her dedication to secular knowledge, the stark renunciation, the selling of her books and other possessions, and the language of contrition in these documents have prompted more questions than they have answered. Was the embattled Sor Juana finally worn down and, essentially, forced to pen these documents? Or was this the culmination of a long process of reconversion to the principles of faith and renunciation of worldly concerns central to her religious vocation? How can one understand their relationship to documents such as the "Letter by Mother Juana Inés de la Cruz" (1681) and the "Response" (1691)? At the present the answers to these questions are necessarily speculative. They depend, in great part, on the level of sincerity one attributes to Sor Juana's adoption of a religious vocation and whether one believes this contradicts or not her more strident expressions of her right to study and write on secular as well as sacred subjects. While undoubtedly marking a radical change of course in Sor Juana's life, the documents do have notable stylistic and rhetorical resonances with her previous writings.

Juana Inés de la Cruz, the most unworthy and ungrateful creature of the many created by your Omnipotence, the most unknown of all those cradled in your love, I appear before your divine and sacred Majesty in the best manner and form that the just law of your mercy and infinite clemency permit. Prostrating my soul with all reverence before the Most Holy Trinity, I declare:

In the suit pursued by your Just Tribunal against my grave, enormous, and unparalleled sins, I find myself convicted by all witnesses in Heaven and on Earth. For the crimes alleged by the Criminal Prosecutor of my own conscience, I find I ought to be condemned to eternal death, although even that would be granting myself clemency, since infinite Hells would not suffice for my innumerable crimes and sins. Though I find myself convicted on all counts, and

---

† From Sor Juana Inés de la Cruz, *Obras Completas*, 4 vols., vol. 1 (México: Fondo de Cultura Económica, 1951), pp. 520–21. Copyright © 2009, Fondo de Cultura Económica. All rights reserved. Mexico, D.F. Translated for this edition by Isabel Gómez. Sor Juana uses the formulas of legal language to compose her spiritual petition. She positions God the Holy Trinity as a divine tribunal judging her case; the prosecutor is her own conscience, and her lawyers are Saint Joseph and Saint Jerome [*Translator's note revised by Editor; all further notes are Editor's*].

recognize I deserve no pardon nor hearing from you, still: I know your infinite love and tremendous mercy, that as long as I live I have time, and that the statute of limitations has not yet expired for me to appeal the sentence to the Tribunal of your Mercy. I do so now, entreating you to admit my appeal on the grounds of that intense and incomprehensible act of love through which you have suffered such a shameful death on my behalf. I offer this—as one who has the right to do so—in justification of my grave sins and with it, I offer all your merits, the very love you have for me, and the merits of your Blessed Virgin Mother, my Lady of Mercy, and her husband and my beloved lawyer Saint Joseph, my Sainted Guardian Angel, and of my devotees[1] and the Community of Blessed Souls in Heaven.

I offer so much that your Justice might be fully satisfied, vested with the force and vigor of my right as daughter and heir to your Glory, reflected in me. Yet still, as you know, for many years I have lived in religion, not only without Religion, but worse than a pagan. To atone some for my share in falling so far short, and to recommit to those obligations to which I am beholden and have fulfilled so poorly, it is my will to take up the Habit once more and to spend a year in probation, during which, your Minister and the father of my soul in your holy office as my Confessor must examine the will and freedom of my state. As for my dowry, I offer all the alms of virtue the Blessed Souls have given me, at my request; and whatever may remain will be paid by my Mother and yours, the Holy Virgin Mary, and her husband my father, the glorious lord Saint Joseph, who (as I trust in their mercy) will commit themselves to said dowry, wax, and other offerings.

For this purpose, I beg your Consecrated Majesty to concede your license, consent, and permission to all the saints and Angels, especially those associated with making vows, so the whole Celestial Community may recommend and receive my vows, and once this is done as I trust in your mercy it will be, let me be given the sacred Habit of our father Saint Jerome, in whom I place my trust as lawyer and intercessor, not only so that I may be received in his holy Order, but also so that in the company of my mother Saint Paula,[2] he might beseech you for perseverance and increased virtue, as is my constant request. Through all this, I will gladly receive the charity of your infinite clemency, which you most fittingly provide. I beg mercy for it all, etc.

Juana Inés de la Cruz

1. Secular supporters charged with the consolation of specific nuns. Saint Joseph was husband to the Virgin Mary.
2. Companion to Saint Jerome and the patron saint of Sor Juana's convent. Saint Jerome was a Doctor of the Church and founder of the Hieronymite order to which Sor Juana's convent pertained.

Document in the Book of Professions in the Convent of Saint Jerome†

I, Juana Inés de la Cruz, professed nun of this Convent, not only do I ratify my vocation and renew my vows, but I also take oath once more to believe and defend that my Lady Virgin Mary was conceived without the stain of original sin in the first instant of her conception in virtue of the Passion of Christ. And so do I swear to believe any honor of hers, for one does not oppose the Holy Church. In witness of which I signed with my blood on the eighth of February of 1694: Juana Inés de la Cruz. May all flow to the defense of this truth, for her love of us all and of her Son.

Let it be inscribed here the day, month, and year of my death. For the love of God and his most Immaculate Mother, I beseech my beloved sisters, the nuns here now and those who shall be, commend me to God: I, who have been and remain, the worst that has ever been. I beg their pardon for the love of God and his Mother. I, the worst woman in the world.

Juana Inés de la Cruz.

Ballad 51‡

First published after her death in *Fame and Posthumous Works* (1700), this ballad refers to the praise Sor Juana received during her lifetime. While the humility the poem displays was a part of conventional rhetoric of her time, Sor Juana adds her own perspective by highlighting her situation as a self-educated female poet writing an ocean away from the Spanish metropolis where her works were published. She returns to some of the themes of her "Response" in this poetic description of her untutored writings, here in relation to the praise of her intellectual community instead of the censure of her religious authorities. This *ballad* also includes a trope central to "First Dream": the episode of Phaethon. Here, the mythological scale of her intellectual striving is united with an articulation of her position as a woman and as a *criolla*.[1] In one of the verses of the poem, the poetic voice wanders "as though a stranger to myself" through writings that praise her; recognizing that

---

† From Sor Juana Inés de la Cruz, *Obras Completas*, 4 vols., vol. 1 (México: Fondo de Cultura Económica, 1951), pp. 522–23. Copyright © 2009, Fondo de Cultura Económica. All rights reserved. Mexico, D.F. Translated for this edition by Isabel Gómez. This restatement of faith followed the first signature Sor Juana left in the Book of Professions when she entered the convent and signed on February 24, 1669.

‡ First published in *Fame and Posthumous Works* (1700). Introduction and translation for this edition by Isabel Gómez. All notes are the translator's unless otherwise indicated.

1. A term used in colonial Spanish America to refer to American-born persons of European descent [*Editor*].

they cannot see her, the poem measures the distance between their image and her own. Although the poem has become one of her most famous, it is impossible to know whether it was printed in its final form or not.

In recognition of the inimitable Quills of Europe, whose unending praise enhances her Works: a ballad found unfinished.

When, Numina most divine,
sweetest Swans, oh when
did ever my paltry verse deserve
to occupy your attention?
5   From where has come all this acclaim?
From where such high tribute?
Could it be that distance embellish
my portrait to this extent?
What stature have you given me?
10   What Colossus have you mounted:
oblivious to the lowly height
of the source from where he came?
I am not she of whom you think,
unless over there you give me
15   another being through your plumes,
on your lips, another breath,
as though a stranger to myself,
among your quills I wander,
not as I am, but as you see
20   and what you wished to imagine.
Had you but judged me by accounts,
I would not have been astonished:
full well I know the way affection
can make their measure larger.
25   But if you saw the very blots
on my most humble serifs,
the scribbles of my idle time,
my careless squandered hours,
what could there be to move you so
30   to applaud my little merit?
In truth, can courtly praise be won
should it be compelled by force?
Why to a woman ignorant,
whose study has not surpassed
35   rare moments poorly pilfered from
her rightful natural tasks;
why to the rude, abortive issue

of these infertile fields—
because I too was born in them,
40 were left all the more depleted;
        why to an education so uncouth
its infancy was tasked
with deep reflection: all the work
a teacher should have had;
45   why should the most lucid Geniuses
direct toward her their praise,
when in Pulpits and Universities
the World venerates them as sage?
        Which was that ascendant Star of mine
50 so dominating the Cosmos,
inclining you to my favor, making
you choose what should be forced?
        What magical infusions made
by Indian herbalists,
55 what enchantment from my Patria did
they spill among my works?
        What distance, what proportion makes,
thereby modulating the sound
that all my deeds, cacophonous,
60 may be tuned into harmony?
        What perspectives, what suspect slants,
on a body half composed,
can give such apparent ornament
to its few indistinct lines?
65   Oh, how so ever many times
between the many waves
of undeserved encomia,
of praises ill employed;
        Oh how so ever many times,
70 dazzled so by a gulf of rays
I would have perished, Phaethon-like,[2]
an endangered Narcissus[3] been—
        if I did not have within myself
a remedy close at hand:
75 I know myself, like the peacock

---

2. Phaethon was the son of Helios, god of the sun (a Greek deity later conflated with Apollo). When his father allowed him to drive the chariot of the sun, he lost control and fell to his death. For more on Phaethon within Sor Juana's work, see Paz on p. 255.
3. Narcissus falls in love with his own reflection in a pool, rejecting the nymph Echo. The myth from Ovid's *Metamorphoses* ends when he is transformed into the narcissus flower. Sor Juana's mystery play, *The Divine Narcissus*, employs the myth in an extended allegory of Christ's love for the Church [*revised by Editor*].

who can see his feet are foul![4]
Shame and disgrace you all cause me
with your celebration,
since your illumination brings
80   also to the light my errors.
When the Sun tries to penetrate
and enter opaque bodies,
that which appears a benefit
tends to result in harm:
85   for the unrefined, the densely coarse,
will just resist the light,
the intromission of the rays
to narrow, winding pores,
admitting only surface touch
90   and superficial light:
illumination only serves
to emphasize its shadows.
So it is that, in the light
of your gallant panegyrics,
95   my obscure blots are left exposed
as paltry deformed traces.
Such honorific monuments
to rigid, frozen cadavers
are your encomia most high
100   to all my soulless conceits.
Pantheons most elegant
of jasper stone and marble,
superfluous custodians
rule over inanimate dust.
105   Everything that one receives
is measured not by the size
true to itself, but in the way
it fits the receiving vessel.[5]
That all of you conceived of me
110   in your way is no surprise
but the greatness of those concepts must
perforce be miraculous.
The image of your own idea
is all that you've been praising—
115   and being yours, it quite deserves

---

4. A common story about the peacock, found in emblem literature of Sor Juana's time [*Editor*].
5. Méndez Plancarte notes the similarity of this verse to a scholastic maxim: *Quidquid recipitur, ad modum recipientis recipitur* (whatever is received, is received according to the manner of the recipient). Cruz, *Obras completas*, 1, 448 [*Editor*].

all of your own applause.
    Celebrate, then, your very own
selfsame imagination,
as simulacrum, so that thus
120 the laurel can return to stay.
    Unless it is my sex has tried,
or has wanted to be able
to let the strange, the rare, achieve
the status of the perfect,
125   then just to be pleasing, this alone,
would clearly be prize enough,
without your lavishing me with such
involuntary accolades.
    Whoever may see that such great minds
130 are occupied in my praises,
What will they say but only that
taste rules over intelligence?

Background

OVID

From the *Metamorphoses*†

Publius Ovidius Naso (43 B.C.E.–17 C.E.), or Ovid, was a Roman poet later canonized as one of the greatest Latin authors. A prolific writer, he became best known for the *Metamorphoses,* a fifteen-book poem in epic verse recounting over 250 stories from Greek and Roman mythology. The central components of Ovidian myths are transgression and punishment by transformation. Despite his reputation for lasciviousness, Ovid remained surprisingly popular in medieval and Renaissance Europe; the *Metamorphoses* in particular was continually published and translated, serving as the inspiration for art and literature throughout the period.

References to Ovid's works, especially to the *Metamorphoses,* appear throughout Sor Juana's writings. It is unclear how much of Ovid she read in the original, however. The Renaissance compendia of myths such as Natale Conti's *Mythologiae* or Baltasar de Vitoria's *Teatro de los dioses* (Theater of the gods) that she cites in *Allegorical Neptune* contained extensive passages from Ovid. In "First Dream," her repetition of an error suggests that she was reading Jorge de Bustamante's 1545 Spanish translation of the *Metamorphoses.* Yet Sor Juana's fascination with Ovid was great, and she did read Latin. In several works she ambiguously turns to the figure of Phaethon as a symbol of hubris and overreaching. The full account of this Ovidian myth gives context to her succinct allusions but also suggests poetic resonances, particularly with "First Dream."

Phaëthon

There stood the regal palace of the Sun,
soaring upon its many lofty columns,
with roof of gold and fire-flashing bronze,
and ceilings intricate with ivory,

† From Ovid, *Metamorphoses,* trans. Charles Martin (New York: Norton, 2004), pp. 51–59, 61–64. Copyright © 2004 by Charles Martin. Used by permission of W. W. Norton & Company, Inc. Notes adapt Martin's glossary, unless otherwise indicated.

5   and double-folding doors that shone with silver.
         Its art surpassed the stuff that it was made of,
    for Vulcan[1] had engraved upon those doors
    the seas that gird the middle of the earth,
    the circling lands and the overhanging sky.
10   The waves displayed their gods of cerulean hue:
    harmonious Triton, inconstant Proteus,[2]
    huge Aegaeon,[3] who lifts enormous whales,
    and Doris[4] with her daughters, the sea nymphs;
    some are depicted swimming, others sit
15 upon a rock to dry their sea-green hair,
    and others are shown riding upon fishes,
    their features neither utterly alike
    nor wholly different, but rather mixed,
    as those of sisters ought to be.
                                    On land
20 were scenes of men in cities, beasts in forests,
    rivers and nymphs and rural deities;
    and over this he set the zodiac,
    six figures each upon the left and right.
         Soon as the son of Clymene[5] had climbed
25 the steep path leading to the dwelling place
    of his reputed parent,[6] he went in
    and turned at once to meet his father's gaze—
    though at some distance, for he could not bear
    such brightness any closer.
                                 Phoebus sat
30 in robes of purple high upon a throne
    that glittered brilliantly with emeralds;
    and in attendance on his left and right
    stood Day and Month and Year and Century,
    and all the Hours, evenly divided;
35 fresh Spring was there, adorned with floral crown,
    and Summer, naked, bearing ripened grain,
    and Autumn, stained from treading out her grapes,
    and Winter with his grey and frosty locks.
         And sitting in the middle of these figures,
40 the all-seeing Sun looked upon that youth,
    who quaked with terror at such novel sights.

---

1. God of fire; armorer of the gods.
2. Shape-shifting sea god. Triton was the son of Neptune, the god of the oceans.
3. Son of Neptune, a hundred-armed giant.
4. Daughter of Oceanus and Tethys and mother of the Nereids.
5. Wife of Merops and mother of Phaethon and the Heliades.
6. Phoebus, the sun god; Phaethon was born out of wedlock.

"What brings you here?" he asked. "What do you seek
in this high tower, Phaëthon—you, an heir
no parent would deny?"
                        The youth responded:
45 "O Phoebus, our universal light,
and father—if you let me use that name!
—If Clymene is not concealing guilt
under false pretenses, then give me proof
by which I might have credibility
50 as your true son, and free my mind of doubt!"
So the boy spoke.
                    The father put aside
his shining crown and told him to draw nearer
and took him in his arms: "It would not be
appropriate for me to disavow
55 our relationship," he said, "for Clymene
has spoken truly of your parentage.

    "But so that you may have no doubts at all,
whatever gift you ask me will be given you;
and this I promise by the marshy Styx,[7]
60 which all of the immortals swear upon—
a sight which I, of course, have never seen."

    He'd scarcely finished speaking when the boy
asked for his father's chariot—and permission
to guide his winged horses for a day.
65 The father's oath now filled him with regret;
three times and four he struck his lustrous brow:
"Your deed reveals the rashness of my speech!
Would that I were permitted to rescind
the promise I have given! I confess
70 that this alone I would deny you, son!

    "At least I am permitted to dissuade you:
what you desire is most dangerous!
You seek a gift that is too great for you,
beyond your strength, beyond your boyish years;
75 your fate is mortal: what you ask for isn't.

    "Out of your ignorance, you seek much more
than even gods are able to control,
for though each god may do just as he pleases,
none but myself may set his heel upon
80 the fire-bearing axle. No—not even he
who governs vast Olympus[8] and who flings

7. River in the underworld. An oath made upon Styx was sacred and could not be broken
or withdrawn.
8. Mountain in Thessaly; home of the gods.

the thunderbolt may drive this chariot:
and what force is more powerful than Jove?[9]
   "The journey starts off steeply, and my team,
85 emerging from their stables in the morning,
must struggle to ascend—and barely do:
the midpoint of the heavens is so high
that when I look down on the earth and seas,
fear often makes me tremble, and the heart
90 within my breast is seized with palpitations!
   "The last part of the journey is a steep
descent that needs a skilled hand on the reins;
then, even Tethys,[1] waiting to receive me
beneath the waves, must fear that I will crash!
95   "Besides, there is the whirling vault of heaven
that draws the stars along and sets them spinning;
I press against this force which overcomes
all others, and I overcome it by
opposing the revolving universe.
100   "Suppose the chariot were in *your* hands:
what would *you* do? Would you have the power
to go against the whirling of the poles,
lest their rotation sweep you off completely?
   "Perhaps you think that there are sacred groves
105 and cities of the gods along the way,
temples displaying all the gifts of wealth?
Not so: your path is full of lurking perils
as well as images of savage beasts.
   "And if you hold this course unswervingly,
110 you'll find the horns of Taurus in your way,
the Archer and the gaping jaws of Leo,
and Scorpio, whose long and curving arms
sweep one way, while the curving arms of Cancer[2]
sweep broadly in the opposite direction.
115   "Nor will you find it easy to control
my fire-breathing steeds, who challenge me
to hold them back when they get heated up,
and their wild necks rebel against the reins.
   "I would not be the giver of a gift
120 that would prove fatal to you, son—beware,
and change your asking while it may be changed!

---

9. Ruler of heaven.
1. Sea goddess; wife of Oceanus and mother of Clymene, hence Phaethon's grandmother.
   She attends the sun as he rises out of the water and returns at the end of the day.
2. Along with Taurus, the Archer, Leo, and Scorpio, celestial configurations of the zodiac
   [*Editor*].

You seek assurance that you are my son?
I give you such assurance by my fears,
and by my dread, I show myself your father.
125   Look, look, upon my countenance—I wish
that you could look into my heart as well,
and there discover my paternal cares!
      "Whatever wealth this ample world affords
is yours to have: just cast your eyes about
130   the plentitude of sky and earth and ocean
and ask for any of the goods you see:
I will deny you nothing that you wish.
      "Only one thing I beg you not to ask for,
a punishment, if truly understood,
135   and not a gift, although you think it so—
a punishment indeed, my Phaëthon.
      "Why do you throw your arms around my neck,
you foolish child? Why do you beseech me?
It will be given to you! Have no doubt!
140   I've sworn it by the waters of the Styx,
whatever you wish for—only wish more wisely!"
But his rebellious son refused to listen
and adamantly kept to his design,
so great his passion for the chariot.
145   And so, after delaying for as long
as possible, the father led his son
to Vulcan's gift, the noble chariot.
Golden its axle, golden too, its shaft,
and golden the outer surface of its wheels,
150   adorned with radiating silver spokes;
its yoke, inlaid with golden chrysolites,
returned the light of Phoebus in reflection.
      And while the overreaching Phaëthon
gazed upon it in admiration, look—
155   Aurora, wakeful in the gleaming east,
has once more opened wide her purple gates,
and now her rosy courtyard is displayed;
the stars all scatter, and bright Lucifer[3]
brings up the rear, the last to leave his post.
160   When the father noticed that the morning star
was setting, and the world was growing red,
and the Moon's pale horns were vanishing, he ordered
the passing Hours to prepare his steeds.
Swiftly they brought his fire-breathing horses

3. The morning star.

165 from the lofty stalls where they had been well fed
     on heavenly ambrosia, and harnessed them:
     they shook their jangling reins impatiently.
         Then Phoebus smeared his son's face with an ointment
     to keep him safe from the consuming flames,
170 and placed the radiant crown upon his head.
     Foreseeing grief, his breast heaved as he spoke:
     "You have so far ignored your father's warnings,
     but listen now, and—if you can—heed these:
     spare the whip, boy, and rein your horses in,
175 for on their own, they will go fast enough—
     your task is to restrain them in their flight.
         "Do not attempt to go directly through
     the five zones of heaven, but rather take
     the curving route that leads through only three,
180 and thus avoids extremes of north and south.
         "That is the right way—you will clearly see
     the ruts worn in the pathway by my wheels.
     To heat the earth and sky both evenly,
     don't hug the earth, don't rise to the upper air
185 or you will either set the sky ablaze
     or the earth below: the middle way is safest.
         "Avoid the coiled-up Serpent on your right
     and the low-lying Altar[4] on your left—
     keep in between! I leave the rest to Fortune,
190 and trust that she will be a better guide
     than you yourself have been.
                                   "But while I speak,
     the humid night has reached the western shore—
     we may delay no longer. We are called:
     Dawn is conspicuously present now,
195 and shadows all are fled. Take up the reins,
     or, if that heart of yours can be persuaded,
     take my advice—and *not* my chariot!
         "Change your mind now, while change is still permitted,
     while both your feet are firmly on the ground—
200 before you mount and set out on this course
     which, in your ignorance, you foolishly desire—
     look on in safety while I light the world!"
     But the boy is in the chariot already
     and stands there proudly as he takes the reins

---

4. Along with the Serpent, constellations that illustrate the extremes of the highest and
   lowest points of heaven.

205 and offers thanks to his unwilling father.
     Meanwhile, the flying horses of the Sun,
     Pyrois, Eous, Aethon, and Phlegon,
     filled all the air with fiery whinnying,
     and kicked the bars that held them back.
                                 When Tethys
210 (not knowing what her grandson's fate would be)
     released them, and all heaven opened up,
     they took off with their hooves shredding the mists
     of morning in their way as they flew past
     the east winds in the quadrants where they rise.
215   But the burden that the horses of the Sun
     were used to bearing was much heavier,
     and their yoke lacked its customary weight;
     just as a ship that is unballasted
     rolls all about, unsteadied by its lightness,
220 and goes off course, so too the chariot,
     without the weight it usually carries,
     leaps in the air, bucking, tossed all about
     as though it had no passenger at all;
     and once they're all aware of this, the horses
225 bolt from the rutted track in four directions.
         Now terrified, it is impossible
     for him to use the reins that he was given,
     or find his way; nor, if he were to find it,
     could he control his steeds. For the first time, then,
230 the Great and Little Bears[5] knew the sun's heat
     and tried—in vain, for it was not permitted—
     to plunge into the sea. And the Serpent, who
     lies nearest to the frigid northern Pole,
     and who has been, in sluggish hibernation,
235 a threat to no one, suddenly became
     a raging terror, stirred up by the heat.
     Folks say that even you, Boötes,[6] fled,
     slow as you are, and hampered by your oxcart.
         But when, from heaven's summit, he looked down
240 at the lands that lay so distantly beneath him,
     unlucky Phaëthon at once turned pale,
     and suddenly his knees began to shake
     with terror, and his eyes were darkened by
     excessive light; and now the god's true son

5. Two northern constellations that had never previously experienced heat.
6. The plowman tries to flee from the catastrophe but is hindered by his slow oxen.

245 regrets he ever touched his father's horses,
      is sorry to have found his origins,
      and sorry that his prayer was ever answered;
      he wishes to be called the son of Merops,[7]
      this boy now like a ship caught in a gale
250 and driven by the furious north wind,
      whose helmsman lets the useless tiller go
      and puts his trust in heaven and in prayer.
         Much of the sky already lies behind him,
      much more remains ahead: what can he do?
255 He turns this matter over in his mind,
      now looking to the west (which he is fated
      never to reach), now looking eastward: no
      solution to his problem may be found,
      and stunned by ignorance, cannot decide
260 if he should hold the reins or let them go—
      he doesn't even know his horses' names!
         And scattered everywhere throughout the sky,
      he sees the terrifying images
      of enormous beasts, which aggravate his fears.
265 There is a place where two gigantic arms
      bend into bows, and arms and tail extended,
      Scorpio wholly occupies two zones:
      when the boy sees this venom-sweating monster
      bend its tail back to strike at him, his mind
270 goes blank with icy fear. He drops the reins,
      which slackly lie upon the horses' backs;
      and now his steeds, completely unrestrained,
      go galloping off course through the unknown
      regions of the upper air, wherever
275 impulse proposes, purposeless, and knock
      against the fixed stars set within the sky,
      dragging their chariot through trackless space.

                     *   *   *

               Kind Mother Earth, surrounded
      by the sea and by the waters of the deep
      and by her streams, contracting everywhere
      as they took shelter in her shady womb,
365 though heat-oppressed, still lifted up her head
      and placed a hand upon her fevered brow;
      and after a tremor that shook everything

7. Ethiopian king, husband of Clymene and putative father of Phaethon.

had subsided somewhat, she spoke out to Jove
in a dry, cracked voice:
                              "If it should please you
370 that I merit this, greatest of all gods,
why keep your lightnings back? If I must die
of fire, why not let me die of yours:
knowing that *you* are author of my doom
will make it more endurable to me.
375 I'm scarcely able to pronounce these words—"
(through choking smoke)
                              "—Just look at my singed hair,
the glowing ashes in my eyes and face!
    "Do I deserve this? Is this the reward
for my unflagging fruitfulness? For bearing,
380 year after year, the wounds of plow and mattock?
And for providing flocks with pasturage,
the human race with ripened grain to eat,
the gods with incense smoking on their altars?
    "But even assuming I deserve destruction,
385 why is your brother equally deserving?
Why are those waters, which were his by lot,
so much diminished, so far now from the sky?
    "If neither Earth nor Sea deserve your favor,
have pity on the heavens! Look around you!
390 Both poles are smoking now! If flames destroy them,
the palaces of heaven will collapse!
    "Atlas[8] is scarcely able to support
the white-hot heavens on his bare shoulder!
Now if the sea, the lands, the heavens perish,
395 all will be plunged in chaos once again!
    "Save from the flames whatever is still left,
take measures to preserve the universe!"
    So spoke the Earth, and with no more to say,
unable any longer to endure.
400 the heat, retreated deep within herself
and took up chambers nearer the underworld.
    Before he would commit himself, however,
the father almighty made the other gods
(especially the god who gave his son
405 the chariot) swear that the gravest fate
hung over all, unless he should take action.
    And then he sought the pinnacle of heaven,

8. Giant who supported the weight of the heavens on his shoulders.

whence he was wont to parcel out the rain clouds
widely over the earth, and whence he moved
410 the thunder and sent forth his lightning bolts;
but now he had no rain clouds to distribute,
nor any rain to send down from the heavens;
and so he thundered and released a bolt
of lightning from beside his ear that drove
415 the hapless driver from his spinning wheels
and from his life: fires put cruel fires out.
    In consternation then, his horses reared
and slipped their yoke and fled from their restraints;
the chariot breaks up now: here the reins
420 come falling from the sky, and here the pole
now breaks off from its axle, and the spokes
of the shattered wheels fall to another spot,
and wreckage litters a wide area.
    But Phaëthon, his bright red hair ablaze,
425 is whirled headlong, and tracing out an arc,
seems like a comet with a tail of fire,
or like a star about to fall that doesn't.
In Italy, far distant from his homeland,
the river Eridanus [now the Po]
430 receives his corpse and bathes his seething face.
    Italian naiads lay his broken body,
still smoking from that three-forked thunderbolt,
within a tomb prepared for it and carve
this epitaph in verse upon the stone:

435   YOUNG PHAËTHON LIES HERE, POOR LAD, WHO DREAMT
      OF MASTERING HIS FATHER'S SKY-BORNE CARRIAGE;
      ALTHOUGH HE SADLY DIED IN THE ATTEMPT,
      GREAT WAS HIS DARING, WHICH NONE MAY DISPARAGE.

      His miserable father, sick with grief,
440 drew his cloak up around his head in mourning;
for one whole day then, if the tale is true,
the sun was quite put out. The conflagration
(for the world was still ablaze) provided light;
that was a time some good came out of evil.
445   After Clymene said what might be said
of such an awful situation, she
wandered the world, her mind quite gone with grief,
beating her breast, and seeking first to gather
his lifeless limbs, then to collect his bones;

450 which she at last found in a foreign tomb;
     collapsing, she threw herself upon the stone
     that bore his name, and bathing it in tears,
     she pressed her naked breast on the inscription.

                    *   *   *

JUAN LÓPEZ DE PALACIOS RUBIOS

The Requirement[†]

The *Requirement* was a Spanish juridical document originally written in 1513 by Juan López de Palacios Rubios of the Council of Castile. Spanish conquistadors were required to read it aloud before they entered into unconquered regions in the Americas. It demanded that all indigenous peoples submit to the Spanish Crown and permit the entrance of friars who would proselytize Christianity. If they did not comply, it justified Spanish war. More than an effective act of communication with indigenous communities, it was a document meant to control the actions of Spanish conquistadors by justifying war only when indigenous peoples actively resisted voluntary submission.

The *Requirement* was the object of derision even at the time: in his *Brevísima relación de la destrucción de las Indias* (Very Brief Account of the Destruction of the Indies, 1552), the crusading Dominican Friar Bartolomé de las Casas, for instance, enumerated ways in which it was continually contradicted by Spanish practices and insisted that conversion to Christianity be voluntary and peaceful. In accordance with Las Casas's complaint, in her *"Loa to the Mystery Play The Divine Narcissus,"* (on p. 66) Sor Juana represents conversion as the ultimate goal of Spanish presence in the Americas and, therefore, suggests the illegitimacy of violent conquest. By the time that Sor Juana wrote, however, Las Casas had fallen from favor in Spanish writings and it is likely that her stance reflects the general way that his critique had been incorporated into Spanish imperial jurisprudence rather than a direct citation of his position.

Text from 1513; reproduced with names changed for New Spain in 1518 and 1523; for Tierra Firme in 1526; and for Peru in 1533. This Requirement must be made to the Indians so that they may submit.

On behalf of his Highness the most powerful Catholic Defender of the Church, always the victor and never vanquished, the great

---

[†] *Provisiones, Cédulas, Capítulos de Ordenanças, Instruciones y Cartas libradas y despachadas en diferentes tiempos por sus Magestades* (Provisions, documents, chapters of ordinances, instructions, and letters signed and sent at different times by their majesties) (Madrid: En la Imprenta Real, 1596), IV, pp. 226–27. Available online at www.cervantesvirtual.com/bib/historia/CarlosV/9_1.shtml. Translated for this edition by Isabel Gómez. All notes are the editor's unless otherwise noted.

King Don Ferdinand the Fifth of Spain and the Second of Sicily and Jerusalem and of the Islands and Tierra Firme[1] and the Ocean, etcetera, subduer of all barbarous nations, and for his dearly beloved daughter Doña Juana, Queen of Castilla y León, I, Pedro Arias Dávila,[2] their servant, messenger, and Captain, do notify you and make you aware as best I am able:

That our Lord God is the one true God, now and forever, who created Heaven and Earth, and one man and one woman,[3] from whom we and you and all humankind on earth were and are descendants and progeny, along with all those who shall come after us. Because of the multitudes of generations descended from them in the five thousand years or more since the world was created, some men went to one part and others to another by necessity: they divided themselves into many realms and provinces, for they could not sustain and preserve themselves in one place alone.

Out of all these people, our Lord God put one in charge named Saint Peter,[4] so that he could be Lord of all men on Earth and obeyed by all as their Superior. He was the head of all human lineage; wherever men may go, in any law, sect, or creed, he was given by God all the world for his Reign and jurisdiction. As he wished, he commanded him to found his seat in Rome, the place most prepared to rule the world— but he also permitted him to put his seat in any other part of the world and to judge and govern all people: Christians, Moors, Jews, Gentiles, or those of any other sect or creed there may be. He was called Pope because it means great and admirable Father, governor of all men.

This man Saint Peter was obeyed by all, and they took him as Lord King and universal Superior in their time; and in the same way, all those who came after him and were chosen for the Papal seat were honored by all, and so it has been to this day and so it shall be until the world comes to an end.

One of the previous Pontiffs who succeeded him to this dignity and seat that I have said, as Lord of the world, decreed that all these islands and lands across the Ocean be given to the aforementioned King and Queen and their successors in these realms, with all that may be in them, as it is said in certain writings that are about this topic, as has been said, which you can see if you wish.[5]

1. "Tierra Firme" (solid ground) was the name given to the Spanish colonial province that included territories on Caribbean islands, the north coast of South America, and what is now the Isthmus of Panama [*Translator*].
2. Pedro Arias de Ávila (ca. 1468–1531), also known as Pedrarías Dávila, was the Spanish conquistador of Panama and Darien. Ferdinand II (1452–1516) of Aragon with his wife, Queen Isabella, were called the "Catholic Kings." In 1468 Ferdinand became king of Sicily and in 1474 Ferdinand V of Castile. Juana (1479–1555), Ferdinand and Isabel's daughter, who was also known as "Juana the Mad."
3. Adam and Eve.
4. One of the twelve Apostles of Christ and recognized by the Church as the first pope.
5. The *Intercaetera* Bull of 1493 issued by Pope Alexander IV granted Spain all lands west and south of the Canaries and Azores Islands. It was augmented in 1494 by the Treaty

Thus, Their Majesties are kings and lords of these islands and lands by virtue of said Papal bull. Some other islands, and almost all those that have been notified, have received Their Majesties as kings and lords, and have obeyed and served them, and do serve them as subjects ought, with good will and without any resistance or delay. As they were informed of the aforementioned, they obeyed and received religious men sent by Their Highnesses to preach and teach them our Holy Faith. And all of them became Christians of their glad free will, without any rewards or conditions: they are now Christians, and Their Majesties receive them gladly and benignly, ordering that they be treated just as all their other subjects and vassals. And you are all obliged to do the same.

Consequently, as best as we are able, we beg and require you to understand well all that we have said to you. Take and deliberate on it, to understand it in due time, so that you recognize the Church as your Lady and Superior of the Universe and the World, and in her name the Supreme Pontiff known as the Pope; recognize the King, the Queen Doña Juana, and our Lords in their place, as superiors and kings of these islands and these lands by virtue of the aforementioned papal bull; and consent and make room for these religious fathers to declaim and preach the aforementioned to you.

If you do so, you do well and that which you are required and obliged to do, and Their Highnesses and we in their name will receive you with all love and mercy. We will leave your women, children and possessions to you, free and without servitude, so you may be at liberty to do with them as you wish and for your own benefit.[6] And you will not be compelled to become Christians, unless—since you are now informed of the truth—you all wish to convert to our holy Catholic Faith, as almost all of your neighbors from the other islands have done. Their Majesties will confer on you all these privileges and exemptions and more, for they will do you many favors.

However, if you do not submit, or if you maliciously pursue delay, I swear to you that with the help of God we will enter powerfully against you, and we will make war on you in all places and in every way that we are able. We will subject you to the yoke[7] and obedience of the Church and Their Majesties, and we will take your people, your women and children, and make them slaves to sell and dispose of them however Their Majesties command.[8] We will take all your

---

of Tordesillas, which granted Portugal lands to the east of the line. Until Charles V, the so-called papal donation was one of the primary forms by which Spain justified its sovereignty in the Americas.

6. Enslavement was considered a victor's right in the case of a "just war," the latter juridically limited to cases of active resistance or rebellion of indigenous peoples.

7. A common metaphor for sovereignty. Often texts spoke of the hard yoke, forced sovereignty, or the soft yoke, voluntary sovereignty.

8. See above n. 6.

goods and we will do all the evil and harm we possibly can, as we would to any vassals who do not obey or receive their Lord but instead resist and deny him. We profess that all the death and damage that may come from this will be your fault—not that of their Majesties, nor ours, nor any of the knights that come with us.

And so we ask the scribe present here to give us in a signed document that we say and require this, and we beg all those present to be our witnesses.

SAINT TERESA OF ÁVILA

From The Life[†]

Saint Teresa of Ávila (1515–1582) was a Spanish Discalced Carmelite nun and author. She was especially known for her mystical encounters with the divine, which she described in several treatises. Although she was canonized in 1622, not long after her death, in life Saint Teresa's mysticism was viewed with suspicion by some sectors in the Catholic Church. Lutheran Protestantism made accounts of direct contact with God dangerous, and over the course of the sixteenth century the Church condemned various movements that espoused individual forms of worship. Saint Teresa was investigated by the Spanish Inquisition, although not condemned, the mystical fervor she inspired among Catholic faithful eventually made her a useful tool for the Counter-Reformation Church.

Once canonized, Saint Teresa became the model for Catholic women, although mysticism itself continued to be viewed as potentially heterodox. The selection printed here from Saint Teresa's autobiography, *The Life*, is representative of the "rhetoric of femininity"[1] condoned by the Church. Female mystics practiced a form of holy ignorance and bodily abnegation: women were particularly able to approximate God because of their ability to do away with earthly obstacles such as the mind and the body. Saint Teresa alternates between a posture of humility and insignificance and the powerful discourse of a woman authorized by direct experience of the divine. Sor Juana appropriates and distances herself from this feminine discourse which by her time had become generic. Saint Teresa's account of mystical "rapture" in this section of *The Life* provides a notable contrast with Sor Juana's account of her natural impulse to study in the "Response" and her account of the soul's attempts to gain absolute knowledge in "First Dream," in which, as

---

[†] From *The Life of Saint Teresa, Written by Herself*, trans. Reverend John Dalton (London: C. Dolman, 1851), pp. 154–61, 164–71. All notes are by the editor.
1. See Allison Weber, *Teresa de Ávila and the Rhetoric of Femininity* (Princeton: Princeton University Press, 1989).

opposed to Saint Teresa's account, the soul never fully abandons the body through union with the divine.

* * *

Chapter XX.

THE SAINT TREATS OF THE DIFFERENCE WHICH EXISTS BETWEEN UNION AND RAPTURE, ETC.

I should be glad to know how to explain, by the divine assistance, the difference there is between union and rapture, or, as it is called, elevation of the soul, for these mean one and the same thing. It is also called an "Ecstasy:" the names are different, but they signify one and the same thing. The advantage arising from "Rapture" is very great. The effects, likewise, as well as many other operations which it produces, are much greater, for "Union" seems to be the same both in the beginning, in the middle, and in the end, and it takes place in the interior.

But as a "Rapture" is an elevation of the soul in a much higher degree, it produces effects both interior and exterior. May our Lord enable me to explain this part of the subject, as He has assisted me in the rest; for, certainly, if His Majesty had not made me understand, by what means and in what manner it might be done, I should not have been able to say anything.

Let us now consider that this last water (of which I have been speaking)[2] is so very plentiful and abundant, that if we were capable of receiving it, we should believe the cloud of that divine Majesty were with us, which waters our soul here upon earth. And thus, when we are grateful to our Lord for this great blessing, and acknowledge our gratitude by our good works, according to our strength, our Lord attracts that soul, just in the same way as the clouds attract the vapours from the earth, and mount up towards heaven: and so He takes the soul along with Him himself, and begins to show her the riches of that kingdom which He has prepared for her. I know not if the comparison be just and suitable, but this happens truly and really. In these raptures, it seems as if the soul did not animate the body: it feels very sensibly the want of natural heat, and becomes cold, though possessing the greatest sweetness and delight.

Here there is no means of resisting, though in "Union" (being then in our own country) there is a remedy; and so we may almost always resist, though not without pain and using some violence.

---

2. Saint Teresa is continuing a previous discussion in which she refers to the concession of divine favor as water from a well.

But here, for the most part, there is no remedy at all; for very often the rapture happens without our thinking of it, or employing any means of bringing it on: and then there comes such a quick and strong impetuosity, that you see and feel this cloud raising itself up, or rather, this strong eagle carries you away between her wings (and this is understood), for you know you are carried away, though you know not whither, because though you may feel delight, yet so great is the weakness of our nature that it makes us fear at first. Hence it will be necessary for the soul to be much more determined and courageous than she was when in the degree of union, in order to be able to hazard everything, and to abandon herself entirely into the hands of God, and willingly to go wheresoever she shall be carried, though they will take her whether willing or no. Sometimes the rapture was so great that very, very often I wished to resist, and employed all my strength for this object (especially when the raptures happened in public, and many other times also when they were private), fearing lest I might be deluded. Sometimes I was able to make a slight resistance, but it cost me great trouble; for it seemed like one fighting with a strong giant, so that afterwards I found myself very tired: but at other times it was impossible to resist, for my soul was carried quite away; and generally even my head, and sometimes my whole body, were raised from the ground. This last happened but seldom: it happened once, however, when we were altogether in the choir, and when I was on my knees (being then about to receive the Blessed Sacrament). I was exceedingly troubled thereat; and as it seemed to me to be a very extraordinary circumstance, and that great notice might be immediately taken of it, I commanded the nuns not to speak of it; and this I did because I then held the office of prioress. But, at other times, when I began to see that our Lord was about to do the same again (once in particular, during a sermon, being the feast of our patron, and in the presence of many ladies of quality), I cast myself on the ground; and though the Religious came and kept my body down, yet the rapture was easily perceived. I accordingly besought our Lord that He would no more grant me such favours as would bear exterior demonstrations, because I was already very weary by being so watchful over myself, and His Majesty could not bestow such favours upon me without their being known. And it seems that, through His goodness, He has heard my prayer, for since that time I have had no raptures of the kind, though it is not long since the last happened.

But when I wished to resist, there seemed to be something under my feet of such great strength, that I know not what to compare it to; and it came with much greater impetuosity than any other thing which I ever experienced in my soul: hence I was torn, as it were, to pieces, because the combat is terrible. In a word, all my resistance was of little use, because when our Lord wishes to do anything, no power can stand against Him. At other times He is pleased to content Himself with letting us see that He desires to do us this favour, and that it only remains for us to receive it from His Majesty; and when we resist for the sake of humility, the same effects follow, as if we had entirely consented. These effects are very great: first, the great power of our Lord is made manifest thereby: second, that when His Majesty wishes, we are as little able to detain our bodies as our souls; that we are not masters of them, but that there is a Superior by whom all these favours are given; and that, being nothing ourselves, we can do nothing. These considerations fill us with deep humility: and I acknowledge that these raptures excited in me great fear; and at the beginning I was extremely terrified to see a body raised from the earth; for though it is the spirit which draws it after her, and this with great feelings of delight if no resistance be made, yet we do not lose our senses; at least, I had mine in such a manner that I was able to understand I had been raised up. There also appears so great a majesty in Him who can do this, that it makes even the hair of one's head stand on end; and there remains a great fear of offending so mighty a God: this fear, however, is accompanied by an exceeding great love, which the soul conceives again for Him, who she sees bears so deep a love for such a wretched worm; for He seems not content with really drawing the soul to Himself, but He wishes to draw the body also, even when it is mortal and composed of such filthy dust as we have made it by our sins. This also leaves in the soul a particular disengagement from all things in the world, but I cannot explain what it is. I think however I may say, that it is not only in some degree a different, but also a much greater kind of favour, than any of those other things which act on the soul alone; for though in those other visitations, there is also, as far as relates to the soul, a total disengagement from the things of this world, yet here, it seems, our Lord is pleased, that even *the body itself* should act in the same manner: it likewise excites such a new aversion for the pleasures of this life, that it makes life itself much more painful to us. It afterwards gives another pain, which we can neither procure when we have it not, nor free ourselves from when we have it. I should be very glad to be able to make this "great pain" understood, but I think I shall not be able; still, I will say something, if I can.

I must remark, that these things now happen at the very last, after all those visions and revelations whereof I shall write, and during the time when I am in prayer, when our Lord is accustomed to give me very great sweetness and caresses; and though I sometimes continue to experience the same sweetness, yet the pain of which I shall now speak comes upon me much more frequently. It is sometimes less and sometimes greater. I now wish to speak of the greater, because though I shall treat hereafter of those great impetuosities which I experienced, when our Lord was pleased to give me those raptures; yet, in my opinion, there was as little resemblance between them, as there is between things spiritual and corporal. I believe I do not at all exaggerate the matter, because this pain seems to be such, that though the soul feels it, yet she feels it together with the body, and so both of them share in it; but she feels not that extremity of abandonment which this pain causes, and in which (as I have already mentioned) we have no part ourselves. But there often comes unexpectedly a kind of transport, the cause of which I know not; and this transport, which penetrates the whole soul in an instant, begins to agitate the soul to such a degree, that she rises above herself and all created things; and God makes her so disgusted with them, that however much she may strive, she cannot find on earth any creature for a companion; and even if she could, she would prefer to die in that solitude. If people speak to her, or if she employed all the power which she could possibly possess, in speaking to others, it would be of little use, for her spirit (however much she may strive) is still attached to that solitude. And though it seems to me, as if God were there at a very great distance from her, yet at times He communicates His greatness to her, in a manner the most extraordinary that can be imagined or expressed; and I think that he only can believe or understand it who has experienced it himself; for it is no communication to give comfort, but only to show the reason which he has to be afflicted, on account of being absent from that good which comprehends all good.

By means of this communication, the desire increases of remaining in that extreme solitude in which the soul finds herself, together with a pain which is so very acute and penetrating, that she may then, I think (being placed in this desert), literally make use of these words: "I have watched, and become as a sparrow all alone on the house-top."[3] These words the royal prophet, perhaps, spoke when he was in the same solitude; but being a saint, our Lord made him feel them in a more sensible manner. This verse comes into my mind, because it seems as if I see myself in it; and I am consoled in seeing that other persons also have found themselves in such great solitude, and the greatest saints more than any one else. And thus it appears that the soul in this state is raised, not only above all created things, but even above herself.

At other times, the soul seems to find herself in the very extremity of misery, asking herself this question: "Where is thy God?"[4] I must remark, that I did not understand the meaning of these words

3. Psalm 102:7.
4. Psalms 42:3 and 42:10.

in the Psalms; but after they were explained to me, I was much com-
forted in seeing that our Lord brought them to my memory, without
any endeavour on my part. At other times, I remembered the words
of St. Paul, "that he was crucified to the world."[5] I say not that I was
crucified, for I see clearly I am not; but it seems to me, that the soul
in this case is, as it were, crucified, and suspended between earth
and heaven; and hence no comfort comes from heaven, because she
is not there, nor from the earth, because she is no longer upon it;
and she suffers all the time, without receiving any succour from
either place. That which does come to her from heaven is so great a
knowledge of God, that she loses herself in the contemplation of His
infinite greatness; and this knowledge increases rather than dimin-
ishes her pain, because her desire of possessing Him increases in
such a manner, that, in my opinion, the excessive pain sometimes
takes away her senses; but she remains without them only a little
while. This state seems to be the very agony of death itself; and yet
it is accompanied with such a great pleasure and content in suffer-
ing, that I know not what to compare it to. It is a sharp and yet a
delightful kind of martyrdom, since everything relating to this world
which can possibly be represented to the soul, even though it were
the most delightful object, is on no account admitted, but rather it
is immediately cast away from her. She understands well, that she
cares for nothing but for her God; and yet she loves in Him no par-
ticular perfection, but all His perfections together; still, she knows
not what she wishes or desires. I say, she knows not, because her
imagination represents nothing to her; and during all the time she
remains in this state, the powers of the soul do not (in my opinion)
produce that joy which is felt in union and rapture; the pain entirely
suspends them.

✳ ✳ ✳

I think I have wandered from my subject, for I began by speaking
of raptures; but what I have just been speaking of is much greater
than raptures, and so it leaves those effects in the soul, which I have
been relating. I will now speak of these raptures, and of that which
usually happens therein. I wish to mention then, how the rapture
often left my body so light, that all the weight thereof was quite
taken away, and sometimes to such a degree, that I hardly knew how
to set my feet on the ground. But when the soul is in a rapture, the
body remains as it were dead, being often unable to do anything at
all of herself; and as it happens to be at the time, so it remains,
whether it be in a sitting posture, or whether the hands be opened
or closed; for though she loses her senses a few times (and the same

5. Galatians 6:14.

has happened to me now and then), yet they have been seldom *entirely* lost, and then only for a short time. The usual effect is, that she is disturbed a little; and though she can do nothing of herself, as far as regards the exterior, yet, she is able both to understand and to hear, as if something were spoken to her from afar off. I say not that she understands and hears when she is in the very height of her rapture (I use the words, "the very height"), at that time when the faculties are lost, because they are very closely united with God; and then, in my opinion, she neither sees nor hears. But, as I mentioned in the former prayer of Union, this total transformation of the soul into God continues only for a short time; but, as long as it lasts, no power of the soul either feels or knows what passes there. And it seems to be for this object, that as long as we live in this world, it is not God's will we should understand what passes there, because we are not capable of understanding it; at least, I myself have experienced this.

But your Reverence will perhaps ask me, how is it that raptures should sometimes last so many hours? I answer, that what happened to me very often (as I have mentioned in the former prayer) is this: that we enjoy raptures only by intervals, and the soul often engulfs herself, or rather (to speak more correctly) our Lord engulfs the soul in Himself; and as He keeps her there for awhile, there remains only her will which she can make use of. As to the exercise of those other two powers, it seems to me to be like that of a needle on a sun-dial, which never stands still; but yet when the Sun of Justice wishes, He makes them stop. This, I say, lasts but for a short time. As, however, the impulse and exaltation of the spirit were great, the will remains engulfed, and acts like a sovereign lady over all the operations of the body, because those other two restless powers wish to disturb her: the senses, however, do not disturb her. And thus they also are suspended, because our Lord is so pleased. The eyes, too, are mostly shut, though we may not wish to shut them; and if sometimes they be open, yet, as I have already mentioned, the soul does not consider nor advert to what she sees.

The body is now much less able to do anything of herself; and even after the three powers[6] have been united, it can do but little. Let him, therefore, to whom our Lord shall grant this favour, not be astonished when he sees the body so weak for many hours, and his memory and understanding sometimes so apt to wander. True it is, that souls are ordinarily, in this state, *drowned* in the praises of God, and in desiring to comprehend or understand what has taken place in them; and even for this object they are not wholly awake, but like a person who has slept and dreamt a great deal, and is not yet quite

---

6. Memory, will, and imagination in scholastic psychology.

awake. I have thus explained myself at some length, because I know there are persons at this time, and even in this place, on whom our Lord has bestowed these favours; and if those who direct these religious[7] have not experience in these matters, they will perhaps think, especially if they be not learned, that in these raptures the persons are as it were dead. It is a subject of grief to consider how much one suffers from such confessors, who do not understand these matters, as I shall afterwards mention. Perhaps I know not what I say; but your Reverence will understand if I should say anything to the purpose, since our Lord has already given you experience herein; though as it is not long since you began, you may not perhaps have considered the subject so much as I have. But though I endeavoured to do so very often, and to the best of my power, yet the body has not strength enough to stir itself, for the soul takes all its strength away with her. Thus a sick person often recovers his health, and she who was full of weakness and pain regains her strength, because great favours are given in this state. And sometimes (as I was saying) our Lord is pleased that the body also should experience a certain degree of joy, because it obeys what the soul desires. When she has returned to herself, it may happen (if the rapture has been great), that she will go for a day or two, or even for three days, with the powers so absorbed, and as it were engulfed in God, that she seems out of herself.

But in this state she feels it painful to be still obliged to live in the world; for now, having lost her weak feathers, others have come strong enough to enable her to fly well: now the banner of Christ is so directly unfurled, that there seems to remain nothing more but that the captain of this fort may either ascend himself, or be carried up to the highest tower, there to plant this standard for the glory of God. She now looks upon those who are below as one who is already in safety; for so far is she from fearing danger, that she rather wishes it, like one for whom victory is secured in a most certain manner. Now she sees very clearly how little all worldly things ought to be esteemed, and what a "nothing" they are. He who is in a high place sees many things. Now she does not wish to have any other will but the will of our Lord, and she gives Him the keys of hers. From being a gardener, she has now become a governor; she wishes to do nothing but the will of God, nor does she desire to be the governor of herself, nor indeed of anything, not even of a single well in this garden; and if there be anything good in it, she wishes His Majesty to divide the fruits thereof; for, from that time forward, she desires nothing of her own, but only that all things may be done in conformity with His will and for His glory. Everything happens in this way

7. Confessors.

truly and really, if the raptures be real, and the soul enjoys the effects and advantages which I have mentioned. But if such are *not* the effects, I should doubt much whether the raptures come from God, but should rather be inclined to fear they were of that kind of ravings whereof St. Vincent[8] speaks. This I know, and through experience I have seen that here the soul remains a queen over all things, and acquires in less than an hour so much liberty, that she is not able to know herself. But yet she knows well all this is not her own; nor does she know how she came to obtain so great a blessing: still she understands clearly the exceeding great advantage which every one of these raptures brings with it. No one can believe all this but he who has experienced it himself; and therefore men cannot believe that a poor soul, which they knew was before so wicked, can so soon undertake to do such wonderful things, because she immediately resolves not to be content with serving our Lord in small things, but to serve Him in most difficult matters also. But men are apt to imagine that such resolutions are only temptations and foolishness. But if they would consider that they come not from herself, but from our Lord, to whom she has already given up the keys of her will, they would not wonder so much at it. I am of opinion, that a soul which arrives at this state neither says nor does anything of herself, but this Sovereign King takes care of everything which is to be done. O my God! how clearly does a soul see here the meaning of that verse, "Who will give me the wings of a dove?"[9] The prophet David had reason to make this request, and so have we all. That "flight" is clearly meant which the soul takes, in order to raise herself above all creatures, and before all things above herself: but this "flight" is sweet; it is a pleasant flight, and a flight without noise. What dominion does such a soul possess which our Lord conducts to this degree, that she looks down upon all things without being entangled by them! How full of confusion is she for the time in which she was entangled by them! How astonished at her blindness! How full of compassion for those who still remain in this blindness, especially if they be people of prayer, and such as God is pleased to caress! She desires to cry aloud, that so all may understand how much they have been deceived, and this she does sometimes; and then men pour down upon her head a thousand persecutions; they treat her as having but little humility, and as one who wishes to *teach* those from whom she ought rather to learn, especially if she be a woman, then they condemn her; and perhaps they have reason for so doing, because they know not by what impulse she is moved. And as she

---

8. Saint Vincent Ferrer (1350–1419), Dominican friar from Valencia. Rosa Navarro Durán claims that the citation is from his *Libellus de Vita Spirituali* (Pamphlet on the Spiritual Life). Saint Teresa of Ávila, *La vida/Las moradas* (Madrid: Planeta, 1989), 115 n. 49.
9. Psalm 55:6.

knows not how to help herself on the one hand, so on the other she cannot forbear undeceiving those persons whom she loves, and whom she desires to behold free from the prison of this life, for the state wherein she was seems neither more nor less than a prison.

She is much afflicted at the thought of that time in which she attended to points of honour; and for the error and deceit into which she fell, by believing *that* to be honour which the world calls honour. She sees that it is a very gross lie, and that all men live in the practice of it. But now she understands that real honour is not false, but true; and she esteems *that* to be worth something which indeed is so, and considers that to be nothing which is in reality so; since all is nothing, and less than nothing, which will one day have an end, and because it does not please God. She laughs at herself for the time in which she made any account of money, and had a desire for it: though in this particular I do not believe (and this is the truth) that I ever had any fault to confess; but it would have been a fault to have esteemed or desired money in any way. If by means of it I could have purchased those blessings which I now see in myself, I might have valued it very much; but the soul now perceives that such blessings are purchased best by leaving all things. And what is that which can be purchased by this money, which men so much desire? Is it anything of value? Anything durable? And for what object do we desire it? A miserable repose is purchased, and dearly does it cost us; for often do we purchase hell by it, endless torments in everlasting fire! O! that all men, then, would resolve to consider it as earth, which is good for nothing! In what harmony would the world then move! How free from unjust contracts! In what friendship would all men live, if they would not hanker after honours or riches! In that case I think every evil would be remedied.

The soul also sees that there is great blindness respecting the delights of this world, and that by them nothing is purchased, even for this life, but trouble and affliction. What trouble, and what little pleasure! What labour in vain! Here she perceives not only the cobwebs of her soul,—that is, her great faults,—but even the smallest grain of dust, because the Sun is very bright. And so, however much the soul may have laboured to perfect herself, if this same Sun should truly strike her with its beams, then she sees how dusty everything is. It is like a glass full of water, which you think to be very pure and clear, if the sun do not shine upon it; but when the sun does shine, you find it to be all full of animalculæ. This comparison is literally true; for before the soul is in this ecstasy, she thinks that she has been very careful not to offend God, and that she endeavoured to do so to the best of her power. But when she has arrived so far, that this Sun of Justice makes her open her eyes, then she sees so many motes in them that she would be glad to shut

them again; for she has not yet become so strong, like the coura-
geous eagle which bred her, as steadily to fix her eyes on this Sun.
But however little she may open them, she sees herself covered with
imperfections, and then she remembers the verse, "Who shall be
pure in Thy sight?"[1] When she beholds this Divine Sun, she is daz-
zled by the brightness thereof; but when she looks upon herself, her
eyes are stopped up with clay; and so this little dove is blind. And
sometimes it happens that she remains entirely blind, being
absorbed, amazed, and as it were out of herself, at all the greatness
that she beholds. Here true humility is acquired; for she cares not
either about speaking well of herself, or about others doing it: she
wishes our Lord, and not herself, to divide the fruits of the garden,
and so nothing sticks to her fingers. All the good that she has is
directed and referred to God; and if she should say anything of her-
self, it is for His glory, for she knows that she has nothing of her
own: of this she cannot be ignorant, even if she would, because she
knows it by the very sight of her eyes, which are shut to the things
of this world, but open for understanding the truth, whether she is
willing or no.

*   *   *

DIEGO CALLEJA

Approval of the Most Reverend Father
Diego Calleja of the Society of Jesus[†]

Father Diego Calleja (1639–1729) was a Spanish Jesuit and playwright.
His approval of the final volume of Sor Juana's works contains her
earliest biography. Printed in the same volume as the "Response," it
augments and repeats much of what Sor Juana writes. Its tone, however,
is hagiographic and clearly attempts to exculpate Sor Juana from the
attacks she had received during her life.

Very Powerful Señor:
   By the orders of Your Highness, I have read the book titled *Works
and Posthumous Fame of Mother Sor Juana Inés de la Cruz* [sic], which
the Doctor Don Juan Ignacio de Castorena y Ursúa,[1] Honorable
Chaplain of your Majesty, wishes to bring to press. Be assured that I

1. Psalm 143:2.
† First published in *Fame and Posthumous Works* (1700). Translated for this edition by
   Isabel Gómez. All notes are the editor's.
1. Juan Ignacio María de Castorena Ursúa y Goyeneche (1668–1733): Mexican-born bishop
   of Yucatan and patron of Sor Juana who edited the posthumous publication in which
   Calleja's biography appears.

have read it and find nothing within that would oppose the upright sentiments of our Holy Faith or the purity of good customs, but rather much instruction, adding judgment to spirituality. For these reasons it merits the license requested by the supplicant. Given that there are many lords in the Council, whose severity as judges does not interfere with their good taste as courtly gentlemen, it will not be too inappropriate (or, who knows, perhaps obsequious), if, on returning this Approval, I also inform them (with such proofs as will be seen) of the beginnings, development, and death of this most ingenious woman who, through the works of her other two volumes, presently fills both Spains[2] with the reputation of her admirable wisdom. I recount her life story with plain simplicity. Not because wasting words would betray lack of faith in the intelligence of my reader, but rather because elaborate praise steals thunder from her eulogists.

Forty-four years, five months, five days, and five hours: for this duration, the life of this rare woman illuminated her era, born to this world for prodigious feats as the pride of nature.

Two mountains lie twelve leagues from Mexico City, capital of New Spain. Almost contiguous, they make good neighbors despite their different qualities—one is always covered with successive snowfalls, the other constantly erupts with fire[3]—instead of clashing, they conserve the peace through their extremes and create a zone of benign temperance in the small distance that divides them. In their foothills on the border between excessive hot and cold, as in spring, the homeland of this marvel was a well-run farmstead known as San Miguel de Nepantla.[4] There Mother Juana Inés was born in the year 1651,[5] on Friday, November 12 at eleven at night. Born in a bedchamber known as "The Cloister," in the very same homestead, she fell in love with the monastic life with her first breath, because this coincidence showed her that to be alive meant breathing convent air. Her father, don Pedro Manuel de Asbaje, native of Villa de Vergara in Guipuzcoa Province, crossed over to the Indies with the desire to overcome the faults in the heart of his motherland, which was as fertile in nobility as it was sterile in wealth. There, this blessed Basque married doña Isabel Ramírez de Cantillana, daughter of Spaniards and native to Yacapistla in New Spain. From their legitimate union was born our peerless poetess, among other children: she did have blood parity, though her soul may not seem to admit human parentage.

2. Spain and New Spain.
3. The snow-capped peaks of Iztaccihuatl ("the white woman," in Nahuatl) and the volcanic Popocatepetl ("the smoking mountain," in Nahuatl).
4. Signifies "between" in Nahuatl, and Calleja is most likely conscious of this wordplay. "Marvel": Sor Juana.
5. Calleja is the source for this birthdate; the baptismal records of Nepantla show a Juana baptized in 1648.

At age three, when she had run away from her mother to school with her sister, she gave her mind its first breath of life: she saw them giving lessons to her sister. As though she already knew the age of majority is in the soul and not in years, she believed herself to be ready to learn and asked that they give her lessons too. The matron refused, because in her little girl stutter it was not yet possible to discern more than prattle or ignorance, but she was soon disabused of that impression. At her first lessons, without having been subjected to the tiresome process of sounding out words, she read with effortless fluency, and in two years she learned to read, write, count, and all the other trifles of intellectual labor—all with such precocious skill that it would have been her legacy had this remained her only task.[6] The first light of her wit shone on Spanish poetry; everyone who saw her at such a tender age was rightly awed to see the facility with which rhyme and meter flowed from her mouth and pen, as if she found them fully formed in her memory and they cost her no effort at all.

To achieve poetic genius, this facility with poetry alone is enough, and can do without the expression of subtle conceits or elevated thoughts, much less heroic episodes, because without going beyond the grasp of an elevated fantasy, any material can reach the sphere of its perfection when it is accompanied by a profound and clear intellect. To treat a subject celebrated throughout the ages, the poet must add the perspicacity of a fertile mind and the enlightenment of a variety of knowledge, particularly in the language of composition.

Before she turned eight, the Holy Sacrament festival offered Mother Juana a book as a prize, a treasure she always ardently desired, and she composed a *loa*[7] with all the qualities required of a complete poem. The Reverend Father Master Friar Francisco Muñiz witnessed this; he was a Dominican vicar in the town of Amecameca, four leagues from the homestead where Mother Juana Inés was born. She herself tells us that, at that age, if she heard a particular sweet would cause ignorance, she would flee from it as though it were a poison that would infect her intelligence if eaten. She begged her parents to send her to the University of Mexico,[8] dressed as a man, to study the many subjects she had heard were taught there. In this way, her spirit revealed the impetuous energy growing impatient with the limits imposed by nature trapped in her petite body. She did not anticipate that such superior intelligence could, in the shrewdness of its understanding, contain all knowledge as if in a seed, giving copious fruit even with light cultivation. In this way, it

---

6. See the "Response," on p. 97.
7. A short prologue preceding a mystery play. Sor Juana wrote several later in life but this one, if it was written, is now lost. See headnote to "*Loa* to the Mystery Play" on p. 66.
8. See the "Response," on p. 96.

requires only the explanations of tutors as gentle limits and guidance that contribute to usage if not to natural intelligence. This prodigious woman always lacked teachers, but she never suffered from their absence. Her capacious mind was in itself equivalent to a university professor and an auditorium: enough to learn the major sciences with the supreme intelligence always demonstrated in her writing. She was simultaneously her own argument, response, reply and satisfaction, as if she had learned everything in the guise of Poetry,[9] without instruction.

When she was eight years old, her parents took her to live with a grandfather in Mexico City. In his house she found a few books, whose greatest destiny was weighing down the side table, and with these fed her hunger for knowledge. For years she endured the punishment of studying at the mercy of books not of her choosing. According to the testimony of Martín de Olivas, the university student who taught her Latin, she knew the language with distinction after only twenty lessons. Since her education had been left in her own hands, she added her own effort as taskmaster: she would cut her hair, vowing that if it grew back to a certain length measured on her shoulder before she learned what she had set as her goal, she would cut it again.[1] Perhaps she never needed to: where other women might lose their senses to such a rich treat, she availed herself of this to awaken her memory from its light sleep.

Rumors flew about her abilities, so uncommon at such a young age. As she grew in years, careful study augmented her intelligence just as nature did her beauty, not wishing, in her case, for an envious dissimulating body to conceal so much subtly of spirit, the way inside the rough, uncouth earth a rich treasure can be hidden from the covetous. As soon as her relatives recognized the risk that she might be disgraced for her intelligence—and, with no less disgrace, pursued for her beauty—they ensured both extremes at once by introducing her into the palace of his Excellency the Lord Marquis de Mancera,[2] Viceroy of Mexico at that time. She entered palace life with the title of the favorite of her lady the Vicereine.[3] Here I regret having discarded the flattering style of a eulogist, because I cannot believably describe without hyperbole how much affection—why not even call it veneration, because there are ways of serving that dominate the wills of one's rulers—their Excellencies were repaid just by seeing her and which was returned when, without being ordered, she obeyed them. Her lady the Vicereine seemed unable to

9. That is, as though from a Muse.
1. See the "Response" on p. 97.
2. Antonio Sebastián Álvarez de Toledo Molina y Salazar, Marquis de Mancera (ca. 1608–1715), viceroy of New Spain (1664–1673).
3. Leonor Carreto (1616–1673), Marquisa de Mancera, patroness of Sor Juana, and "Laura" in Sor Juana's poems.

live a single instant without her Juana Inés, but this never meant she
lost time from her studies: rather, she continued them through con-
versation with the Vicereine. At this point, either to avoid creating
the suspicion that I am an overly credulous admirer or to erase any
remaining doubts about what I have already said, I must refer with
indisputable certainty (such is the utmost faith I have in the witness)
to a fact that without such corroborating support I would suppress.
His lord the Marquis de Mancera (may he live for many years to
come, as his favored vassals say) told me a number of times how (with
an admiration far from the common, being that of his Excellency) he
would see that Juana Inés was so well informed in a variety of sub-
jects, so apparently accurate in her logic, and well founded in all,
that he wanted to disenchant himself once and for all, to discover
whether her wisdom was so truly admirable—whether mystical,
acquired, artificial, or supernatural. One day, he brought all the
learned men from the University and from Mexico City to the palace.
Together, they numbered up to forty and their professions were
various: theologians, scriptural experts, philosophers, mathemati-
cians, historians, poets, and humanists. There were also not few of
those known by the allusive appellation *tertulios*, who have no offi-
cial university studies but with their great wit and some application
tend to achieve effective and sound reasoning on all things. These
highly acclaimed and prudent men did not disdain the youth—at
that point Juana Inés was no more than sixteen years old—of the
one who was not so much embattled as she was examined. Neither
did they discourteously avoid the intellectual competition with a
woman, as they were Spaniards. They convened on the planned day
for the examination of such a curious marvel, and according to the
Lord Marquis, what he saw there escapes human understanding.
Citing the words of his Excellency, he said: *just as a royal galleon
would defend herself from small vessels charging at her, so did Juana
Inés dispatch the questions, arguments, and replies that her many
examiners posed to her, each according to their abilities.* What study,
what understanding, what capacity and memory would be neces-
sary to be capable of this? The reader can reason for himself; I can
only affirm that such triumph left Juana Inés (as she herself wrote,
when I asked) with only as much satisfaction as she would have if at
school she had more skillfully completed an open-work hemstitch.

This most genteel woman lived among the flatteries of such an
elevated atmosphere, where everyone wished to see the brilliant
mind they had heard about. She was well aware that the very ten-
derness of green youth is a threat to its own survival; that there is
no April that lasts longer than a month, nor can any morning out-
last the day; that beauty is a gift of such villainous pride that it is

only esteemed if allowed to wither on the vine; that the lovely face of a poor woman is a white wall where every fool wants to make his mark; that even the measure of her honesty can put her at risk, for some eyes will slip all the more on ice; and finally, that the most beautiful flowers, once handled, are lost, but when placed in altar urns are divine worship. Knowing all this from such a young flowering age, she dedicated herself to serve God in a religious cloister without ever giving any signs of considering marriage. Perhaps the American Phoenix[4] was persuaded by her secret knowledge that this bond was impossible for someone who could find no peer in this world.

Mother Juana Inés made this decision in spite of her awareness that it would contradict her vehement inclination toward study. She feared that the unavoidable crowd would neither leave her time nor alleviate her fervor to employ her whole self in her books. To dedicate herself to religious life with such an obstructed desire would be to take as her relief a continuous regret, a torment that would fill the lives of even the most vigorous of souls only with sighs, unable to breathe. This is especially so when the repressed desire is not understood as a type of sin, for then, with broad concessions the greatest minds find the resistance to their desire beyond their reach.

In those days, the wise and virtuous Antonio Núñez[5] of the Jesuits in Mexico City was venerated by all and served as confessor for their Lords the Viceroyalty. Juana Inés communicated her doubts about her vocation to this august man, and he dispelled her fear like a light: as confessor for so great a family, it clearly would not have appeared unusual to him that so many talents of wisdom would be conjoined with religious virtues in one soul. If the former opposed the latter, he told her, it was preferable to hide her talents. With this, Juana Inés overcame her repugnance and resolved with pious daring to leave behind her inclination for human wisdom. With every book she abandoned, she cut the throat of another Isaac in sacrifice to God.[6] His Majesty paid her for this courtesy by, during those brief periods meant for idleness or rest, adding to her wisdom the capacity to learn more new material within the religious community than so many who in school chip away at time, eventually whittling themselves down to the trunk.

The San Jeronimo convent in imperial Mexico City was a peaceful sea enclosing this rare pearl, where she would grow. There, she

4. That is, Sor Juana.
5. António Núñez de Miranda (1618–1695), Jesuit priest in New Spain and Sor Juana's confessor when she entered the convent and then again at the end of her life. See "Letter by Mother Juana Inés de la Cruz" on p. 144.
6. The biblical story of Abraham, whom God orders to sacrifice his only son, Isaac (Genesis 22:9–12).

professed her vows and don Pedro Velásquez de la Cadena[7] was favored to pay her dowry—as such expenditures do enrich—a kindness for which the Mother Juana Inés was always grateful, as if to a patron who had saved her from a foreseeable tempest. Ingratitude would have debased the value of such a rich jewel whose great understanding was adorned with equally precious qualities. For this reason, when she realized the sciences she had studied were of no benefit to her religious family, where music was practiced with such edifying care, she immediately began to study this art with great purpose, to thank the loving sisters for the caring hospitality they all showed her. She achieved it with such ease that she composed another simpler form to perfect the skill without the circumlocutions of the old method—an achievement so highly praised that those who understand this art say that this alone would have been enough to bring her fame the world over.[8]

She lived for twenty-seven years in the religious community—without the seclusion that earns the glory and renown of the ecstatic—but effectively fulfilling the obligations of her religious state, in whose common observance Mother Juana Inés kept her place among the best. Her most intimate and familiar interactions were with books, where she fruitfully spent her time; but she ceded all to the community activities that gained her eternity. Charity was her crowning virtue: she did not leave the bedsides of the sick except to prepare food or dispense remedies. Poor nuns, followed by the needy in the city, were the first deserving beneficiaries of the presents and rich treasures constantly given to her. She would distribute this charity gradually, as some religious women, trusting that they have food—and how doubtful is that security!—have suffered grave scarcity. But her liberality was so humble that she did not even keep for herself the veneration or vanity of a reputation as an almsgiver or a generous person.

Fortune is under oath to Nature, as we know, and the shining target of great ability is that which luck uses to aim her shots. Those that fly highest in the atmosphere of a community deserve the commiseration found in Cicero and Aristotle,[9] afflicted when present and praised when absent.

Mother Juana Inés received contradictory authorization for the verses she composed, a fact we need not lament here: either because those who approved her first volume fought this battle for her, or

---

7. Captain Don Pedro Velásquez de la Cadena was the secretary of governance and war of New Spain and paid Sor Juana's dowry for entrance into the convent.
8. Sor Juana's musical abilities were well known.
9. Greek philosopher (384–322 B.C.E.), considered to be the most important in Sor Juana's time. Marcus Tullius Cicero (160–43 B.C.E.): Roman philosopher and statesman, model of rhetoric for the Renaissance.

because the good taste of poetic spirits tends to convert such grief into witty seasonings, referring to them in harmoniously happy complaints that lighten sorrow. We should only regret the period of time during which Mother Juana was banned by an in-house mandate from studying the major sciences. This was doubtlessly concocted by certain souls whose judgment only knows how to stop at the most assured, as though human behavior could be limited on these subjects, or as though obedience could still be praiseworthy when it is entirely certain—and this especially when the most learned minds opine that between two extremes, "more" and "less," will affect only perfection and not legality. As her doctors testified, this prodigious woman fell sick from not being able to work on her studies. To revive her from her fatigue, the Superiors had to give her permission and she returned to her books with thirst for the prohibited. She made rigorous rules that no one should enter her cell: so beloved was she by all that no one could depart quickly once they entered. She needed more patience during visits in the *locutorio*:[1] the personalities who frequented her audience did not know when to leave her, nor could she lose their respect by excusing herself. Only when responding in verse and prose to the letters she received from the two Spains, even dictating her thoughts aloud, could the scribe have a more solitary task to occupy her labor.

Even with such weight on her shoulders, this robust soul did not surrender: she always studied and always wrote, and both so well that these appeared to be done little and with leisure.

It would be disgraceful not to provide some reflection here on two of her works that show her to be as ingenious as she was wise. One is the *Critique* in which, with sharp scholastic rigor, she disagrees with the content and reasoning of a sermon by father António Vieira.[2] First, it is so well written that even the most highly versed scholar of syllogistic forms cannot surpass the exactness, correctness, and clarity with which Mother Juana syllogistically distributes the terms of her argument. Second, anyone can see how convincing her argument is in light of the following witness. The most Reverend Master Father Francisco Morejón,[3] whose wisdom and other good qualities are renown in Madrid—and whose rigor has had painful consequences for so many—after reading this work by Mother Juana arguing against the sermon of father Vieira, said that four or five times she convinced him with her evidence. So I heard from this

---

1. Reception rooms in convents that allowed visitors to converse with nuns who remained behind a grille.
2. António Vieira (1609–1697), Portuguese Jesuit known for his oratorical skills. His 1650 Maundy Thursday sermon was the object of Sor Juana's critique in her *Athenagoric Letter* (1690), or "Response." The latter was published under the title *Crisis de un sermón* (Critique of a Sermon) in her *Second Volume* (1692).
3. A Spanish Jesuit, Rector of the Colegio de Murcia and Provincial of Toledo.

most solemn mind. In order that an overabundance of support does
not weaken the credit of the poetess among those who require the
report of others to consider her a scholastic,[4] I do not to refer to the
many others who, learned and with correct judgment (two names
will suffice for the many: Francisco Ribera and Father Sebastián
Sánchez[5]), having read this paper the *Critique*[6] were overwhelmed by
praise, with the certainty that to admire the intelligence of a women
without formal schooling but who reasoned with such formal preci-
sion, it mattered little whether this was on a sermon of Vieira or not,
since it would be incorrect to distinguish whether or not an arrow
hit its mark according to the distinct targets, calling it "perfect
marksmanship" to hit a pomegranate but "delirium" to hit a pearl.[7]

Whoever wants complete satisfaction to the objections of those
who pass off their superficial reading for finished judgments, should
read the *Response* by Mother Juana to the illustrious Filotea, printed
to the unique honor of this third volume. There you will see that
the objection to the idea that a woman should dare to boast of
formal scholasticism is just as irrational as scolding an iron mine
because it meddled with producing gold, against its nature. There
you will see that Mother Juana Inés did not intend this writing to
be published, but that an illustrious writer offered the printed ver-
sion to her hand, not according to her desires. There you will see
that with the response of the poetess to father Vieira, even he who
washed snow with ink[8] remains more illuminated by the defense she
wrote. There you will see, finally, that in this admirable woman there
is a humble candor so measured that she does not refuse to defend
her own offense, even refusing to disdain the Herostratus,[9] who,
with boorish momentum and the smoldering embers of a casuistic
style, wished to gain fame by burning this marvel.

Another work we must consider is *The Dream*, which she herself
describes as the only one written solely from her own volition. The
basis of this *Dream* is knowledge of all the subjects contained in the
books of *On the Soul,*[1] many that cover mythology, physics—even
that of medical books, secular and natural histories and other types

---

4. Scholasticism is the school of rational theology that followed the work of Saint Thomas
   Aquinas (1225–1274).
5. There is no further information on these men.
6. See p. 191 n. 2.
7. That is, Vieira's work.
8. An apparent reference to a phrase by the pre-Socratic philosopher Anaxagoras, repeated
   by authors from Cicero to Saint Augustine, for an absurd position: that snow is black.
   Ignacio Arellano has identified the same reference in a poem by Sor Juana. Ignacio Arel-
   lano, "La nieve negra de Sor Juana: de Anaxágoras a Enrique Lihn, pasando por San
   Agustín a Ramírez de Prado," *Romance Notes* 54, no. 2 (2014).
9. Greek arsonist who burned the Temple of Artemis, he represents one who commits a
   criminal act for fame.
1. Aristotle's *De Anima* (On the Soul) was the basis for scholastic physiology and psychol-
   ogy, or study of the soul.

of elevated erudition. The meter she uses is the *silva*,[2] freed from the restriction of consonant rhymes in a fixed number of verses, the same metrical form used by poetic genius don Luis de Góngora in his *Solitudes*, the imitation of which surely animated Mother Juana in this *Dream*. Though the latter may not be equally sublime, nobody who understands it well would deny that both soar in the same sphere. We do not challenge the possible (even great) superiority of don Luis, but we must also consider their topics. Although poetry itself disregards its contents, some subjects are more capable than others of giving vent to the pen. Don Luis took these as his subject matter when he composed his *Solitudes*, while the majority of the topics chosen by Mother Juana Inés for her *Dream* are by nature so arid that simply making them flower so beautifully is a marvelous argument for the fecundity of her cultivation. What could be further from the airy discourse of the poetic spirit than the principles, means, and ends with which the stomach digests its sustenance, making substance out of alimentation? Or what happens to sensible species during thought production, from the external senses to the common, to the intellective agent, to understanding? And other things of this nature—merely that our poetess was able to elaborate such elegant delicacies from such a dismal basis is reason enough for admiration. Don Luis is justly praised for the spirit with which he adorned two events of such little consequence with such copious elegance of periphrasis and fantasy.[3] Mother Juana had no more grounds for her composition than this: *as night had fallen, I slept and dreamed I once desired to understand everything that made up the Universe. I failed, both divided in its categories and as one single object. Morning arrived, and, disenchanted, I awoke.* She reduced a great sea of erudition, subtleties, and elegance to this extremely narrow riverbed, and so her result had to be profound, and by consequence, difficult to understand for those who mistake depth for obscurity. But those who know the meaning of the schools of thought, histories, and fables that she touches on will understand her translations of allegorizing and allegorized extremes, resulting in their meeting. It is clear that our poetess never wrote another work that allows us to see the grandness of her subtle spirit with such lucidity.

Despite all these works that made Mother Juana Inés beloved and venerated by the noblest personages, she lived in ignorance of all praise, as if she had entered among the nuns to be no more than one of them. She did not wish to become the Mother Superior, nor

---

2. The metrical form of "First Dream," used also by Luis de Góngora in his *Soledades* (*The solitudes*) (1613).
3. The events depicted in de Góngora's unfinished *Solitudes* include a shipwrecked pilgrim washing ashore, attending a country wedding, departing with fishermen, and watching a hawking hunt taking place on land from the boat [*Translator*].

194   Diego Calleja

have any advantage or be singled out, as it is common that the spite
of fortune blocks such superior understanding from ruling. We even
mark slaves with letters, as though to say: this one was born to be
commanded. Those who knew her affirm that they had never seen
an equally perspicacious intelligence together with such naturally
clear candor. Nobody ever heard her utter a complaint or an impa-
tient remark; her comfort was her library, where she received the
consolation of four thousand[4] friends, which was the number of
books she gathered almost without cost, because there was no printer
who did not contribute a volume to her library, as they would to the
copyeditor.

In the year 1693, the divine Grace of our Lord settled its founda-
tional dwelling in the naturally clear and composed disposition of
our Sister Juana.

She took account of herself, recognizing that until then she had
only given God merely punctual payment in observation of the
law, an ungenerous repayment of her debts for His divine mercy.
Promising never to err by excusing licit actions with good motives,
she began her supererogation as carefully as if it were required. The
first diligence she made to declare war and conquer herself once and
for all without leaving hidden enemies was a general confession of
her past life. She took advantage of her prodigious memory, never
again dedicated to such an end, to take inventory of her life without
any dissembling. This general confession lasted several days, and
neither her condition nor her ignorance made her hesitate: to such
an illustrious mind, no demand seemed excessive in the examina-
tion of a life in which the tepidness, the confidences, the omissions
and paltriness mark a conscience with more than a few secret stains.
No air is so pure that you cannot feel the roiling of its atoms when
bathed by the sun. Since even this general confession failed to satisfy
this fearsome penitent, she then presented to the Divine Tribunal,
in the form of a juridical petition, a supplication limited neither by
discretion nor fervor. It will be printed in this third volume along
with other spiritual tracts and with two *Protests of Faith* that she
wrote in her blood, drawn without pain and reviewed with tenderness
every day.[5]

Mother Juana made her bitterest sacrifice, which she suffered
without showing the slightest tremor, when she unburdened herself
of her beloved books the way someone at the dawn of a clear day
might snuff out the now useless artificial light. She left a few for

4. Generally believed to be an exaggeration. See Marie-Cécile Bénassy-Berling, *Human-
ismo y religión en Sor Juana Inés de la Cruz*, trans. Laura López de Belair (México:
UNAM, 1983), 106–07.
5. See "Petition in Juridical Form" on p. 153.

her sister nuns and sent a copious number to the archbishop of Mexico to be sold as charity for the poor, so that in this way their contents could be used to more advantage than through study. This good fortune also befell her many rare and precious musical and mathematical instruments. The treasures, the trifles, and all other goods sent to her even from afar by illustrious personages, devotees of her famous name: she reduced it all to money which she offered as succor to many poor people, buying patience for them and salvation for herself. In her cell, she left no more than three books of devotion and several hair shirts and scourges.

Armed with this nakedness she entered into battle with herself. Her most continuous victory was to avoid appearing particularly spiritual before her sister nuns even while she was working to become spiritual in essence. Given that the many fasts and penances she undertook necessarily showed in her demeanor, she made even more effort to assure that this took on its old semblance and her conversation its light sweetness so that vanity would not devalue her virtue by dislodging its calm state.

Only her confessor—from whom it was neither possible nor desirable to hide the pitiless rigors with which she treated herself—knew about these and he tried to persuade her to diminish them. He was the aforementioned virtuous and wise father Antonio Núñez, who as we have already mentioned had directed her as a girl to leave behind her secular state and persuaded her that the best way to spurn the world was not to walk upon it.[6] It is worthy of admiration that this illustrious man, having demanded at the beginning of her youth that Juana Inés cut her hopes to the quick, could hardly convince through reasons, persuasions and even pleas, that the same woman, now another person, temper the rigor of her penitence. It must have been an attention-worthy performance to hear the results of this experienced man, so used to governing spirits, arguing in his venerable old age that the fervor of her beloved and fearful penitence was an indiscretion and she responding in his favor, and so against herself, with fervent solutions that even the arguer judged convincing, each leaving the pacific battle, she disconsolate in her relief and he praising God for creating a woman with such a profound intellect and wisdom and nevertheless such docile judgment.

His sainted family of Jesuits once asked father Antonio Núñez how it was that Mother Juana strove for perfection. And he responded: *it is necessary to mortify her so that she does not mortify herself excessively, keeping a firm hand on her penitence so that her health is not incapacitated, for Juana Inés does not run toward virtue: she flies.*

6. Sor Juana recounts the same in her "Letter by Mother Juana Inés de la Cruz," on p. 149.

Mother Juana spent her two last years in this fervent intimacy with God, such a desirable place to await death for those who do not fear it as the end of life but rather as the beginning of eternity. She survived through the end of 1695, a fertile one for heaven when there was a great harvest of pure souls from the convent of Saint Jerome and the city of Mexico. As pious reason might expect, even if it does not desire, one of them was Mother Juana Inés, who, like the wife in the Song of Songs[7] in proximity to other flowers, fell sick through her charity.

The convent was infected by such a pestilential epidemic that out of ten nuns who fell ill, only one recovered. It was a very contagious disease. Mother Juana, compassionate by nature and zealously charitable, ministered to everyone, without tiring from the continuous effort or guarding herself from infection. To advise her (as many did) that perhaps she should not get so close to the most afflicted was as useless as dressing her in the wings of a bee to convince her to flee from flowers. In the end, she fell ill. When the danger was recognized, the convent and city filled with prayers and offerings for her health; she was the only one who accepted her death, which everyone else feared, with hope. She ministered to herself with continual and painful remedies, chosen by her and in the same style as her painful and continued penitence. She received the final Sacraments just in time and with Catholic zeal; during the Eucharist she demonstrated her faith in his great tenderness, saying farewell to her spouse to see him soon and closer at hand. The severity of her illness, which was enough to take her life, could not cause even the slightest disturbance in her metal faculties. Like a faithful friend, her mind kept her company to the last cold and labored breaths she drew, after receiving extreme unction, but less than the prayers to Christ and his blessed Mother, which she did not let out of her hand or her mouth. Up to the end she showed her awareness, responding promptly and to the point to prayers for her soul. Once she passed away, these returned her spirit, not just in serene conformity but with active signs of desire, to the hands of her creator, at four in the morning on the seventeenth of April, Sabbath of the Good Shepherd in the year 1695.

---

7. Also called Song of Solomon; book of the Bible in which a husband expresses love for his wife through metaphors of flowers.

Historical Context

MARÍA ELENA MARTÍNEZ

From The Initial Stages and Socioreligious Roots
of the *Sistema de Castas*[†]

Testimonies to the Spanish colonial project to create a dichotomous
model of social organization, the first Mexican parish books contain-
ing baptismal, marriage, and death registers were divided into *libros
de españoles* (books of Spaniards) and *libros de indios* (books of Indi-
ans). During the first half of the seventeenth century, however, par-
ishes in different parts of New Spain started to keep separate records
for people of mixed ancestry, the "castas," who previously had tended
to be included in the books of Spaniards. Scholarship on colonial
Mexico has generally interpreted this change as a sign that the
sistema de castas had crystallized.[1] The system began to unfold in
the second half of the sixteenth century, a period that witnessed the
growth of a "mixed" population as well as a nomenclature referring
primarily to descent. By the end of the century, main colonial cat-
egories of difference, including *mestizo* and *mulato*, started to appear
in administrative records on a regular basis.

Spanish colonial categories of "mixture" partly drew on metro-
politan traditions. Beginning with the Council of Elvira (circa 314
C.E.), sexual intercourse between people of different religions was
the subject of continual ecclesiastical prohibitions, and eventually
marriages between Christians, Jews, and Muslims were not per-
mitted. The persistence of interreligious sexual unions during the

---

[†] From Chapter 6 of *Genealogical Fictions: Limpieza de Sangre, Religion, and Gender in
Colonial Mexico* (Stanford, CA: Stanford University Press, 2008), pp. 142–43, 161–67.
Copyright © by the Board of Trustees of the Leland Stanford Jr. University. All rights
reserved. Reprinted by permission of the publisher.
1. See, for example, Patricia Seed, *To Love, Honor, and Obey in Colonial Mexico: Conflicts
Over Marriage Choice, 1574–1821* (Stanford: Stanford University Press, 1988), p. 251 n.
25; and Cope, *The Limits of Racial Domination*, p. 24. Note that in certain places, par-
ish books for people of mixed ancestry were never kept, and in those that they were
(mainly in larger cities), the timing varied.

medieval period gave way to new terms for their "hybrid offspring" (*híbridos*), including that of *mozárabe* (mixed Arab), which initially referred to the children of a Christian and a Muslim.[2] This classificatory impulse intensified when the Spanish Inquisition began its genealogical investigations and efforts to determine people's degrees of Jewish, Christian, and Muslim blood. Given early modern Spain's acute concerns with lineage, purity, and categorization, the emergence of the colonial *sistema de castas* was perhaps to be expected. But the rise and form of that system can be explained only by social, political, and religious developments in Spanish America and the dynamic interaction of local and transatlantic processes, among them those set in motion by the African slave trade.

This chapter charts the origins of the *sistema de castas* in central New Spain. It first discusses main classificatory trends in sixteenth-century parish records, particularly the shift from a somewhat fluid system of categorization in which paternal ancestry was privileged, but not always, to a more rigid model based on both bloodlines. Focusing mainly on mestizos, this section attributes the shift at the end of the sixteenth century to processes of economic and political exclusion as well as to the establishment of the Inquisition and accentuation of Spanish anxieties over the religious proclivities and genealogical origins of the native populations. The chapter then examines the role of slavery in determining the juridical-theological status of blacks vis-à-vis that of the native people and more generally the place that African descent occupied within colonial society and its gendered order of blood symbols. The final section analyzes the Spanish colonial language of "race," particularly the concepts of raza and casta, and the influence that religious notions of blood purity had on the system of classification's principal categories.

⁎ ⁎ ⁎

Raza, Casta, and Limpieza de Sangre:
The Spanish Colonial Language of Race

Raza and *casta*, terms central to early modern Spain's lexicon of blood, both referred to breed, species, and lineage, and could thus be used interchangeably to describe groupings of animals, plants, or humans.[3] Their uses and connotations were not identical, however. Whereas the first became strongly identified with descent from

2. AHN, Inquisición, libro 1266. The word *mozárabe* eventually came to designate Christians who had lived under Muslim rule (especially in Toledo) and adopted aspects of Islamic culture.

3. Corominas, *Diccionario crítico etimológico de la lengua castellana*, pp. 722–24. Corominas disagreed with Covarrubias's claim that the word *casta* derived from the Latin *castus*, which alluded to chastity.

Jews and Muslims and acquired negative connotations, the second remained more neutral and was hence more frequently applied to Old Christians.[4] But *casta* also had multiple meanings. If as a noun it was usually linked to lineage, as an adjective it could allude to chastity, nobility ("good breeding"), and legitimacy, and more generally to an uncorrupted sexual and genealogical history. *Casta* was thereby able to give way to the term *castizo*, which referred to notable ancestry.[5] By implication, the mother of a castizo would have been casta, a woman who had remained faithful to her husband. When applied to humans, then, the sixteenth-century Spanish word *casta* and its various connotations were alluding to a system of social order centered around procreation and biological parenthood, one in which reproducing the pure and noble "caste" was mainly predicated on maintaining the chastity of its women. Whether in Spain or Spanish America, notions of genealogical purity and their privileging of endogamic marriage and legitimate birth were never divorced from discourses of gender and female sexuality, from a sexual economy constituted by gendered notions of familial honor.

In the colonial context, Spaniards came up with even more uses for the word *casta*, for by the mid-sixteenth century it was functioning, in the plural, as an umbrella term for the children of "mixed" unions.[6] In Mexico, this application of the term began around the mid-sixteenth century, almost simultaneous with the rise of a nomenclature distinguishing people of different lineages, its first and most enduring terms being *mestizo* and *mulato*. Hence, when later in the sixteenth century Diego de Simancas, a man of Spanish and native parentage, was tried by the Mexican Inquisition for allegedly believing that Jesus was not the true son of God, he was asked to declare not his "race," but his "caste."[7] The dominant colonial usage of the term *casta* simultaneously signaled the importance of reproduction and sexuality to the colonial order and the increasing

4. Domínguez Ortiz made the same observation in *La clase de los conversos en Castilla en la edad moderna*, p. 55.
5. "Castizos," stated Covarrubias, "we call those that derive from good lineage and caste." *Tesoro de la lengua castellana*, p. 282.
6. Because the word *casta* referred to people who were "mixed," it meant the opposite of what *caste* meant when the British (who borrowed it from the Portuguese) applied it to the Hindu system of social differentiation, which was based on endogamous social groups. In Spanish America, then, the *sistema de castas* was a function of the instability, not rigidity, of "caste." See Julian Pitt-Rivers, "On the Word 'Caste,'" in *The Translation of Culture: Essays to E. E. Evans-Pritchard*, ed. T. O. Beidelman (London: Tavistock, 1971), pp. 234–35. Iberians also used the word *casta* to designate the place of origin of slaves who had been born in Africa (as in *casta angola*) and thus applied it to "pure" blacks. According to Leslie Rout, all blacks were considered part of the castas, even if they had no native or Spanish ancestry, because it was African blood itself, not necessarily mixture, that was deemed to have a degenerating effect. Leslie B. Rout, *The African Experience in Spanish America* (Cambridge: Cambridge University Press, 1976), p. 127.
7. AGN, Inquisición, Caja 163, fols. 1–37v.

anxieties about being able to control them. The Augustinian friar Nicolás de Witte expressed these anxieties in 1552, when he wrote about the difficulty of maintaining peace in Mexico. The land, he noted,

> is engendering and is being populated by a mixture of evil people. For it is clear that this land is full of mestizos, who are [born] so badly inclined. It is full of black men and women who derive from slaves. It is full of black men who marry Indian women, from which derive mulattos. And it is full of mestizos who marry Indian women, from which derive a diverse caste [casta] of infinite number, and from all of these mixtures derive other diverse and not very good mixtures.[8]

The emerging system of classification relied on the idea that each of the three main colonial categories—Spaniards, Indians, and blacks—was characterized by a unity of substance that was maintained through endogamy but could be broken through sexual intercourse outside the group. As other naturalizing discourses, the sistema de castas[9] held sex as a productive act that could pollute or dilute blood, which in turn could generate sick and degenerate beings, or at the very least pose classificatory problems within the hierarchy of allegedly natural categories.[1] Indeed, the system allowed for a virtually infinite number of castes to be produced. Did the premises of the sistema de castas and in particular the belief in discreet human groups challenge the theory of monogenesis? Not according to Gregorio García. Realizing the dangerous theological implications of applying the concepts of purity and mixture to people, he pointed out that mestizo animals could come from distinct creatures but be part of the same species. Likewise, individuals could belong to different "nations" or "lineages" but be part of the same Adam-derived human species.[2] García seemed to be echoing Fray Juan de Pineda's discussion, in his *Diálogos familiares de la agricultura cristiana* (1578–1580), of marriages between Old Christians and New Christians and in particular his comparison of horse breeding with human reproduction to argue that even though all people derived from the founding biblical couple, some lineages were better than others and therefore should avoid mixing with lesser ones. The influence of understandings of reproduction in the natural world on Spanish thinking about human reproduction proved to be even stronger in the colonial context, as evidenced, for example, by the numerous casta categories created from zoological terms.

8. AGI, México 280. The author's translation and interpolations.
9. Literally, caste system, or racial taxonomy [*Editor*].
1. See Williams, "Classification Systems Revisited," pp. 201–36.
2. García, *Origen de los indios del Nuevo Mundo*, p. 65.

Once the term *casta* was applied to people of mixed ancestry, it began to acquire negative connotations, but it remained distinct from the concept of raza and its religious undertones. Hence, mestizos, mulattos, and in a general sense also Spaniards and Indians were considered castes, lineages, but not necessarily races. Or rather, not all of these categories were thought to have "race." Anthropologist Laura Lewis is thus partly correct when she asserts that early modern Spain elaborated an exclusionary discourse on race within its peninsular borders at the same time that it created a more inclusive system of caste in the Americas, one that allowed the different castas to claim to be connected through genealogical or symbolic kinship ties.[3] Such a rigid distinction between the two systems of differentiation cannot be drawn, however. Not only did caste in the colonies become racialized over time, an increasingly naturalizing discourse, but as stressed earlier, by the late sixteenth century, Iberian notions of race and impurity had started to be used against persons of African ancestry. This use was captured in the probanzas de limpieza de sangre. In 1599, for example, Cristóbal Ruiz de Quiroz submitted his genealogical information to the Franciscan Order in Puebla in order to prove that he descended from "a clean caste and generation, without the race or mixture of Moors, mulattoes, blacks, Jews or the newly converted to the Holy Catholic Faith."[4] The following year, Pedro Serrano, a native of Seville who applied to be a royal secretary in the Philippines, submitted his genealogical information in order to establish that his ancestors had not been tried by the Holy Office and that they were pure Old Christians, "clean from the races of moriscos, Jews, blacks and mulattoes."[5]

The extension of Castilian notions of race and impurity to persons of African ancestry was also reflected in casta nomenclature. For example, the term *mestizo*, which surfaced in the 1530s and by the next decade had become almost synonymous with illegitimacy, simply meant "mixed" and had been used in Spain mainly to refer to the mixture of different animal species.[6] The category of *mulato*, which in the Spanish colonies appeared on a regular basis only as of 1549, referred to the children of Spaniards and blacks and in general to anyone with partial African ancestry. In both Mexico and Peru, it was initially applied to persons of either black–Spanish or

3. Lewis, *Hall of Mirrors*, pp. 22–25.
4. JCBL/LI, vol. 1, fols. 487–91. Also see JCBL/LI, vol. 2, fols. 207–14: información of Alonso Gómez, made in the Villa de Niebla (Spain), 1617.
5. AGI, México 121, r. 1.
6. Covarrubias Orozco, *Tesoro de la lengua castellana*, p. 751. For Corominas, the word *mestizo* was of uncertain origin, but he speculated that it might have come from the Latin *mixtus*. Corominas, *Diccionario crítico etimológico de la lengua castellana*, vol. 3, p. 359.

black–native parentage, but in the seventeenth century, a separate, though sporadically used, category for the latter was created, that of *zambahigo* (*zambo* in Peru).[7] According to Solórzano Pereira, the term *mulato* was used to describe the offspring of Spaniards and blacks because they were considered an uglier and more unique mixture than mestizos and because the word conveyed the idea that their nature was akin to that of mules.[8] Although both *mestizo* and *mulato* derived from a zoological vocabulary and implied crossbreeding, their use marked an important difference in Spanish attitudes toward reproduction with blacks and indigenous people.

Covarrubias, who also linked the word *mulato* to that of *mule*, pointed out that mules were bastard animals, a "third species" that was produced by the crossing of horses with donkeys and that could reproduce only under extraordinary circumstances.[9] As such, the term was reminiscent of *alboraico* (or *alboraique*), a pejorative name for conversos. Originally the word referred to the Prophet Muhammad's fabled animal, which was neither horse nor mule, but in fifteenth-century Spain, it was used to convey that the New Christians were neither Jews nor Christians but a kind of unnatural or third species, one that presumably had difficulties reproducing. In the case of the term *mulato*, its trope of infertility perhaps served the same function in the Spanish colonial world that it had in the French colonies: simultaneously easing white anxieties about the uncontrolled growth of populations descending from slaves and sanctioning the continued sexual exploitation of enslaved women by their masters.[1] What is clear is that the word *mulato*, which for some Spaniards connoted ugliness, was inextricably linked to social and reproductive relations promoted by the institution of slavery and incipient Western notions of beauty and race.

Spanish views about reproduction with blacks versus native people become even more evident in the next two casta categories that surfaced in central Mexico: castizo and morisco. These for the most part did not appear in early parish registers but were used in some colonial administrative and Inquisition documents. *Castizo*, which emerged in the last third of the sixteenth century, referred to the

7. Forbes writes that, in Mexico, the term *mulato* continued to be used for the descendants of blacks and Indians into the 1650s and that within the Spanish empire, the term generally meant a person who was half African and half something else. As such, it could be applied to various combinations. Jack D. Forbes, *Black Africans and Native Americans: Color, Race and Caste in the Evolution of Red-Black Peoples* (New York: Basil Blackwell, 1988), pp. 162–65. Forbes also notes that the term *mulato* initially appeared in legislation relating to the Americas (p. 173), but it is not clear whether it was first used in the colonial or Iberian context.
8. Solórzano Pereira, *Política Indiana*, vol. 1, p. 445.
9. Covarrubias, *Tesoro de la lengua castellana*, p. 768.
1. See Doris Garraway, "Race, Reproduction and Family Romance in Moreau de Saint-Méry's Description . . . de la partie française de l'isle Saint-Domingue," *Eighteenth-Century Studies* 38, no. 2 (2005): 227–46.

child of a Spaniard and a mestizo, that is, to someone who was three-quarters Spanish and one-quarter Indian.[2] *Morisco* was at first more ambiguous, for it was associated with Islam, blacks, or both.[3] In New Spain, it continued to be applied to Muslim converts to Christianity. Thus, in the early 1600s, María Ruiz, a morisca residing in Mexico City and native of Granada, Spain, was tried for being a follower of the "sect of Muhammad."[4] In subsequent decades, the word *morisco* increasingly referred to the children of Spaniards and mulattos. For example, in 1631, the Mexican Inquisition tried Agustín, a "morisco or mulatto," for idolatry; in 1658, it reviewed the case of Beatriz de Padilla, "an unmarried morisca, daughter of a Spaniard and a free mulata"; and in 1693, it tried Francisca de Chiquacen, a "mulatto of the morisco race" (*"mulata de raza morisca"*) for sorcery.[5]

Needless to say, the terms *castizo* and *morisco* carried significantly different cultural baggage. In Spain, the first had been used to describe a person of good lineage and caste and the second to designate ex-Muslims, thus carrying connotations of religious infidelity. It is true that when Mexican Inquisition officials first explained the meaning of *castizo* in their 1576 letter to the Suprema, they did not associate the category with any redeeming qualities. Nevertheless, the displacement of a word that in Castile mainly had positive connotations onto the children of mestizos and Spaniards was no linguistic accident. It not only acknowledged the aristocratic bloodlines of some castizos, descendants of Spanish conquerors and noble native women, but also signaled the construction of a specific type

2. The Mexican Holy Office, for instance, used the word *castizo* in the 1570s and stated that it was a term commonly applied in New Spain to the children of mestizos (and presumably Spaniards). AHN, Inquisición de México, libro 1047, fols. 430–34: Correspondence from the Mexican Inquisition to the Supreme Council of the Inquisition, November 5, 1576. Also see AHN, Inquisición, libro 1064: Summary report of the bigamy case against Bartolomé Hernández, "castizo," native of the city of los Ángeles (Puebla), 1578.
3. In 1539, for example, Viceroy Mendoza instructed Mexico City, Puebla, and other cities not to allow *negros* or *moriscos*, whether free or slave, as well as Indians, to carry arms without special permission. BNAHMC, Serie Puebla, roll 81, fol. 12v. Viceroy Mendoza also ordered that any "negro, negra o morisca" who made pulque be punished with two hundred lashes. Condumex (Mexico City), Fondo CMLXI-36, fol. 46. Also see AAPAC, vol. 1, doc. 234: Puebla's city council orders penalties for anyone helping "runaway moriscos or black slaves," March 2, 1537. Noting the association that Spaniards in Peru made between blacks and moriscos, Lockhart speculated that the latter, who were usually described as white, were either Muslim Spaniards or slaves from Morocco, but in Mexican sources there is not enough information to determine whether that was the case. James Lockhart, *Spanish Peru, 1532–1560* (Madison: University of Wisconsin Press, 1974), p. 196.
4. See AHN, Inquisición, libro 1064.
5. AGN, Inquisición, vol. 372, exp. 14; AHN, Inquisición, libro 1065; and AGN, Inquisición, vol. 684, exp. 4. Note the deployment of the word *raza* to describe moriscos. For more on Beatriz de Padilla's case, see Solange Alberro, "Beatriz de Padilla, Mulatta Mistress and Mother," in *Colonial Spanish America: A Documentary History*, eds. Kenneth Mills and William Taylor (Wilmington, DE: SR Books, 1998), pp. 178–84.

of discourse of "mixture," one that recognized the purity, or potential purity, of native lineages (especially if they were noble).

Indeed, in the last decades of the sixteenth century, royal policies began to privilege castizos over other castas, namely, by making them eligible for the priesthood and (like mestizos) exempt from paying tribute.[6] Furthermore, the Holy Office started to consider them eligible for the status of purity of blood. Thus, in 1590, the canon Santiago was commissioned by the Mexican Inquisition to investigate the purity of blood of Juan de Reina and his wife in order to determine if he was eligible to work for the Holy Office. After some inquiries, Santiago wrote to the Suprema requesting instructions because he had discovered that Reina's wife was not a "castiza hija de mestiza," but a "mestiza hija de India." She was not the product of a union between a Spaniard and a mestiza, as he had assumed, but rather of a union between a Spaniard and an Indian woman.[7] Santiago's letter clearly implied that the category of castizo was compatible with the status of purity of blood. In the early seventeenth century, the Suprema received a number of similar letters, which led it to instruct colonial Inquisition officials to grant purity certification to those candidates for offices or familiaturas who had no more than one-fourth Indian blood (cuarto de indio). Other colonial establishments, including the Franciscan Order, instituted the same policy.[8]

Although the sistema de castas lent itself to the production of a great number of classifications, only a handful appeared in a consistent fashion in Mexican colonial records such as parish registers, tax lists, and censuses. Besides Spaniard, Indian, and black, these categories mainly consisted of mestizo, mulato, castizo, morisco, and zambahigo (or zambaigo), and in the eighteenth century, also lobo, coyote, pardo, moreno, and occasionally chino.[9] That a relatively small number of terms figure in legal records does not mean, however, that others were not in everyday use. As numerous documents

---

6. See, for example, Philip II's 1582 letter to Mexican secular and religious officials, which clarifies that any previous decrees limiting the access of mestizos to the priesthood should be understood to apply only to the children of Indian and Spanish unions, not to their subsequent descendants. See Konetzke, *Colección de documentos para la historia*, pp. 543–44.

7. AGN, Inquisición, vol. 82, exp. 4, fol. 118.

8. See AHN, Inquisición de México, libro 1057; and Morales, *Ethnic and Social Background of the Franciscan Friars in Seventeenth-Century Mexico*, pp. 16–17.

9. *Lobo* (wolf) and *coyote* are zoological terms, while *pardo* and *moreno* refer to skin color and were applied to people of partial African descent. In casta paintings, the classification *chino* was designated to the child of a black and native woman, but colonial officials often used it as a generic name for Asians, particularly from the Philippines. Thus, when the religious official in charge of the Provisorato or Inquisition for indigenous people changed his title in the eighteenth century, he became "Provisor de Indios y Chinos del Arzobispado" because his jurisdiction extended to the Philippines. AHN, Inquisición, leg. 2286 (1).

containing legal petitions or witness testimonies indicate, categories such as "mestiza coyota," "mulato lobo," and "coyote mestizo" circulated among the population, and composite zoological names became increasingly common in the second half of the colonial period.[1] But the appearance and relevance of certain terms varied by region and period. The system of classification was even less rigid in the northern Mexican frontier, for example, than it was in central New Spain.[2] Even within the same region, their use was often inconsistent and influenced by a number of subjective and situational factors.[3] The process of recording caste classifications in parish archives was itself fraught with complications. Ancestral information provided at the time of a birth or marriage was not always trustworthy, for example, and parish priests were sometimes less than rigorous in their use of categories.

If in practice the use of classifications tended to be anything but systematic, the sistema de castas was nonetheless a system, an ideological complex constituted by a set of underlying principles about generation, regeneration; and degeneration. These principles linked main casta categories with specific proportions of Spanish, Indian, and black blood; made certain mixtures compatible with purity; and distinguished between people who descended from Spaniards and Indians and those who had African ancestry. Although they did not go unchallenged, the organizing assumptions behind the sistema continued to operate throughout the colonial period, influencing colonial power relations, individual and group identities, and Mexican definitions of purity, race, and nation.

1. See AGN, Bienes Nacionales, vol. 578, exp. 21; and AHN, Inquisición, libro 1067, fols. 316–18, and 500–500v. Casta nomenclature came mainly from a zoological vocabulary, particularly from the breeding of horses and cattle. See Nicolás León, *Las castas del México colonial* (Mexico City: Talleres Gráficos del Museo Nacional de Arqueología, Historia y Etnografía, 1924), p. 27; and Daisy Rípodas Ardanaz, *El matrimonio en Indias: Realidad social y regulación jurídica* (Buenos Aires: Fundación para la Educación, la Ciencia y la Cultura, 1977), p. 26.

2. Ramón A. Gutiérrez, *When Jesus Came, the Corn Mothers Went Away: Marriage, Sexuality and Power in New Mexico, 1500–1846* (Stanford, CA: Stanford University Press, 1991), pp. 196–200; Jackson, "Race/caste and the Creation and Meaning of Identity," p. 155; and Steven W. Hackel, *Children of Coyote, Missionaries of Saint Francis: Indian-Spanish Relations in Colonial California, 1769–1850* (Chapel Hill: Omohundro Institute of Early American History and Culture and University of North Carolina Press, 2005), pp. 59–60.

3. See, among others, Patricia Seed, "Social Dimensions of Race: Mexico City, 1753," *Hispanic American Historical Review* 62, no. 4 (1982): pp. 568–606; Cope, *The Limits of Racial Domination*, pp. 49–67; Schwartz, "Colonial Identities and the *Sociedad de Castas*," pp. 185–201; and Richard Boyer, *Cast [sic] and Identity in Colonial Mexico: A Proposal and an Example* (Storrs, CT; Providence, RI; and Amherst, MA: Latin American Studies Consortium of New England, 1997).

ASUNCIÓN LAVRIN

From Sor Juana Inés de la Cruz: Obedience and Authority in Her Religious Context[†]

Almost three hundred years after her death, the figure of Sor Juana Inés de la Cruz continues to prove elusive for historians. The search for traces of trustworthy historical information on which to support new inferences has not yielded much fruit.[1] Sor Juana gave us her own autobiographical writing—which continues to occupy the passions of eminent critics, but has engaged historians more sparsely— yet she kept silent on many key aspects of her life that could have given us a better understanding. In her recent analysis of two Sor Juana biographies by Dorothy Schons and Octavio Paz, Georgina Sabat-Rivers[2] demonstrates the way two eminent scholars confronted and resolved in their own ways the challenge of recreating her life with the scarcity of verifiable facts—and the problems that arise from that situation.

For the historian, the most accessible objective is to come to a better understanding of the reality in which Sor Juana lived, delving into archives to illuminate anything that could bring us closer to the ways she and her contemporaries lived, thought, and felt. This work is elliptical and does not spare me from having to interpret, but I believe my contribution will make the ground we tread on more certain. In a work from 1982, I framed Sor Juana within the category of other nun writers to underscore differences between her and her

---

[†] From Asunción Lavrin, "Sor Juana Inés de la Cruz: Obediencia y autoridad en su entorno religioso," *Revista Iberoamericana* 61.172–73 (1995): 605–09, 611–12, 614–15. Translated for this edition by Isabel Gómez. Reproduced by permission of the Instituto Internacional de Literatura Iberoamericana. All notes are Lavrin's unless otherwise indicated.

1. The search for material in the archives of Mexico and Spain brought to light much information about the family and birth of Sor Juana. The most recent find is the so-called "Letter of Monterrey." No new documents have been found that reveal more historical data about her. See Aureliano Tapia Méndez, ed. *Carta espiritual de Sor Juana Inés de la Cruz a su confesor: Autodefensa espiritual* (Monterrey: Impresora Monterrey, S.A. 1986); Guillermo Ramírez España, *La familia de Sor Juana Inés de la Cruz: Documentos inéditos.* México: Imprenta Universitaria, 1947. 12–21. The "Letter of Monterrey" has been translated to English by Nina M. Scott, "If You Are Not Pleased to Favor Me, Put Me Out of Your Mind . . . ," Gender and Authority in Sor Juana Inés de la Cruz, *Women's Studies Forum.* 11.5 (1988): 429–38. [The "Letter by Mother Juana Inés de la Cruz," on p. 144, is also known as the "Letter of Monterry"—*Editor*]

2. "Biografías: Sor Juana vista por Dorothy Schons y Octavio Paz" in Georgina Sabat-Rivers, *Sor Juana Inés de la Cruz y otros poetas Barrocos de la Colonia.* Barcelona: PPU, 1992. 327–39. Schons fictionalized on the basis of scant historical detail, but she managed a noteworthy and empathetic approximation. Paz wraps his work in a more ample cover of academic studies, presenting us with a much more extensive investigation that is also woven through with his own reading. All of us who approach this multifaceted writer must take flight through interpretation when information is lacking, and consequently, we must accept that there is space for other interpretations.

cloistered companions. In another more recent and still unpublished work, I was supported by knowledge of women and gender relations in the mid-seventeenth century to evaluate the extent to which certain traits of her life as a woman were shared with other women of her time.[3] In the present work, I explore the theme of religious obedience and disobedience in the relationship between prelates, nuns, and royal authorities, using examples primarily from the seventeenth century. I use this information to revise one critical aspect of the life of Sor Juana and all nuns: the duty to obey ecclesiastical authority as opposed to the urgency to reaffirm their own existence through intellectual and spiritual expression.

To consider the tension between these conceptual poles, we must keep in mind that it involved the prelates as much as the nuns. The sisters saw the binary authority-obedience as a personal relationship with their confessors and as a community facing orders from religious superiors or the representatives of civil authority, acting in the name of the interests of the state. For their part, the prelates assumed broad dominion over their spiritual daughters, but that implied responsibility to guide them towards the clearly defined goal of the salvation of their souls and not a mere exercise of power. The prelates were also members of a sociopolitical hierarchy, which made them responsible for the interests of their corporation in relation to other entities and authorities. This web of obligations led the bishops, archbishops, and provincial ministers of the religious orders into frequent conflict and the need to confront problems of authority, obedience, and disobedience in relation to the community of nuns and the Crown.

The importance of studying the religious context of Sor Juana resides, for me, in an attempt to comprehend her special relationship with the men who had decisive influence over her life. I think it is possible and desirable to reconsider the frequently debated topic of the relationship Sor Juana had with Bishop Manuel Fernández de Santa Cruz (and with her confessor Antonio Núñez)[4] through the prism of religious vows and the significance of concepts of obedience and authority. The study of religious writing by Sor Juana and its possible theological vein is quite recent, and it is still fitting to ask: what do we know about her life as a nun or her relationships

---

3. "Sor Juana Inés de la Cruz: A Woman Among Women," Paper given at Pomona College, March 3–4, 1989, Conference on "Sor Juana Inés de la Cruz: Portraits and Perspectives"; "Unlike Sor Juana? The Model Run in the Religious Literature of Colonial Mexico," *University of Dayton Review*, 16:2 (Spring 1983), 75–92. Reissued in Stephanie Merrim ed., *Towards a Feminist Understanding of Sor Juana Inés de la Cruz* (Detroit: Wayne State University Press, 1990), 61–85.

4. Antonio Núñez de Miranda (1618–1695), Jesuit who wrote several treatises on feminine spirituality and served as Sor Juana's confessor at the beginning and end of her years in the convent. Manuel Fernández de Santa Cruz (1639–1699), bishop of Puebla [*Editor*].

with those who directed her?[5] Little or nothing, until the discovery of the so-called *Letter of Monterrey*, and, of course, the "Response" to Bishop Fernández de Santa Cruz. As far as strictly historical material—not writing of a religious quality—we have very little.

Prelates in the seventeenth century, and even into the eighteenth, brought from Spain a vision of religious life rooted in the Counter-Reformation, and they found a very different reality in the New World. Their work was to execute a cultural-religious transference and to guide their new flock within Catholic orthodoxy, yet without overlooking what was suitable in America. Did they achieve this, or not? We cannot yet answer this question thoroughly, without knowing much more about pastoral writing and the practice of spiritual direction exercised by archbishops and bishops over their religious daughters during the seventeenth century to begin to untangle spirituality and the practice of episcopal authority and religious obedience in the Baroque world of New Spain. But, judging by the information at hand, there were many hurdles in the path to perfection caused by the mismatch between peninsular and American [cultures] that, joined by the personal and institutional problems cited above, make the study of religious life a task full of surprises.[6]

I approach the theme of the ecclesiastical context in which Sor Juana lived through my investigations in Spanish and Mexican archives, using the religious literature of that time to support my version of a few key moments in her life. It is important to begin with a reminder of the significance of one of the four essential vows of monastic life: the vow of obedience. Antonio Núñez de Miranda of the Society of Jesus defined it as the renunciation of one's personal will to subject oneself to the will of one's prelates; it was a mortal sin to fail to comply perfectly. For this Jesuit, as much as for other theologians contemporary to Sor Juana, the prelates including the

5. George H. Tavard, *Juana Inés de la Cruz and the Theology of Beauty* (Notre Dame, Indiana: University of Notre Dame Press, 1991); Georgina Sabat-Rivers, "Ejercicios de la Encarnación: sobre la imagen de María y la decision final de Sor Juana" in Sabat-Rivers, *Sor Juana Inés de la Cruz y otros poetas*, 257–82; Amanda Powell, "Women's Reasons: Feminism and Spirituality in Old and New Spain" *Studia Mystica* 15:2–3 (Summer–Fall 1992): 58–69; Josefina Muriel, "Sor Juana Inés de la Cruz y los escritos del Padre Antonio Núñez" in Sara Poot Herrera, ed., *Y Diversa de mi misma entre vuestras plumas anto: Homenaje internacional a Sor Juana Inés de la Cruz* (Mexico: El Colegio de Mexico, 1993), 71–84.
6. Marie-Cécile Bénassy-Berling, *Humanisme et Religion chez Sor Juana Inés de la Cruz: la femme et la culture au XVIIè Siècle* (Paris: Publications de la Sorbonne, 1982); José L. Sánchez Lora, *Mujeres, conventos y formas de la religiosidad baroca* (Madrid: Fundación Universitaria española, 1988); Electa Arenal y Georgina Sabat-Rivers, eds., *Literatura conventual femenina: Sor Marcela de San Félix, hija de Lope de Vega. Obra Completa* (Madrid: PPU, 1988); Manuel Ramos Medina, *Imagen de santidad en un mundo profano* (México: Universidad Iberoamericana, 1990); Clara García Ayluardo y Manuel Ramos, coord., *Manifestaciones religiosas en el mundo colonial americano*, Vol. I (México, 1993); Kathleen Myers, *Word from New Spain: The Spiritual Autobiography of Madre María de San José (1656–1719)* (Liverpool, UK: University of Liverpool Press, 1993).

Abbesses in their function as the highest authority within the convent, exercised their authority in the name of Jesus. The nun as a religious subject was obliged to do whatever they ordered, promptly and gladly, judging theirs better than her own opinion. In particular, she owed her confessor obedience to the letter.[7]

* * *

Obedience had its limits. It did not negate sovereignty of being, the authority every individual holds over him or herself in the full capacity of free will. All people maintain that God-given faculty: the freedom to make decisions, and the decision to obey is, in itself, irrevocably and appropriately individual. When an order opposed an established rule, or carried with it a capital sin, one could disobey.[8] This theoretically small escape-hatch was utilized frequently—as much by religious subjects as by the New Spanish prelates—when the circumstances required it and also when the reasons were not so clear or self-evident. Precisely because authority was not exercised without challenge, nor was obedience given unconditionally, there existed many administrative and personal tensions within the religious state. Modes of disobedience existed within parameters of obedience, which permitted prelates and religious subjects to avoid one another or avoid their superiors and pursue their own courses of action. Although it is still not fully appreciated, this play on the limits of obedience and authority was a determining factor that oriented historical events.

* * *

Other sources of friction between authority and obedience from the first decades of the seventeenth century included observance of the rules related to the number of servants and laypeople of all ages who could be housed in convents, the cut and fabric used to make habits, and the receipt of visitors in the convent *locutorios*,[9] realities that in the Bishop's opinion "relaxed" the observance of religious discipline, materially and spiritually. For more than a century and a half, Mexico received patents and orders from Spain, directed to seated Bishops and regulars, about the necessity of reforming such customs. Mexican nuns were recalcitrant when it came to defending

---

7. Antonio Núñez, *Plática doctrinal . . . en la profesión de una Señora religiosa del convento de San Lorenzo* (México, 1710), 6; *Cartilla de la doctrina religiosa* (México, 1708), 12.
8. In 1803, the archbishop of Mexico Francisco Javier Lizana y Beaumont (1802–11) explained that the only valid way to depart from the precept of obedience was when to obey would put one at risk of breaking other vows. Obedience should be based on judgment, free will, and effort, like that of the sheep who listens to her shepherd. See: *Carta pastoral a las RR.MM. superioras y súbditas del Arzobispado de México*. México, 1803. 19–22.
9. Reception rooms in convents that allowed visitors to converse with nuns who remained behind a grille [*Editor*].

their interpretation of the rules and their right to maintain servants as well as orphans and pupils in their cloisters.

During his prelature in Puebla, Juan de Palafox y Mendoza (1640–1655) made a pragmatic concession to the reality he found in his diocese. He concluded that, while the nuns did keep many servants in their convents in the Indies, this was also a very "difficult abuse to remedy without serious scandal, and therefore it will be better to guide the manner in which it is carried out. Since it is no longer possible to do away with it, it is better that it be supervised . . ." In other words, let the abuse be well regulated.[1] On the other hand, other prelates arrived from Spain with a degree of intolerance in this matter that created friction with their spiritual daughters who resisted the discipline they wished to impose on them. In 1677 the Franciscan nuns of Mexico [City] and Querétaro found themselves embroiled in a legal battle against their own prelate, Fray Hernando de la Rúa, who insisted they reduce the number of servants in the convents. That year the orders about observance given by the General Commission of the Indies in Spain in 1639 were reinstated; among them was the reduction of the number of laypeople of all categories in convents. In Santa Clara of Querétaro, the nuns erected a memorial to the King in which they argued that they had professed [their vows] with the understanding that they would have the help of servants, and that these girls were not against the rules.[2]

This same year, the Franciscan convents San Juan the Penitent and Santa Isabel sent appeals to the General Commissary of the Indies to the King,[3] defending the practice of having servants as a custom of that land since its foundation eighty years before. Any changes to the internal observance or regulation of convent life needed to be calibrated to the "characteristics of the region and its customs." The nuns of Santa Isabel complained that the Provincial Commission had prohibited them from dressing in linen, consuming chocolate, keeping girls in the convent to receive an education, and that they had been ordered to expel all their servants. Since many other holy men had approved their observance, how could La Rúa presume that he was holier than those others? This underhanded commentary was aimed at reducing his authority. Nevertheless, La Rúa was not a friend of ceding authority: he simply excommunicated the protesters, and took steps to remove them from their offices within the convent.

---

1. Juan de Palafox y Mendoza, Bishop of Puebla, *Obras del Ilustrísimo, Excelentíssimo, y Venerable Siervo de Dios, Tomo III, Part I, Direcciones para los señores obispos,* Madrid: Imprenta de Gabriel Ramírez, 1752. 46.
2. Biblioteca Nacional de México, Fondo Franciscano, Box 75, Leg. 1257, fols. 12–22.
3. In the Franciscan order, the official charged with oversight of the Americas [*Editor*].

This scandalous process involved the Viceroy Marquis de Mancera (1664–1674), who sought to be an intermediary between the religious communities, their Prelate, and the council. Putting himself on the side of the nuns, he ordered the Commissioner to lift the excommunication. La Rúa tried to not obey the order of the Council, accusing the nuns of "obstinate disobedience" contrary to the "monastic moderation needed in these regions." Obviously there is an underlying consciousness of the difference between religious observance on the Peninsula and that followed in "these regions," which the Spanish prelates were trying to erase. Behind the whole process there is a vein of incipient *criollismo*[4] that was not exploited openly by any of the parties, although its presence is perceptible.

The prelate lifted the excommunication, but the last word arrived from Spain. When the highest power of the Viceroyalty intervened, this implied an interference of secular power in ecclesiastical matters that did not pass unnoticed. The Crown reprimanded the Council for taking steps beyond their proper domain and left the prelate at liberty to direct his flock.[5] The rift between rule and observance, prelate and subject, remained open. In the Santa Clara convent of Querétaro, it was reduced to nothing once the nuns resorted to a direct appeal to the Pope, going over the heads of the Archbishop and the Royal Council to obtain ratification from His Holiness about the number of servants they argued they should be able to have.[6]

* * *

These frictions have revealed themselves little by little through archival research, and some stand out with far more stridency than the disagreement between Sor Juana and Father Antonio Núñez, which, although we did not study it here, did not have the social repercussions of the former cases. Convinced by this evaluation, I want to revisit the celebrated exchange between Sor Juana and the Bishop Manuel Fernández de Santa Cruz,[7] and reframe it within the context of religious life of her time. Departing from the premise that Sor Juana, as subject to her prelates and as a nun, was obliged to obey her religious superiors and although she could not legitimately evade fulfilling this essential element of her condition, she could

4. In this context refers to ways of thinking, being, or identifying within the culture of individuals born in the New World to Spanish parentage but differentiating themselves from the Spanish peninsular culture and worldview. A person born in the Spanish colonies could be a *criollo* and might exhibit *criollismo*, as in this example, where there is a growing belief that the convents of New Spain should regulate themselves based on their own circumstances. This should not be confused with the French words *creole* or *créolité*, terms developed in the Francophone Antilles that tend to refer to ideas of culture derived from racial and ethnic mixture [*Translator*].
5. AGI (Archivo general de Indias), Escribanía de Cámara, leg. 175 A.
6. AGI, Mexico, Leg. 306.
7. See headnote on p. 83 [*Editor*].

certainly express her doubts in that respect. Within the imperative of obedience, her spirit forced her to live out her freedom and establish respect for her intellectual free will. The battle was hard fought, and the episode with the Bishop is an example of a reality that other nuns also lived. As has been observed, there are subtle differences between the defiant letter to Father Núñez and her correspondence with the Archbisop. Sor Juana had to take a different position before them, given that the Bishop did not have the same spiritual intimacy with her that Núñez had.[8]

The relationship between Fernández de Santa Cruz and Sor Juana was special to the extent that Sor Juana was not a spiritual daughter or subject of the prelate, which limited him to merely canonical authority over her, giving Sor Juana more space for intellectual dialogue. Regardless, the relationship between a prince of the Church and a nun, whether or not she was a subject of his order, demanded respect to the hierarchies of ecclesiastics and of gender that characterized Catholic Christianity. It also involved the use of methods established by the religious canon to resolve transgressions and stabilize relationships. The act of contrition is the most orthodox method for a Catholic who had broken any Church precept, whether it be disobeying an ethical command, religious dogma, or behavioral norm within the institution. Contrition is the renunciation of sin, an essential process for returning to the grace of God. During the High Medieval period and until the Council of Trent, the state of attrition was also considered a state of shame in which renunciation is less complete, part of a process that leads to contrition. One of the era's most influential theologians, Duns Scotus,[9] considered attrition to be sufficient to justify the sacrament of penitence. The Council of Trent (1540–63) defined attrition as voluntary act that did not affirm or exclude the evolution from one state to another.[1]

My hypothesis is that in the correspondence between Fernández de Santa Cruz and Sor Juana there is a mix of obedience and disobedience, of attrition and challenge that cannot be ignored. This internal tension better explains the personality of Sor Juana as a nun of her time than the interpretation of the nun herself and her writings as an example of open rebellion. The text of both pieces has been widely analyzed by many pens and the tone of reprimand by

8. Tapia Méndez, *Carta de Sor Juana Inés de la Cruz a su confesor*, 29–42.
9. Franciscan theologian (1266–1308), who followed the positions of Saint Augustine, emphasizing freedom in divine and human will [*Editor*].
1. *Catholic Encyclopedia* (Washington: The Catholic University Press, 1967. 4:278). One characteristic of medieval thought was to see attrition as part of a process that culminated in contrition. The controversy over these degrees of renunciation of sin and error continued even after the Council of Trent. It was debated whether attrition and contrition were motivated by disinterested love of God or by fear of punishment, and some theologians were inclined to separate the sequence attrition–contrition.

the Bishop has not escaped anyone. José Pascual Buxó[2] has done an intelligent and well-founded analysis of all the arguments offered to explain the origin of the interchange between Sor Juana and the Bishop and the decision to turn herself over entirely to the faith. Buxó asks himself at one point if there was no way at all to "reduce a disobedient nun to silence and obedience . . ." The truth is that, although there were ways, they did not always render the desired effect, as the cases cited above demonstrate. And, precisely, in the *Athenagoric Letter* as much as in the "Response" there are elements of the strategies developed by nuns and prelates before and after Sor Juana in points of dissention, contradiction and solution to problems of observance.

CHARLENE VILLASEÑOR BLACK

Portraits of Sor Juana Inés de la Cruz and the Dangers of Intellectual Desire[†]

The most famous portrait of celebrated writer and nun Sor Juana Inés de la Cruz (1648–1695) was painted by renowned Mexican artist Miguel Cabrera (1695–1768) fifty-five years after the sitter's death (Figure 1). The depiction is unique among existing portrayals of Mexico's famed "Tenth Muse," and also among portraits of nuns. Seemingly, Cabrera's image was intended as a pictorial commemoration of Sor Juana's final conflict with the Catholic Church,[1] perhaps even as a painted exoneration, as close visual reading of the painting and related sources suggest. Cabrera's portrait thus visualizes the dangers of intellectual desire for women of the time.

The portrait is large, approximately life size. In it, Sor Juana sits regally at her writing table, surrounded by books, ink wells, and plume pens. Sixty books from her personal library, said to have numbered four thousand volumes, appear in the background, their leather spines inscribed with titles and authors.[2] She wears the black and white habit of the Hieronymites, one of the wealthiest and most elite orders in the Spanish empire. A swag of red drapery in the right corner, a convention borrowed from royal portraiture, proclaims her

---

2. Jose Pascual Buxó, "Sor Juana: monstruo de su laberinto," in Sara Poot Herrera, ed., *Y diversa de mi misma entre vuestras plumas ando: Homenaje internacional a Sor Juana Inés de la Cruz* (Mexico: El Colegio de Mexico, 1993), 43–70 [*Editor*].

† Written for this Norton Critical Edition. All notes are Villaseñor Black's unless otherwise indicated.

1. For the historical controversies surrounding Sor Juana's final years, see the Introduction, on p. xvi [*Editor*].

2. Francisco de la Maza, *Sor Juana Inés de la Cruz ante la historia* (Mexico City: Universidad Nacional Autónoma de México, 1980), 303.

Figure 1. Miguel Cabrera, *Sor Juana Inés de la Cruz*, 1750, oil on canvas, 81½ by 58¼ inches (207 by 48 cm), Museo Nacional de Historia, Mexico City, Mexico.

status. She seems assured, seated in an open, commanding pose, her gaze direct and assertive. Her arm is confidently laid over an open book, her fingers about to turn the page, indicating that the viewer has interrupted her reading. The setting—library, desk, open book, writing accoutrements—is striking for its insistence upon Sor Juana's status as an intellectual.

Cabrera's unique approach in this portrait is thrown into relief when it is viewed in the context of other portraits of nuns, a notable genre in colonial Mexico. Most Mexican nun portraits, produced during the vibrant flowering of conventual culture that marked vice-regal New Spain, conform to one of three types: profession portraits, posthumous portraits, or founder portraits. The most frequent type is the profession portrait, as seen in Mexico's famous "crowned nuns" (monjas coronadas), which represent the sitter richly costumed and wearing an elaborate floral crown, her last act of worldly vanity before profession.[3] Posthumous portraits of nuns are less frequent, a genre reserved for particularly notable sisters.[4] In these paintings, the deceased reclines upon her deathbed or bier, again crowned with flowers. The third portrait type, commissioned by and displayed in convents, commemorates important founders of nunneries or religious orders.[5] Cabrera's portrait of Sor Juana, with its assertion of her status as an intellectual, fits into none of these categories of Mexican colonial nun portraiture.

How did the eighteenth-century viewer understand Cabrera's painting? Although painted fifty-five years after her death, Cabrera's stylistic choices, as well as specific details in the painting, suggest that it was intended to commemorate her final conflict. His pictorial strategies—the austere palette, exacting realism, the sober use of light and shade, and the overall mood of gravity—would seem to date the canvas to the seventeenth century, that is, during Sor Juana's lifetime. The palette, in particular, is more in keeping with seventeenth-century taste, and less in tune with the softer, frequently pastel colors and smoky modeling of the eighteenth century. Cabrera thus intentionally employed an archaizing Baroque Realist style to historicize his subject.

3. Sources include Josefina Muriel de la Torre and Manuel Romero de Terreros, Retratos de monjas (Mexico City: Jus, 1952); Alma Montero Alarcón, Monjas coronadas (Mexico City: Círculo de Arte, 1999); Kristen Hammer, "Monjas Coronadas: The Crowned Nuns of Viceregal Mexico," in Elizabeth P. Benson et al., Retratos: 2,000 Years of Latin American Portraits, exh. cat. (New York: El Museo del Barrio, 2005); and James Córdova, The Art of Professing in Bourbon Mexico: Crowned Nun Portraits and Reform in the Convent (Austin: University of Texas Press, 2014).
4. Muriel and Romero, Retratos de monjas, 30.
5. Muriel and Romero, Retratos de monjas, 29; Noemí Atamoros Zeller, Nueva iconografía de Sor Juana Inés de la Cruz: 1695–1995, Trescientos años de inmortalidad (Mexico City: Química Hoechst de México, Hoechst Marion Roussel, 1995), 29.

What sources did Cabrera employ to create his portrait of Sor Juana, and what do these sources reveal about its intended meaning? A prominent inscription in the middle of Cabrera's canvas proclaims that the work is a *"fiel copia"* (faithful copy) of a now lost portrait, formerly in the Hieronymite convent of Mexico City. Most scholars associate this lost original with the painting now in the Rector's Office at the Universidad Nacional Autónoma de México, attributed to Juan de Miranda, and dating to the early eighteenth century (Figure 2). Some scholars have further related Miranda's image with a supposed self portrait referred to by Sor Juana in her writings, no longer extant.[6] How does Cabrera's portrayal compare to the rendition attributed to Miranda, its possible source?

The obvious differences between the two portraits highlight Cabrera's emphasis on Sor Juana's status as an intellectual. In Miranda's painting, in which Sor Juana appears as a full-length figure standing in her cell, only thirty of her books are visible behind her. Cabrera amplified the number of books to sixty. Furthermore, in Miranda's portrait, Sor Juana is depicted in the act of writing a sonnet, *Verde embeleso de la vida humana* (Sonnet 152, Green rapture and delight of human life).[7] Three additional volumes of her own works, published in 1689, 1692, and 1700 (the latter issued five years after her death), can be found on her writing desk.[8] Notably, in Cabrera's image, Sor Juana is not in the act of writing, but is reading. Whereas Miranda has characterized the sitter as a famous poet, highlighting her writings, Cabrera, in contrast, emphasizes Sor Juana's scholarly life. Finally, the lengthy inscription, which proclaims the painting a "faithful copy" (*fiel copia*), in Cabrera's portrait is unique. The inscription in Miranda's painting, on the left, also begins with the proclamation "faithful copy," but is drawn from the first biography of Sor Juana, written in 1700 by the Jesuit Diego de Calleja.[9] The author of Cabrera's inscription, which has yet to be entirely deciphered, remains unknown. A recent scholar who has studied its enigmatic numerical references has suggested that the digits refer to the years of the sitter's birth and death, as well as the number of years she lived.[1] It is the only portrait of Sor Juana that does not bear Calleja's inscription.

Miranda's characterization of Sor Juana as a famed writer is the most frequent strategy employed by artists to depict the sitter.

6. Donna Pierce, Rogelio Ruiz Gomar, and Clara Bargellini, *Painting a New World: Mexican Art and Life 1521–1821* (Austin: University of Texas Press, 2004), 209; Octavio Paz, *Sor Juana, Or, The Traps of Faith*, trans. Margaret Sayers (Cambridge, MA: The Belknap Press of Harvard University Press, 1988), 231 ff.
7. Stephanie Merrim, *Early Modern Women's Writing and Sor Juana Inés de la Cruz* (Nashville, TN: Vanderbilt University Press, 1999), 187.
8. Paz, *Sor Juana*, 234; and Ruiz Gomar, *Painting a New World*, 209.
9. Paz, *Sor Juana*, 234.
1. Ruiz Gomar, 209.

Figure 2. Attributed to Juan de Miranda, *Sor Juana Inés de la Cruz,* early eighteenth century, oil on canvas, Rector's Office, Universidad Nacional Autónoma de México, Mexico City, Mexico.

Figure 3. Lucas Valdés, *Sor Juana Inés de la Cruz*, 1692, engraving, frontispiece, *Second Volume* (Seville, 1692), Edward E. Ayer Collection of The Newberry Library, Chicago. Courtesy of The Newberry Library, Chicago. Call no. Ayer 888 .J91 1692a.

It is, in fact, a description that dates back to the first extant portrait of her—the only one created during her lifetime—the engraved frontispiece by Lucas Valdés, published in the first edition of the second volume of her works in Seville, Spain, in 1692 (Figure 3). Here, Sor Juana is presented bust length in an oval frame, flanked by Mercury and Minerva, her right hand reaching out to pen the encircling inscription. The characterization of Sor Juana as author distinguishes most portraits of the nun, as we see in

Figure 4. Fray Miguel de Herrera, *Sor Juana Inés de la Cruz*, 1732, oil on canvas, private collection. Courtesy of Art Resource, NY.

examples by Mexican colonial painters Fray Miguel de Herrera, Nicolás Enríquez, and others (Figure 4).[2] One final portrait, which postdates Cabrera's work and was clearly based on it, painted by Mexican artist Andrés de Islas (Figure 5),[3] provides a fascinating comparison. As in Cabrera's portrait, Islas portrayed Sor Juana sitting at her writing desk, although unlike its source, the nun is represented in the act of writing. Thus, Islas's portrait, like the other representations of the celebrated nun, showcases her literary fame, not her learnedness or piety, throwing into relief Cabrera's unique interpretation of the "Mexican Phoenix" as an intellectual, in the act of reading, not writing.

Sor Juana's *escudo*, or nun's badge, encodes additional commentary on writing. This oval shaped insignia, worn at her throat, was part of the attire of the Hieronymite Order. It usually proclaims

2. Clara Bargellini identified the work by Enríquez, "La colección de pintura colonial de Robert Lamborn en el Philadelphia Museum of Art," in *Patrocinio, colección y circulación de las artes*, ed. Gustavo Curial (Mexico City, UNAM, IIE, 1997), 573–93; and Pierce, Ruiz Gomar, and Bargellini, *Painting a New World*, 209. For the other paintings see Atamoros Zeller, *Nueva iconografía*, 14.

3. It was formerly in the collection of Francisco Antonio de Lorenzana, archbishop of Mexico City, in 1776; he took it back with him to Spain. Atamoros Zeller, *Nueva iconografía*, 5.

Figure 5. Andrés de Islas, *Sor Juana Inés de la Cruz,* 1772, oil on canvas, 41⅓ by 33 inches (105 by 84 cm), Museo de América, Madrid, Spain. Courtesy of Album/Art Resource, NY.

a nun's favorite devotion,[4] the vast majority at the time depicting the Immaculate Conception, the Virgin of the Apocalypse, or the Virgin of Guadalupe.[5] In Cabrera's painting, the *escudo*, so large that it competes with the sitter's face, represents the Annunciation to the Virgin, a very unusual subject for a nun's badge. How would the period viewer have understood Sor Juana's choice of this image? What role did this theme play in Sor Juana's life?

The scene of the Annunciation, described in the Gospel of Luke (1:26–39), narrates the angel Gabriel's appearance to the Virgin Mary to announce that she will be the mother of God. At this moment, the Incarnation, or miraculous impregnation, occurs. We see the announcement rendered in the *escudo*: the angel Gabriel flies in from top right, to hail Mary, who, like Sor Juana, is seated at a desk, reading. According to tradition, Mary is reading Isaiah 7:14, a prophecy of the coming of the Messiah. The Annunciation scene thus encodes important allusions to the significance of text, for at the moment of the Incarnation, the Word that is Christ became flesh in Mary's womb. In "Response of the Poet," Sor Juana described Mary as "the Mother of the Word."[6] In addition, she penned three *villancicos* (carols) on the theme, including one in which she described Mary as the person who made "man out of word," her womb the site of this miraculous transformation.[7]

Despite the inscription on Cabrera's portrait identifying it as a "faithful copy," this close visual reading demonstrates that Cabrera's rendition of Mexico's "Tenth Muse" is strikingly different from other extant portrayals; perhaps it reflects a lost original. Although Cabrera included her inkwell and pens, he did not depict among the sixty books a single work by Sor Juana herself; nor is she shown in the act of writing. Why not? After all, she was a renowned late Baroque poet famed throughout the Spanish empire. Why is Cabrera's portrait so different from other renditions, which portray the nun in the act of writing, or highlight her literary production?

Cabrera's emphasis on Sor Juana as reader, not author, is further accentuated when the portrait is compared to possible sources, namely, images of clerics or theologians, the ultimate inspiration for Cabrera's portrayal. In such images, which are plentiful in European

4. On the *escudos*, Elizabeth Perry, *"Escudos de monjas* Shields of Nuns: The Creole Convent and Images of Mexican Identity in Miniature," Ph.D. dissertation, Brown University, 1999; and "Convents, Art, and Creole Identity in Late Viceregal New Spain," in Kellen Kee McIntyre and Richard E. Phillips, eds. *Woman and Art in Early Modern Latin America* (Leiden and Boston: Brill, 2007), 321–413; and Muriel and Romero, *Retratos de monjas*, 203–04.

5. Perry, in Pierce, Ruiz Gomar, and Bargellini, *Painting a New World*, 230.

6. See "Response," p. 91 [*Editor*].

7. See Villancico II (*Letras sagradas para cantar, A la encarnación*), [Juana de Asbaje] Sor Juana Inés de la Cruz, *Obras completas*, ed. Alfonso Méndez Plancarte (Mexico City: Porrúa, 1989), 315.

art from the Middle Ages on, figures in clerical garb appear seated at their writing desks surrounded by books, inkwells, and plume pens. Often, the figures are shown reading, just like Sor Juana. Clearly, the similarities between these images and Cabrera's Sor Juana indicate that the artist chose this format in order to underscore his sitter's learnedness, as well as her piety. One very significant difference has yet to be mentioned, though: all of the sitters portrayed are men. Cabrera's portrait is thus unique in that it employs a portrait type usually reserved for male sitters to depict a woman.

One theologian frequently rendered in this scholar portrait type merits special mention—Saint Jerome (ca. 347–420), Doctor of the Church, and translator of the Bible into Latin. Sor Juana clearly identified with Jerome. She was, after all, a member of the Hieronymite order, and when she professed, she made a special vow to Saints Jerome and Paula, the order's co-patrons.[8] In "Response of the Poet," Sor Juana repeatedly referred to Jerome as her father and described herself as his daughter.[9] Like Sor Juana, Jerome, too, had come under attack by the Catholic Church for his intellectual endeavors. In a vision inspired by his guilty love of classical literature, an angel accused Jerome of preferring Cicero to the Bible, a story she recounted in "Response of the Poet." Sor Juana compared her difficulties with the Church to those of Saint Jerome, writing: "For me, not the knowing . . . but only the desire to know has been so difficult that I could say with my father Saint Jerome . . . : *The labor it has cost me, the difficulties I have endured, the times I have despaired, and the other times I have desisted and begun again, all because of my determination to learn.*"[1] Sor Juana also admired Saint Jerome as a promoter of women's education. In the juridical style typical of her defense, she cites Jerome's various letters to female followers in "Response of the Poet." Several of them, and especially his *Letters* to Leta, Paula, and Eustochium, address the importance of the education of women. She argues that if Jerome were alive today he would be an ardent supporter of the education of women, girls, and especially nuns.[2]

The analogy to Jerome is strengthened by the visual evidence of Cabrera's portrait, which, like many paintings of Saint Jerome, depicts its sitter in a study intently reading, surrounded by books and the objects of scholarly life. The similiarities strengthen by association the idea that like Saint Jerome, Sor Juana was also a learned scholar. The books depicted by Cabrera in the background reinforce this connection. Of the sixty texts represented, patristic texts by the

---

8. Paz, *Sor Juana*, 124.
9. See "Response," pp. 91, 98, 102, 114, 115, 120, 122, and 125 [*Editor*].
1. See "Response," p. 102 [*Editor*].
2. See "Response," p. 115 [*Editor*].

Church Fathers are given a position of prominence in the center of the painting.[3] One volume, however, is missing here: the writings of Saint Jerome. This is, in fact, the text that Sor Juana is reading. Close examination of the painting reveals the exact title of the text— Saint Jerome's commentary on Psalm 50, the great penitential psalm, now numbered 51 in the Western Church: *Miserere mei, Deus, secundum magnam misericordiam tuam* (Have mercy on me, O God, according to thy great mercy).[4] That Cabrera took pains to identify the text Sor Juana reads—a detail not found in one single other painting—indicates his association of her learnedness with her religious piety. This intepretation is confirmed by the lengthy inscription in the center of Cabrera's painting, which highlights her dedication to "sacred learning": *"LA MADRE JUANA INES DE LA CRUZ . . . en quien vinculó el tesoro de su Saviduria sirvien- dose de ella para fecundar su portentoso Entendimiento con la noticia de la Escritura divina, y toda Erudicion Sagrada en la carrera de qua- renta, y quatro años . . . "*[5] (The Mother Juana Inés de la Cruz . . . in whom was perpetuated the treasure of her wisdom, employed to fer- tilize her prodigious intellect with the light of divine scripture and all sacred learning during her life of forty-four years . . .).

Two other sources for Cabrera's portrait of Sor Juana merit exam- ination: depictions of Saint Teresa of Ávila, the great sixteenth- century Spanish mystic, writer, and reformer of the Discalced Carmelite Order, as well as the Spanish writer-visionary-nun Sor María de Ágreda. Both were also portrayed using the scholar por- trait compositional type (see Figure 5), and both were among the female role models singled out by Sor Juana in "Response of the Poet."[6] Saint Teresa seems to have been the first female sitter depicted using this portrait type, and thus, images of her may have been a source for Cabrera's unusual portrait. The correspondences between Cabrera's Sor Juana and depictions of Saint Teresa are striking. Both represent the two nuns as scholars seated in their studies, surrounded by the trappings of intellectual life.[7] Portraits of Teresa, though, usually

3. The books on the shelves have been identified by Maza, *Sor Juana Inés de la Cruz ante la historia*, 303.
4. The psalm is numbered 50 in Saint Jerome's text because he used the earlier Greek num- bering of the *Septuagint*. J. P. Migne, ed., *Patrologiae Cursus Completus, Sancti Eusebii Hieronymi. Opera Omnia*, Vol. VII (Paris: Garnier Fratres, 1884), 1030, Psalm L.
5. The inscription is transcribed in Abelardo Carrillo y Gariel, *El pintor Miguel Cabrera* (Mexico City: Instituto Nacional de Antropología e Historia, 1966), 52.
6. See above, p. 118 [*Editor*].
7. On images of Saint Teresa in Mexican art, see Christopher C. Wilson, "Mother, Mis- sionary, Martyr: St. Teresa of Ávila in Mexican Colonial Art," Ph.D. dissertation, George Washington University, 1998; "Saint Teresa of Ávila's Martyrdom: Images of Her Trans- verberation in Mexican Colonial Painting," *Anales del Instituto de Investigaciones Esté- ticas* 74–75 (1999): 211–34; "From *mujercilla* to *conquistadora*: St. Teresa of Ávila's Missionary Identity in Mexican Colonial Art," in McIntyre and Phillips, eds., *Woman and Art in Early Modern Latin America*, 419–41.

Figure 6. Francisco de Zurbarán, *St. Teresa of Ávila,* ca. 1640, oil on canvas, Cathedral, Seville, Spain. © Fundació Institut Amatller d'Art Hispànic. Arxiu Mas.

focus on the sitter's role as writer, as seen in a famous example by Spanish painter Francisco de Zurbarán, which dates from around 1640, eighteen years after Saint Teresa's 1622 canonization (Figure 6). In this work and others, Zurbarán presented Saint Teresa in the act of writing, prominently holding aloft her pen, as she looks up to the dove of the Holy Spirit, her source of inspiration. Depictions of Sor María may have been another source of inspiration for Cabrera, and indeed, the mystical "Nun of Ágreda," as Sor Juana herself pointed out in "Response of the Poet," had been allowed by the Church to write and study.[8] Images of her similarly employ this scholar-cleric compositional format, but once again, feature the sitter holding up her pen, emphasizing her occupation as writer.

When Sor Juana's image is compared to other writer portraits, be they depictions of male or female clerics or scholars, as well as other portraits of the sitter herself, the omission of the act of writing in Cabrera's painting becomes even more striking. Writers are almost always portrayed with pen in hand, showcasing the act of writing and the instrument of their creativity and fame.[9] Most of the possible visual sources—images of clerics, theologians, Saint Teresa, and Sor María de Ágreda—represent the sitter writing. Cabrera's omission of the act of writing in his portrayal of Sor Juana was clearly intentional. Why did he represent her in this way?

Cabrera's amplification of the number of books in this portrait provides a starting point to understand these questions. The great number of books depicted signals Sor Juana's learnedness, and functions to underscore an interpretation of her as an intellectual, not a writer. Books occupied a similar position of importance in Sor Juana's life. Reporting on her childhood, she recalled that as a teenager, "I continued my studious effort . . . to read and read some more, to study and study some more, with no teacher other than the books themselves."[1] Finally, Cabrera's display of books attests to Sor Juana's claims that she was first and foremost a scholar, and not a worldly poet, an assertion central to her self defense: "All that I have wished is to study in order to be ignorant about less," she claimed.[2]

Cabrera also seems to marshall the Virgin Mary in defense of Sor Juana, a strategy also inspired by the nun herself. In the Annunciation scene featured on Sor Juana's *escudo*, Mary appears not only

8. See "Response," p. 118 [*Editor*]. Thank you to Mario Ortiz for pointing out the relevance of portraits of María de Ágreda. On the so-called Lady in Blue, the author of *The Mystical City of God*, see Marilyn H. Fedewa, *María of Ágreda: Mystical Lady in Blue* (Albuquerque: University of New Mexico Press, 2009).
9. Charlene Villaseñor Black, "Pacheco, Velázquez, and the Legacy of Leonardo in Spain," in Claire Farago ed., *The Historical Reception of Leonardo da Vinci's Treatise on Painting: Art as Institution* (Aldershot, UK: Ashgate, 2009), 361–63.
1. See "Response," p. 97 [*Editor*].
2. See "Response," p. 118 [*Editor*].

as reader, but, one could argue, also as author. According to the Gospel of Luke, after the Annunciation occurred, Mary visited her cousin Elizabeth, who was the first to recognize the miraculous pregnancy, exclaiming: "Blessed art thou among women, and blessed is the fruit of thy womb" (Luke 1:42). Mary replied (Luke 1:46–48): "My soul doth magnify the Lord. And my spirit hath rejoiced in God my Saviour. Because he hath regarded the humility of his handmaid; for behold from henceforth all generations shall call me blessed."[3] These words constitute the *Magnificat*, one of the oldest hymns in Christianity. And in the "Response of the Poet," Sor Juana defended her right to pen poetry by reporting that "The Queen of Wisdom and Our Lady, with her sacred lips, intoned the Canticle of the Magnificat."[4] In other words, Mary wrote in verse, just like Sor Juana. What more efficacious defense of a woman's right to poetry could be found?

The *escudo* encodes yet another layer of meaning. In her guise as the word bearer, Mary is an image of the Holy Mother Church. How could the Church, embodied literally by the pregnant Virgin Mary, displayed prominently on the nun's badge in the center of Cabrera's painting, refuse her daughter Sor Juana the right to a scholarly life? Sor Juana asks this very question of her detractors: "If she, with her most holy authority, does not forbid me to do so, why should others?"[5] Her devotion to and connection with Mary is further emphasized by the fact that with one hand Sor Juana clasps her rosary as her other hand rests on Saint Jerome's text.

Does Cabrera's failure to reference her writing indicate his understanding of Sor Juana's conflict with the Catholic ecclesiastical hierarchy? Has Cabrera represented the Church's silencing of Sor Juana's pen? Seemingly so. Writing was, after all, the source of her repeated conflicts with the Church.[6] Cabrerea's omission of writing in the portrait finds a parallel in Sor Juana's "Response of the Poet," in which she repeatedly asserts that she has neither the desire nor the talent to write: "Writing has never been by my own volition but at the behest of others; for I could truthfully say to them: *Ye have compelled me*."[7] Instead of drawing attention to her literary fame, Cabrera follows Sor Juana herself, presenting her as a scholar, shown in the act of reading, surrounded by books on theology, science, philosophy, and rhetoric. This shift in emphasis mirrors the strategy of the "Response of the Poet" to focus on Sor Juana's right as a woman to a life of study. Furthermore, it mirrors her argument that studying

3. All quotations taken from the *Douay-Rheims Bible*, with Bishop Richard Challoner's notes from the eighteenth century: www.drbo.org.
4. See "Response," p. 121 [*Editor*].
5. See "Response," p. 119 [*Editor*].
6. See "Response," p. 93 [*Editor*]. "I know very well that your most sage warning is not directed at it [her letter] but at how much you have seen of my writings on human affairs."
7. See "Response," p. 95 [*Editor*].

secular letters was a path to the sacred: "In this way I proceeded, always directing the steps of my study to the summit of sacred theology, as I have said . . ."[8]

A close rereading of Cabrera's portrait of Sor Juana Inés de la Cruz in conjunction with related portraits and other possible visual and textual sources opens up new understanding of the image. Painted in 1750, fifty-five years after her death during an epidemic, it seems to function as a pictorial vindication of Mexico's most famous writer and nun. The mystery, though, of the painting's original commission remains to be clarified. Who was its patron and what were the circumstances of its commission? Until the felicitous discovery of a new document, the reasons for the portrait's creation must remain speculative. Circumstantial evidence suggests that it was commissioned by a powerful patron. We do know that it was painted while Miguel Cabrera's was the *pintor de cámara* (court painter) of the powerful archbishop of Mexico City, Manuel José Rubio y Salinas, who was an important patron of the Church and promoter of education during his tenure from 1749 to 1765.[9] In 1751 Rubio y Salinas founded in Mexico City the Casa y Colegio de San Ignacio (called "de las Vizcainas") and the Oratory of San Felipe. In 1754, he supported the founding of La Enseñanza; in 1755 consecrated the Royal Convent of Santo Domingo, and in 1755 founded the new church of *San Fernando*.[1] Cabrera worked for other powerful patrons, though, too, including Viceroy Francisco de Güemes y Horcasitas, whose portrait he painted, and which, like Sor Juana's portrait, is housed in Mexico's National History Museum.[2] The current location of Cabrera's rendition of Sor Juana, part of a collection of portraits of viceroys, a bishop and archbishop, as well as other powerful figures, including a lawyer, a friar, and others, provides an additional clue. Its inclusion in this group might indicate that it, too, like these other works, has a distinguished provenance. Cabrera's relationship with his major ecclesiastical patrons, the Jesuits, also merits further investigation.[3] The circumstances of the commission

---

8. See "Response," p. 98 [*Editor*].
9. Francisco Sosa, *El episcopado Mexicano. Biografía de los Ilustrissimos Señores Arzobispos de Mexico desde la época colonial hasta nuestros días*, vol. II, 3rd ed. (Mexico City: Jus, 1962), 95–113.
1. Sosa, *El episcopado mexicano*, 109.
2. Raúl Cruz Aguillón, *El maestro don Miguel Cabrera* (Mexico City: Museo de Arte Prehispánico de México, 1993), 37.
3. This suggestion was made by Cruz Aguillón, *El maestro*, 25. He notes that Bernardo Couto, writing in the 19th century, commented on Cabrera's Jesuit patrons: "*Cabrera fue el pintor de la Compañía, y entre el artista y aquella sábia corporación mediaron relaciones estrechas. Las casas de los jesuitas estaban llenas de cuadros suyos . . .*" (Cabrera was the painter for the Society [of Jesus], and there was a close interaction between the artist and that wise corporation. Jesuit houses were full of his paintings . . .) [*Translated by Editor*]. Bernardo Couto, *Diálogo sobre la historia de la pintura en México* (Mexico City: Secretaría de Fomento, 1889), 63–64.

of such a commanding, life-size portrait in 1750 are made more puzzling by the fact that Sor Juana's literary work lay forgotten in relative obscurity from the mid-eighteenth century and throughout the nineteenth century. The last time her work was published in the eighteenth century was in 1725, and no modern edition was issued until 1940.[4] This lends additional weight to the notion that the commission came from an ecclesiastical patron.

In conclusion, close visual analysis of Cabrera's *Portrait of Sor Juana Inés de la Cruz*, including identification of the text she is reading and analysis of the books in her library, in addition to comparison to other nun portraits, including portrayals of Sor Juana herself, reveals Cabrera's unique characterization of his sitter as both learned and pious. His portrayal has more in common with representations of clerics and theologians, and especially Saint Jerome, than with existing genres of nun portraiture. These visual strategies echo Sor Juana's own writings. In fact, Cabrera's portrait seems to constitute a visual analogue of "Response of the Poet," suggesting as it did that intellectual desire and piety can complement each other. One wonders if the clock, placed prominently on the left, right above the text Sor Juana reads, was intended as an additional symbol in the portrait. A well recognized sign of temperance, the clock also references the vanity of worldly triumphs.[5] Perhaps it alludes to the bishop's accusation of vanity on the part Sor Juana. Might it also suggest that time reveals truth? Cabrera's portrait therefore seems to function as a pictorial exoneration. At the same time, though, the reference to Saint Jerome's commentary on Psalm 50/51 indicates that the portrait is in line with official Church versions of her life that claimed that Sor Juana felt true remorse at the end of her life for her devotion to secular matters. Thus Cabrera's portrait also makes clear the dangers of intellectual desire.

Works Cited

Armella de Aspe, Virginia and Guillermo Tovar de Teresa. *Escudos de monjas novohispanas*. Mexico City: Fernández Cueto, 1993.
Atamoros Zeller, Noemí. *Nueva iconografía Sor Juana Inés de la Cruz: 1695–1995, Trescientos años de inmortalidad*. Mexico City: Química Hoechst de México, Hoechst Marion Roussel, 1995.

---

4. Paz, *Sor Juana*, 63, refers to Ermilo Abreu Gómez, ed., *Poesías completas* (Mexico City: Botas, 1940). But on 510, Paz describes an earlier edition of selected works: Juan León Mera, *Obras selectas de la célebre monja de México, Sor Juana Inés de la Cruz*, published in Quito in 1873.
5. James Hall, *Dictionary of Subjects and Symbols in Art*, rev. ed. (New York: Harper & Row, 1979), s.v. "Clock," 72.

Bargellini Clara. "La colección de pintura colonial de Robert Lamborn en el Philadelphia Museum of Art." *Patrocinio, colección y circulación de las artes*. Ed. Gustavo Curial. XX Coloquio Internacional de Historia del Arte. Mexico City: UNAM, IIE, 1997. 573–93.

Bergmann, Emilie L. "The '*Sueño*' of Sor Juana Inés de la Cruz: Dreaming in a Double Voice." *Women, Culture, and Politics in Latin America*. Ed. Seminar on Feminism and Culture in Latin America. Berkeley: University of California Press, 1990. 151–72.

Black, Charlene Villaseñor. "Pacheco, Velázquez, and the Legacy of Leonardo in Spain." *The Historical Reception of Leonardo da Vinci's Treatise on Painting: Art as Institution*. Ed. Claire Farago. Aldershot, UK: Ashgate, 2009. 349–74.

Carrillo y Gariel, Abelardo. *El pintor Miguel Cabrera*. Mexico City: Instituto Nacional de Antropología e Historia, 1966.

Colonial Latin American Review 4.1 (1995). Special issue: Pórtico: Homenaje a Sor Juana Inés de la Cruz. Georgina Sabat de Rivers and Raquel Chang-Rodriguez, eds.

Córdova, James. *The Art of Professing in Bourbon Mexico: Crowned Nun Portraits and Reform in the Convent*. Austin: University of Texas Press, 2014.

Couto, Bernardo. *Diálogo sobre la historia de la pintura en México*. Mexico City: Secretaría de Fomento, 1889.

Cruz, Sor Juana Inés de la. *Obras completas*. Ed. Alfonso Méndez Plancarte. 4 vols. Mexico City: Porrúa, 1989.

———. *Sor Juana Inés de la Cruz: Selected Works*. Trans. Edith Grossman. New York & London: Norton, 2014.

Cruz Aguillón, Raúl. *El maestro don Miguel Cabrera*. Mexico City: Museo de Arte Prehispánico de México, 1993.

Fedewa, Marilyn H. *María of Ágreda: Mystical Lady in Blue*. Albuquerque: University of New Mexico Press, 2009.

Hammer, Kristen. "*Monjas Coronadas*: The Crowned Nuns of Viceregal Mexico." *Retratos: 2,000 Years of Latin American Portraits*. Ed. Elizabeth P. Benson et al. exh. cat. New York: El Museo del Barrio, 2005. 86–101.

Kirk, Pamela. *Sor Juana Inés de la Cruz: Religion, Art, and Feminism*. New York: Continuum, 1999.

Martí Cotarelo, Mónica. *Miguel Cabrera, un pintor de su tiempo*. Mexico City: Consejo Nacional para la Cultura y las Artes, 1999.

Maza, Francisco de la. *Sor Juana Inés de la Cruz ante la historia*. Mexico City: Universidad Nacional Autónoma de México, 1980.

Merrim, Stephanie. *Early Modern Women's Writing and Sor Juana Inés de la Cruz*. Vanderbilt University Press, 1999.

Metropolitan Museum of Art, New York. *Mexico: Splendors of Thirty Centuries*. exh. cat. New York: Little, Brown, 1990.

Migne, J. P. ed. *Patrologiae Cursus Completus, Sancti Eusebii Hiero-nymi. Opera Omnia*, Vol. VII. Paris: Garnier Fratres, 1884.

Montero Alarcón, Alma. *Monjas coronadas*. Mexico City: Círculo de Arte, 1999.

Muriel, Josefina. *Cultura feminina novohispana*. Mexico City: Universidad Nacional Autónoma de México, 1994.

Muriel de la Torre, Josefina and Manuel Romero de Terreros. *Retratos de monjas*. Mexico City: Jus, 1952.

Ortiz, Mario A. "Sor Juana Inés de la Cruz: Bibliography." *Hispania* 86.3 (September 2003): 431–62.

Paz, Octavio. *Sor Juana, Or, The Traps of Faith*. Trans. Margaret Sayers Peden. Cambridge, Mass.: The Belknap Press of Harvard University Press, 1988.

Perry, Elizabeth. "Convents, Art, and Creole Identity in Late Viceregal New Spain." *Woman and Art in Early Modern Latin America*. Ed. Kellen Kee McIntyre and Richard E. Phillips. Leiden and Boston: Brill, 2007. 321–41.

———."*Escudos de monjas*/Shields of Nuns: The Creole Convent and Images of Mexican Identity in Miniature." Ph.D. dissertation. Brown University, 1999.

Pierce, Donna, Rogelio Ruiz Gomar, and Clara Bargellini. *Painting a New World: Mexican Art and Life 1521–1821*. Austin: University of Texas Press, 2004.

Prendergast, Ryan. "Constructing an Icon: The Self-Referentiality and Framing of Sor Juana Inés de la Cruz," *Journal for Early Modern Cultural Studies* 7.2 (fall–winter 2007): 28–56.

Ridderbos, Bernard. *Saint and Symbol: Images of Saint Jerome in Early Italian Art*. Trans. P. Waard-Dekking. Groningen: Bouma's Boekhuls, 1984.

Sosa, Francisco. *El episcopado Mexicano. Biografía de los Ilustrissimos Señores Arzobispos de Mexico desde la Época Colonial hasta Nuestros Días*. vol. II. 3rd ed. Mexico City: Jus, 1962.

Tapia Méndez, Aureliano. *Autodefensa espiritual de Sor Juana*. Monterrey: Universidad de Nuevo León, 1981.

Wilson, Christopher C. "From *mujercilla* to *conquistadora*: St. Teresa of Ávila's Missionary Identity in Mexican Colonial Art." *Woman and Art in Early Modern Latin America*. Ed. Kellen Kee McIntyre and Richard E. Phillips. Leiden and Boston: Brill, 2007. 419–41.

———. "Mother, Missionary, Martyr: St. Teresa of Ávila in Mexican Colonial Art." Ph.D. dissertation. George Washington University, 1998.

———. "Saint Teresa of Ávila's Martyrdom: Images of Her Transverberation in Mexican Colonial Painting." *Anales del Instituto de Investigaciones Estéticas* 74–75 (1999): 211–34.

CRITICAL TRADITIONS

Criticism

MARCELINO MENÉNDEZ Y PELAYO

From Anthology of Hispanic American Poets[†]

Marcelino Menéndez y Pelayo (1856–1912) was a leading Spanish philologist and a founder of Hispanic literary history. His description of Sor Juana's works is the first to engage them systematically after their relative disregard during the eighteenth and nineteenth centuries, when they were associated with what was deemed the obfuscation and excess of seventeenth-century verse. Even though he praises many of Sor Juana's works, Menéndez y Pelayo's criterion continues to be clarity of expression and thus he critiques some of her writings as ornate paeans to courtly culture.

Sor Juana Inés de la Cruz lived in such a pedantic atmosphere of literary aberration that her very existence possesses something of the supernatural and extraordinary. Not because she was free of bad taste—such a prodigy would be wholly unbelievable—but her lively intelligence, witty imagination, and above all the impetus and ardor of her sentiment for secular and mystical writing all demonstrate what she could have been with a different education and in better times. Her varied and vast learning—while not very selective—did manage to give several of her compositions a durable and absolute poetic worth. To be honest, only a few of her works can be extracted from her three published volumes by someone of truly scrupulous taste, and even these will not be exempt of defects including over-elaboration, recherché style, or an excess of complex conceits. Even still, one could compile quite a respectable volume with two dozen of her lyric poems, a few mystery plays such as *The Divine Narcissus*, her charming comedic play *The Trials of a House*,[1] and her letter to the

† From *Antología de poetas hispano-americanos. Tomo I. México y América Central* (Madrid: Real Academia Española, 1893), pp. lxvi–lxxiv. Translated for this edition by Isabel Gómez. All notes are the editor's unless otherwise indicated.
1. A secular courtly drama first published in *Second Volume* (1692). "Mystery plays": religious allegorical dramas that sought to explain Church dogma such as the Eucharist.

bishop of Puebla, which would be admirable if it could be unbur-
dened of its extemporaneous citations and unnecessary erudition.
This volume would earn her the credit of her name *Tenth Muse of
Mexico*, and the high opinion of her formed by Father Feijóo would
prevail over the rigorous sentence pronounced by Doctor Juan Nica-
sio Gallego.[2] Driven by his rigorous classicism, he declared that
"bloated with extravagance, her work has languished in dusty librar-
ies since the restoration of good taste."

To declare Sor Juana superior to all poets during the reign of Car-
los II damns with faint praise: her era was certainly unfavorable for
the literary arts, although it was not as bad for other branches of
our culture, nor did it produce as much material. But whatever it
may be worth, nobody can deny her this laurel in the realm of lyric
poetry, just as Bances Candamo must be granted the same in dra-
matic poetry, and Solís[3] in prose. One cannot condemn Sor Juana
for her symbols and hieroglyphs, her *Allegorical Neptune*, her *ensal-
adas* and *villancicos*, her verses in rhymed Latin, or for any of the
innumerable qualities of trivial and homespun poetry which fill
the ballads and *décimas*[4] with which she entertained the soirées of
the Viceroys the Marquis de Mancera and the Count of Paredes.[5]
All this is merely a curious document in the history of colonial court
life and a clear testimony to the way the tyranny of environment can
deform even the most privileged nature.

For Sor Juana was undoubtedly this[6]—what is most interesting
in her works is that most rare psychological phenomenon offered by
the personality of their author. In our literary history, there are abun-
dant examples of nuns who write, not only on subjects limited to
the mystical but also on secular and profane topics. The Portuguese
Sor Violante do Ceo,[7] almost contemporary to Sor Juana, had a
poetic talent that matched or even surpassed hers. But the exemplary
quality of scientific curiosity, all-encompassing and overwhelming,

2. Spanish priest and poet (1777–1853). The following citation is from his prologue to *Poe-
sías de la Señorita Gertrudis Gómez de Avellaneda* (Poems by the Señorita Gertrudis
Gómez de Avellaneda, 1841). Father Friar Benito Jerónimo Feijóo y Montenegro (1676–
1764), Galician monk and leading figure of the Spanish Enlightenment. His *Teatro
crítico universal* (1726–1739) mentions Sor Juana.
3. Antonio de Solís y Ribadeneyra (1610–1686), Spanish playwright and historian of the
Historia de la Conquista de México (History of the Conquest of Mexico) (1684). Fran-
cisco Bances Candamo (1662–1704), Spanish playwright.
4. Lyric form composed of ten octosyllabic lines per stanza with the consonant rhyme
scheme ABBAACCDDC. Often set to music. "Ensaladas": literally, salads. A genre of
lyric poem characterized by mixture, either of verse forms, speaking voices, or even
citations of other lyrical composition [Translator]. "Villancicos": carols performed on holy
and feast days [Editor].
5. Tomás de la Cerda, Marquis of la Laguna, Count of Paredes (1638–1692), viceroy of
New Spain from 1680 to 1686. Antonio Sebastián Álvarez de Toledo Molina y Salazar,
Marquis de Mancera (ca. 1608–1715); viceroy of New Spain from 1664 to 1673.
6. That is, a privileged nature.
7. Violante do Ceo (1601 or 1607–1693): Portuguese nun and poet.

dominated Sor Juana from her early years and drove her to trample
any obstacle put in her way by concern or custom until the end of
her days. She never allowed anything to chill this ardor: not exter-
nal repression or her own scruples; not ascetic fervor, scourges, or
hair shirts once she entered into convent life; not the tumult and
pomp of the worldly life that occupied her youth, nor the cloud of
hopes and desires that she dragged behind her in the Viceregal
Court of Mexico; not the human love that she seemed to have felt
so deeply that her verses include tones that could not have come
from literary imitation alone; not spiritual love, the only one that
ultimately proved sufficient to fill the immense capacity of her
soul. She is something so new, so unusual and out of this world,
that if she had not written her own confessions with such candor
and simplicity, they would seem to be immoderate hyperboles of her
eulogists.

* * *

The secular love poems by Sor Juana are among the most subtle and
delicate to be penned by a woman. One can find the bad habit of
affectation in her *arte mayor*[8] compositions. But in her admirable
ballad known as "Absence," which would be better titled "The Fare-
well," and in the *redondillas*[9] in which she describes the "symptoms
of love," all or almost all of it is spontaneous and comes from the
soul. For this reason she hits the target many times with a felicitous
expression or unique turn of phrase, the true touchstones of sincer-
ity in affective poetry.

This quality is no less present in her mystical verses, expressions
of her changeable spiritual state and doubtlessly born from her
reactionary personality that arrived at its sharpest crisis two years
before her death. She was moved to sell her library of more than four
thousand volumes to benefit the poor, along with her musical and
scientific instruments, her jewels, and whatever else she had in her
cell, without preserving more than "three little devotional books and
many hair shirts and scourges." Then, she made a general confes-
sion that lasted for many days, wrote and signed with her blood two
Professions of Faith and a *Juridical Peticion* to the Divine Tribunal.
She also began to torment her flesh so harshly that her superiors
had to take her in hand for the excesses of her penitence. As Father

8. A line of poetry written in *arte mayor* has nine or more syllables [*Translator*].
9. Lyric form composed of four-line octosyllabic stanzas with the consonant rhyme scheme
ABBA. Her most famous *redondilla* is the celebrated "*Hombres nécios*" or "O foolish
men." Menéndez y Pelayo describes this work as "the only composition by Sor Juana still
popular today in Spain" (lxxv). "Absence": Menéndez y Pelayo refers to the lyric poem that
begins "*Divino dueño mío*" (My divine owner). While he calls it a *romance* or a ballad,
it is actually an *endecha*, another musical verse form typically composed of four lines
with six or seven syllables per line [*Translator*].

Núñez, her confessor, said: "Juana Inés did not run toward virtue; she flew." Her death was the crowning achievement of her life: she died in an epidemic, tending to her sisters.[1]

In my opinion, the most beautiful of her spiritual poems can be found in the songs interspersed in the mystery play the *Divine Narcissus*, full of apt imitations of Song of Songs and of other commonplace topics from biblical poetry. They are so beautiful, so generally unadorned with affectation and *culteranismo*, that they seem to belong more to the sixteenth century than the seventeenth, and they recall some disciple of Saint John of the Cross and Luis de León more than an overseas nun whose verses were printed with the title *Castalian Inundation*.[2] Such talents were at work in this humble nun, just as in other nuns who were almost her contemporaries (Sor Gregoria of Santa Teresa, Sor María do Ceo,[3] etc.). Their elevated purity and heightened spiritual sense were conserved, along with certain genres of the literary tradition that are healthy and in good taste, through reading devotional books from the previous century. But in Sor Juana these qualities are doubly praiseworthy, because the ears of those other brides of Christ[4] rarely heard the accents of secular poetry, and it was very difficult for the contagion of bad taste to reach their peaceful seclusion. Quite to the contrary, Sor Juana always lived in the midst of literary life, in correspondence with the scholars and poets of the Peninsula, including the most emphatic and pedantic, and in daily contact with those from Mexico, who tended to exaggerate even more the aberrations of their models. Surely they all admired Sor Juana even more when, setting out to imitate the *Solitudes* by Góngora in "First Dream," her results were more inaccessible than her model, or when in the *Allegorical Neptune, Ocean of Colors, Political Simulacrum*, she pushed her imagination to invent disparate emblems for the triumphal arch constructed to celebrate the entrance of the Viceroy Count of Paredes. [How different from] her humble ballad, where she exclaimed to the divine with such luminous intuition:

> In order to see into hearts
> You need not attend to them;

1. In this paragraph, Menéndez y Pelayo paraphrases Diego Calleja's posthumous biography (see p. 196).
2. The first volume of Sor Juana's works, published in 1689. "*Culteranismo*": an ornate style of poetry associated with Luis de Góngora (1561–1627). Saint John of the Cross (1542–1591), Spanish mystic and poet. Luis de Léon (1527–1591), Spanish poet and Augustinian friar.
3. Portuguese nun, poet, and playwright (1658–1752). Gregoria de Santa Teresa (1653–1736), Sevillian nun and poet.
4. That is, nuns.

for You they are as apparent
as the entrails of the Abyss.[5]

Therefore our *Anthology* includes a small selection from her sacred
and secular verses; the Mexican Parnassus[6] begins with them and
loses nothing by being under the protection of such an agreeable
patroness. If our collection expanded to include dramatic poetry, we
could have also allowed entrance to one of her mystery plays, such
as the one dedicated to Saint Hermengildo, perhaps a prologue to a
mystery play,[7] and above all her fascinating imitation of the cloak
and dagger comedies by Calderón [de la Barca] titled *The Trials of a
House*. Perhaps even another comedy of hers, *Love Is More Like a
Labyrinth*,[8] belongs, although it is notoriously inferior to the former.
Its defects including a mythological plot, the vice of *culteranismo*,
weak dramatic structure, and above all the extremely unfortunate
second act that ruins it—which is not by the nun but by her collabo-
rator the scholar Don Juan de Guevara. There is still something worth
praising in it: a robust and Calderon-like quality in the story of
Theseus and in the speech by the ambassador of Athens.

Even in a chronological sense, Sor Juana marks the end of seven-
teenth century poetry.

IRVING A. LEONARD

From Baroque Times in Old Mexico[†]

Irving A. Leonard (1896–1996) was a historian and literary critic who
specialized in Hispanic American literature. His work on seventeenth-
century Mexico was important for bringing authors such as Sor Juana
to the attention of North American scholars. While Leonard did much
to further historical documentation of the period, at times his narrative
historiography led him to exaggerate evidence and often he ignores the
rhetorical context of statements, interpreting them as expressions of an
interior psychology. He also shared the eighteenth- and nineteenth-
century dismissal of seventeenth-century verse and scholastic thought as

5. This verse is cited from her Ballad 58 with the first line "*Amante dulce del alma,*" or
"Sweet beloved of the soul," and refers to the actions of Christ on behalf of human souls,
specifically the Sacrament of Communion figured as the gift of divine love (*Obras*, Vol. 1,
169, verses 25–8) [*Translator*].
6. Collection of verse.
7. A *loa* is a genre of brief dramatic verse that serves as a prologue introducing a mystery play
or comedia. The genre often praised a benefactor or presented an allegory [*Translator*].
8. *Amor es más laberinto* (Love is a greater labyrinth), a comedic play first published in
Sor Juana's *Second Volume* (1692).
† From Irving A. Leonard, *Baroque Times in Old Mexico: Seventeenth-Century Persons,
Places, and Practices* (Ann Arbor: University of Michigan Press, 1959), pp. 182–92, 242.
Copyright © by the University of Michigan, 1959. Reprinted by permission of the pub-
lisher. All notes are Leonard's unless otherwise indicated.

superficial and convoluted. Continuing a narrative begun by Menéndez y Pelayo (see p. 235), Leonard promoted Sor Juana as a figure leading toward the Enlightenment, an exception in what he characterized as a century of Baroque obscurity.

A Baroque Poetess

✻   ✻   ✻

It was Sister Juana's fate to have her being in this age when, even in Old Mexico, though ever so slightly, the long accepted and sole approach to truth was beginning to be threatened by a new way, a new method. Almost imperceptibly the traditional scholastic and authoritarian concepts of revealed knowledge were yielding to the more sensate procedures of scientific observation and analysis. In the Mexico City of her time there was greater awareness of this intellectual revolution than commonly believed, and the capital had a tiny group of savants who were abreast of contemporary thought, even that of non-Catholic Europe. The comparatively free circulation of nontheological books during the sixteenth and seventeenth centuries,[1] the frequent presence in the viceroyalty of transient men of learning from the Old World, and the personal correspondence of local scholars with thinkers abroad, had all contributed to a more vital mental climate in the New World centers than the contemporary dominance of a medieval Church was thought to permit. A small number of Creole *sabios* were already familiar with the ideas and writings of Erasmus, Copernicus, Kepler, and particularly Descartes,[2] whose philosophies they discussed among themselves in comparative freedom and even cited in their published writings.

   Most conspicuous of this intelligentsia of New Spain was Don Carlos de Sigüenza y Góngora.[3] He was a professor of mathematics

1. Cf. Irving A. Leonard, *Books of the Brave* (Cambridge: Harvard Press, 1949), *passim*. Regarding works in Sister Juana's library, see E. Abreu Gómez, *Sor Juana Inés de la Cruz. Bibliografía y Biblioteca*. Monografías Bibliográficas Mexicanas, 29 (Mexico City, 1934), *passim*.
2. A list of early modern thinkers who defied Church dogma. Erasmus of Rotterdam (1466–1536), Dutch Catholic theologian who advocated for reforms similar to those promoted by Protestants. Nicolaus Copernicus (1473–1543), whose heliocentric model of the universe challenged Church doctrine. Johannes Kepler (1571–1630), German mathematician who advanced a theory of planetary motion. René Descartes (1596–1650), French philosopher considered the founder of modern philosophy. There is no way to ascertain that Mexico City authors actually discussed these authors, as Leonard claims. Leonard was probably thinking of Carlos de Sigüenza y Góngora's oft-cited reference to Descartes in the *Libra Astronómica* (Astronomical balance, 1690). There is no indication that Sigüenza approved of Descartes's thought, however, and it is likely that he knew of the French philosopher only through the many anti-Cartesian writings that circulated among Jesuits. "*Sabios*": savants [*Editor*].
3. Mexican mathematician and university professor (1645–1700) known for his wide range of interests. It has been difficult to determine the exact relationship between Sor Juana and Sigüenza y Góngora, and Leonard's account of their conversations in the *locutorio* and Sigüenza's gifts of mathematical instruments is speculative [*Editor*].

in the University of Mexico, renowned for his studies of astronomy, archaeology, history and natural philosophy, and also an intimate friend of Sister Juana. Living at the Hospital del Amor de Dios where he served as chaplain, he was a frequent visitor at the Jeronymite convent a few blocks away where the nun-poetess had her cell. It appears that these two intellectually gifted and lonely people enjoyed long discussions together in the locutory of the convent. Sigüenza, a very minor poet, was encouraged in these exercises by Sister Juana, while she in turn received his stimulation and training in scientific disciplines. It is likely that she acquired the mathematical instruments and some of the books said to have furnished her cell as a result of this association. Indeed, the attainments of these two figures working together have moved a discerning critic to comment that they were ". . . the first ones (in Mexico) in whom the modern spirit appears or manifests itself."[4] It was Sigüenza who most often brought visiting savants to her convent, including the great mission-founder of the American Southwest, Father Eusebio Francisco Kino.[5] And it was he who initiated the exceedingly intelligent nun into the new methodology propounded by Descartes, of which there are faint indications in her verse.[6] Doubtless it was he who understood her enthusiasm for, and encouraged her in, the performance of such simple experiments in physics as she mentions in her *Reply to Sister Philotea*. And it was he who shared her love for the dawning Age of Enlightenment of which they both were unconscious precursors in Mexico.

The inherent critical capacity of Sister Juana, coupled with omniverous reading, moved her to welcome a more pragmatic approach to truth. Latent in her mind was a healthy skepticism regarding the effectiveness of purely verbal rationalization, and her eager curiosity was insidiously drawn to experimentation and direct observation. A scrutiny of Sister Juana's verse and prose tends to support the conviction that she felt an instinctive distrust of the scholasticism dominating the intellectual life of viceregal Mexico. Her deeper regard for observation and a more scientific analysis seems apparent when, in the *Reply*, she emphasizes the importance of varied studies and methods in throwing light on speculative learning, particularly theology, and her underlying preference is revealed when she adds: ". . . and when the expositors are like an open hand and

---

4. López Cámara, p. 129.
5. Austrian Jesuit (1645–1711) who passed through Mexico City on the way to the missions in Sonora [*Editor*].
6. *Ibid.*, pp. 122–23. Sigüenza cites Descartes in his *Libra astronómica y filosófica* (Mexico City, 1690). [The conjecture that the reference to method in the "First Dream" (ca. 1691) held resonances with Cartesianism has been generally dismissed, as Sor Juana clearly refers to scholastic logic—*Editor*.]

the ecclesiastics like a closed fist."[7] Her reactions to the specious learning and rhetorical ratiocination around her, characterized chiefly by polemical disquisitions with ostentatious displays of classical quotations and cloudy verbosity, emerge clearly in the ballad beginning with the pathetic verse. "Let us pretend that I am happy."[8] The wordy debates of bookish pedants and charlatans of the so-called intelligentsia filling the air about her with their din move her to exclaim metrically: "Everything is opinions and of such varied counsels that what one proves is black, the other proves is white."[9] And regarding these doctrinaire pundits she would surely have agreed with Alexander Pope's caustic couplet:

> The bookful blockhead, ignorantly read,
> with loads of learned lumber in his head.[1]

This universal penchant for splitting hairs in interminable disputes to the neglect of essentials vexes the sound intellect of Sister Juana. "If their soaring rhetoric steeped in false subtleties be not abated, the essential is forgotten in the concern for the accessory."[2] She seemed to feel that these disputants, to borrow a phrase from Bacon,[3] worked at their endless dialectics ". . . as the spider worketh its web, bringing forth cobwebs of learning, admirable for its fineness of thread and work, but of no substance or profit." The pedantry exhibited in the profusion of Latin and Greek quotations, of classical allusions, and of florid circumlocutions irked the wise nun. "If a trained hand does not prevent the foliage of the tree from becoming too dense, its wild tangle will rob the fruit of its substance."[4] All this specious erudition moves her to ask: "What silly ambition sweeps us away, forgetful of ourselves? If it is for so short

7. "Response," p. 101 [Editor].
8. Ballad 2, p. 5, v.13–16 [Editor].
9. Todo el mundo es opiniones,
   de pareceres tan varios
   que lo que el uno, que es negro,
   el otro prueba que es blanco.
1. From Essay on Criticism (1709) [Editor].
2. Y si el vuelo no le abaten
   en sutilezas cebado,
   por cuidar de lo curioso
   olvida lo necesario.
3. Francis Bacon (1561–1626), English philosopher and prominent example of the new science, particularly in his espousal of skepticism and empiricism. The following citation is found in his Advancement of Learning (1605). Leonard slightly rephrases the original citation: "as the spider worketh its web, then it is endless, and brings forth indeed cobwebs of learning, admirable for the fineness of thread and of work but of no substance or profit" [Editor].
4. Si culta mano no impide
   Crecer al arbol copado,
   Quita la sustancia al fruto
   la locura de los ramos.

a life, what good is it to know so much?"⁵ And in despair she cries: "Oh, if there were only some seminary or school, as there is for knowledge, where they would teach ignorance of such learning!"⁶

In the *Reply* she comments, with veiled scorn, on the affectation that passed as learning in the excessive number of quotations from authorities: ". . . and I add that their education is perfected (if nonsense is perfection) by having studied a little Philosophy and Theology, and by having a smattering of languages, by which means one may be stupid in numerous subjects and languages because the mother tongue alone is not room enough for a really big fool." Mindful, likewise, of the self delusion facilitated by the verbalism of scholasticism; Sister Juana believed that everyone should keep within his own mental limitations. If this were so, she tartly exclaims: "How many warped intelligences wandering about there would not be!"⁷

Perhaps the most penetrating stanza of this same ballad is the one in which she puts her finger on the core of true wisdom, the development of sound judgment: "To know how to make varied and subtle discourses is not knowledge; rather, knowledge simply consists of making the soundest choices."⁸

These and other passages in the writings of Sister Juana reflect a disaffection with the prevailing scholastic methods of thinking in her world and an impatience with an intellectual age which she could not know was passing. She yearned for a newer, freer era of widening horizons, of a differing approach to truth which she did not realize was beginning. But the religious institution, of which she was a part and which was so concerned for her salvation, was wholly identified with the old ways of thinking that did not attract her. Rather, her attachment to the unorthodox kind of thinking became a compulsion against which she struggled constantly, fearful of its implications for her eternal security in its radical departure from ecclesiastical authoritarianism. Her intellectual soul was enamored of this new and scientific approach to truth, but there could be no reciprocation in such a passion for one so closely held in the embrace of medieval tradition as a nun. For her only the concept of knowledge revealed by

5. *Que loca ambición nos lleva*
   de nosotros oluidados?
   Si es para vivir tan poco,
   de que sirue saber tanto?
6. *Oh, si, como hay de saber,*
   hubiera algún seminario
   o escuela donde a ignorar
   se enseñaran los trabajos!
   [Ballad 2, (Finjamos que soy feliz)—*Editor*.]
7. "Response," p. 114 [*Editor*].
8. *No es saber, hacer*
   discursos sutiles vanos;
   que el saber consiste sólo
   en elegir lo más sano.
   [Ballad 2—*Editor*.]

242

authority and scholastic methods was proper and permissible. Consequently, she feared this urge to think by unhallowed procedures, and she buried herself deeply in her books in the vain effort to banish such ideas from her mind. Yet this analytical mania obsessed her. "This way of observing everything happened to me and it always happens to me without my having any control in the matter . . . And, continuing on the subject of my cogitations, I must state that this is so constant with me that I do not need any books . . ."9 When deprived of her reading, as happened for a period, her mind seemed to accelerate its activity in this manner. "Even though I did not study in books I kept studying everything in God's creation, the individual objects serving me as words and the whole universal scheme as a book. Nothing did I look at and nothing did I hear that I did not speculate on, even the smallest and most material things . . . And so, I repeat, I looked at everything and I wondered about everything . . ."1 Even in sleep this process operated: ". . . not even in slumber was my mind free of this continuous movement. On the contrary, it seems to operate more freely and unimpeded, bringing out these objects with even greater and more undisturbed clarity than in the daytime."2

Thus it appears that Sister Juana found herself not only torn between "reason" and "passion," but also between *two methodologies of reason.* The time-honored dialectics and syllogisms of scholasticism were still entrenched as the accepted means of rationalization in the Church of Christ which held her in its protective arms and to which she was irrevocably bound by vows. This great institution sheltered and loved her, and obedience to its authority and ways was her ineludible obligation. Yet, deep within, she could not reciprocate its love. Instead, she seemed possessed by a way of thinking that threatened to undermine the assumptions on which the Faith rested. On the true object of her affections, the new concept of experimentalism relying on the senses rather than on authority, her benevolent guardian, the Church, severely frowned. Such intellectual exercise might well be inimical to the divine science of theology, and it was potentially, if not actually, heretical. Adherence to such thinking could seriously jeopardize her eternal salvation, which was infinitely precious to her. In her religious play, *The Divine Narcissus,* she wrote: "Behold that what I yearn for I am powerless to enjoy, and in my anxious longing to possess it, I suffer mortal pangs."3

In this torturing dilemma Sister Juana, in her long letter to the Bishop of Puebla, sought to rationalize her predilection when she asked how the "Queen of Sciences," that is, Theology, could be

9. "Response," pp. 109–110 [*Editor*].
1. "Response," p. 108 [*Editor*].
2. "Response," p. 110 [*Editor*].
3. *El Divino Narciso* (1689). The citation has not been located [*Editor*].

understood without knowledge of a series of secular disciplines including Logic, Rhetoric, Physics, Arithmetic, Geometry, Architecture, History, and others.[4] This passage seems a faint echo of the Third Precept of Descartes which reads: ". . . to conduct my thought in such order that, by commencing with objects the simplest and easiest to know, I might ascend little by little and, as it were, step by step, to the knowledge of the more complex, assigning in thought a certain order even to those objects which, in their own nature, do not stand in a relation of antecedence and sequence."[5] But, however cogently she might argue for more pragmatic learning and greater intellectual freedom, the heavy odds of the traditions of her time, place, vocation, and sex were overwhelmingly against her. Inevitably, she fell prey to torturing uncertainty, guilt, and despair, from which she sought release in her more intimate poetry. These inner rendings of her being resulting from the many dualisms of her complex personality became chronic and, in time, made her long for death. In one of her poems appear these words: "I am dying (who will believe it?) at the hands of the thing that I love most, and what is killing me is the love I have for it."[6] And in a secular play[7] of hers occurs the line: "I am dying for the sake of one who is not dying because of me."

Repeatedly in verse and in prose her guilt complex and torment are revealed by the phrase: "I am my own executioner," which seems a cry of anguish, though "I do not study in order to write, and much less to teach, for that would be unpardonable arrogance in me, but just to see if by studying, I can be less ignorant."[8] In her constricted world with its low, arching dome of heaven,[9] there was no space for her privileged spirit to soar. With deepening despair she knew that such a strange preoccupation with her mind was unseemly in a woman, especially one in religious reclusion; it erected barriers of intercourse with her uncomprehending sisters in the community in which she lived, and their jealousy and envy of her recognized superiority did not grow less. "Let not the head which is the repository of knowledge expect any other crown than that of thorns,"[1] she wrote bitterly, for she had known the reprobation of her superiors. Indeed,

4. See "Response," p. 98 [Editor].
5. In Descartes' Discourse on Method (1637), he presents four precepts to orient philosophical inquiry, the third of which Leonard cites [Editor].
6. Muero (y quién lo creerá?) a manos
   de la cosa que más quiero
   y el motivo de matarme
   es el amor que le tengo.
   [Ballad 56, "Traigo conmigo un cuidado"—Editor.]
7. Most likely Los empeños de una casa (The house of trials, 1692). The following citation has not been identified [Editor].
8. Both citations are from the "Response" (p. 103 and p. 95) [Editor].
9. A reference to the celestial spheres of the Ptolemaic universe, discredited by seventeenth century new science, but in Sor Juana's period still considered orthodox by the Catholic Church [Editor].
1. See "Response," p. 106 [Editor].

the chiding letter of the Bishop of Puebla was probably mild and gentle in comparison with the admonitions of her confessor and of the convent sisters. The bishop had reproved her cultivation of "profane letters," by which it was clear that he included her preoccupation with a secular rationalization. He had urged her to confine herself to the exercise of theological scholasticism of which she had given such proof of her skill in her telling critique of the sermon of the celebrated Portuguese Jesuit.[2]

But Sister Juana's mind and heart responded instinctively to a more experimental pragmatism, and she could not bring herself wholly to surrender to the verbal hairsplitting of the intellectual life about her. In many of her poems she used the poetical name "Fabio" as the figure she adored and Silvio, Feliciano and others as the ones she disdained or abhorred. "My will belongs to Fabio, and may Silvio and the world forgive me,"[3] are two typical verses. That her preference for "Fabio" stems from its similarity to the Spanish word *sabio*, the wise or learned, is a possibility. Silvio, like other designations, may well refer to the pedants that she could not esteem. But convent-bound in the medieval atmosphere of the ecclesiastical society of Mexico City she could only feel at war with it and with herself. The love and kindliness implicit in the Church's paternalism claimed her gratitude and, of course, her vows compelled obedience to it. Yet the persistent longing for a freer expression of her intuition and for another and more open avenue to truth and to God prevented complete reciprocation and submission in her heart. The sensate experimentalism and scientific methodology of a dawning age beckoned her, while the secular world, which was giving birth to it, was indifferent and unaware of the love of a lonely woman deeply enmeshed in the toils of rigid medievalism. It seemed only to disdain her and, inevitably, Sister Juana's was a blighted love— rejection by the beloved and possession by the unloved—a triangular antithesis. Rarely did she experience even a momentary relief from the incessant conflict within her and, in time, it undermined her health and hastened her death. In this unhappy state of *encontradas correspondencias* she could only externalize her dilemma in verses of obscure symbolism but unmistakable feeling which voiced her suffering repeatedly. In the poignant sonnet, "Who thankless flees me, I with love pursue," the "Who" was, perhaps, experimentalism, a secularized freedom, and a newer age; and in "Who loving follows me, I thankless flee," the "Who" was possibly scholasticism, ecclesiasticism, and medievalism; the first the avenue to salvation by knowledge, the second the avenue to salvation by *faith*.

2. António Vieira (1609–1697), author of the 1650 Maundy Thursday sermon critiqued by Sor Juana in the *Athenagoric Letter* (1690); see p. 83 [*Editor*].
3. Ballad 4, "Supuesto discurso mío" [*Editor*].

Who thankless flees me, I with love pursue;
Who loving follows me, I thankless flee;
To him who spurns my love I bend the knee,
His love who seeks me, cold I bid him rue.
　　I find as diamond him I yearning woo,
Myself a diamond when he yearns for me:
Who slays my love I would victorious see
While slaying him who wills me blisses true.
　　To favor this one is to lose desire,
To crave that one, my virgin pride to tame;
On either hand I face a prospect dire;
　　Whatever path I tread, the goal the same;
To be adored by him of whom I tire,
Or else by him who scorns me brought to shame.[4]

As the dawn of April 17, 1695 was casting a wan light over the troubled City of Mexico the wracked and broken spirit of Sister Juana quietly claimed its longed-for release from the prison of her aloneness. "See how death eludes me because I desire it," she had exclaimed in one of her poems, "for even death, when it is in demand," she had added, "will rise in price." Over the long years of her short life she had struggled against the viselike prejudices and incomprehension of her time and place. She had dreamed of a liberation from the shackles of static traditions and stultifying conventions. She had dared to rebuke the men of her society for their double standard of morality and had thus struck a first blow for women's rights.

Which has the greater sin when burned
by the same lawless fever:
She who is amorously deceived,
or he, the sly deceiver?

Or which deserves the sterner blame,
though each will be a sinner:
She who becomes a whore for pay,
Or he who pays to win her?[5]

---

4. Sonnet 168, "Al que ingrato me deja, busco amante" [Editor].
5. Cuál mayor culpa ha tenido
　　en una pasión errada:
　　la que cae de rogada,
　　o el que ruega de caído?

　　O cuál es más de culpar
　　aunque cualquiera mal haga:
　　la que peca por la paga
　　o el que paga por pecar?
Translation of Robert Graves, in Encounter, no. 3 (December, 1953), and quoted with his permission. [Redondilla 92—Editor.]

But more than all else she had struggled for a freedom of thought for all. "There is nothing freer than the human mind,"[6] she had proclaimed to a world that could not comprehend these words, or could only hear them as subversive of a God-given truth. Against her the odds were too great and their relentless pressure brought at last a total renunciation of all effort and a complete submission of her intellect. The passionate woman in her capitulated to the devout nun and this surrender left her bereft of life. Physically she survived herself briefly.

To the unhappy nun-poetess during the last four or five years of her existence the world outside must have seemed a projection of her own inner turmoil and affliction. A series of disasters and phenomena were then plaguing the city and its environs, bringing suffering, fear and violence. Heavy rains in 1691 brought successively ruinous floods, crop destruction, famine, and pestilence, while a total eclipse of the sun stirred panic fear. Sullen discontent and mounting tensions erupted into mass riots that nearly toppled Spanish authority in the land.[7] As these sinister events darkened the world without, the storm, so long brewing within Sister Juana Inés, broke.

In 1690 she inadvertently brought to a head the disapproval and hostility of her religious associates slowly gathering over the years. In some way she was induced to write a successful rebuttal of certain views set forth long before in a sermon by a famous Portuguese Jesuit, Father Vieira. Her skill in manipulating the methods of neo-scholasticism evidently pleased the Bishop of Puebla who took it upon himself to publish her paper. At the same time, in the guise of "Sister Philotea," he wrote her a letter chiding her alleged neglect of religious literature and her fondness for profane letters. "You have spent a lot of time studying (secular) philosophers and poets, and now it would seem reasonable to apply yourself to better things and to better books."[8] Clearly, this was a reproof from a superior high in the hierarchy and it could not fail to distress a nun tormented by guilt feelings. Through months of declining health she brooded on a reply to the Bishop's censure. Finally, under date of March 1, 1691, it took form in her famous *Reply* in which, with many autobiographical details and with alternate humility and boldness, she defended herself from the prelate's strictures.

Obscure complications followed this epistolary exchange, chief of which was the withdrawal of her confessor, Father Antonio Núñez de

6. Ballad 1, p. 3 [*Editor*].
7. The 1692 riot in Mexico City, the largest in the colonial period, was recounted in detail by Carlos de Sigüenza y Góngora in his letter to the Admiral Pez. Rioters stormed the main plaza (*zócalo*) and burned the marketplace and the viceregal palace [*Editor*].
8. "Letter from Sor Filotea," p. 88 [*Editor*].

Miranda,[9] who had influenced her decision to enter the convent and had counseled her over the years. Vainly he had urged her to turn from what he considered worldly matters and apply her great talents to things eternal. All her devoted supporters, it seemed to her, were falling away through absence, desertion, or death. And she had never enjoyed the favor of the misogynistic Archbishop Aguiar y Seijas,[1] who had involved her in his frenzied almsgiving. In 1693, as if to remind everyone of her worldliness, a second edition of a volume of her poems,[2] which the vicereine, her friend and patroness, had extracted from her, appeared in Spain, and copies doubtless reached Mexico City soon after. This intended kindness may have hastened her final surrender. On February 8, 1694, using blood from her veins as ink, she indited an abject reaffirmation of her faith and renewed her vows, which she signed: "I, Sister Juana Inés de la Cruz, the worst in the world."[3] She renounced all her possessions, the gifts and trinkets of her admirers, the mathematical and musical instruments that she had so long studied and used, and—the most painful wrench of all—those silent and precious companions of her cell, her beloved books. All were sold and the proceeds given to charity. With this bitter deprivation, she gave herself to excessive acts of penance, self-flagellation, and mortification of the flesh. The coveted death of the body came at last during her tireless ministrations to sisters of her community decimated by a pestilence sweeping the city.

The one kindred spirit that had most nearly understood her, Don Carlos de Sigüenza y Góngora, delivered the funeral oration[4] at her grave. Even his sympathy was denied her in those final, bitter years when his absence on an expedition to Florida,[5] and the preoccupation of public service, private family, and declining health kept him away. The words uttered on the melancholy occasion of her interment are lost but, even more feelingly, they probably echoed sentiments he had expressed in 1680 when both were rising to fame. "There is no pen that can rise to the eminence that hers o'ertops," he had written, and then added, with a sincerity that shines through his pedantic style: "I

9. Confessor (1618–1695) and advocate for Sor Juana early on, who was apparently dismissed by her around 1681, in the "Letter by Mother Juana Inés de la Cruz" (p. 152). She accepted him again as confessor at the end of her life. Leonard did not have access to this letter, which was discovered in 1981, and therefore believes that Núñez continued as confessor to Sor Juana through the period of the "Response" [Editor].
1. Francisco Aguiar y Seijas (1632–1698), Spanish Jesuit who was archbishop of New Spain from 1680 until his death. He was famous for his misogyny and alms giving [Editor].
2. Segundo volumen (Second volume), published in 1692 through the patronage of the Countess of Paredes upon her return to Spain at the end of the reign of her husband as viceroy of New Spain [Editor].
3. See Petition on p. 155 [Editor].
4. This has never been found. It is a strong piece of evidence of his admiration for Sor Juana, but Leonard's characterization of their strong friendship is speculative [Editor].
5. In 1693 Sigüenza y Góngora traveled to Pensacola Bay in Florida to map the region and investigate the possibility of fortifying the northern territory against the entrance of other Europeans [Editor].

should like to omit the esteem with which I regard her, the veneration that she has won by her works, in order to make manifest to the world how much, in the encyclopedic nature and universality of her letters, is contained in her genius, so that it may be seen that, in one single person, Mexico enjoys what, in past centuries, the graces have imparted to all the learned women who are the great marvels of history." And he concluded prophetically that the name and fame of "Mother Juana Inés de la Cruz will only end with the world."[6]

OCTAVIO PAZ

From Sor Juana or, The Traps of Faith[†]

Although constructed with deliberate and rigorous objectivity, *First Dream* is threaded with personal emotion. The daring of the soul, its ecstasy, its doubts, its vacillations, and the praise of the tragic figure of Phaethon are a true intellectual confession. To confirm this we need only compare the poem with what Sor Juana says in the *Response* about her desire for learning, her psychic wavering, her method of study, meditations, and reasonings. In the space of an ideal night, in a consciously abstract manner, Juana Inés recounts her intellectual life. The poem ends inconclusively: the soul does not know what path to choose—all are "quicksand and reefs"[1]—the body awakens and the dream dissipates. The abrupt awakening puts an end to the dream, not to the intellectual adventure of the soul. This explains and justifies the adjective *primero*, first. But *First Dream* also portrays the history of a defeat, although some Catholic critics, contrary to what is explicit in the text, insist in seeing in the poem the "beautiful embrace of faith and piety."[2] What, then, is the meaning of that "defeat"?

The idea that learning is impossible divides into two other ideas: either man cannot know because he is man, or he is precluded from knowing by some particular circumstance—for example, in Sor Juana's case, because she was Sor Juana. This is the distinction perceptively set forth by José Gaos in his essay "El sueño de un sueño"

6. Carlos de Sigüenza y Góngora, *Teatro de virtudes políticas,* in Francisco Pérez Salazar, *Obras de Carlos de Sigüenza y Góngora* (Mexico City, 1928), p. 38.
† From Octavio Paz, *Sor Juana or, The Traps of Faith,* trans. Margaret Sayers Peden (Cambridge: Belknap Press, 1988), pp. 377–85, 533. Copyright © 1988 by the President and Fellows of Harvard College. Reprinted by permission of the publisher. Editor's notes include contributions by Isabel Gómez.
1. From *First Dream,* lines 827–28 in the original poem, translated in this volume in lines 704–05 as "But while choice foundered, confused, among the reefs, / touching sandbars of courses impossible" (see p. 63) [*Editor*].
2. Paz does not name the author of this quotation [*Editor*].

("Dream of a Dream").[3] According to Gaos, "Sor Juana did not phi-
losophize in verse on the limits of human knowledge . . . but on the
primary experience of her life: the failure of her quest to learn."
And he adds, "Is this failure of a woman's desire to learn the result
of being a woman or of being the woman she is? A feminist or a
personal skepticism?" As a person, Sor Juana was "inclined toward
learning," but soon she realized that "being female was a basic bar-
rier to the realization of that desire. She attempts to neutralize being
female by means of religion . . . but even this neutralizing fails."
Gaos does not clarify whether this barrier was natural for Sor
Juana—that is, her condition as a woman—or imposed by society.
Sor Juana's texts make clear that she did not believe that being a
woman was a natural barrier: her obstacles originated in customs,
not in her femaleness. That is why she turns to religion: to neutralize
the social barrier. Furthermore, the protagonist of *First Dream* is
not the female soul but the human soul that for Sor Juana—it cannot
be repeated too often—has no gender. The barrier is not her wom-
anhood but the fact that the soul is prisoner of the body. Failure
derives not from her sex but from the limitations of human compre-
hension. The defect of "not knowing in one instant the whole of
creation,"[4] as we read in the middle section of the poem, is a defect
of fallen man. Sor Juana did reflect on the limitations of reason:
this is the theme of her poem and is at the center of her inner life.

Most critics believe that the poem is about "the dream of knowl-
edge." They immediately invest the word "dream" of the title with
the sense of illusion and vanity. The soul "dreams" of knowing, fails,
and, now awakened, realizes that knowledge is a delusion. Sor Juana's
skepticism, like that of so many others, leads to surrender to God.
At the end of her life, faced with the failure of her dream of learning,
Sor Juana renounces human studies, renounces the word itself,
to enter the silent world of contemplation and charity. This is the
opinion of Ricard, Ramón Xirau, and Gaos as well: "from vital and
intellectual disillusion, to mystic release, refuge in God."[5] *First
Dream* is the poem of Sor Juana's intellectual crisis and the initial
act of her conversion. This proposition has a corollary: the poem is
yet another example, the most radical, of the baroque poetry of
disillusion.[6] It must be said, first of all, that this idea has no basis in

3. José Gaos, "El sueño de un sueño," *Historia Mexicana* 10, 1 (1960): 54–71. Paz does not
indicate page numbers for his citations of Gaos's article [*Editor*].
4. Refers to lines 590–92 in the original poem; lines 506–07 in the translation in this
volume (see p. 58) [*Editor*].
5. Ramón Xirau, *Genio y figura de sor Juana Inés de la Cruz* (Buenos Aires: Editorial
Universitaria de Buenos Aires, 1967). [Robert Ricard (1900–1984), French scholar of
Hispanic literature and author of several important essays on Sor Juana—*Editor*.]
6. Disillusion (*desengaño*) was a widely used trope in seventeenth-century Spanish litera-
ture; it refers to the moment of consciousness that the world is an illusion and that
ultimate truth comes after death [*Editor*].

chronology: many years passed between the writing of *First Dream* and the crisis of 1693. The causal relation between the poem and the so-called conversion, therefore, is tenuous. An even more pertinent question: are the dream and vanity of knowledge actually the theme of the poem?

I believe that the interpretations to which I have just referred are a reading we have imposed on the poem in order to make it coincide with the baroque poetry of disillusion and the view of skepticism as a road toward faith. Sor Juana tells us a dream about the voyage of the soul through the celestial spheres, her bedazzlement, and her efforts to convert her *vision* into *idea*: Intellect sees but Reason does not comprehend what it sees. The dream the poem relates is an allegory of the *act of knowing*. It describes the vision, the difficulties encountered by Reason, its wavering and its daring, its heroic spirit; it yearns to know, although it is aware in advance that surely it will fail. The model of the soul—the prototype, Sor Juana emphasizes— is Phaethon, the youth Jupiter strikes down, but who is immortalized in his fall. Earlier, she had compared the aspiration of the soul toward the First Cause[7] to the Egyptian pyramids. The symbolic model of spiritual yearning is the pyramid: the mythic model is Phaethon, with whom—for reasons I shall explain in a moment— Sor Juana secretly identifies. The poem is all upward impulse: there are falls, yes, but again and again the soul is determined to soar.

The parallel between *First Dream* and the *Response* is complete. In the latter, written years after the poem, Sor Juana, in closing, says that *she will continue to write*: there is not the slightest sign of any intention to stop writing, nor is there any notice of a renunciation or a surrender to silence. In *First Dream*, more profound and intimate in its abstraction and objectivity (she is talking with herself, not with a prelate), she makes the same affirmation, but in a tragic vein: she is determined to persist in her endeavor, and she spells out her glory in her fall. No: *First Dream* is not a poem about knowledge as a vain dream, but a poem about the act of knowing. This act adopts the form of a dream, not in the sense of an ordinary dream or of an unrealizable illusion, but in the sense of a spiritual voyage. During the dream the soul is awake, something most critics forget. The voyage—a lucid dream—does not end in a revelation, as in the dreams of hermetic and Neoplatonic tradition; actually, the poem does not *end* at all: the soul hesitates, recognizing itself in Phaethon, whereupon the body awakens. An epic of the act of knowing, the poem is also the confession of the doubts and struggles of

---

7. The Aristotelian concept of the prime mover, defined as God by the scholastics [*Editor*].

Reason. A confession that ends in an act of faith: not in learning but in the desire to learn.

Góngora's *Solitudes*[8] is the great poem of Spanish disillusion. Góngora's disenchantment—his skepticism—ends not in an act of faith but in aesthetic affirmation. In the *Solitudes* there is no desire for learning, but neither is there faith. For Góngora there is neither a *here* (world and history) nor a *there* (Heaven or Platonic idea) but only the word: light and air. Góngora responds to the horror of the world and to the nothingness of the beyond with a language beyond language, that is, with words that have ceased to be communication to become spectacle. The sign becomes an enigmatic object that, once deciphered and seen, we admire. *First Dream* recounts the confrontation between the human spirit and the cosmos: Sor Juana does not want to clothe nothingness in a language of equivocal splendor, she wants to penetrate being. Sor Juana's vertigo has a different name: poetic rapture. Like all unique and singular works, *First Dream* cannot be reduced to the aesthetic of its time—that is, to the poetry of disillusion. This is true of all great poets; they express their age but simultaneously transcend it; they are its exception, everything that in some way escapes the tyranny of styles, tastes, and canons. Without denying Sor Juana's debt to her time, Vossler[9] has said that *First Dream* prefigured the philosophical poetry that was to follow: "The cosmic poem of the Mexican nun was, historically, both late and premature: a late fruit of the baroque and the jubilant precursor of the Enlightenment." The great German critic is right in pointing out that the poem is doubly displaced in time, but wrong as to the nature of that displacement. Although it takes the form of Gongorist poetry, *First Dream*'s ties are to the tradition of the voyage of the soul belonging to the ancient hermeticism rediscovered by the Renaissance. It is a prophecy not of the poetry of the Enlightenment, but of the modern poetry that centers on the paradox at the heart of her poem: the revelation of nonrevelation. In this sense *First Dream* resembles Valéry's *Le cimetière marin* (*Graveyard by the Sea*) and, in the Hispanic world, José Gorostiza's *Muerte sin fin* (*Death without End*) and Vicente Huidobro's *Altazor*.[1] And, above all, the poem in which all that poetry is subsumed: Mallarmé's *Un coup de dés*.[2] Sor Juana's poem inaugurates a poetic mode

---

8. An unfinished poem (1613) considered the best example of the ornate style of Luis de Góngora (1561–1627) [*Editor*].
9. Karl Vossler (1872–1949), German literary critic of Sor Juana. The following citation comes from the essay "Die Zennte Muse von Mexico, Sor Juana Inés de la Cruz" (1934) [*Editor*].
1. "The Graveyard by the Sea" by Paul Valéry (1920), "Death without End" by José Gorostiza (1939), and *Altazor* by Vicente Huidobro (1919–1931) [*Editor*].
2. "A Throw of the Dice [Will Not Abolish Chance]" by Stéphane Mallarmé (1897) [*Editor*].

that is central to the modern age; more precisely, a mode that *defines* modern poetry in its most radical and extreme form: the very antithesis of the *Divine Comedy*.[3]

A baroque poem that negates the baroque, a belated work that prefigures the most modern modernity, *First Dream* is a verbal obelisk rising out of a nebulous zone of mist, precipices, and dizzying geometry. Like its author, it is of the dusk and the dawn. If we are to understand its unique situation better, we must again turn to Sor Juana's cosmography. Was it really Ptolemy's cosmography?[4] Yes and no. That traditional image of the universe instilled a security we have lost. The earth was in the center, surrounded by seven planets, from the moon to Saturn; beyond, the firmament of fixed stars and the empyrean, with the Prime Mover. A finite universe, with well-defined limits and a center. A harmonious universe. The distances between the earth and the stars were enormous but, as C. S. Lewis[5] says, man experienced no fear: the cosmos, like one of the walled cities of the Middle Ages, protected and defended him. Everything changed with the Renaissance: the walls crumbled and the center vanished. It is clear that Sor Juana had information, even though imperfect and vague, of the changes in the status of the earth, the sun, and the planets. Kircher alludes in his works to the new astronomy, although with prudence; he lived in Rome, where they had burned Bruno and tried Galileo.[6] Sor Juana's reserve on these themes should not surprise us; it was typical of her class and her world. We must not forget, in addition, that she was familiar with Neoplatonism,[7] which exercised a decisive influence in changing the image of the universe.

It is customary to attribute the triumph of the new image to the diffusion of the ideas and discoveries of Copernicus, Galileo, Kepler,[8] and others. This is only partly true. According to modern historians, Neoplatonism was the true source of that change. This philosophical and spiritual current had been repressed throughout the Middle

3. By Dante Alighieri (ca. 1265–1321), Italian author and first major poet of European modernity [*Editor*].
4. Refers to the model of the universe created by the Ptolemy (90–ca. 168 c.e.), Greco-Egyptian mathematician from Alexandria. His was considered the orthodox model until it was displaced by the Copernican [*Editor*].
5. Oxford medievalist, novelist, and poet (1898–1963) [*Editor*].
6. Galileo Galilei (1564–1642), Italian mathematician persecuted by the Catholic Church for his support of Copernicanism. Athanasius Kircher (1602–1680), Jesuit polymath and author of more than forty treatises on natural philosophy, music, optics, astronomy, and other subjects. Giordano Bruno (1548–1600), Italian Dominican friar burned at the stake by the Inquisition for his version of Copernicanism [*Editor*].
7. A revival of Platonic philosophy that sometimes bordered on hermetic and occult beliefs [*Editor*].
8. Johannes Kepler (1571–1630), German mathematician who studied planetary motion and prepared the way for Newton's theory of gravity. Nicolaus Copernicus (1473–1543), Polish mathematician who placed the sun rather than the earth at the center of the universe [*Editor*].

Ages but toward the end of the fifteenth century resurfaced with renewed vigor to win the best minds of the sixteenth century. In refuting Scholasticism,[9] it outlined a different idea of the world, one linked with the new physical and cosmographic sciences. We know that the great scientific innovators were greatly indebted to Neoplatonism. What determined the image of the world that displaced the Ptolemaic finite universe, therefore, was not so much the heliocentrism of Copernicus, which was rather slow to be accepted, as certain propositions that were not, strictly speaking, derived or deduced from the new science: the infinity of the universe, the lack of a cosmic center, the plurality of inhabited worlds.[1] More than in Copernicus and Galileo, the new ideas originated in Neoplatonism and in the speculations of philosophers like Nicholas of Cusa, who had postulated the coincidence of opposites. Cusanus, several centuries before Kant,[2] confronted the antinomy of the infinite and attempted to negate it with the paradox of the circle whose center is everywhere. The circle does not enclose the infinite, does not *define* it, but it is an image that allows us, if not to think it, to *intuit* it.

The new universe was a challenge to man's reason as well as his sensibility and fantasy. The extreme attitudes it produced are exemplified in two minds, Bruno and Pascal.[3] They are divided not by a century but by something more profound: temperament. They are like hot and cold, wet and dry. Giordano Bruno was a passionate defender of the astronomy of Copernicus, but he also, and with still greater passion, believed in an infinite and decentralized universe with a plurality of inhabited worlds. His spiritual relationship to Nicholas of Cusa was more profound than the merely intellectual ties that joined him to Copernicus. His reasons for postulating an infinite universe were not what today we would call scientific, but rather ontological, moral, and temperamental: "it is incomparably better that Infinite Excellence should express itself in innumerable individuals than in some finite number of them . . ."[4] Bruno rejoiced in the idea of an infinite universe, and in that idea there is an echo of Plato: all that exists, even the bad, is good. Again and again he repeats that there are no differences, everything is center, and all is

9. The rational theology that followed from the adaption of Aristotle to Christian dogma by Saint Thomas Aquinas (1225–1274); considered orthodox by the Catholic Church during Sor Juana's time [*Editor*].
1. Lovejoy, *Great Chain of Being*.
2. Immanuel Kant (1724–1804), German philosopher whose theory of the sublime is found in *Critique of Pure Reason* (1781). Nicholas of Cusa (1401–1464), German theologian and mathematician associated with hermeticism and Neoplatonism (he is also called *Cusanus* [Latin]) [*Editor*].
3. Blaise Pascal (1623–1662), French Jansenist philosopher who provided a rational defense of Christianity [*Editor*].
4. Cited in Arthur O. Lovejoy, *The Great Chain of Being* (*A Study of a History of an Idea*) (Cambridge: Harvard University Press, 1964), p. 119 [*Editor*].

circumference. Lovejoy comments that there is "an essentially cos-
mical piety" in Bruno, but "to Pascal's imagination the vision of the
infini créé is not exhilarating but oppressive."[5] The infinite does
not elate Pascal; it humbles him. The image of the circle reap-
pears in the French philosopher but with a negative coloration: "It
[the universe] is an infinite sphere, of which the center is every-
where and the circumference nowhere . . . What is a man, in the
midst of infinity?" Confronting this infinite and incomprehensible
universe, Pascal, in order to become a *chrétien soumis*, chooses first
to be a *pyrrhonien accompli.*[6] Was Pascal's experience shared by
Sor Juana?

It is impossible to confuse the world of *First Dream* with that of
traditional cosmography. In her descriptions of celestial space Sor
Juana never alludes to the discoveries of the new astronomy, and we
do not know what she really thought about controversial and dan-
gerous subjects such as heliocentrism, the infinity of the universe,
and the plurality of inhabited worlds. No matter; her emotions and
sentiments about the cosmos tell us as much as her ideas. First of all,
her world has no clear outlines or precise limits. This distinguishes
it radically from the traditional cosmos, which was a harmonious
world. Another difference: distances are not only immense but
immeasurable. Last—and this is a modern characteristic—her world
lacks a center and man feels lost in its uninhabited spaces. It is a
world that, if not infinite, produces sentiments and images that are
a response to infinity. This is why Sor Juana, in order to think about
the infinite, turns quite naturally to Nicholas of Cusa's paradox
of the divine circle: she does exactly the same as Bruno and Pascal,
who did believe in an infinite universe. Sor Juana feels that the
"machinery of the world" is both "immense and terrifying." Her emo-
tions are not those of a Dante, or even a Fray Luis de León:[7] neither
metaphysical certainty nor supernatural rapture. The cosmos no
longer has shape or measure; it has become unfathomable, and
the Intellect itself—not even Neoplatonism can rescue her at this
point—has experienced vertigo confronting its abysses and myri-
ads of stars. Sor Juana is awe-struck. But this emotion soon
becomes a different sentiment that is neither the jubilant elation
of Bruno nor the melancholy depression of Pascal. The sentiment
appears in the last part of *First Dream*, when everything seems
about to end on a Pascalian note. It is rebellion. Its emblem is
Phaethon.

5. Here and two sentences on, Paz paraphrases Lovejoy's comments. See Lovejoy, p. 126 [*Editor*].
6. Meaning he prefers to go through the experience of being an "accomplished Pyrrhonist [a confirmed Pyrrhonist skeptic]" for his conversion into a "submitted Christian." Paz paraphrases, without citing, Lovejoy, p. 130 [*Editor*].
7. Spanish Augustinian friar and poet (1527–1591). "Dante": see p. 252, n. 3 [*Editor*].

In the myth of Phaethon, Sor Juana is appropriating a motif from the poetry of her time, a very popular theme during the Golden Age. In Alciati's *Emblemata*[8] he appears as an example of temerity; the Spanish translator, Bernardino Daza, turns the myth into a model for "the vain princes" who "destroy their kingdoms" and then "plummet to the earth and die." In the poetry of the sixteenth and seventeenth centuries there are innumerable sonnets, *décimas*, and *romances* on the theme of Phaethon and his fall. Francisco de Aldana[9] wrote a long and ponderous *Fábula de Faetonte*, a free translation from the Italian, which is one of the least felicitous compositions by this great poet. In contrast, *Fábula de Faetón* by Juan de Tassis Peralta, Count de Villamediana, is, in the words of Juan Manuel Rozas, "one of the most ambitious endeavors of our baroque lyric."[1] Rozas points out that the myth "serves some as a moral; for others it is an exemplum for lovers; and finally it is a model of glory and honor, of the desire to climb to the heights and undertake great enterprises." Villamediana's Phaethon fits the latter category. Epaphus[2] having questioned whether Phaethon is the son of Apollo, the youth goes to his father's palace to seek recognition; the god grants it willingly, but for Phaethon this satisfaction is not sufficient. He yearns to show the world—and himself—that he is worthy of being Apollo's son and capable of driving his chariot through the sky. The theme of questionable birth is allied with that of honor, and both are allied to the theme of forfeiting life for a glorious death: "You have fallen, Phaethon, you have yielded to your fate . . ."[3] Sor Juana's hero is more complex; Phaethon is herself. Although she is moved by the desire for glory, she is attracted by a passion unknown to Villamediana: love of knowledge.

A new passion in the history of our poetry appears with *First Dream*: love of learning. Let me clarify. The passion, of course, was not new; what was new was that Sor Juana used it as a poetic theme and invested it with the fateful intensity of erotic love. For her, intellectual passion is as strong as the love of glory. In the best Platonic tradition, intellectual passion—reason—enlists the spirit to accompany it in its adventure. But the next step is an even greater break with tradition: if knowledge seems unachievable, one must somehow outwit fate and dare to try.

8. Andrea Alciato (1492–1550), commonly known as Alciati, Italian humanist and inventor of emblems, iconographical puzzles that became popular in the sixteenth and seventeenth centuries [*Editor*].
9. Francisco de Aldana (ca. 1537–1577), a Spanish courtesan and poet [*Editor*].
1. *Obras* of Juan de Tarsis y Peralta, Conde de Villamediana, edited with an introduction and notes by Juan Manuel Rozas (Madrid: Editorial Castalia, 1969). [Paz does not identify the pages of the citations. Villamediana: Juan de Tassis y Peralta, El Conde de Villamediana (1582–1622), Spanish poet who wrote in the florid *culturanista* style—*Editor*.]
2. Son of Zeus and Io who doubted Phaethon's heraldry [*Editor*].
3. The verses are from Villamediana's *Fábula de Faeton* (1617) [*Editor*].

Daring becomes defiance, rebellion: the act of knowing is a transgression. The infinity of the universe elates Bruno and depresses Pascal. In *First Dream* Sor Juana moves from inspiration to fall, and from fall to defiance. Hers is an intellectual and lucid hero who wants to learn even at the risk of falling. The figure of Phaethon influenced Sor Juana in two ways. First, as the intellectual example that joins love of learning to daring: reason and spirit. Second, because he represents freedom in its most extreme form: transgression.

The theme of Phaethon appears several times in her work, always as an image of the freedom that dares to cross boundaries. I have commented on sonnet 149, which portrays her envy of the person bold enough to seize the reins of the chariot of the Sun, "heedless of the danger," and who does not, like her, resign himself to a "state to last his span."[4] A terrible confession for a nun. Phaethon attracted her in still another way: for her, too, the question of birth, bastardy, was a sensitive one.[5] But, as we have seen, she transcended the theme of honor; her theme was learning. This may be why she does not share Pascal's dilemma; Sor Juana is not torn between "total Pyrrhonism" and "submissive Christianity." She separates the two orders, the religious and the strictly philosophical; she is a Christian but, in a different sphere, she is *un*submissive. This sentiment was the secret core of her psychic life. Very early, as I attempted to demonstrate in Part Two, Juana Inés proposed to transcend her allotted role, and identified with her grandfather and with the masculine world of learning and books. Her choice of Phaethon, in her mature years, realizes her childhood desire in the world of symbols. Juana Inés saw herself in three figures: in the pythoness of Delphi, in the goddess Isis, and in the youth Phaethon. The three images are interwoven with literature and knowledge: the maiden of Delphi is inspiration; Isis[6] is wisdom; and Phaethon is the unfettered desire for learning.

The act of knowing, even if it ends in failure, is learning: the nonrevelation is a revelation.

---

4. Lines from Sonnet 149 (see p. 36) [*Editor*].
5. Sor Juana is believed to have been born out of wedlock [*Editor*].
6. Egyptian goddess of magic and nature central to the argument of *Allegorical Neptune* (on p. 138). The oracle of Delphi was found at the temple to Apollo near the Castalian spring, referenced in the title of Sor Juana's first published collection *Castalian Inundation* (1689) [*Editor*].

STEPHANIE MERRIM

From Toward a Feminist Reading of Sor Juana Inés de la Cruz: Past, Present, and Future Directions in Sor Juana Criticism†

✻ ✻ ✻

K. K. Ruthven has written in *Feminist Literary Studies*, "Every critical method is a scanning device for picking up particular types of information which it logs by means of a technical vocabulary specially invented for this purpose. The point of inventing a new device is to reveal what was previously invisible, and in that way to articulate a new kind of knowledge."[1] In this spirit and with similar intentions we now approach the next phase of this essay, which involves laying further, and explicit, groundwork for a feminist reading of Sor Juana Inés de la Cruz's oeuvre.[2] From my foregoing discussion the reader will have gained a sense of the axial issues and possibilities for such a reading; in what follows, I will both build on and depart from what has already been written to suggest what have struck me (and I emphasize the personal, and thus circumscribed, nature of these observations) as productive directions for future investigations. Here I will essentially be mapping directions as well as asking questions, briefly outlining a working plan for a feminist reading—and, tacitly, inviting the reader further to develop these ideas—rather than proposing in any way a definitive strategy.

Two emblems, of sorts, preview the shape of my argument. The first is Paz's incisive formulation regarding Sor Juana's double-edged relationship to the female condition—"Sor Juana's contradictions: . . . a deliberate exaltation of the female condition that, simultaneously, expresses a no less deliberate will to transcend that condition" [Span., p. 232; Eng., p. 171][3]—which suggests the manner in which

---

† From *Feminist Perspectives on Sor Juana Inés de la Cruz*, ed. Stephanie Merrim (Detroit, MI: Wayne State University Press, 1991), pp. 20–25, 34–35. Copyright © 1991 Wayne State University Press. Reprinted by permission of the publisher.
1. K. K. Ruthven, *Feminist Literary Studies* (Cambridge: Cambridge University Press, 1984), p. 24.
2. My notion of feminist criticism with respect to this essay is broad-based and fluid but gravitates toward those critical postures that are more practical than theoretical in nature, and which are relevant to the context and concerns of a seventeenth-century Hispanic writer such as Sor Juana. The kinds of questions I ask and the directions I propose in this essay will give the reader a better sense of what is meant here by feminist criticism. [The first section of Merrim's essay has discussed the ambivalent reception and possibilities of Octavio Paz's 1982 study of Sor Juana for feminist criticism—*Editor*.]
3. Octavio Paz, *Sor Juana Inés de la Cruz o las trampas de la fe* (Barcelona: Seix Barral, 1982). Page references to Paz's book will henceforth be included in the body of the essay. The English versions are largely taken from Margaret Sayers Peden's translation of Paz's book, *Sor Juana* (Cambridge, Mass.: Harvard University Press, 1988), and page

Sor Juana, also in literary terms, moves between two worlds. The second is the exquisite and unresolvable multivalence of the last lines of the *Primero sueño* (First Dream) quoted as the epigraph to this essay, in relation to the poem they conclude.[4] A coda, a surprise ending, (as has been widely observed) these lines contain the poem's first and only "yo" or "I" as well as its only first person feminine adjective, and thus indication of its female authorship. The last lines explode the poem. Do they set the feminine quest for knowledge, and perhaps, by extension, the feminine, on an equal continuum with the masculine? Or do they privilege the female, feminizing and/or personalizing the quest? The rich indeterminacy of these lines provides us with both the crux and the categories for our discussion, as we proceed to raise questions regarding Sor Juana's relation to male literary tradition, her relation to female literary tradition, and the representation of her own personal circumstances. Throughout, the purpose remains to awaken the feminine in Sor Juana criticism, to "restore" Sor Juana as a woman writer and as a woman writing.

How to arrive at a fuller understanding, perhaps even a theory, of the terms that Sor Juana negotiates with the male literary tradition? In Sor Juana's time and space, institutionalized literary culture (this, of course, is not to deny the existence of a women's writing, which we shall address shortly), the cultural hegemony, was overwhelmingly masculine. Then, even as now, the great masters—Lope de Vega, Góngora, Quevedo, Calderón[5]—dominated the Spanish and Mexican cultural scene. In practical terms, we cannot forget that it was patronage and acceptance by the court that allowed our nun the considerable autonomy from conventual strictures so essential to her intellectual endeavors. In philosophical terms it might be said that, for Sor Juana, to accede to knowledge involved allying herself with the reigning (masculine) tradition.[6] Writing, then, at the very end

---

references to the English are also included in the body of the essay. Since the English version is a revised edition of the original, not all of the material I quote from the Spanish appears in it. Those citations that are a mixture of Peden's translations and my own are identified as "trans. augmented"; those entirely my own list only the page reference for the Spanish edition. My sincere thanks to Maud Wilcox of Harvard University Press and Enrico M. Santí of Georgetown University for making available to me a prepublication copy of the translation.

4. Paz, as might be expected, would resolve this ambiguity. In viewing the impersonality of the bulk of the poem as an expression of Sor Juana's notions of androgyny and her own ungendered state, he plays down the impact of the coda: "This information doesn't alter the impersonality of the poem" [Span., p. 481]. In philosophical terms, his argument may be well taken; in poetic terms, I believe that it is counterproductive to explain away the rich dynamics of the dramatic ending.

5. Pedro Calderón de la Barca (1600–1681), one of the most important Spanish playwrights of his time, responsible for courtly theater. Felix Lope de Vega (1562–1635), a Spanish playwright and poet who wrote popular and courtly theater. Luis de Góngora (1561–1627), a Spanish poet known for his florid and difficult style. Francisco de Quevedo (1580–1645), a Spanish poet, satirist, and moralist who rivaled Góngora [*Editor*].

6. Paz incisively notes in this regard, "How, in a civilization by and for men, can a woman obtain to learning without making herself masculine?" [Span., p. 94].

of an illustrious era, Sor Juana bows to the weight of prior literary tradition: in one of her "ovillejos" she exclaims, "¡Oh siglo desdichado y desvalido / en que todo lo hallamos ya servido / pues que no hay voz, equívoco ni frase / que por común no pase / y digan los censores: / ¿Eso? ¡Ya lo pensaron los mayores!" (Oh disgraced and destitute century in which everything we find has already served, for there is no word, pun or phrase that doesn't pass as a commonplace and of which the censors don't say: *That? It was already thought up by our elders!*).[7] Rather than denying the past, she self-consciously absorbs and recapitulates the century's literary languages through explicit imitations both stylistic and thematic, verbal allusions, hidden polemics, and so on. Thus, José Lezama Lima's famous characterization of the New World as a gnostic space or incorporative protoplasm[8] is well applied to Sor Juana—a ventriloquist whose voice is to a significant degree configured by other voices, other texts.

When essayed by a woman of Sor Juana's sensibility and self-consciousness, I believe that such "textual friendships"[9] take on a greater resonance, exceeding the condition of simple admiring imitation. Rather than projections, displacements of the self onto the other, they may entail "introjections" of sorts, wherein qualities belonging to an external object are absorbed and unconsciously regarded as belonging to the self.[1] Let me explain. Sor Juana, we have seen, adheres to male literary languages, eschewing that "negative" function of rejecting the ruling cultural values that Julia Kristeva would attribute to women's writing.[2] Further, in her poetry and thinking, Sor Juana both ascribes to a neoplatonic notion of androgyny according to which the soul has no sex ("las almas / distancia ignoran y sexo," souls transcend distance and sex),[3] and describes herself as androgynous ("y sólo sé que mi cuerpo, / sin que a uno u otro se incline, / es neutro, o abstracto, cuanto / sólo el Alma deposite," and I only know that my body, not inclining to one man or another, is neuter or abstract, solely the dwelling of my soul).[4] In

7. Sor Juana Inés de la Cruz, *Obras completas de Sor Juana Inés de la Cruz*, Vol. I (*Lírica personal*), ed. by Alfonso Méndez Plancarte (Mexico: Fondo de Cultura Económica, 1951). Ovillejo 214, lines 39–44. All quotations of Sor Juana's poetry are taken from this edition and volume.

8. José Lezama Lima, "Sumas críticas del americano," in *La expresión americana* (Santiago: Editorial Universitaria, 1969), pp. 112 ff.

9. I owe this felicitous phrase, as well as many other insights, to my colleague at Brown University, Professor Alan S. Trueblood, Golden Age scholar and translator of Sor Juana.

1. Elizabeth Wright, writing about Melanie Klein, in *Psychoanalytic Criticism: Theory in Practice* (London and New York: Methuen, 1984), p. 80.

2. Ann Rosalind Jones, "Writing the Body: Toward an Understanding of l'Ecriture feminine," in *The New Feminist Criticism*, ed. by Elaine Showalter (New York: Pantheon, 1985), p. 363, quotes Julia Kristeva: "If women have a role to play . . . it is only in assuming a *negative* function: reject everything finite, definite, structured, loaded with meaning, in the existing state of society."

3. Romance 19, lines 111–12.

4. Romance 48, lines 105–8.

writings such as her *Respuesta* and the *Autodefensa espiritual* (Spiritual Self-Defense), Sor Juana militantly defends a woman's right to education and, by implication, participation in the male order. All of this together, added to the example of her own literary life, but substantiates the obvious: that—as is entirely natural in view of the context in which she wrote—rather than asserting or projecting women's "difference," both ideologically and literarily Sor Juana sought to *negate* their difference, to introject or appropriate the masculine realm for the feminine and to place them on the same continuum. For Sor Juana, to write with the words of the ruling order may well have entailed claiming the woman's equal rights to write in that world; and signaled, as Virginia Woolf's notion of literary androgyny would have it, her belief that "it is fatal for one who writes to think of their sex."[5]

The foregoing discussion by no means purports to deny Sor Juana's originality as a writer vis-à-vis her literary precursors. In fact, now that we have analyzed the similarity of Sor Juana's writings to accepted forms of discourse, let us explore certain aspects of their difference from tradition. In this regard, not only Paz's book but, notably, Georgina Sabat-Rivers's *El "Sueño" de Sor Juana Inés de la Cruz: Tradiciones literarias y originalidad* (Sor Juana Inés de la Cruz's 'Dream': Literary Tradition and Originality), as well as Marie-Cécile Bénassy-Berling's *Humanisme et religion chez Sor Juana Inés de la Cruz* (Humanism and Religion in Sor Juana Inés de la Cruz) document our author's innovations with impressive authority, though without undertaking theoretical conclusions.[6] Arthur Terry has noted that Sor Juana's "best verse succeeds precisely because her imagination is able to find new patterns in traditional clusters of thought without accepting them schematically."[7] Following Terry's remarks (as well as the excellent information provided by the longer studies) through to their logical conclusions, we might attempt to arrive at a more global and systematic understanding of the shape(s) of Sor Juana's "swerves" from tradition through an investigation,

5. Virginia Woolf, *A Room of One's Own* (New York: Harcourt, Brace and World, 1957), p. 108. As Sor Juana noted in her *Autodefensa espiritual,* "pero los privados y particulars estudios ¿quién los ha prohibido a las mujeres? ¿No tienen alma racional como los hombres? ¿Pues por qué no gozará el privilegio de la ilustración de las letras con ellos?" (but private and individual study, who had forbidden that to women? Like men, do they not have a rational soul? Why then should they not enjoy the privilege of the enlightenment of letters with them?) [p. 642; trans. p. 499].
6. Georgina Sabat-Rivers, *El "Sueño" de Sor Juana Inés de la Cruz: Tradiciones literarias y originalidad* (London: Tamesis, 1976). Jean Franco's excellent *Plotting Women: Gender and Representation in Mexico* (New York: Columbia University Press, 1989) appeared after this book was written. See her Chapter 2, "Sor Juana Explores Space," for a sophisticated theoretical and textual analysis of the nun's interventions in the "language games" [p. 25] of her times: Professor Franco examines the ways in which Sor Juana "destabilizes" the male and female literary languages of her times.
7. Terry, "Human and Divine Love," p. 303.

for example, along the lines of Harold Bloom's *The Anxiety of Influence*, which would ask: in *general* and to what end does Sor Juana modify, complete, or selectively reject the courses set by her strong precursors?[8]

More particularly, feminist criticism has taken up Bloom's notion of the "swerve" from literary tradition, adapting it to the woman writer's situation. Pre-twentieth-century women authors in particular, Sandra Gilbert and Susan Gubar observe, "'swerved' from the central sequences of male literary history, enacting a uniquely female process of revision and redefinition . . ." which allowed them self-expression, ostensibly within the bounds of the acceped code.[9] Such, we must note, are the verbal stratagems of the oppressed in general, not just of women. The Baroque of colonial Mexico, with its cryptic anagrammatic forms and always contending with the shadow of the Inquisition, especially invited such ciphering.[1] Whether the encodings of a woman writer or of a colonial Mexican, it is something of a truism by now that Sor Juana's Baroque, as manifested in the forbidden scientific explorations of the *Primero sueño*, surreptitiously filled the empty Spanish forms with audacious new content. Fleshing out this truism, we might seek out other messages ciphered into other texts, as well as examining in detail those verbal strategies, so akin to dreamwork,[2] by means of which Sor Juana processed her models in order to achieve self-expression within another's language. Is it her own tale, as Irving Leonard[3] in his reading of the Fabio sonnets (and I, rather less directly, in my other essay in this volume) would have it, that Sor Juana is telling? To what degree and in what contexts does she deflect, as in the *Respuesta*, her own most dangerous thoughts onto others' words?[4] And, importantly, in what ways does Sor Juana avail herself of poetic topoi and conventional forms, such as the courtly love sonnet or portrait poem, only to subvert

---

8. Harold Bloom, *The Anxiety of Influence: A Theory of Poetry* (New York: Oxford University Press, 1973). Bloom presents these questions in a far more detailed and technical fashion.

9. Sandra M. Gilbert and Susan Gubar, *The Madwoman in the Attic: The Woman Writer and the Nineteenth-Century Literary Imagination* (New Haven: Yale University Press, 1979), p. 73. Such "swerves," in Gilbert and Gubar's interpretation [p. 73], created "palimpsestic" works "whose surface designs conceal or obscure deeper, less accessible (and less socially acceptable) levels of meaning." "Thus," they comment, "these authors managed the difficult task of achieving true female literary authority by simultaneously conforming to and subverting patriarchal literary standards."

1. As Mariano Picón-Salas observes of the New World Baroque, on p. 127 of his *De la conquista a la independencia* (Mexico: Fondo de Cultura Económica, 1944; cited in the Bibliographical Note): "The form is cryptic, exceedingly ornate and obscure, for two reasons: because they have nothing to say or don't mean to say anything, or because they are guarding themselves from danger with the most complex tangle of forms."

2. Akin to dreamwork, as understood by Freud, in the sense that one seeks an acceptable set of images to express a dangerous personal content.

3. See "A Baroque Poetess," p. 244 [*Editor*].

4. See Arenal's "The Convent as Catalyst for Autonomy" for a discussion of these tactics in the *Respuesta*.

them to her own purposes? (I shall have more to say on this subject.) Such investigations should confirm what we will call, thinking of *El Divino Narciso* (The Divine Narcissus),[5] the echolalic nature of Sor Juana's language: for Echo/Eco, the quintessenial trope, only manages to speak by repeating others' words. Like Sor Juana, as one critic puts it, Echo deconstructs words "into their hidden but operative ultimae."[6]

Also standing inside and outside of literary convention, as we began to see in examining Paz's reflections on the subject, is Sor Juana's treatment of female characters and her depiction of their passions. In reconstructing legendary female figures as the embodiment of knowledge, and particularly in the "Villancicos a Santa Catarina" (Villancicos to Saint Catherine),[7] Sor Juana performs a revisionary reading of the female which should be understood as a necessary complement to the views expressed in the *Respuesta*. Sor Juana also flies in the face of conventions, past and present, to portray women as the locus of reason in the wars of love. Secular love, in our author's (anti-romantic) conception, is a battleground—invariably problematic, fueled by unreason, fraught with tensions—where in males and females enact that eternal strife to which the Fall condemned them.[8] A battleground and an illness, marked by "desasosiego" (restlessness), "desvelos" (sleeplessness), "tibiezas" (indifference), and proceeding "hasta que con agravios o con celos / apaga con sus lágrimas su fuego" (until injuries or jealousy extinguishes its fire with their tears).[9] The female *yo* of the love poems rails against and attempts to defend herself from "mad love's" ravages, as in Décima 99 ("Que demuestra decoroso esfuerzo de la razón contra la vil tiranía de un amor violento," Which demonsrates the decorous efforts of reason against the vile tyranny of a violent love) which postulates, "En dos partes dividida / tengo el alma en confusión: / una, esclava a la pasión, / y otra, a la razón medida." (In two parts divided is my soul in confusion; one, a slave to passion, and the other, gauged to reason). The poem concludes in reason's favor, "Y así, Amor, en vano intenta / tu esfuerzo loco ofenderme: / pues podré decir, al verme / expirar sin entregarme, / que conseguiste

5. Sor Juana's 1689 mystery play, which allegorizes Christ's love for the Church through the myth of Narcissus and Echo [*Editor*].
6. John Hollander, *The Figure of Echo: A Mode of Allusion in Milton and After* (Berkeley: University of California Press, 1981), p. 12.
7. *Villancicos* to Saint Catherine were theatrical carols written in 1692 in praise of Catherine of Alexandria, the fourth-century martyr [*Editor*].
8. As Sor Juana wrote paraphrasing Genesis in her *auto sacramental*, *El cetro de José* (*Obras completas*, Vol. IV, p. 205), "Quebrantará, altiva, / tu cuello orgulloso; / y a su carcañal / le pondrás estorbos" (Arrogant, the woman will break your prideful neck, and at her heel the man will place obstacles). [Auto sacramental: mystery play, in English, was a theatrical allegory of Christian dogma—*Editor*.]
9. Sonnet 184, lines 7–8.

matarme / mas no pudiste vencerme" (And thus, Love, in vain does your mad effort attempt to offend me: because I can say, seeing myself expire without surrendering, that you tried to kill me but couldn't defeat me).[1] In like manner, the third-person voice of the famed *redondilla* "Hombres necios" (Foolish Men)[2] through biting logical argumentation exposes the absurdities of the male's double standard. As this last point suggests, both the content and the impeccably logical form of Sor Juana's poetry argue for the female as a bastion of reason: the poet "cannibalizes" the topic of love, using it as a pretext for philosophical debates and as a showcase for her own lucid reasoning.

Much remains to be said about the construction of the female as well as the male, and about notions of androgyny in Sor Juana. In this light, for example, one could consider the author's manipulation of gender switches (in voice and in characters), of the stock figure of the *mujer varonil* (manly woman) in her plays and other writings, of the courtly love tradition when addressed to a female by a female, or of patristic mariolatry—which Sor Juana reshapes to her own needs and beliefs.[3] All of this may well necessitate a further act of revision, that is, a re-viewing of the canon of Sor Juana's works in accordance to their relevance to a feminist reading. Such a reading would accord new prominence to works, notably to Sor Juana's devotional writings (which Paz finds "insignificant": "They are interesting neither as literature nor as examples of ascetic or mystical writing. Prose for devout old ladies" [Span., p. 550; Eng., p. 538]),[4] so important for their elevation of the female and previously considered to be of little interest. Further, it incites us to cross parochial critical lines, tracing the continuity between Sor Juana's religious and secular writings, between her prose, poetry, and theater.

1. Décima 99, lines 21–24, 45–50.
2. See p. 20 [*Editor*].
3. See Electa Arenal's excellent, "Sor Juana Inés de la Cruz: Speaking the Mother Tongue," *University of Dayton Review* 16, 2 (Spring 1983): 93–102. On p. 101 of the article she characterizes Sor Juana's special mariolatry as having "accomplished what a twentieth-century North American feminist theologian insists women must do to legitimize and authorize themselves—to go beyond the father." My essay in chapter 5 in this volume contains further discussion of Sor Juana's mariolatry.
4. Paz, in keeping with his analysis of Sor Juana's forced "abdication," likens these writings to Soviet confessions made under duress, finding them impersonal and formulaic [p. 602].

GEORGINA SABAT de RIVERS

From Sor Juana and Her Love Sonnets[†]

Sor Juana, in the history of Hispanic poetry, was clearly the last great poet in the tradition that had begun in Spanish with Boscán and Garcilaso[1] and that came to an end with her death on this side of the Atlantic Ocean, in New Spain, as Mexico was then known. Although she was well acquainted with the Petrarchan tradition, reflected in her poetry (Rabin 1993), her love sonnets do not form a *canzoniere*.[2] We may group her sonnets by the persons to whom they are addressed, but when we consider her sonnets as a whole, we find that they are addressed to many different persons, and although they do not constitute a love story, they do reflect her social and personal relations with a number of other people.

Sor Juana was thoroughly familiar with the sonnets written by the great poets of Europe, and by minor poets both in Spain and in the colonies.[3] Her poetry echoes the traditions of New Spain; in her literary world she was the poet who commanded the widest range of previous poetry. She was of course conversant with the Renaissance practice of *imitatio*,[4] which in her case was never servile. She adapted to her own purposes a wide range of models from different sources, addressing a public that ranged from the clerical writer, the aristocratic courtier, and the learned scientist to the more modest world of musicians and poets involved with cathedral carol sequences and street recitations. Her world of poetry was international, according to Eugenio de Salazar's *Epístola a Herrera*[5] (Méndez Plancarte 1942–44, 1:67), ranging from the "mil riquezas" of Spain and "las lindezas" of Italy to the poetry of Provence and of Greece. In New Spain there had lived sonneteers from Seville, such as Gutierre de Cetina and Juan de la Cueva; local poets,

---

† From *Colonial Latin American Review* 4.2 (1995): 104–05, 109–11, 116–21. Article translated by Elias L. Rivers. Reprinted by permission of the publisher, Taylor & Francis Ltd. Editor's notes and several translations include contributions by Isabel Gómez.

1. Garcilaso de la Vega (1501–1536), generally considered the greatest lyric poet in Renaissance Spain. Íñigo López de Mendoza y de la Vega, Marquis of Santillana (1398–1458), Castilian poet and admirer of Dante and Petrarch. Juan Boscán Almogàver (1490–1542), Castilian poet responsible for introducing the Italian sonnet and Petrarchan cycle into the Spanish court [*Editor*].

2. Francesco Petrarca (1304–1374), or Petrarch, Italian humanist and poet whose lyric cycle addressed to Laura became the model for Renaissance courtly poetry. Petrarch's cycle of love poems, called the *Canzoniere* (Songbook) or *Rime sparse* (Scattered rhymes), was dedicated to Laura [*Editor*].

3. For colonial poetry in Mexico, see Méndez Plancarte 1942–44; Pascual Buxó 1986; González Boixo 1988 and 1989; and Frenk 1989. See also my chapter on "La poesía popular y la poesía culta," written many years ago and soon to be published in a history of Spanish American literature edited by Amos Segala (UNESCO). To what extent was Sor Juana familiar with this colonial poetry, which circulated principally in manuscripts? Margit Frenk tells us, for example, that González de Eslava frequently visited the Jeronimite convent, where he had many readers: he probably left manuscripts of his poetry with the nuns. [For González de Eslava, see p. 265, n. 6—*Editor*.]

4. A value drawn from classical rhetoric and poetics; imitation, either of previous models or of nature, was the primary goal of Western art before the eighteenth century [*Editor*].

5. Spanish poet (1530–1602) who lived in Mexico City between 1581 and 1600 and became the chancellor of the Royal and Pontifical University of Mexico [*Editor*].

such as Francisco de Terrazas, Francisco Bramón, Miguel de Guevara; as well as others from Spain who had become fully adapted to the *criollo* world, such as Bernardo de Balbuena, Fernán González de Eslava, and the bishop of Puebla and viceroy Juan de Palafox y Mendoza.[6] Later, there were other Mexican-born sonneteers such as Catalina de Eslava (the author of a sole surviving sonnet on the death of her uncle), María de Estrada, and Sor Juana's contemporary Diego de Ribera.[7] Such poets as Luis de Sandoval Zapata (see note 3),[8] for example, had written sonnets shortly before Sor Juana did. Thus, we see that her local poetic environment, which directly influenced her sonnets, was a rich one. The diversity of themes, motifs, and voices which she appropriates as a poet give evidence of this whole literary world as transformed by a learned Mexican-born writer,[9] conscious of her unique role as an intellectual woman. She tells us in her *Respuesta* that she could not help being a writer; she wrote many different sorts of sonnet, seeking recognition, within her convent and outside, of her right to be a writer.

Before beginning to analyze Sor Juana's sonnets, we should emphasize one of their most unusual aspects: the fact that the poetic self who speaks is in her case not masculine but feminine. The courtly love tradition, including Petrarch,[1] had always been based on the premise of a poet-lover who was male and adored his lady. But Sor Juana inverts or varies this established norm, speaking in different voices: the poetic self is sometimes feminine and addresses a male beloved; it is sometimes masculine and tells his lady of his suffering; it is sometimes ambiguous, of unidentifiable gender; and occasionally, whether male or female, it simply reflects upon a love situation.

Turning now to the study of Sor Juana's love sonnets, we may note that she normally follows the tradition of posing a problem in the octet and, after the usual pause or transition, of resolving the problem in the sestet.[2] But sometimes the posing of the problem continues into the tercets, as is frequent in Baroque sonnets, and the resolution or reversal comes only in the final lines.

6. The influential bishop of Puebla and viceroy (1600–1659) also wrote spiritual verse. "Criollo" originally described any person born in the Americas, but came to signify Americans of Spanish descent or Spaniards who lived permanently in the Americas. Francisco de Terrazas (1525–1600 or 1604), soldier in Cortés's army, mayor of Mexico City, and author of epic and lyric poems. Francisco Bramón (d. 1664), Mexican-born author of lyric and drama. Miguel de Guevara (ca. 1585–ca. 1646), Augustinian friar, relative of Hernán Cortés, poet and philologist of indigenous languages. Bernardo de Balbuena (1561–1627), Spanish poet who lived in Guadalajara and Mexico City before becoming bishop of Puerto Rico; author of *Grandeza mexicana* (Mexico's grandeur, 1604) and other works. Fernán González de Eslava (ca. 1534–1601), Spanish poet who lived in Mexico [*Editor*].
7. Mexican-born author of an extensive array of verse (1630–1688). Catalina de Eslava, niece of Fernán González de Eslava included in his compendium. María de Estrada Medinilla, poet who wrote a homage for a viceregal entrance in 1660 [*Editor*].
8. Poet from New Spain (ca. 1620–1671), recognized in his time as a "Mexican Homer" [*Editor*].
9. Concerning the *criollo* aspect of Sor Juana's writings, see my article of 1992. ["*Criollo*": American born of European descent—*Editor*.]
1. See p. 264 n. 2.
2. In a sonnet, the two final stanzas of tercets (three verses each). "Octet": in a sonnet, the first two quatrains (four verses each) [*Editor*].

* * *

The sonnet that we will now read is one of Sor Juana's most famous (number 165), and justly so:

Que contiene una fantasía contenta con amor decente.

> Detente, sombra de mi bien esquivo,
> imagen del hechizo que más quiero,
> bella illusión por quien alegre muero,
> dulce ficción por quien penosa vivo.
> 5   Si al imán de tus gracias atractivo
> sirve mi pecho de obediente acero,
> ¿para qué me enamoras lisonjero
> si has de burlarme luego fugitivo?
>   Mas blasonar no puedes, satisfecho,
> 10 de que triunfa de mí tu tiranía:
> que aunque dejas burlado el lazo estrecho
>   que tu forma fantástica ceñía,
> poco importa burlar brazos y pecho
> si te labra prisión mi fantasía.

[Which restrains a fantasy by making it content with decent love.

> Halt, O faint shade of my elusive love,
> image of the enchantment I love best,
> fair illusion for whom I gladly die,
> sweet fiction for whose sake I live in pain.
>   If th'attraction, the magnet of your charms
> draws my heart as if it were made of steel,
> why woo and win me over with flattery
> if then you will deceive me, turn and flee?
>   But, satisfied and proud, you cannot boast
> that your tyranny triumphs over me:
> for though you escape and slip through the tight cords
>   that bind your imagined form in fantasy,
> it matters not if you elude my arms,
> my dear, when thought alone can imprison you.][3]

In this sonnet the poet overtly adopts the feminine voice (with the usual pronouns "yo / tú"). The key words used in the first quatrain ("sombra," "imagen," "ilusión," "ficción"[4]) have Latin roots and are

---

3. Translation by Edith Grossman. See p. 37.
4. For the definitions of these words I have consulted the *Diccionario de Autoridades* and the Covarrubias *Tesoro de la lengua castellana o española* and have chosen those definitions

based on Aristotelian concepts dealing with the mind, which the poet uses at the same time to address her beloved. In the second quatrain the virtues of the beloved become a magnet that attract her breast, enclosing her heart, which responds as a piece of steel, conveying the idea of armor against the attacks of love, quite different from the soft wax ("cera") used by Garcilaso de la Vega in one of his sonnets.[5] The idea of his virtues as a magnet that attracts her is related to what we have seen in her "rational love": he has sufficient merits to be loved, but he does not love her in return. We discover the reason for the opening imperative "detente" when we reach the reproachful question of the final two lines of the second quatrain: Why do you make me fall in love with you if you then run away from me? His flight explains why she has had recourse to complex mental concepts (note 4). The feminine voice of the poet, aware of her beloved's deceitful game, decides in the sestet to teach him a lesson: your tyrannical treatment, she says, cannot triumph over me, for, although you attempt to flee me, my "fantasía" can hold you fast, in spite of yourself. She is triumphant because of her mental possession of the beloved's image. Note that the "forma fantástica" that runs away from her arms is already a product of her imagination; being fantastic, his form can be captured by her mind. My inner self, she tells him, imprisons you, and this establishes a close relationship between the sentiments of love and the faculties of the mind.

This sonnet, highly intellectual and at the same time highly lyrical, can be compared, in the attitude that it expresses, with the *Carta Atenagórica* and the "Carta de Monterrey";[6] it is one more expression

---

most appropriate to this sonnet. "Sombra" (from *umbra*) is the equivalent of "spectre" or "phantasm"; "imagen" (*imago*) is the "figura, representación, semejanza y apariencia de alguna cosa" (figure, representation, similitude and appearance of some thing); "ilusión" (*illusio*) is a deception, a false image, a deceptive apparition; "ficción" or "ficón" (*fictio*) is a "simulación con que se pretende encubrir la verdad o hacer creer lo que no es cierto" (simulation that seeks to veil the truth or have one believe a falsehood). "Imaginación" (*imaginatio*) is the "potencia con que el alma representa en la fantasía algún objeto" (potential by which the soul represents some object in the fantasy); Covarrubias equates this word with "fantasía" (from Greek *phantasia*) or "visio, imago rerum animo insidentium." In *Autoridades* we find for "phantasia" this definition: "La segunda de las potencias que se atribuyen al alma sensitive o racional, que forma las imágenes de las cosas" (The second of the powers (*potencias*) attributed to the sensitive or rational soul that forms images of things), adding: "Cuando no hay sustento en el estómago, para que el calor natural se ocupe en él, se ocupa en representar, juntamente con el ánima, al sentido común, o *phantasia*, diversos simulacros de cosas" (When there is no sustenance in the stomach, such that natural heat might be used there, it is used to represent, together with the soul, diverse simulacra of things to the common sense or phantasia). This "sentido común" (common sense) is the inner sense that combines the sensations received via the five physical senses (sight, hearing, taste, etc.). All of this leads us to the scholastic language that Sor Juana uses in her *Sueño*, terms taken from Aristotelian physiology by the nun and converted into poetry.

5. "Si a vuestra voluntad yo soy de cera" (If to your will I am as if formed of wax) (Sonnet XVIII) [*Editor*].

6. See "Letter by Mother Juana Inés de la Cruz" on p. 144. "Athenagoric Letter": Sor Juana's critique of the Maundy Thursday Sermon of Father Antonio Vieira (see p. 83) [*Editor*].

of Sor Juana's intellectual self-confidence, of her faith in the triumph of mind over matter. The mind is so powerful that it can destroy prisons as well as create them; as she says in poem 42, which seems to anticipate this sonnet:

> Para el alma no hay encierro
> ni prisiones que la impidan,
> porque sólo la aprisionan
> las que se forma ella misma.[7]

> [For the soul there is no enclosure
> nor prison that can impede it,
> because she may only be incarcerated
> by those she creates for herself.]

Among the many excellent examples of related topics in previous authors that Méndez Plancarte[8] cites in his notes (Cruz, *Obras completas*, 1:529–30), the following seem particularly appropriate: Martín de la Plaza's "Amante sombra de mi bien esquivo" (already noted by Abreu); Quevedo's "A fugitivas sombras doy abrazos / . . . / Búrlame y de burlarme corre ufana"; Calderón's "Adorando estoy tu sombra, / y, a mis ojos aparente, / por burlar mi fantasía / abracé al aire mil veces" and his "Detente, espera, / sombra, illusión . . ."[9] These concepts, drawn from Aristotelian psychology, were a common patrimony; Sor Juana uses them in a splendid sonnet, adding as a personal note the great power of the mind; her originality lies in the fact that she centers the action within herself, a woman in love, and not in the beloved who flees and who, in the final analysis, cannot escape her mind.[1]

There are two other poems by Sor Juana, a group of *décimas* (number 101)[2] and a *glosa* (number 142), in which she deals with

7. Ballad 42, verses 25–28. Cruz, *Obras completas*, 4 vols., vol. 1, 2nd ed. (Mexico: Fondo de Cultura Economica, 2009), p. 170 [*Editor*].
8. Alfonso Mendez Plancarte (1909–1955), editor of the *Complete works of Sor Juana Inés de la Cruz*, first edition, published by Fondo de Cultura Económica between 1951 and 1957 [*Editor*].
9. Pedro Calderón de la Barca (1600–1681), Spanish playwright and poet. The previous citations are from his *El mayor monstruo del mundo* (The greatest monster of the world) and *Las tres justicias en una* (Three justices in one). Luis Martín de la Plaza (1525–1577), Spanish poet from Málaga. Francisco de Quevedo (1580–1645), Spanish author of poetry and prose, known for his metaphysical wit. The previous citation is from his sonnet 358 [*Editor*].
1. In this love sonnet the poet expresses a highly positive view of the mind's supreme power; in her poem the *Sueño*, concerned with questions of scientific knowledge, she reaches the conclusion that the mind's power has its limits. It is one thing for the mind to contain the image of a person, and quite another for it to intellectually attempt to contain the universe.
2. Décima 101, verses 51–55: "Partid, en fin, confiado / en mi voluntad constante, / de que, aunque estéis muy distante / nunca estaréis apartado." (Leave, finally, with confidence / in my constant and loyal will / from which, although very distant / you are never separated) [*Editor*].

similar ideas in connection with the theme of absence. The lover, by means of thought, never leaves the beloved, no matter how far away he may be; she says that she will have "siempre el pensamiento en ti, / siempre a ti en el pensamiento" [always have a thought for you / and always have you in my thoughts]. She converts the philosophical ideas of our sonnet into an almost religious love, when she says "Acá en el alma veré / el centro de mis cuidados / con los ojos de mi fe: / que gustos imaginados, / también un ciego los ve" [There in my soul I can see / the center of my affections / with the eyes of my faith: / such imagined pleasures, / *even the blind can see them*].[3] But our sonnet is poetically superior to these two poems.

We should not forget that Sor Juana's *Sueño* contains some of the same topics that we find in the sonnet, including the word "imán" [magnet], in connection with the lungs that attract air; more important, there is a passage in which the Pharos of Alexandria is compared with the faculty of Phantasia. The stomach, says the poet,

> al cerebro envïaba
> 255 húmedos, mas tan claros, los vapores
> de los atemperados cuatro humores,
> que con ellos no sólo no empañaba
> los simulacros que la estimativa
> dio a la imaginativa
> 260 y aquésta, por custodia más segura,
> en forma ya más pura
> entregó a la memoria que, oficiosa,
> grabó tenaz y guarda cuidadosa,
> sino que daban a la Fantasía
> 265 lugar de que formase
> imágenes diversas . . . [4]

> [. . . transmitted to the brain
> the damp but most clear vapors
> of the four tempered humors
> that not only did not cloud the semblances
> the intellect gave to imagination

3. The cited lines are from Glosa 142, "Aunque cegué de mirarte." They are the last four lines of the last stanza.
4. The four humors were blood, phlegm, choler, and melancholy, which were the "vapores" in the mechanical process of Aristotelian psychology. In this passage the "estimativa" seems to be the equivalent of the faculty of phantasia or common sense, which combines the data (or species) provided by the five senses of the body to form simulacra in the imagination, from which they go to the memory; the memory stores and purifies them, as Sor Juana says, until they are taken up again by the phantasia (the active aspect of the imagination) and makes new combinations with their images. See Méndez Plancarte's note on lines 256 and 258–65 of the *Sueño* and also my book (1976, 135–36), as well as note 4 above. [See p. 51, lines 232–42—*Editor*.]

> which, for safer keeping and in purer form,
> presented them to diligent memory
> that etched them, tenacious, and guards them with care,
> but permitted fantasy
> to form diverse images.]

In both the sonnet and the *Sueño*, Phantasia—capitalized as a per-
sonified character—mediates between thought and the sensations
received by the five physical senses, as the "common sense" that
combines them. In the sonnet, Phantasia forms the image of the
beloved and has it retained by Memory. This faculty of the human
mind plays a leading role in our sonnet; once again Sor Juana con-
verts scientific terms into love poetry.

*   *   *

The European Tradition and Sor Juana
in Her World of New Spain

The masochistic suffering of courtly love took different forms in
different poets and periods, from the theological spiritualization of
Dante to the humanistic introspection of Petrarch[5] to the burlesque
indecency of unprintable sonnets (Alzieu 1975). The love sonnet, with
its medieval roots, was the most widely known poetic genre, and one
of the most prestigious, during the sixteenth and seventeenth cen-
turies. In studying Sor Juana's love sonnets we should always keep
in mind that Renaissance and Baroque poetry has little to do with
the cult of sincerity and autobiographical directness that became
popular during the Romantic period, which cultivated a sensibility
much closer to our own. From the simple objective idealism of the
neo-Platonic Renaissance we move to the complex, disillusioned
subjectivism—dynamic and Protean—of the Counter-Reformational
Baroque period. Reality can no longer be trusted; Sor Juana's many
voices do not give us accounts of personal experiences, which come
to the surface only as remembered fantasies. In our case, these fan-
tasies take concrete form as sonnets, with strict formal rules; they
are often poetic games invented to amaze and astound. Baroque
poetry, to which we attribute such complex and interrelated tenden-
cies as both "conceptismo" and "culteranismo," reflects a perplexed
and tortured world-view, according to Maravall,[6] and a need to

5. See p. 264 n. 2. "Dante": see p. 252 n. 3 [*Editor*].
6. José Antonio Maravall (1911–1986), Spanish historian and author of an influential study
   of seventeenth-century Spanish culture, *Cultura del barroco* (Culture of the Baroque,
   1974). "Culteranismo": florid style associated with the Spanish poet Luis de Góngora
   (1561–1627). "Conceptismo": witty style associated with the Spanish poet Francisco de
   Quevedo (1580–1645) [*Editor*].

exercise and cultivate the mind during a difficult cultural crisis; Gracián[7] urges the intellectual to be highly attentive and on guard, so as to be able to decipher the traumatic events that take place, events that cause one to doubt the evidence of one's own senses. Baroque wit thrives on contradictions.

In this study, we have separated Sor Juana's love sonnets into two major groups. We have called the first group orthodox or idealistic; it evokes a pure, disinterested, and permanent love, or a rational love based on the merits of the beloved. The second group is heterodox in the sense that love is seen as problematic and relativistic, mixed with hate, aware of its own impermanence.

The most noteworthy fact is that Sor Juana is a woman who reinvents love poetry from a feminine perspective; she knows the established tradition, but she finds herself immersed in the disquieting Baroque world that we have described. She sometimes assumes the traditional male voice of the courtly love tradition; sometimes she applies to love her knowledge of scholastic science to characterize it as incorruptible and based on reason. In her more unorthodox phases, we hear the same voices—masculine, feminine, or ambiguous—insisting now on love as subject to time and change, as subject to practical decisions based on the human understanding. Her language, though complex, reflects at times lovers' contact with the everyday world.

In her sonnets we can see that, from within her cloister, Sor Juana took a leading role in the cultural life of New Spain; she exchanged with the outside world not only sonnets but other manuscripts and probably books. Her poetry reflects this cultural world and shows pride in her personal knowledge of intellectual trends, both scholastic and more recent. But it also allows us to see her social role as a female arbiter and adviser in a real world of courtly gossip and family intrigue, of flirtation and changing relations among aristocrats born in Spain or in the New World; she taught lessons to others on how to react in the face of amorous deception, how to break off a sentimental engagement, why one should reject an unworthy beloved and recognize love's time-bound nature. As is shown in the case of the *Enigmas* that Sor Juana wrote for a group of Portuguese nuns (Martínez López 1968 and Alatorre 1994), who knew they could find in her poetry the answers to her riddles, she was widely known for her mental agility and respected for her writings, which had a strong influence on people even before they were printed.

---

7. Baltasar Gracián (1601–1658), Jesuit author of the moral treatise *Oraculo manual y arte de prudencia* (Manual oracle and art of prudence, 1647) [*Editor*].

As for the unique poem that stands out amidst all of her sonnets, "Detente, sombra de mi bien esquivo,"[8] which has been called "the masterkey to her love poetry" (Paz 1982, 380–83), it is a compendium of the poet's own literary and personal characteristics, among which we will point out again the following two. First, she emphasizes the inner life of the mind, analyzed here in terms of Aristotelian psychology: she reviews the process by which memory stores the "sombras," illusions and fictions that have been caught by the senses and converted into the "imagen del hechizo que más quiero,"[9] becoming in this way imprisoned by fantasy in her mind, from which there is no escape. And, second, she emphasizes the feminine perspective: in this sonnet she ignores the will of the male beloved and acts with a profoundly and daringly "feminist" determination. This sonnet reflects not only her pride as an intellectual woman capable of analyzing the mind with an erudition acquired by her own independent studies, but also her ability as a plain and simple woman to find a way to escape the "tyranny" of a fleeing lover and win the upper hand over him.

Sor Juana's intellectual and literary creativity takes advantage of a long, rich tradition to rise to new poetic heights as she analyzes with great sophistication the sentimental relationships between people belonging to her world of New Spain; she knew this world well, she was thoroughly familiar with the literary tradition dealing with questions of love, and she had a powerful human intuition that took poetry to levels that cannot be excelled.

YOLANDA MARTÍNEZ-SAN MIGUEL

From American Knowledge: The Constitution of a Colonial Subjectivity in the Writings of Sor Juana Inés de la Cruz[†]

The majority of critical studies on Sor Juana's *villancicos*[1] have emphasized their popular characteristics and capacity to represent marginalized voices in colonial society. Alfonso Méndez-Plancarte

8. "Halt, O faint shade of my elusive love," analyzed on p. 266 [*Editor*].
9. "image of the enchantment I love best," in the sonnet, the second verse. "Sombras": shadows [*Editor*].
† From Yolanda Martínez-San Miguel, *Saberes americanos: subalternidad y epistemología en los escritos de Sor Juana* (Pittsburgh: Instituto Internacional de Literatura Iberoamericana, 1999), pp. 151–59. Translated for this edition by Isabel Gómez. Reproduced by permission of the Instituto Internacional de Literatura Iberoamericana. All notes are Martínez-San Miguel's unless otherwise indicated.
1. The *villancico* is a lyric form of popular song that originated in the Spanish Middle Ages. Today, the term is associated primarily with Christmas carols, but the form was originally used to celebrate a range of Christian festivals [*Translator*].

contextualizes these lyric songs in their development and cultivation in Spain. In his detailed introductory study to the *Obras completas* [Complete Works] of Sor Juana, he emphasizes the origin of the term *villancico* as describing a "diminutive of a *villano*: a rustic villager or Spanish commoner—and his characteristic songs, percussion, or dances—or a basically artificial imitation of them" (*Obras*, Volume 2, xi). This definition by Méndez-Plancarte establishes a link between the genre, its use of colloquial speech, and its representation of popular sectors of urban society. Originally, the content of these compositions could be sacred or secular, and their primary interest was a representation of rustic common speech, following the model of *sayagüés* that Encina[2] had elaborated and institutionalized as a religious composition to be sung in church during Christmas and other festivals (*Obras*, Volume 2, xiii). By 1660–1750 the *villancico* had already become a specialized poetic composition, exclusively interspersed within the matins for liturgical festivals. Later on, these religious *villancicos* were composed of cycles made up of eight to ten carols organized in the following way: "three Nocturnes, each one with three Psalms and three lessons interspersed with a Response after each one, which served as their polyphonic climaxes" (*Obras*, Volume 2, xvii–xviii).

Most carol cycles ended with an *ensalada*,[3] which represented the multiplicity of voices from marginal sectors of urban society (OC, II, XVIII). Georgina Sabat Rivers has shown how the *ensalada* is characterized by a mobility and polyphony that incorporates and places a wide variety of voices and races typical to the makeup of New Spanish society ("Blanco, negro, rojo" 248). On the other hand, José Antonio Mayoral has studied the structure of these *ensaladas* in Sor Juana's *villancicos*, and he demonstrates that this mixture of voices responds to a specific structure that was definitive of that poetic genre and cultivated widely when Sor Juana composed her *villancicos* (224–26). According to Mayoral, the introductory stanza for each *ensalada* explains and distributes the diverse voices, especially determining who will intervene in the debate or dialogue, establishing the last part of the song cycle (230). In this sense, the incorporation of subaltern voices in the *villancico* simultaneously opens up the religious discourse to incorporate the contributions and perspectives of marginalized individuals, but also positions

2. *Sayagüés* refers to the rustic speech of a person from the Sayago region of Zamora in central Spain. Juan de Encina (ca. 1468–ca. 1529) was the poet and playwright known for writing in a literary representation of this regional Spanish dialect [*Translator*].
3. *Ensalada* literally means "salad" and refers to a specific subgenre of the *villancico* that includes representations of popular voices and often also a greater mixture of lyric meters and stanza forms [*Translator*].

or defines specific locations occupied by these subjects within the social order of colonial New Spain.

I am interested in reading of some of the texts by Sor Juana precisely from this starting point of the structure of the *villancico* as a song cycle. It is important to remember here that the main purpose of these religious *villancicos* was to transmit some lesson of dogma or Catholic belief to the public gathered in the church. In this way, as the epigraph from Muriel emphasizes,[4] the inclusion of "popular" voices indicates the necessity of identifying registers and models of community self-expressions in order to transmit to the common people a doctrinal teaching that would unify them:

> *villancicos* were directed at a heterogeneous community which was nevertheless, in that historical moment, fundamentally harmonious: as a community so singularly enclosed within its limits as a distant Viceroyality and in its leisure as a minor court, it was open, at all levels, to the refined and sumptuous tastes of the Baroque (Puccini, "Los 'villancicos' de Sor Juana Inés de la Cruz" 231).

In accordance with this "unifying" purpose, the *villancicos* compensated with a centralizing voice of the metropolitan Catholic faith that, as the song cycle went on, progressed into a dispersion of voices and culminated with the *ensalada* or the mix of diverse popular voices. The *villancico* would rehearse, over the course of its nine compositions, a series of simultaneous explanations that transmit one doctrinal or dogmatic truth crafted in diverse verbal and intellectual registers. This diversified didactic reinforcement was central in the cultivation of the *villancico* in Spain and in the American colonies. The inclusion of black or indigenous voices was not exclusive to the *villancico* in colonial America, as Georges Baudot points out.[5]

We all know that the *villancico* was Spanish and the themes and forms it exploited were fully conventional: it used and

4. The epigraph to this section of Martínez-San Miguel's book, a citation of Josefina Muriel's *Cultura feminina novohispana,* reads: "The common people filling the cathedrals heard a voice that was theirs, they understood and felt something they could identify with. They may not have understood the Latin of the matins, but they did follow Spanish, Nahuatl, mixed jargons, and the simplicity of what was said—this is what conveyed the larger theological lesson" [*translated by Editor*].

5. Alfonso Méndez-Plancarte suggests this same idea in "Estudio liminar" to the second volume of the *Obras completas;* Fernando Benítez in *Los demonios en el convento* (73–82), where he cites lines by Góngora that use black speech, and the study by Rosa Valdés Cruz, "La vision del negro en Sor Juana." Some of these studies, nevertheless, emphasize how the black and indigenous voices in Sor Juana are more subversive because they openly complain against the system of slavery. In my reading, I emphasize, in spite of this, the formation of an intermediary colonial identity, and how the representation of these voices permits the articulation of the particular space of mediation corresponding to this social sector.

sometimes abused literary conventions including the "half language" of African slaves, speech delivered "in the manner of a black person" or in the "portuñol" of Portuguese inflected Spanish; and even in Spain, poets used sayings "in the Aztecan way" as in the Nahuatlized *tocotín* imported to Cadiz by José Pérez de Montoro around 1680, proclaiming that it came from "Chapurtepeque" ("El barroco mexicano" 110).

Therefore I am not as interested in emphasizing the use and representation of certain "subaltern" voices in Sor Juana's *villancicos*, given that European and American authors had already made ample use of this literary device (Jones 67, Wilson 93). The point is to examine the use of this verbal and literary strategy when it is integrated in a colonial context. In that context, the representation of "subaltern" voices in their specific locations in the structure of villancico cycles produces a diversifying epistemology hidden within the common denominator of Catholic dogma in order to propose a new mode of approaching the problem of knowledge. The *villancico* cycles, therefore, may indicate through their very structure a journey toward the articulation of an "intercultural epistemology" in which the *villancico* is a space for the confluence of a variety of paradigms and an intersection of subjects of knowledge.

In this sense, my reading coincides with Puccini's analysis of the *villancico* as a double project of transculturation in Sor Juana's work: she directs her mystery plays to one select public and her *villancicos* to another more massive one:

> The mystery play and its prologues were dedicated to a different public, or one that imagined itself to be different, more select than that which was called to sing and listen to the *villancicos*: Sor Juana develops an act of transculturation on two distinct fronts that are actually parallel underneath. In the *villancicos*, the popular interventions exclude the more problematic and immediate positions. As actors and spectators at the same time, indigenous and mestizo people revive the legend of Christmas, the myth of the purity of Mary, the exemplary histories of the Saints, both in a direct figuration of pure fantasy and in a simple, immediate, emblem-like performance (Puccini, "Los 'villancicos'" 236).

Beneath this supposed unification through knowledge of the Catholic faith, the *villancico* executes a process of diversification in the acquisition of knowledge, which unfolds in various successive narrations that use different registers to articulate themselves to the heterogeneous sectors of colonial society. I am interested, therefore, in reading parts of four *villancico* song cycles by Sor Juana in order to trace the articulation of the "intercultural epistemology" these texts indicate through their generic constitution. In this sense, my analysis does not posit that the gesture of producing new paradigms of knowledge is exclusive to the work of Sor Juana. Rather, it is the result of a colonial or multiracial context that promoted a new epistemological and pedagogical paradigm through intercultural contact.

My reading here also takes into account the ambiguous and problematic representation of the cultural elements of New Spain, either as indications of differences, or as spaces for the negotiation of an inscription into the colonial circuit. The epistemological subjectivity articulated in these texts, therefore, breaks down into multiple positions that on some rare occasions reach a point of complete polarization of the metropolitan and American sectors.

* * *

This cycle [of the *villancico* for the Feast of the Assumption, 1676][6] closes with an *ensaladilla*[7] that is divided into three vocal registers: the Queen, the Blacks, and the Indigenous. This diversification of voices indicates an amplification of linguistic and semantic registers that aspires to transmit its praise of the Virgin to a heterogeneous public. The entrance of the "Plebeian humanity" into the *villancico* culminates the symbolic journey from Castilian Spanish and Latin to the Nahuatl that ends the song cycle. We will examine the final *villancico* more closely.

The "Introduction" functions to distribute the voices that can participate in the religious ceremony: "To the festive acclamation / of the Oath of our Queen / the common people come together / with the Angelic Nobility / since she is Queen of everyone / they celebrate her coronation / in majesty of many voices / they sing her Magnificent songs": (Cruz, *Obras completas,* Volume 2, 14). After that, the *villancico* is divided into three songs. The first speaker is a "Queen" who offers the Virgin her obedience in exchange for protection and peace for humankind, defending their lives against violence. Notice here that a Queen is the figure chosen to represent secular power and offer obedience to the Divine. The Queen appears to be the first iteration of "Plebeian humanity" congregated in the church, which emphasizes the marginality of the female subject within secular power structures. After the Queen's song, the black slaves enter and praise the Virgin Mary, but also mourn her ascent to heaven that leaves them alone as enslaved labor:

6. Martínez San-Miguel has been analyzing the different sections that make up Sor Juana's first *villancico* (1676) in celebration of the Catholic Feast of the Assumption, which celebrates Mary in her bodily ascent into heaven [*Translator*].
7. For the definition of *ensalada* in the context of the *villancicos,* see n. 3 on p. 273 [*Editor*].

"Pilico, les all go singin
for da Queen she be leavin,
an give us all together
a blessed good evenin."
          "I be cryin all da same
Flacico, of da pain
in da dark she lef behin
all us black people."
          "If she be goin to Heaven
an God he take Her der,
what you be cryin for
if our Queen She be glad?"
          "Go on an let me cry
Flacico, I cryin for Her—
when she go an leave us here
da Oblaje be left to us."

The first thing that stands out in the text are the linguistic markers that separate the rough Spanish of the black slaves from the Castillian Spanish that opens and predominates in most *villancicos* in this cycle.[8] This representation of the particularized speech of a black individual differs from other stylized representations of indigenous speech that appear in the prologues and the mystery plays. In this case, the *villancico* draws in a public to the Church by means of the inclusion of marginal characters who pay their respects to the Virgin on her ascent to Heaven at the same time as they lament the distancing of the Catholic religion from the suffering of their lives as slaves. The slaves' song is in two voices: one which seems to conform to the Virgin's side and another which laments her distance and forgetting of black slaves. This structure produces a polyphony of opinions that does not permit the homogeneous participation of the black slave in the religious ritual. The final stanza of this section unifies both voices through the racial identification of the Virgin with the slaves: "—Uh, uh, uh / she ain white like you, / ain no Spanish, that no good, / so she say: 'I dark-skinned too / cause the Sun been lookin at me'" (Cruz, *Obras*, Volume 2, 16). Perhaps the only possible way to achieve total union was by severing the link between the Virgin Mary and the white and Spanish race associated with the enslaving power of the Viceroyality, instead associating her with the black race.

8. In her book, Martínez-San Miguel includes the original verses by Sor Juana along with a version rendered in more standard Spanish to clarify meaning. Both texts have influenced this translation. See p. 132, n. 5 for the translation of stereotyped speech in the *villancicos* [*Translator's note revised by Editor*].

In this subtle way, the *villancico* points toward the religious syn-
cretic practices that transformed saints and divine figures in Catholi-
cism into equivalents among the African deities. By transforming the
Virgin racially, the text adds this metamorphosis and likens it to the
previous series of transformations the Virgin experienced—first into a
teacher, then a knight errant—all of which are used to allegorize and
enumerate her virtues. In the same way, the text places syncretism in
an evangelical context, where depicting the Virgin as a dark-skinned
morena not only makes her comprehensible for a slave public but also
converts her into a motif that conflates the official religious prac-
tices of the colony. Enacted here in its racial dimension, syncretism
becomes another evangelical strategy that unifies the diverse voices of
the *villancico* in the common space of the Catholic faith. One could
say that the *villancico* takes advantage of Christian religious senti-
ment in this moment as a mediating discourse in which it aspires to
harmonize all the heterogeneous racial make-up that characterizes
New Spanish culture (Meléndez 88). In this sense, religion continues
to function as an incorporating force that permits the scenic and
verbal space to open up to the diverse voices, races, and world-
views that make up colonial society, without fragmenting the cen-
tral meaning in these texts. Evangelization, incorporation, and
domination continue to be very strong elements in the *villancicos* by
Sor Juana.

It is important to emphasize the way her onomatopoetic represen-
tation of black voices, on one hand, intends to bring out the repre-
sented subject as an individual, but on the other hand, also performs
an erasure that distances the black subject as such by assuming his
particular and different mode of talking with a rhythmic sound linked
to African ritual dances. In this way, the onomatopoeic language
points precisely to her limited knowledge of the slave. While it
attempts to open up a dramatic space for him, the result is very frag-
ile because of its link to humor and farcical joking: "Baroque authors
saw the black person as humorous figure full of lightheartedness: he
was the ignorant fool who pertained to an inferior class and occupied
a world with a social sphere like that of the rustic villager and the
shepherd" (Valdés-Cruz 209). The black slave does not intervene
on the same rational and epistemological level as the pedagogi-
cal Latin or the allegories presented in Castillian Spanish, but
rather as rhythm, oration, and musicality that create variety in the
villancico.

Nevertheless, the verses sung by black slaves register a social cri-
tique that indicates a critically thinking mentality, one that resists
the prevailing social and political system and is capable of trans-
forming the metropolitan referents for a very specific usage within

their social sector. Race is identified as a value that polarizes social spaces, another indication of the way the black subject participates in the catalogue of allegories and debates through which the Virgin Mary's virtues are thematized.

Finally, this song cycle closes with a *tocotín*[9] in Nahuatl that asks the Virgin to remember her indigenous supplicants and places her in a mediating position between Christ and humanity in a way that is very similar to the traditional Marian cult of the metropolis.[1] The Virgin occupies, therefore, that space of intercession that allows for the salvation of faithful indigenous peoples: "Well, for all peoples / she supplicates him: / and if he doesn't want to / she reminds him / that your flesh / You gave it to him / your milk / he drank it, while dreaming, / and when he was a little one" (from the Spanish translation by Angel Garibay, Cruz, *Obras*, Volume 2, 365). This closing song stands out for the way it introduces the "Mexican language"[2] (Cruz, *Obras*, Volume 2, 16): by means of the strangeness of the language for a metropolitan and *criollo*[3] public, it transmits content that is fairly typical for the religious poetry of the Medieval and Renaissance Europe. This gesture seems to place the indigenous subject as more easily assimilated to the European religious tradition than the African syncretist. The villancico also differentiates the spaces that indigenous subjects and African subjects occupy, another way to emphasize the great degree of hierarchical ordering in the New Spanish cultural experience. Closing the *villancico* in a different language culminates the intercultural epistemological process with which I characterized the *villancico* cycles from the start of this reading. The text moves from the framework of Castilian Spanish and Latin toward other registers that are disciplinary, colloquial, and popular, followed by the rough Spanish of enslaved black people, and ending with an encounter between languages when Nahuatl is introduced. The structure of the text can be summarized as follows:

---

9. A Mexica dance with its accompanying music [*Editor*].
1. For a study of the use of Nahuatl in Sor Juana's work, see the article by Georges Baudot, "La trova náhuatl de Sor Juana Inés de la Cruz," and the presentation by Frances Karttunen, "The Nahuatl Language in the Works of Sor Juana." The two studies express opposite arguments about the skill and usage of Nahuatl in Sor Juana's works, and they analyze the few texts by this writer that we have in this language.
2. That is, Nahuatl. In the seventeenth century, *Mexican* referred almost exclusively to the Nahuatl-speaking peoples of the central valley [*Editor*].
3. A term used to describe an American-born person of European descent [*Editor*].

Villancico I: Appeal to Heaven and Earth	Castilian Spanish
Villancico II: The Ascension of Mary	Latin
Villancico III: Allegory of University Life	Castilian Spanish and Latin
	Disciplinary vocabulary
Villancico IV: Musical Allegory	Castilian Spanish and Latin
	Disciplinary vocabulary
Villancico V: Allusion to the "Song of Songs"	Castilian Spanish
Villancico VI: Allegory of War	Colloquial Spanish
Villancico VII: Rhetorical Allegory	Castilian Spanish
	Disciplinary vocabulary
Villancico VIII: Little Salad	Castilian Spanish, black speech and Nahuatl

The Nahuatl finale of the *villancico* cycle completes the journey that begins in the Spanish metropolis and ends in America. It also characterizes religion as the link that unifies all these diverse modes of expression and articulations of knowledge through one aspect: the Virgin Mary and her virtues. In this way, the text recuperates a multiplicity of knowledge that can be disciplinary, racial, and regional, which all "converge" in the space of religion.

A similar structure can be observed in her *villancicos* dedicated to the "Conception" (1676); "Saint Peter Nolasco" (1677); "Saint Peter the Apostle" (1677); "Assumption" (1679); "Assumption" (1685); and "Saint Joseph" (1690). This structural similarity suggests that the *villancico* as a genre draws together distinct points of contact and allows for encounters between different fields of knowledge production, be they religious or secular, metropolitan or colonial. The evangelical project in the text unfolds through the multiplicity of linguistic registers and sites of knowledge, which question the hierarchies of social, racial, and institutional factors that consolidate colonial power. This questioning, while not necessarily subversive, does indicate a desire to expand the spaces of debate for knowledge to include a whole series of regional variants, both American and European.

Contemporary Influences

EMILIE BERGMANN

From Abjection and Ambiguity: Lesbian Desire in Bemberg's *Yo, la peor de todas*†

In a slow-paced scene of domination and seduction in María Luisa Bemberg's film about Sor Juana Inés de la Cruz, the poet's patroness, the vicereine of Nueva España,[1] declares her desire for intimate knowledge of her brilliant protégée: "Jamás he conocido a una mujer como tú: más poeta que monja, más monja que mujer. Hace años que me pregunto: ¿Cómo es Juana cuando está sola, cuando nadie la mira?" [Never have I known a woman like you: more poet than nun, more nun than woman. For years I have asked myself: what is Juana like when she's alone, when no one is looking at her?]. After commanding the nun to remove her veil, performing an awkward striptease from the neck up, the condesa kisses her, claiming "Esta Juana es mía. Solamente mía" [This Juana is mine. Only mine]. Staging the attempt to fix an identity for this elusive figure as object of desire, Bemberg's imperious vicereine repeats a gesture enacted by generations of readers, critics, novelists, and dramatists in search of a Sor Juana of their own.

Yo, la peor de todas is shaped by a narrative of female abjection, the defeat of a risk-taking, exceptionally gifted, and accomplished woman crushed by the patriarchal social order. The film draws heavily on the textual source cited in the opening credits, Octavio Paz's *Las trampas de la fe* (*The traps of faith*).[2] Bemberg, however, goes farther than Paz to posit a causal relationship between this defeat and the homoeroticism that can be read in some of Sor Juana's poems

† From Emilie Bergmann, *Hispanisms and Homosexualities*, ed. Sylvia Molloy and Robert McKee Irwin (Durham, NC: Duke University Press, 1998), pp. 229–31, 236–47. Copyright 1998, Duke University Press. All rights reserved. Republished by permission of the copyright holder. All notes are Bergmann's unless otherwise indicated.
1. New Spain. The film is *Yo, la peor de todas* (I, the worst of all) (1990). "Patroness": Maria Luisa Manrique de Lara (1645–1715), the Countess of Paredes, vicereine of New Spain from 1680 to 1686 [Editor].
2. See Paz, p. 248 [Editor].

to her patronesses. Thus, Bemberg's project is implicated in Paz's
homophobic readings of Sor Juana's expressions of passionate friend-
ship toward the vicereine, despite her earlier creation of what was
probably the first significant and sympathetic role for a homosexual
character in Argentine cinema, in *Señora de nadie* (1982).[3]

Bemberg's condesa problematizes Sor Juana's gender in the scene
described: as nun, her sexuality is neutralized; as poet, she engages
in a masculine activity, and the condesa wishes to uncover the
woman behind these social roles. But the shorn head of the unveiled
Sor Juana reveals submissiveness rather than a desiring female body.
This scene and the selection of poems in *Yo, la peor de todas* exem-
plify the problem of representing lesbian desire:

> The difficulty in defining an autonomous form of female sex-
> uality and desire in the wake of a cultural tradition still Pla-
> tonic, still grounded in sexual (in)difference, still caught in the
> tropism of hommo-sexuality, is not to be overlooked or willfully
> bypassed. It is perhaps even greater than the difficulty in devis-
> ing strategies of representation which will, in turn, alter the
> standard of vision, the frame of reference of visibility, of *what
> can be seen.* (de Lauretis, "Sexual Indifference" 152)

Bemberg's film creates the fleeting image of two women looking at
each other with a desire that is historically situated and not "hommo-
sexual" but homoerotic. Her choice of poetic texts recited by the
actors and her statements about the film obscure the lesbian read-
ing of that image.

Because public recognition and scholarly work were generally
limited to men in the early modern period, Sor Juana's erudite
poetry, publication, and fame within her lifetime created gender
troubles that haunt her earliest biographies, including her own self-
representations. Central to Bemberg's representation is the attribu-
tion of sexual desire, both heterosexual and homosexual, to the
Condesa de Paredes[4] while characterizing the homoeroticism of Sor
Juana's poetry as sublimated, distanced, and "Platonic." Bemberg
stages a causal connection between Sor Juana's passionate poems to
the condesa and her persecution by ecclesiastical authorities, which
requires that Sor Juana's devotion to the condesa be perceived as
threatening to the social order. The film's characterization of the

---

3. Production of "Señora de nadie" was postponed because the military regime considered
the protagonist's separation from her husband and her friendship with a homosexual to
be subversive: "They told me that it was a very bad example for Argentine mothers and
that we couldn't put a maricón (which is a terrible word for a homosexual) in the film.
The colonel said that he would rather have a son who had cancer than one who was
homosexual, so I couldn't do it" (Whitaker, 115).
4. María Luisa Manrique de Lara y Gonzaga, Marquesa de la Laguna by marriage and
Condesa de Paredes through her mother's lineage, was the wife of Tomás Antonio de la
Cerda, Viceroy of Nueva España from 1680 to 1688.

condesa as bisexual reflects fairly accurately an early modern context in which, as Valerie Traub suggests, "desire may have been allowed to flow more freely if less sensationally between homoerotic and heterosexual modes," as long as homoeroticism was not "perceived as a threat to the reproductive designs of heterosexual marriage" (78–79).[5] The cinematic interpretation of the relationship between patroness and poet ensures that this threat is only a delusion of leering, misogynistic clerics and does not implicate Sor Juana as desiring subject.

* * *

One conventional answer to generations of readers' questions about the nature of the eroticism in Sor Juana's poems dedicated to the marquesa is that, whatever one or both might have felt, they were separated by the convent walls and the bars of the *locutorio*, the visitors' room that served as Sor Juana's salon. Novelists and playwrights have contrived various means to penetrate that barrier or to allow their Sor Juana a physical or imaginary escape.[6] Early in the film, Bemberg introduces the framing device of the gleaming iron bars of the *locutorio*, the grillwork that divides visitors from the cloistered women in the convent. In her first visit to the convent, as the vicereine notes the similarities in their restricted lives, the grillwork dominates the scene, and other iron bars are visible behind the vicereine. A few scenes later, Sor Juana and her confessor Antonio Núñez de Miranda[7] are in sharp chiaroscuro, with the camera as well as the light on Sor Juana's side of the bars while from the darkness Núñez (called "Miranda" in the film) warns her about her secular poems to the viceroy and his wife. Bemberg explains in an interview that this scene symbolizes the entire story of the film, placing Sor Juana in the context of medieval women persecuted as witches and accomplices of the devil. The filmmaker concludes: "È l'oscurantismo che vince" [It is the darkness that wins] (Vernaglione 480).[8]

5. Traub chooses the term *homoeroticism* to avoid the historical specificity of terms like *homosexual* and *lesbian* and to include possibilities still relatively unexplored in the early modern period. Although her study of feminine homoeroticism is limited to early modern England and France, Traub's argument is useful in studying the instability of gender within categories of sexuality and articulating a "discourse of desires and acts" (64) in this period in Spain and Colonial Spanish America.
6. The scenes in two plays based on Sor Juana's life, Rosario Castellanos's *El eterno femenino* (1975) and Coral Aguirre's *La cruz en el espejo* (1988), for example, involve dream and memory to transcend the limitations of physical space and verisimilitude. Alicia Gaspar de Alba's "Sapphic Diary" uses letters and memory to cross those boundaries.
7. Jesuit priest (1618–1695) and confessor to Sor Juana; she most likely dismissed him around 1681 and he became her confessor again only at the end of her life [*Editor*].
8. How great a threat the Inquisition posed to Sor Juana's intellectual activity is debatable: it was not the Holy Office itself that placed pressure on her.

The ominous confrontation between the poet and her religious adviser is immediately followed by a scene in which the condesa appears within Sor Juana's light-filled study, without revealing the opening through which she, in her voluminous brocaded gown, managed to penetrate the division of secular world from cloister. With her strong Habsburg[9] chin and a history of films in which she plays coldly beautiful women who make dangerous object choices (*The Garden of the Finzi-Continis, The Conformist*), Dominique Sanda is cast as the sexually aggressive bisexual vicereine. The poet, played by Assumpta Serna, seems much younger than the vicereine, although historically both women were in their early thirties when they met. Bemberg's Sor Juana is a fresh-faced ingenue, with hardly a trace of the femme fatale—quite literally—that Serna played in Pedro Almodóvar's *Matador*.[1] This Sor Juana has apparently plucked the heavy dark Frida Kahlo[2] eyebrows she has in all her portraits. Her powerful intellectual presence wanes, and she appears increasingly subjugated as the plot unfolds.

Exerting the greater power of the secular state established in the first scene, and unsatisfied with small talk in the convent locutorio, the condesa occupies the exclusively feminine space of Sor Juana's study in the cloister, initiates physical contact, and speaks explicitly about desire. As Sor Juana passes through a gauzy curtain to join her, the condesa explains, "No soporto los barrotes de tu locutorio" [I can't stand the iron bars of your locutory]. The scene in Sor Juana's study is structured around the intellectual danger of books, the sexuality of the pregnant vicereine, and the play of religious and secular authority. Like Núñez in the previous scene, the vicereine cautions Sor Juana, observing dangerous books on her study table: Descartes, Gassendi, Kircher.[3] Her vivid memory of an *auto-da-fé*[4] causes the pregnant vicereine to become faint, and she asks Juana to loosen her bodice. This scene foregrounds the inequalities and differences in temperament and experience between the two women. The dialogue casts Sor Juana as a scholar so absorbed in intellectual passion and ignorant of feminine sexuality that she is shocked by the vicereine's pregnancy. The figure of the vicereine brings together two aspects of feminine sexuality, lesbian desire and maternity, traditionally perceived as mutually exclusive. In addition to

---

9. The royal family that ruled Spain from 1516 to 1700 [*Editor*].
1. A 1986 film by Spanish director Pedro Almodóvar [*Editor*].
2. Mexican artist (1907–1954) whose self-portraits exaggerated her heavy eyebrows [*Editor*].
3. Paz discusses the possibility, still open to debate, that Sor Juana might have read or heard summaries and discussions of prohibited works by these authors (*Traps* 258–59). The film depicts a fallible process of censorship in which Sigüenza y Góngora attempts to slip a few banned books into a stack of approved ones.
4. Public penance and sentencing conducted by the Spanish Inquisition [*Editor*].

positioning the vicereine as desiring subject, this sequence balances her unusual sympathy toward the victims of the Inquisition with her status as noblewoman born and raised to command her social inferiors, and unable to release herself without help from the constrictions of seventeenth-century dress. The dialogue clearly supports a homoerotic interpretation. In response to Sor Juana's need for silence and solitude, the vicereine invokes Nature and God in favor of the "deseo de amar" [desire to love]. As Sor Juana conducts a guided tour of her collection of scientific and musical instruments, the condesa comments, "¡Qué bella eres cuando te apasionas!" [How beautiful you are when you're excited!].

Bemberg does not cite the transgressive poetic portraits of her patronesses that might have accompanied a later scene in which the vicereine sits for a painter. Instead, she invents an exchange in which Sor Juana is the passive recipient of a miniature portrait of the vicereine, which the nun secretly wears around her neck where she would ordinarily wear a scapular. Sitting in a sunny patio outside the palace while the painter works, the vicereine reads Juana's lyrical expressions of the agony and melancholy of love, in her *redondillas*, "En que describe racionalmente los efectos irracionales del amor" [In which she describes rationally the irrational effects of love] (*Obras Completas* 1: 213–16, no. 84; trans. Trueblood 79), a poem probably written at an earlier time.

In this witty appropriation of tropes traditionally used by male poets to complain about their beloveds' "ingratitude," Sor Juana weaves conceptual oppositions of love as suffering, with verbal intricacies of "passion" and "reason," "blame" and "justice." Bemberg reads Sor Juana's poetry in light of Paz's discussion of "Platonic" love[5] and "amorous ambiguity": "Per lei l'amore è una idea e che si tratta di un amore impossibile, ed è l'amore migliore, quello che non tiene ai premi, alle ricompense, agli asservimenti" [for her, love was an idea and she wrote about an impossible love, which is the best, that love whose devotion is not rewarded] (Vernaglione 481). These observations explain why Bemberg chose courtly conceptual wordplay and the absence of graphically physical desire in the verses recited in this scene. Their tone matches the spiritual devotion suggested in Sor Juana's faithful wearing of the miniature, rather than the erotic energy and playfulness of some of the poems explicitly dedicated to the condesa, such as "Lámina sirva el cielo al retrato," and "Lo atrevido de un pincel." The closing quatrain of these redondillas assumes common ground with the male speakers in other Petrarchist poems:[6] anyone who has loved will understand and

5. Unconsumated or chaste love, at a distance [*Editor*].
6. Poems that imitate the lyrics of Francesco Petrarca (1504–1374), or Petrarch, known for his courtly love poetry, especially sonnets [*Editor*].

forgive the speaker's irritability and shifting moods. This is a poem closer to imitation, however problematic, of the masculine poetic tradition than to the confrontation and resistance that characterizes much of Sor Juana's work.

One of the most effective scenes in the film shows Sor Juana's salon in the convent locutory at the height of her poetic powers and social prestige. Her vanity and self-assurance are dramatized as she prepares to meet her visitors, putting cologne on her hands, and a jet bracelet on her wrist, historically accurate details of the relaxed discipline in the Hieronymite convent (Scott, "Sor Juana" 153). She stands on a small platform while her servant brushes her habit. She sits regally in a chair while the camera focuses on her face and then on the faces of her *tertulia* [salon] of male intellectuals. The camera always includes some part of the iron grillwork, no matter what the angle, a semiotically necessary element, however architecturally impossible. Sigüenza y Góngora argues that Phaëton signifies "imprudence," whereas Sor Juana interprets the mythological figure as a symbol of intellectual aspiration and knowledge without limits.[7] Her confessor asks if Phaëton perhaps symbolizes the attraction of the abyss, implying a warning, and Sor Juana replies, "El conocimiento es siempre una transgresión. Y más para una mujer." She pauses a moment, sips hieratically from her elegant porcelain cup, and adds, "Y si no, preguntadselo al arzobispo" [Knowledge is always a transgression. And more so for a woman. And if you don't believe it, ask the archbishop]. At the insistence of her admirers, she recites her sonnet on the risk of undertaking a lifelong commitment to the convent or marriage (*Obras Completas* 1: no. 149), only to be interrupted by the entrance of the condesa, bearing an enormous headdress of quetzal feathers. Fernández de Santa Cruz and Sigüenza y Góngora remark on the appropriateness of the quetzal, which they term "our sacred bird," "the Mexican bird." Sor Juana accepts the gift and steps back from the bars, so that the camera frames her through them. She puts on the headdress, bows, and remarks wittily, "Moctezuma se cae postrado a los pies del conquistador" [Moctezuma falls prostrate at the feet of the conquistador].

The gift of the headdress of quetzal feathers serves multiple purposes: it inscribes this discourse in a Mexican context, it re-creates a gift Sor Juana commemorated in a poem, it pictures Sor Juana as an ingenious rara avis in her cage, and it creates a self-conscious scene of colonial dominance and submission. This episode communicates power and the erotic through the rapt expressions on

7. The reference is to the figure of Phaethon in Sor Juana's "First Dream" (on p. 62). Sigüenza y Góngora (1645–1700), Mexican polymath and contemporary of Sor Juana [*Editor*].

the nun's and the vicereine's faces, and the harpsichord music that announces the vicereine's entrance on the soundtrack. But the episode also corroborates Jean Franco's reading of the passionate friendship between Sor Juana and her patroness as clearly mediated by their hierarchical power relationship in its colonial context: "It is impossible to separate personal love from love of the body politic, and love of the body politic included the recognition of authority" (50).

Although the passionate poems to the vicereine are textually absent, interpretations of them as "Platonic," as courtly performance and as homoerotic, are brought together with the noblewoman's maternity in a scene in the viceregal palace in which a voice-over of Sor Juana recites amorous verses while the vicereine caresses her son's head. The poet's voice and her immediate audience, the condesa, embody and weave together the feminine in the forms of virgin, mother, and wise woman that Sor Juana celebrated in her long philosophical poem *Primero sueño* [First dream]. The setting each one occupies, however, is a scene of patriarchal power that will separate them. The correspondence of sound to image, voice with body, are shattered as the voice changes to the viceroy's and the camera shifts from the vicereine to her husband, reading the same poem aloud.

These shifts in voice and image signal a change in Sor Juana's fortunes. Her poetry is no longer a private form of communication between two women. The viceroy comments urbanely, "¡Qué pasión! Sigues haciendo estragos, María Luisa" [What passion! You keep on breaking hearts, María Luisa]. The lines are the tercets of a sonnet: "Baste ya de rigores, mi bien, baste; . . . pues ya en líquido humor viste y tocaste / mi corazón deshecho entre tus manos" [So, beloved, put an end to harshness now . . . since, in that flood of tears, you saw and touched / my broken heart within your very hands] (*Obras Completas* 1: 287, no. 164, ll.9–14; Trueblood 81).[8] The mental confusion of the lines cited earlier in the portrait scene gives way to suggestively physical imagery in these lines.

The use of voice-overs continues in the transition to the next scene, accompanied by the ethereal sound of the nuns' singing. While Sor Juana sings innocently in choir, her enemies enter her study and copy out her poems to the vicereine. With an implication of causality leading up to Sor Juana's persecution and final renunciation, the poems are examined by a group of clerics convened by the archbishop. Once again, the sonnet chosen for discussion in this scene was not written for the Condesa de Paredes. Its lyric speaker, of indeterminate gender, advises a jealous man, "Alcino," in love with

8. Sonnet 164, on p. 36 [*Editor*].

"Celia," and enumerates the stages of love: "Amor empieza por desa-
sosiego, / solicitud, ardores y desvelos; / crece con riesgos, lances y
recelos, / susténtase de llantos y de ruego" [Love begins with rest-
lessness, / solicitousness, ardor and wakefulness; / it grows with risks,
daring, and misgivings, / and feeds on tears and prayers] Obras Com-
pletas 1: 297–98, no. 184).

The clerics' scrutiny of Sor Juana's poetry initiates a series of
scenes that become increasingly speculative. Núñez, Juana's confes-
sor, affirms the autonomy of poetry. He claims that it is not subject
to religious judgments and insists that he finds no perverse inten-
tion. He rehearses Paz's argument that these tropes of praise and
adoration are still used by poets all over Europe. But two unidenti-
fied clerics leer over the poems, one referring to Sor Juana's "enfer-
miza sexualidad" [diseased sexuality], a term worthy of Pfandl.[9] The
archbishop finds her poetry "profoundly disturbing." In the following
scene, the door to Juana's study is barred and sealed. Núñez, despite
his defense of her writing among his peers, appears to recognize the
homoeroticism in her poems. He warns her, "En el convento esos
desordenes amorosos no pueden llevarte más que al castigo. Tam-
poco en el mundo hay esperanza para ellos" [In the convent those
amorous disorders can lead only to punishment. Nor is there any
hope for them in the secular world]. Bemberg's sequence departs
from Paz's political arguments by implying that Juana's troubles begin
with these expressions of love by one woman to another, and that Sor
Juana's contemporaries did not need to read Diderot[1] to find the
lesbian in them.

In the transition to the next scene, a voice-over of the condesa
assures Sor Juana, "Mientras estemos en Mexico nadie te puede
tocar" [As long as we are in Mexico nobody can touch you]. Her dis-
embodied voice is prophetic of the disasters to follow, because the
viceregal couple is about to return to Spain, leaving Sor Juana with-
out their powerful patronage and protection. The long, slow-paced
scene of seductive domination that follows the debate about the erot-
icism of the nun's poems to the condesa is an ambiguous response
to the question of Sor Juana's sexuality that displaces sexual desire
and agency from the criolla[2] poet to the powerful condesa.

The camera cuts to the condesa in Sor Juana's study, wondering
who this woman is, more nun than woman, more poet than nun,

---

9. Ludwig Pfandl (1888–1942), German Hispanist who argued that Sor Juana was "inter-
   sexual" as a result of an Oedipal drama. Bergmann has previously referred to this theory
   (p. 286, n. 3), noting that the term "was used by early-twentieth-century 'sexologists' to
   refer to sexual deviation toward masculine appearance and behavior among indepen-
   dent women" [Editor].
1. Denis Diderot (1713–1784), French philosopher of the Enlightenment known for secu-
   larism [Editor].
2. A term used to describe an American-born person of European descent [Editor].

then cuts again to the vicereine standing behind Sor Juana with a gaze of power and possession: "Quítate el velo. Es una orden" [Take off your veil. That's an order]. Sor Juana looks submissively over her shoulder and obeys hesitantly, taking off only the outermost layer of her habit. The condesa commands her to remove everything, then turns her around to face her with her shorn hair, completely dominated by her patroness. "Esta Juana es mía, Solamente mía" [This Juana is mine. Only mine], she says before kissing her on the mouth. What the condesa says after the kiss, "Para recordar" [To remember], echoes an earlier flashback of Juana's years at the palace, in which a young man kisses Juana, and she reciprocates with surprising fervor. "Para recordar," she tells him. Thus, the chastity of the Hispanic "Décima Musa"[3] is protected, and she is depicted as acting only on exclusively heterosexual desire: when the Condesa de Paredes kisses Juana, she does not return the physical gesture.

Reiterating her claim to believe that the relationship was "platonic," Bemberg explains why she decided not to film a scene of passion between the two women: "Perché sentivo che sarebbe stata una scelta opportunista." [Vernaglione:] "Nella scena dell'incontro tra Juana e Maria Luisa tutto è esplicito. Si pensa che ci sia un rapporto tra le due donne." [Bemberg:] "Credo che tutte le suore, tutte le donne che portano un abito religioso siano misteriose. Dunque quello che vuole la viceregina è conoscere. Perché conoscere è possedere" [Because I thought it would have been an opportunistic decision. [Vernaglione:] In the encounter between Juana and Maria Luisa everything is explicit. One would think that there was a relationship between the two women. [Bemberg:] I think that all nuns, all women who wear a religious habit are mysterious. Therefore what the Vicereine wants is knowledge. Because knowledge is possession] (Vernaglione 481). Bemberg's response is evasive, in light of the overt homoeroticism in the scene, although lesbian subjectivity is exclusively attributed to the vicereine. The omission throughout the film of the poems Sor Juana dedicated to this powerful noblewoman obscures her role as desiring subject and simplifies the relationship along binaries of political power.

In her interview with Vernaglione, Bemberg defends her avoidance of an explicitly lesbian scene whose physicality could be perceived as "opportunistic." It can be argued that there is historical veracity in the voluminous clothing that surrounds female bodies in almost every scene. The exceptions are not scenes of sensual pleasure, but rather scenes of suffering from an epidemic, accompanied by moaning and vomiting, followed by shots of the nuns' bare backs,

---

3. Tenth Muse, the epithet given to Sor Juana on the title page of her *Second Volume* (1692) [*Editor*].

bloodied from flagellation, and the humble, barefoot bodies of plague victims. Nakedness in this seventeenth-century context connotes degradation and suffering rather than sexual release. The film problematizes twentieth-century encodings of sensuality: once freed of its veil, Sor Juana's dull, unevenly chopped hair presents her vulnerability. The condesa, who earlier expressed identification with her, now expresses a desire to possess the nun's unknowable complexity and commands her to reveal what she is without the trappings of her social status. The only scene in which physical contact is associated with pleasure is the one in the viceregal palace in which the condesa reads Sor Juana's lines, "Baste ya de rigores, mi bien, baste," while stroking her son's hair.

The denouement of the film refers to documented events, adding fictional confrontations to dramatize the filmmaker's interpretation of events. Sor Juana's theological critique of a sermon by the Brazilian theologian Vieyra, who was much admired by the archbishop of Mexico, was probably published as the *Carta Atenagórica* [Athenagoric letter][4] by his rival the bishop of Puebla,[5] who then donned the pseudonymous drag of "Sor Filotea" to reprimand the nun for transgressing the exclusively masculine boundaries of theological discourse. Bemberg includes passages from Sor Juana's strong feminist response to "Sor Filotea" but fabricates an implausibly violent confrontation between Sor Juana and her ecclesiastical superiors. The camera captures Sor Juana from the visitors' side of the iron grillwork. She appears, and behaves, like an animal in a cage, in sharp contrast to the witty urbanity of her salon in better days. Soon after this scene, Núñez resigns as her confessor, and Mexico is devastated by famine, plague, and hunger riots, which contribute to the pressures on Sor Juana that culminate in renunciation and handing over her library to be sold by her ecclesiastical superiors.

In a capsule biography of Sor Juana in her interview with Whitaker, Bemberg does not mention the condesa: "[Sor Juana] ended up looking after the nuns in the convent, which is what the Church wants women to do: to scrub, to sew, to wash, but never to think, to be creative and audacious" (120). Scrubbing is precisely what Sor Juana is doing at the end of the film, but contrary to her summary, Bemberg's version of Sor Juana's abjection focuses on the gesture of renouncing her love for the condesa. The camera angle exaggerates the humiliation of her position at the feet of her confessor, who says

4. The popular but inaccurate translation "Letter Worthy of Athena" has no conceptual or grammatical basis; the allusion is to the second-century Christian apologist Athenagoras.
5. Manuel Fernández de Santa Cruz (1637–1699), author of the "Letter from Sor Filotea," on p. 86. Bergmann refers to the theory by Octavio Paz that the publication of the *Athenagoric Letter* was a way for Santa Cruz to attack a rival ecclesiastic, Francisco Aguiar y Seijas, personal friend of António Vieira [*Editor*].

that he has waited twenty years for this Juana, "abnegada, entregada al servicio de Dios" [self-abnegating, surrendering to the service of God]. In a melodramatic moment, Núñez de Miranda blames her intellectual pursuits and her love of the condesa for the recent floods and plague: "Amaste demasiado a esa mujer" [You loved that woman too much]. Juana's reply is a succinct Neoplatonic theory of love: "Más la amaba, más me sentía cerca de Dios" [The more I loved her, the closer I felt to God]. After agreeing to give up all her worldly belongings, Sor Juana finally tears off the concealed miniature of the condesa she has been wearing around her neck.

The voice-body split in the voice-overs within the film replicates the other contradictions between Bemberg's verbal summaries of the biographical plot of the film and the representation of desire in the film, as well as among the poetic texts included, the circumstances that produced them, the possible interpretations, and the images they accompany in the film. There is, in addition, a curious mismatch between the sound track and the dissonant movements of Dominique Sanda's mouth throughout the film. The final credits resolve that mystery: Cecilia Roth provided her voice, suggesting another, ironic reading to Paz's insistence that only a French woman could have felt the lesbian desire attributed to Sor Juana. After the camera work ends, the epilogue appears on a black screen: Sor Juana died shortly after her profession of faith signed in her own blood, and she was considered "Uno de los más grandes poetas del siglo de oro español" [One of the greatest poets of the Spanish Golden Age]. With the problematic "uno" of this epilogue, both unmarked and marked as masculine, and the assimilation into the peninsular Spanish poetic pantheon, Sor Juana's writing continues to be framed and constricted by gender and by political categories. And she continues to defy them.

Works Cited

Cruz, Sor Juana Inés de la. *A Sor Juana Anthology*. Trans. Alan S. Trueblood. Cambridge: Harvard University Press, 1988.

de Lauretis, Teresa. "Sexual Indifference and Lesbian Representation." *The Lesbian and Gay Studies Reader*, Ed. Henry Abelove, Michéle Aina Barale, and David M. Halperin. New York: Routledge, 1993. 141–158.

Franco, Jean. *Plotting Women: Gender and Representation in Mexico*. New York: Columbia University Press, 1989.

Paz, Octavio. *Sor Juana Inés de la Cruz, o las trampas de la fe*. Mexico City: Fondo de Cultura Económica, 1983.

Scott, Nina M. "Sor Juana and Her World." *Latin American Research Review* 29.1 (1994): 143–54.

Traub, Valerie. "The (In)significance of 'Lesbian' Desire in Early Modern England." *Queering the Renaissance*. Ed. Jonathan Goldberg. Durham: Duke University Press, 1993. 62–85.

Vernaglione, Paolo. "Conversazione con Maria Luisa Bemberg." *Filmcritica* 41.408 (Sept.–Oct. 1990): 480–81.

Whitaker, Sheila. "Pride and Prejudice: Maria Luisa Bemberg." *Monthly Film Bulletin* (Oct. 1987): 291–94. Reprinted in *The Garden of Forking Paths: Argentine Cinema*. Ed. John King and Nissa Torrents. London: British Film Institute, 1988. 115–21.

CHARLENE VILLASEÑOR BLACK

Sor Juana as Feminist Icon in Mexican and Chicana/o Art[†]

Sor Juana Inés de la Cruz is one of Mexico's most visible cultural icons, perhaps best-known as the portrait on Mexico's 200-peso bill. The image is based on the famous portrayal of Sor Juana by Miguel Cabrera painted in 1750.[1] She also appears in Mexican murals, easel paintings, and sculptures. A sculpture of her by Ignacio Asúnsolo can be found in the first courtyard of the Ministry of Public Education, where it was placed in 1924, in the heart of Mexico City.[2] Mexican schoolchildren learn about Sor Juana through the free textbooks used by all public schools.[3] She first appears in the elementary school curriculum, along with a short biography focused on her childhood, drawn from "The Response of the Poet." A handful of her sonnets have been introduced over the years in the standardized Mexican secondary school curriculum, but her best-known poem among Mexicans is "Hombres necios" ("O foolish men").[4] In 1990, her story was popularized on the big screen, and the lesbian subtext of her life given explicit voice, in the film by director María Luisa Bemberg, *Yo la peor de todas* (I, the worst of all). A new

† Written for this Norton Critical Edition. All notes are Villaseñor Black's unless otherwise indicated.
1. Alina Sokol, "Unequal Words: Sor Juana and the Poetics of Money in New Spain," *Early American Literature* 41.3 (2006): 455–71; 468–69; and Emily Hind, *Femmenism and the Mexican Woman Intellectual, from Sor Juana to Poniatowska* (New York: Palgrave Macmillan, 2010), 36–37.
2. After the Mexican Revolution, the Mexican state undertook a wide-ranging project of public art that stimulated the works, especially murals, that still adorn state buildings in Mexico City [*Editor*].
3. Benito Quintana-Owen, "Representaciones de Sor Juana en los libros de texto gratuitos de México (1960–2005)," *Cuadernos de música y artes* 4.1–2 (October 2008–September 2009): 291–317.
4. Quintana-Owen, 303. See Redondilla 92, pp. 20–22 of this edition.

film on Sor Juana's life, based on a screenplay co-authored by Chicana novelist and scholar Alicia Gaspar de Alba, went into production in fall 2014. Inspired by Gaspar de Alba's 1999 novel titled *Sor Juana's Second Dream*, this new film starring Ana de la Reguera as Sor Juana promises to popularize a lesbian interpretation of Sor Juana's life, an interpretation of the writer's life denied by many.[5]

Nearly all colonial era images of Sor Juana were portraits, and most characterized her as Mexico's famed poet.[6] With the advent of the Mexican Mural Renaissance in the 1920s, the iconic image of Sor Juana began to emerge in public mural paintings. An example can be seen in Diego Rivera's *Dream of a Sunday Afternoon in the Alameda Park* of 1947 in which Sor Juana appears among other historical figures of the colonial era (Figure 1). The large fresco, measuring 4.8 by 15 meters (49'3" x 15'9") was originally painted for the Hotel del Prado, a well-appointed tourist establishment across from Mexico City's large public park, the Alameda. The hotel was nearly destroyed in the devastating earthquake of 1985, and the mural, which survived with only a few cracks, was eventually moved nearby to a new building constructed expressly for it, the Museo Mural Diego Rivera.[7] Rivera's mural portrays a dream of Mexico's history, played out in the Alameda, the city's public promenade. Set at the turn of the nineteenth and twentieth centuries, the mural portrays Rivera himself as a child in the right foreground, accompanied by his "parents," the revolutionary-era printmaker José Guadalupe Posada, and Posada's most famous character, "La Catrina," a calavera garbed in Parisian dress, fashionable at the time. His life partner, Frida Kahlo, stands behind him.[8] Behind this central vignette episodes from Mexico's history are arrayed: scenes from the colonial era, the abuses of the Catholic Church, *campesinos*, generals, and members of the bourgeoisie, with the bust of President Benito Júarez rising above all.[9] Sor Juana can be found on the left side, in the middle ground, between

5. For more on the controversy surrounding Sor Juana's sexuality, see Bergmann on p. 284 [*Editor*].
6. For the eighteenth-century portraits of Sor Juana, see Villaseñor Black on p. 213 [*Editor*].
7. William Stockton, "Rivera Mural in Mexico Awaits Its New Shelter," *New York Times*, January 4, 1987. www.nytimes.com/1987/01/04/arts/rivera-mural-in-mexico-awaits-its -new-shelter.html. [Diego Rivera (1886–1957) was one of Mexico's best-known artists, particularly recognized for his murals—*Editor*.]
8. Max Kozloff, "Diego Rivera's *Dream of a Sunday Afternoon in the Alameda Park*," *MoMA* 14 (Summer 1993): 8–11. [Jose Guadalupe Posada (1852–1913) was a Mexican printmaker best known for his satiric skeleton prints published in the popular press. Frida Kahlo (1907–1954) was a well-known Mexican artist who married Diego Rivera in 1929—*Editor*.]
9. Benito Júarez (1806–1872) was of Zapotec indigenous origin and elected president five times after Mexican independence [*Editor*].

Figure 1. Diego Rivera, *Dream of a Sunday Afternoon in the Alameda Park* (detail), mural, 1947, Museo Mural Diego Rivera (formerly the Hotel del Prado), Mexico City, Mexico. © 2016 Banco de México Diego Rivera Frida Kahlo Museums Trust, Mexico, D.F./Artists Rights Society (ARS), New York. Courtesy of Schalkwijk/Art Resource, NY.

an image of the Spanish king and a chilling scene of the Inquisition, in which a victim, blood streaming down his back, is burned at the stake with the assistance of a Catholic friar; behind him others await execution. She is instantly recognizable: Rivera's portrayal is based on colonial era portraits such as that by Miguel Cabrera or Juan de Alameda. She appears in bust-length in her habit, her *escudo* bearing the Annunciation scene, carefully positioned between images representing Church and State. She is flanked on the right by the King, whose representatives, the viceroys and vicereines of New Spain, extended their patronage and favor to Sor Juana.[1] The Inquisition scene on her left not only references colonial Mexico's grisly history, but also Sor Juana's final conflict with the Catholic Church. While singled out as one of Mexico's great colonial writers, one detects a certain ambivalence about her image in Rivera's and other murals. While a great writer and intellectual, she also represents the Catholic Church and the abuses of colonial power that led to Independence in 1821 and later, the Revolution of 1910.[2] Placed by Rivera on the left side of the murals, in the middle ground, she is subordinated to the great political leaders depicted, placed directly next to a grotesque caricature of the Spanish king. Perhaps the fact that Sor Juana was a woman contributes to this ambivalence about her image.

A number of later twentieth-century artists in Mexico produced easel paintings of the nun. These artworks tend to be more inventive in their approach. The artists who depict her focus on the theme of conflict—her final conflict with the Catholic Church and her internal conflict between societal expectations of her as a woman and her intellectual desires. Alfredo Castañeda's 1979 image of her is particularly compelling (Figure 2). Titled *El sueño de Sor Juana* (Sor Juana's Dream), the painting references her most important literary work, "First Dream," a lengthy poem of 975 verses published in 1692 about the journey of the human soul during the course of the night.[3] Employing a hyper-realist style, typical of surrealism, or its Latin American variant, Magical Realism, Castañeda's painting also references dreams more generally, a major concern among surrealist artists.[4] The image haunts the viewer. We see Sor Juana's head lying on its side, separated from her body, its horizontal placement intended to evoke sleep. Her uncanny, open eyes look upward. A plume pen, held in Sor Juana's right hand, is poised to write on a blank page. Castañeda portrays her intellect separated from her body, her mind freed from rules imposed on it because of her biological sex. Castañeda's hyper-realist style belies the dreamlike qualities. The corners of the image, on the verge of dissolving, of coming undone, call attention to the constructedness of the image. The painting is illogical, like a dream. Typical of surrealism, contradictions abound here.

1. For more on the context, painters, and details of the portraits of Sor Juana, see Villaseñor Black on p. 213 [*Editor*].
2. Mexican Independence from Spain in 1821 generated much anti-Spanish resentment and affected depictions of the colonial period. The Mexican Revolution (1910–17) targeted the oligarchic elite [*Editor*].
3. Octavio Paz, *Sor Juana; or, The Traps of Faith*, trans. Margaret Sayers Peden (Cambridge: The Belknap Press of Harvard University Press, 1988), Chapter 24, pp. 357–86.
4. Surrealism was an artistic movement developed in Europe in the 1920s that sought to represent oniric or unconscious images. It indirectly influenced the later Latin American literary movement often called "Magical Realism," which depicts the region as infused with magical beliefs [*Editor*].

Figure 2. Alfredo Castañeda, *Sor Juana's Dream,* oil on canvas, 1979, private collection. Courtesty of Galería de Arte Mexicano.

Surprisingly, though, images of Sor Juana are not very visible in twentieth-century Mexican fine arts. Many of the paintings depicting her are small in size, and most of them are in private collections, not accessible to the public in museums.[5] A comparison to the celebrity and visibility of Frida Kahlo is hard to avoid. The reasons for this merit deeper consideration. Sor Juana's poetry is considered by many to be difficult to understand, perhaps too learned, too baroque for some tastes. And her association with the Catholic Church, in contrast to Kahlo's support of the Mexican Revolution, is difficult for many to embrace. Her status as an intellectual may also limit her popular appeal.[6]

5. The most complete collection of 20th-century images of Sor Juana can be found in Noemí Atamoros Zeller, *Nueva iconografía de Sor Juana Inés de la Cruz: 1695–1995, Trescientos años de inmortalidad* (Mexico City: Química Hoechst de México, Hoechst Marion Roussel, 1995).
6. For more on the representation of Sor Juana in popular art, see the interview with Jesusa Rodríguez on p. 304 [*Editor*].

By contrast, in the U.S. Sor Juana is becoming a major icon in Chicana/o art, an emblem of Chicana feminism. Although not as prevalent as depictions of the Virgin of Guadalupe or as popular as Frida Kahlo, a number of Chicana artists and writers have begun producing works valorizing Sor Juana as a proto-feminist, a hero-ine, or "foremother."[7] One of the earliest and most moving artistic meditations on Sor Juana was that created by artist Amalia Mesa-Bains in her 1994 installation, *Venus Envy II: The Harem and Other Enclosures* (Williams College; Figure 3). The installation featured three different zones, representing women's private spaces—garden, harem, and library. The second of these, entitled "Sor Juana's Library," recreated the writer's desk, complete with books and other scholarly accoutrements, as well as musical and scientific instru-ments and natural science specimens—the objects for which Sor Juana was censured during her life.[8] In addition to the recreation of the writing desk, the installation also included a reading area, where viewers could sit and peruse books and drawings. The artist employed strategies familiar from her other altar-installations, an art form that combines contemporary installation practices with Chicana/o vernacular practices drawn from home altars and *ofrendas*. Here, Mesa-Bains carefully placed and juxtaposed objects meant to recreate the life of Sor Juana.[9] While referencing the historical figure of Mexico's Tenth Muse,[1] Mesa-Bains made clear Sor Juana's relevance to contemporary Chicanas by including newspaper arti-cles about protests at Williams College organized by female stu-dents asking the college to hire a Latina professor. Mesa-Bains juxtaposed video stills drawn from footage of these protests to a copy of a colonial portrait of the nun.[2] The artist thus connected the struggles of Latina scholars to find acceptance in the academy with Sor Juana's battle for acceptance as a female intellectual in the seventeenth century. Mesa-Bains was also careful to highlight the conflict between imposed Hispanic culture and Mexico's indig-enous cultures, a theme that other Chicana artists and writers also associate with Sor Juana. Her work thus asks the viewer to medi-tate on these conflicts—between colonizer and colonized, and

7. Jennifer A. González, *Subject to Display: Reframing Race in Contemporary Installation Art* (Cambridge: The MIT Press, 2008), p. 128. For "foremother," see Alicia Gaspar de Alba, *[Un]Framing the "Bad Woman": Sor Juana, Malinche, Coyolxauhqui and Other Rebels with a Cause* (Austin: University of Texas Press, 2014), p. 48; and Tey Diana Rebolledo, *Women Singing in the Snow: A Cultural Analysis of Chicana Literature* (Tucson: The University of Arizona Press, 1995), p. 60.
8. González, *Subject to Display*, Chapter 3, "Amalia Mesa-Bains: Divine Allegories," pp. 120–62; and especially 144ff; and Laura E. Pérez, *Chicana Art: The Politics of Spir-itual and Aesthetic Altarities* (Durham: Duke University Press, 2007), pp. 60–61.
9. González defines the term in *Subject to Display*, p. 122.
1. During her lifetime Sor Juana was referred to as the "Tenth Muse," an epithet that plays on the title given to the ancient Greek poet Sappho [*Editor*].
2. González, *Subject to Display*, p. 158.

Figure 3. Amalia Mesa-Bains, *The Library of Sor Juana Inés de la Cruz* from the installation *Venus Envy Chapter II: The Harem and Other Enclosures*, Williams College, July 9–December 31, 1994. Museum purchase, Kathryn Hurd Fund (95.8). Photo courtesy of the Williams College Museum of Art, Williamstown, MA. Collection of Richard Bains. Reprinted by permission of the artist.

between conceptions of women's private spaces as both liberating and confining.[3] Like the harem, a site of gynosocial camaraderie, the convent was also a site of patriarchy, the thesis of this installation.[4] Mesa-Bains's installation can also be read as a decolonizing project.[5] The artist attempts to recover and revalorize forgotten Mexican and Latina women from history, to give them agency, to wrest them heteropatriarchal, Eurocentric models of scholarship and art making.

Chicana artists have produced other decolonial artworks, foregrounding the intersectionality of Chicana feminism, an approach to feminism that recognizes the overlapping oppressions facing Chicanas as both women and people of color.[6] In fact, some artists and writers seem to portray Sor Juana as the perfect example of intersectionality. Prolific novelist and scholar Alicia Gaspar de Alba explicitly suggested in her 1999 novel, *Sor Juana's Second Dream*, that the nun was a lesbian, a point of view many leading scholars, most notably Octavio Paz, had taken pains to deny.[7] In fact, Gaspar de Alba has reconfigured the nun as a "Chicana lesbian feminist," indeed, a "lesbian separatist feminist," in some of her theoretical writings, a radical, decolonial approach.[8] This notion seems to have been given visual form in the work of Chicana artists and writers.[9] In a work dated 1999 by Yreina D. Cervantez, *Mujer de Mucha Enagua, Pa'Ti, Xicana*, a serigraph created at Self Help Graphics in East Los Angeles, the notion of intersectionality becomes a focus, perfect for a print dedicated by the artist to other Chicanas (Figure 4). As explained by the artist, the title "Mujer de Mucha Enagua," or a woman with many petticoats, is "a woman of strength, courage, and integrity,"[1] a particular take on a specifically Chicana approach to feminism and activism. Her print represents two major figures: Sor Juana on the left, and a Zapatista, based on Comandante Ramona,

3. González, *Subject to Display*, p. 159.
4. González, *Subject to Display*, p. 159. She describes Mesa-Bains's inquiries into the past as "a decolonizing gesture." Her works help create the "decolonial imaginary" of Emma Pérez.
5. Emma Pérez, *The Decolonial Imaginary: Writing Chicanas into History* (Bloomington: Indiana University Press, 1999).
6. Cherríe Moraga and Gloria Anzaldúa, eds., *This Bridge Called My Back: Writings by Radical Women of Color* (New York: Kitchen Table/Women of Color Press, 1983); and Gloria Anzaldúa, *Borderlands/La Frontera: The New Mestiza*, 3rd ed. (San Francisco: Aunt Lute Books, 2007).
7. The Nobel prize-winning Mexican poet and critic, Octavio Paz (1914–1988) addresses the suggestion that Sor Juana's love poetry to women could imply lesbian desire in his monumental 1982 biography, *Sor Juana; or, the Traps of Faith* [Editor].
8. Alicia Gaspar de Alba, *[Un]Framing the "Bad Woman": Sor Juana, Malinche, Coyolxauhqui and Other Rebels with a Cause* (Austin: University of Texas Press, 2014), pp. 47–49.
9. Rebolledo, *Women Singing in the Snow*, pp. 58–62.
1. Yreina D. Cervantez, "About the Cover," p. x, in Lara Medina, *Las Hermanas* (Philadelphia: Temple University Press, 2005).

Figure 4. Yreina D. Cervantez, *Mujer de Mucha Enagua, Pa'Ti, Xicana,*
serigraph, 1999. Courtesy of California Ethnic and Multicultural Archives.

on the left, two children in tow.[2] In the center, a large hand, the
hand of the goddess according to Cervantez, rises up, decorated with
a spiral form representing timelessness, and a Mayan phrase, "mixik
balamiel," or "the navel of the universe." Below it, an Aztec toponym
represents the mountain of Cihuacoatl, the snake woman.[3] Speech
scrolls issue from the mouths of both the revolutionary and Sor
Juana.[4] Their parallel, symmetric placement suggests visually a cer-
tain equivalence between the two. Sor Juana's struggle is that of the
Zapatistas, and vice versa. Sor Juana's nun's badge, which normally
portrays the Annunciation to the Virgin, has been transformed here
by Cervantez into a portrait of Rosario Castellanos, a Mexican poet
from Chiapas. Text from a poem by her is inscribed on Sor Juana's
figure. Thus, Sor Juana's struggles as a female intellectual in colo-
nial Mexico are explicitly linked to twentieth-century Mexican
women's struggles.

A decolonial approach can also be seen in work by Alma López,
the digital mural print *Las Four* from 1997, and a recent print *La
Peor de Todas* (2013), from a series of the same name (Figures 5

2. Comandante Ramona is the most famous female "Zapatista," or member of the revolu-
   tionary movement EZLN, whose 1992 uprising in Chiapas, Mexico, has created a semi-
   autonomous Mayan community in the state [*Editor*].
3. Cervantez, "About the Cover," pp. x–xii.
4. Speech scrolls are small curled icons placed near subjects' mouths; they were one of
   the typical indicators of pre-Columbian Mesoamerican art [*Editor*].

Figure 5. Alma López, *Las Four,* digital mural print, 1997. Courtesy of and reprinted by permission of the artist.

and 6).[5] *Las Four,* created for the Community Center in Estrada Courts, in the Boyle Heights area of Los Angeles, features a casual scene of four young women seated on a step in the neighborhood, one holding a young child, while their foremothers look on from above. Appearing as floating spirits, the figures of Dolores Huerta, Sor Juana Inés de la Cruz, an Adelita from the Mexican Revolution, and indigenous rights activist Rigoberta Menchú hover above the young women, a ghostly image of the Pre-Columbian goddess Coyolxauhqui rising above them all.[6] The pairing of the four

5. On *Las Four,* see Alma López, "It's not about the Santa in My *Fe,* but the Santa Fe in My *Santa,*" Chapter 11 in Alicia Gaspar de Alba and Alma López, eds., *Our Lady of Controversy: Alma López's Irreverent Apparition* (Austin: University of Texas Press, 2011), pp. 287–88; and Kathleen Fitzcallaghan Jones, "The War of the Roses: Guadalupe, Alma López, and Santa Fe," Chapter 3, pp. 63–65. López's print, *La peor de todas,* was published for the first time by Gaspar de Alba in *[Un]Framing the "Bad Woman,"* p. 246.
6. Dolores Huerta (b. 1930) is a principal leader of the farmworker's movement. Adelita refers to a popular *corrido* (ballad) of the Mexican Revolution recounting a female soldier. Rigoberta Menchú (b. 1959) is a Maya K'iche activist for indigenous rights. In Nahua mythology, Coyolxauhqui is a goddess who led her siblings to attack their mother, Coatlicue [*Editor*].

Figure 6. Alma López, *La Peor de Todas,* print, 2013. Courtesy of and reprinted by permission of the artist.

heroines above suggests the young women's political potential, as their placement creates a revolutionary genealogy for Chicana women. López gave her later print a similar political reading. In it we see two figures: Sor Juana, after Juan de Alameda's portrait, on the left, and a revolutionary Chicana or Mexicana on the right, proudly wearing revolutionary bandoliers of roses. A third, ghostly figure appears in the background, the dismembered goddess Coyolxauhqui, theorized by Chicanas as an anti-war activist.[7] The figures in the print are again posed to suggest a visual connection among them. Both hold outsized plume pens in their hands, the revolutionary's dripping blood to form the words at the bottom, "la peor de todas" (I, the worst of all), a reference to Sor Juana's

---

7. On this idea, see Alicia Gaspar de Alba, "Coyolxauhqui and las Maqui-locas," Chapter 4 in *[Un]Framing the "Bad Woman."*

Figure 7. Alejandro Medina, mural (including Sor Juana Inés de la Cruz), Pilsen, Chicago, Illinois, 2010. Photograph courtesy of Chris Diers. Reprinted by permission of the artist.

signature in blood on a penitential letter she signed in 1694.[8] López's image suggests a continuity between the work of Sor Juana and the revolutionary with her dripping pen and bandoliers of roses, indeed, a continuity with the Pre-Columbian goddess Coyolxauhqui figured in the background.

Not a common subject in the early murals of the Chicano Movement, the image of Sor Juana is beginning to appear now more frequently. Images of her are also beginning to spread from California, a major center of Chicana/o art, to other areas of the United States. In Pilsen, a Latino neighborhood on the lower west side of Chicago, muralist Alejandro Medina has created an enormous tribute to Latina women, including a monumental rendering of Sor Juana Inés de la Cruz (Figure 7).

Sor Juana Inés de la Cruz is poised to become a major figure among Chicana/o artists, much like depictions of Adelita, the Virgin of Guadalupe, or Frida Kahlo. Given a decolonial reading, she has the potential to become a major activist emblem. Her figure argues for women's rights to be intellectuals. As conceptualized by Chicana artists and writers, she is seen as a proto-feminist, an early figure in a proud revolutionary lineage of women with "mucha enagua," a lot of petticoats.

8. The phrase in Sor Juana's petition is often misquoted. It reads, "I, the worst [woman] in the world" [Yo la peor del mundo]. See "Petition" on p. 153 [*Editor*].

HEMISPHERIC INSTITUTE

"First Dream" Performed: Diana Taylor Interviews Jesusa Rodríguez (2010)[†]

Jesusa Rodríguez (b. 1955) is a leading theater director, activist, and performance artist based in Mexico City. In this interview, conducted by performance studies scholar Diana Taylor, Rodríguez explains the context, creative process, and audience response to the performance piece she developed around Sor Juana's poem "First Dream," which she has performed since 2007. The piece consists of Rodríguez dressed as Sor Juana reciting the entire poem as a monologue and tableaux vivant with original music and video components.[1]

In the interview, Rodríguez describes the importance of her performance for the political movement that followed from accusations of electoral fraud in the Mexican presidential contest of July 2006. The political movement Resistencia Creativa began with public meetings at the Mexico City cabaret run by Rodríguez and her wife, the Argentine musician Liliana Felipe, and grew into a sit-in of hundreds of thousands of people in the city's central plaza. For Rodríguez the poem "First Dream" becomes the link among a deep Mexican heritage, a personal encounter through performance, and a tool for public actions that address the unspeakable violence affecting Mexico.

DIANA TAYLOR: I would like for you to tell us a little about your interest in Sor Juana and particularly in "First Dream," which you have spent years working on. I would be very interested to know why Sor Juana, and why this text in particular?

JESUSA RODRÍGUEZ:

[Rodríguez first recounts that she began to memorize the poem at age forty in an attempt to understand the text. When the political movement and the sit-ins began, she realized that the poem enriched her language, and she could use it to speak to the resistance.]

I said to myself, tomorrow I'm going to the Zócalo[2] again, and what do I have up my sleeve to say to the thousands of people who will be there, so eager? I'm the master of ceremonies: it's my great responsibility not to waste their time, to have a proposal, to have something to say to all those people, something that will

---

[†] Transcript translated for this edition by Isabel Gómez. Reproduced by permission of the Hemispheric Institute of Performance and Politics. The translator and editor thank Diana Taylor for reading and commenting on a draft of this translation.

1. Photo stills and a video of the performance from 2007 are available at the Hemispheric Institute Digital Video Library: hemisphericinstitute.org/hemi/en/hidvl-interviews/item/43-jesusa-primero-sueno.

2. The main plaza in Mexico City, in front of the cathedral and offices of the Mexican federal government and an arena for many popular protests [Editor].

serve them. At that time, I was studying the emblems of Alciato[3] to be able to understand one part of the many emblems that Sor Juana uses in "First Dream." In one emblem, I read: "Prudence recommends: without haste, but without respite."[4] Ay, to be able to bring them that treasure to the Zócalo the next day, to stand up there and say: "Our movement is one of resistance, but also prudence. And prudence recommends: go forth without haste— but also without hesitation. We are not going to stop, but we don't need to rush to do anything, because this is an action of resistance. We don't have to hurry, we can't achieve anything hastily, but also: we are never going to stop, ever." This Greek epigram came to me, perhaps from the ancient Egyptians, through Sor Juana.[5]

[I also took insight] directly from the poem. Everyone says: "oh that poem is so cryptic, so difficult," but it says the simplest things. Not only about how the human organism functions: it also says, listen, every time you breathe, you are taking in cold and letting go of heat[6]—but "call no / theft small when oft repeated."[7] Since we have to breathe to live, you keep on losing heat until the day you lose all your warmth and die. But this line "call no / theft small when oft repeated" from "First Dream" can be applied to your entire life, even to the sacking of the nation. Because it is one thing to say: "They are robbing us blind!" But it is very different to say: "Remember what Sor Juana says: 'call no / theft small when oft repeated.' Even though they may only steal a little bit at a time from us, they will end up taking the entire country. Theft is theft, if it is continuous, even if only in small amounts." You suddenly start to see how the poetry of Sor Juana is completely timeless and contemporary; it can help you all the time.

Now I need "First Dream" almost every day of my life to understand situations she can clarify with just one line. In many ways, the poem is more than something for me to put on stage as a theatrical monologue: it has kept me company in my life, as a person at my side who now walks with me forever; it has been a solution for many everyday problems, private and social; and the poem is a

---

3. Andrea Alciato (1592–1550), inventor of the Renaissance emblem, a visual icon representing a moral enigma [Editor].

4. Emblem XX, "Maturandum" is translated as "Sin prisa, pero sin pausa," a saying based on the classical adage, festina lente (make haste, slowly) [Editor].

5. Renaissance emblems were believed to be modern heirs to the Egyptian hieroglyph, in turn thought to be the original Adamic script and thus precursor to Greek knowledge [Editor].

6. This is a paraphrase of lines 218–23 in the original (199–203 in this edition): "making it breathe in the cool surrounding air / that it exhales when heated, / and the air avenges its expulsion by / committing small thefts of our natural warmth / at some time wept for but never recovered."

7. Line 225 in the original, 204–05 in this edition.

compendium of wisdom. You can see that Sor Juana constructed haikus within this *silva* of heptasyllables and hendecasyllables that never end—it is telling you something essential in every moment.

For example, recently I've been seeing the mothers of disappeared children.[8] When Sor Juana talks about Persephone, how her mother goes to the underworld through the fountain of Arethusa to look for her daughter Persephone, she says: "seeking her life but losing it in sorrow,"[9] which is exactly the sentiment of a mother who is looking for her child who has been disappeared. She goes looking for her life, but in the process of looking for her disappeared child, she is losing her own life to that pain. It is incredible that when Sor Juana talks about mythology, metamorphosis, emblems—sciences that are apparently very complex—at the end of the day she is only talking about human beings, their most elemental feelings and their most basic situations.

It is an Aleph.[1] If the words and writings of Foucault[2] are an essay about the Aleph, and Borges approximates it in his story "The Aleph," then Sor Juana constructs it in "First Dream:" it is a constructed Aleph. I truly feel that, in my life, having "First Dream" in my head, memorized . . . it might seem ridiculous to memorize a poem such as "First Dream," but for me it was necessary. Having it inside of me constantly makes me look at things, understand things I don't know if I otherwise would. "First Dream" makes me understand many things in life, as though I had inherited a present, as though Sor Juana had given me an incredibly valuable inheritance and now I have it inside of me.

*   *   *

I am also gravely concerned by the poverty of language you find in movements on the left. I think you need to demand more of yourself, a more elevated language. To stand in front of an audience, you have to raise your sights higher and say something worth the trouble. "First Dream" is such a pinnacle of language and the human mind: its power can help raise the level of language, comprehension, and expression. It helps me in all ways. It also helps me through the sadness that comes with a movement and the moment that Mexico is living through, the enormous pain caused by this despicable political right that is always killing, killing, killing, killing, that causes so much pain, pain, pain. You get

8. Rodríguez refers to the disappearances that have occurred as a result of the drug wars in Mexico [*Editor*].
9. Lines 728–29 in the original, 619 in this edition.
1. An object that contains an infinite world in the short story of the same name (1949) by the Argentine author Jorge Luis Borges (1899–1986) [*Translator's note revised by Editor*].
2. *Les mots et les choses* (The order of things, 1966), by the French philosopher Michel Foucault (1926–1984) refers to another story by Borges [*Editor*].

to a point where you can't stand any more, the pain of the country hurts you and the country so brutally, and you confront the pain of so many people. And so sometimes for me the beauty of the poem is a refuge where I can go at any time to rest. I enter a world, I would almost say it's like asylum, where I can take shelter politically for a while—it's a political asylum. There I am, and all the beautiful things that Sor Juana created come back to me. It also relieves my heart, rehabilitates me and allows me to return to the fight with new energy and new insights.

*   *   *

DIANA TAYLOR: Was there anything you learned about the poem only by doing it, acting it, reliving it, things you might not have understood if you had only memorized it?

JESUSA RODRÍGUEZ: Of course, definitely. I understand so much more onstage—that is what theatrical intuition is like. Someone makes a movie because that's the only way something can be told: if it could be told another way, they wouldn't make it. I make theater because I can't say it any other way, not even to myself. For example, I hung a pendulum on stage because it was necessary for me. Where did that pendulum come from? It must have been from the poem, what do I know? But I hung a sphere, and it became clear. There are moments in the poem when I swing the sphere around and illuminate many things Sor Juana wanted to say. Once I hung that sphere, I've been able to understand many things—which according to my mind I had already understood rationally—but then I saw there was much more to understand. And it's a beautiful theatrical element, which apparently doesn't say anything, but—these are instruments of revelation. For me, theater is an instrument of revelation. And it's my favorite one.

DIANA TAYLOR: In the various ways you've presented "First Dream" that I've seen, you've performed it as a striptease. Even in the first version, or the second. I'm interested to know how the body works, the way the body is so covered up at first when you enter with the whole habit of Sor Juana, and then she begins to strip off clothes. What does this have to do with the poem, and the different layers of reference and meaning?

JESUSA RODRIGUEZ: It occurs to me: this poem is so vast with so many lines, you can never cover everything, you can never be sure to what extent you are even approaching the greatness of the poem, because it is so much more complex than a person can grasp. So the striptease was more a kind of provocation on my part. Nevertheless, for some reason, when I was staging it, something motivated me to take the habit off the nun! All those layers and layers and layers—apparently the habit had thirty-two pieces back

then—I just have thirteen. That necessity to take them off, take
them off, take them off—I don't know where it came from. So I
kept playing with the striptease—when I still didn't even under-
stand the poem—doing my little striptease, which was over by line
180 with hundreds of lines still left.

And suddenly in the final version I realized where that came
from—now you see what I mean, how things come to you. That
moment, in the most recent version, I simply open up and expose
my breasts. In the first versions I would draw lungs and a heart
on my chest while she describes the function of the heart, the
stomach, lungs, and larynx. And that's when I realized why: it
was not a striptease at all. It is a revelation of the viscera, which
is going a little bit further than a striptease. It is taking off the
last of the layers, taking off the skin and showing the function of
internal organs, the functions of breathing and eating, how that
material we eat is converted into fantasy and dream. Which is
ultimately what Sor Juana narrates, that whole process: she tells
you how that cookie you ate becomes a dream, a fantasy, and how
the body does alchemy to transform food into illusion and dream.
It is rather audacious what I am saying. The striptease became a
kind of vivisection, an autopsy: an extreme striptease.

But, there are still all the other lines of the poem; do you see
what I mean? Sor Juana's habit is almost an architectural repro-
duction of the cloister. The poem is a kind of architecture built
on top of that architecture. Much of her whole dissertation in
the poem has to do with the architecture of that house and of
the whole universe. So "First Dream" is like an Aleph, a universe,
infinity in compendium: you can find pathways leading every-
where, until you get to what she said to us, our dear Petrona de la
Cruz Cruz from FOMMA,[3] she said, "oh, obviously, she is a woman
who takes off all the layers of the world to be able to know herself,
and then she puts the world back on so she can go back out in the
street." I think this is a marvelous reading, coming from a woman
who has another worldview, an indigenous worldview, and she was
able to say that to us with such clarity.

There are multiple readings. I can't say definitively that what
Sor Juana does is a striptease of the viscera, but that's where it
took me after studying it for twelve years and staging it. Now I
think that is one of the best moments of the performance, because
when she says "This member, then, the king and living center / of
the vital spirits, with / its companion, a breathing / bellows (the

3. This interview was conducted in Chiapas. Rodríguez and Taylor are referring to a pre-
vious conversation with Petrona de la Cruz Cruz, co-founder of the community theater
organization of Mayan women called FOMMA (Fortaleza de la Mujer Maya).

lung that like a magnet attracts / air"[4] and you can see the actress painting her heart and a lung, you can understand what she is talking about, in spite of the language. If I didn't do what I did, and left the poem just as it is, the spectator would get lost, wouldn't know what she is talking about. You see how effective theater can be, how with staging it can be so effective, because it lets people go on.

During last year's theatrical season, it was incredible, I was thinking—at first I didn't know what was going to happen. I said to myself: this is rather perverse of me, dragging the public here to give this whole poem to them in just one hour. Because the spectator tries to understand, no matter how much I may tell them to listen as though it were a symphonic work. When you listen to a musical composition, you aren't trying so hard to understand what Mozart was saying when he wrote a D flat. You just listen. As much as I tell the audience: listen to the poem and let it enter you through the musical side of your brain—no, the brain wants to understand because it is hearing language. So at first it can pick up on some small phrases: "their calls did not unsettle the quietude."[5] But then immediately after comes "Dead of night had almost passed, the darkness half / concluded"[6] and ay that phrase "dead of night" goes rattling in your brain and "half concluded" what is that, and then it has already passed you by, because the poem has moved on to another thing and now it is saying "when wearied by their daily tasks, / (and oppressed"[7] and what is that word "oppressed" and AY! So the brain suffers, in the theater—but in spite of that, the season was fantastic. In the end, people lived through the experience of the poem. Although many suffered trying to understand, they would end up abandoning themselves to the beauty of the language, just the contemplation of that work she made with that beauty of the combination of sound and meaning. I'm sure that those who may have understood enjoyed even more.

But for me it has been a wonderful experience, staging and bringing this to different places. In fact, next I'm going to perform it in the public square, which is an experience I haven't had yet. They invited me to San Luis de Potosí. I'm going to do it in the Plaza de Armas in San Luis de Potosí[8] and I don't know what is going to happen! It is going to be in open air, in the public square, let's see what happens. But I'm not afraid any more that

4. "First Dream," lines 210–13 (192–96 in this edition).
5. "First Dream," line 24 (23 of this edition).
6. "First Dream," lines 151–52 (142–43 of this edition).
7. "First Dream," lines 153–54 (143–44 of this edition).
8. Capital city of the northern Mexico state of San Luis Potosí [*Editor*].

people will be almost offended and say: "Oye, why did you bring me such a complex poem all the way from the seventeenth century to beat me over the head with! Have mercy, a little compassion— at least explain it to us before you start!" I don't worry about that anymore, because now I know that the experience is different. Yes, on the one hand, it is a horrible arrogance on my part to do this. But I also say that it is our heritage, and we must know it. Although it may take some effort, here it is, this gift from Sor Juana.

Sor Juana Inés de la Cruz:
A Chronology†

1514   The *Requirement* is first read by the conqueror Pedrarías
        D'Avila
1521   Hernán Cortés conquers Tenochtitlan
1551   The Royal and Pontifical University of Mexico is founded
1563   The decrees of the Council of Trent are issued
1585   Third Mexican Council incorporates Tridentine decrees
1623   The Hieronymite convent of Saint Paula is founded in Mexico
        City
1648   Probable birth of Juana Inés de Asbaje, according to a bap-
        tismal record for "Inés, Child of the Church" in the parish
        of San Miguel Nepantla outside of Mexico City
1650   Antônio Vieira preaches the Maundy Thursday Sermon in
        Lisbon
1651   Birthdate of Juana Inés de Asbaje, according to Diego de
        Calleja's biography
1651   Juana Inés learns to read, according to the "Response"
1659   Learns Latin with Martín de Olivas
1664   Arrival of the viceroys Marquis de Mancera, Antonio Sebas-
        tián de Toledo, and Marquise Leonor Carreto de Mancera,
        "Laura" in Sor Juana's poems
        Juana Inés enters the viceregal court in Mexico City as lady-
        in-waiting to the vicereine
1668   Juana Inés enters the San José Convent of the Discalced
        Carmelites in Mexico City in August; she renounces the
        order on November 18 of the same year
1669   February 15: Sor Juana becomes a novice in the Convent
        of Saint Jerome, also called Saint Paula, in Mexico City
1673   Archbishop of Mexico Payo Enríquez de Ribera becomes
        viceroy of New Spain

---

† The following chronology has followed closely that published in Sor Juana Inés de la
  Cruz, *Obra selecta*, 2 vols, ed. Margo Glantz (Caracas: Biblioteca Ayacucho, 1994), pp.
  567–78. Dates in Sor Juana's personal life are approximate: many depend on her birth-
  date, variously understood to have been in 1648 or 1651. This chronology dates early
  events in Sor Juana's life following the generally accepted earlier birthdate.

1674 Death of Leonor Carreto, vicereine of Mancera, in Tepeaca, Mexico

1676 The first set of Sor Juana's *villancicos* are published anonymously

Manuel Fernández de Santa Cruz becomes bishop of Puebla

1677 Sor Juana's *villancicos* for "Saint Peter Nolasco" and "Saint Peter Apostle" are published anonymously

1678 Spanish translation of the sermons of António Vieira is published in Madrid

1679 *Villancicos* for the "Assumption of the Most Saintly Mary" are published under Sor Juana's name

1680 Sor Juana designs one of the two ephemeral triumphal arches for the festivities to receive the new viceroy, Count of Paredes, Marquis de la Laguna

Publication of *Allegorical Neptune,* a description and defense of the arch

Sor Juana becomes friends with the vicereine, Maria Luisa Gonzaga Manrique de Lara, "Lysi" in many of her poems

Debate between Carlos de Sigüenza y Góngora and Eusebio Kino, Austrian Jesuit, over the meaning of the 1680 comet

1681 Sor Juana writes a letter to the Jesuit Antonio Núñez de Miranda, releasing him from his position as her confessor

1682 Francisco de Aguiar y Seijas becomes archbishop of Mexico

1683 *Villancicos* for "Saint Peter" published

Carlos de Sigüenza y Góngora publishes *Parthenic Triumph,* the compendium of poems from the poetic competition at the Royal and Pontifical University of Mexico, including two by Sor Juana who has entered under the pseudonyms Juan Saénz del Cauri and Felipe Salayses Gutiérrez

First performance of Sor Juana's courtly play, *House of Trials*

1685 *Villancicos* for "Most Saintly Mary in Her Triumphal Assumption" printed under Sor Juana's name

1686 Arrival of the new viceroy, Melchor de Portocarrero, Count of Monclova

1688 Sor Juana writes the comedic play *Love Is a Greater Labyrinth* and the mystery play *The Divine Narcissus*

The Marquis and Marquisa de la Laguna leave Mexico; the Count of Monclova is sent to the viceroyalty of Peru; the Count of Galve, Gaspar de Sandoval y Silva, becomes viceroy of New Spain

1689 *Villancicos* for the "Conception of the Virgin" published

Castalian Inundation, a collection of Sor Juana's writings, is published in Madrid

The comedy *Love Is a Greater Labyrinth* is performed in celebration of the viceroy Count of Galve's birthday

1690   *Villancicos* performed in the Metropolitan Cathedral are attributed to Sor Juana
The Divine Narcissus is published in Mexico City
In Puebla, Bishop Manuel Fernández de Santa Cruz publishes Sor Juana's "Critique of a Sermon" under the title *Athenagoric Letter* and includes a prologue under the pseudonym Sor Filotea
Poems of the Singular American Poetess, a revised edition of *Castalian Inundation*, published in Madrid

1691   Pens "Response of the Poet to the Very Eminent Sor Filotea de la Cruz," defending herself against the prologue of the *Athenagoric Letter*; in this, she mentions the circulation in manuscript of her poem "First Dream"
Villancicos for Saint Catherine, sung in the Cathedral of Oaxaca

1692   *Second Volume* of Sor Juana's works is published in Seville
Count of Paredes dies in Spain
June 8: the largest riot in the history of Mexico City occurs following flooding and corn shortages; rioters ransack and burn the central market and viceregal palace

1693   Sor Juana reconciles with her confessor, Antonio Núñez de Miranda
Signs *Petition in Juridical Form*; disperses her library and scientific instruments

1694   Sor Juana ratifies her religious vows and declares her defense of the Immaculate Conception
March 5: Sor Juana signs declaration of faith in blood, declaring that she will abandon profane studies

1695   Antonio Núñez de Miranda, Sor Juana's confessor, dies
April 17: Sor Juana dies as the result of an epidemic in Mexico City; Carlos de Sigüenza y Góngora delivers the funeral oration, now lost

1696   Manuel Fernández de Santa Cruz renounces the archbishopric of Mexico and the viceroyalty of New Spain

1697   António Vieira dies

1698   Francisco Aguiar y Seijas dies

1699   Manuel Fernández de Santa Cruz dies

1700   Carlos de Sigüenza y Góngora dies
Fame and Posthumous Works published in Madrid under the patronage of Juan Ignacio Castrena y Ursua; the publication contains the earliest biography of Sor Juana, written by Diego de Calleja

1713   Juan de Miranda paints a posthumous portrait of Sor Juana

1750   Miguel Cabrera paints a copy of Juan de Miranda's posthumous portrait of Sor Juana

Selected Bibliography

The following bibliography emphasizes key works in English but also includes important materials in Spanish. When possible, selections of scholarship found only in Spanish have been complemented by articles in English on similar themes by the same author.

• Indicates works included or excerpted in this Norton Critical Edition.

Selected Early Editions

• Cruz, Sor Juana Inés de la. *Inundación castálida*. Madrid: Juan García Infanzón, 1689.
• ———. *Fama y obras posthumas del Fenix de Mexico*. Madrid: Manuel Ruiz de Murga, 1700.
• ———. *Segundo volumen de las obras de Soror Juana Inés de la Cruz*. Sevilla: Tomas Lopez de Haro, 1692.

Selected Modern Editions

• Alatorre, Antonio. "La carta de Sor Juana al P. Núñez (1682)." *Nueva Revista de Filología Hispánica* 35.2 (1987): 591–673.
Cruz, Sor Juana Inés de la. *Inundación castálida*. Madrid: Castália, 1982.
———. *Neptuno alegórico*. Madrid: Cátedra, 2009.
———. *Obras completas*. 4 vols. Mexico: Fondo de Cultura Económica, 1951.
———. *Obras completas*. 2nd ed. 4 vols. Vol. 1, Mexico: Fondo de Cultura Económica, 2009.
———. *Obras selecta*. 2 vols. Caracas: Biblioteca Ayacucho, 1994.
———. "Respuesta a la muy ilustre Sor Filotea (1691)." Unpublished edition by Jeremy Lawrance, 2002. http://faculty.arts.ubc.ca/jbmurray/teaching/files/span 364_5.pdf (access date 11/25/2015).
Pérez-Amador Adam, Alberto. *El precipicio de Faetón: Edición y comento de Primero Sueño de Sor Juana Inés de la Cruz*. Frankfurt am Main/México DF: Iberoamericana/Vervuert/Universidad Autónoma Metropolitana, 2015.

Selected Translations

Cruz, Sor Juana Inés de la. *The Answer/La Respuesta*. Trans. Electa Arenal and Amanda Powell. 2nd ed. New York: Feminist Press, 2009.
———. *Poems, Protest, and a Dream*. Trans. Margaret Sayers Peden. New York: Penguin, 1997.
———. *Selected Works*. Trans. Edith Grossman. New York: Norton, 2014.
———. *A Sor Juana Anthology*. Trans. Alan S. Trueblood. Cambridge: Harvard University Press, 1988.
———. *Sor Juana Inés de la Cruz: Selected Writings*. Trans. Pamela Kirk Rappaport. Mahwah, NJ: Paulist Press, 2005.

Scott, Nina. "'If You Are Not Pleased to Favor Me, Put Me out of Your Mind . . .':
Gender and Authority in Sor Juana Inés de la Cruz and a Translation of Her
Letter to the Reverend Father Maestro Antonio Núñez of the Society of Jesus."
Women's Studies International Forum 11.5 (1988): 429–38.

Criticism

Alatorre, Antonio. *Sor Juana a través de los siglos (1668–1910)*. 2 vols. Mexico:
Colegio de Mexico, Colegio Nacional, UNAM, 2007.
Arellano, Ignacio. "La nieve negra de Sor Juana: de Anaxágoras a Enrique Lihn,
pasando por San Agustín a Ramírez de Prado." *Romance Notes* 54.2 (2014):
169–76.
Arenal, Electa. "The Convent as Catalyst for Autonomy: Two Hispanic Nuns
of the Seventeenth Century." *Women in Hispanic Literature: Icons and
Fallen Idols*. Ed. Beth Miller. Berkeley: University of California Press, 1983.
147–83.
———. "Where Woman Is Creator of the Wor(l)d, or, Sor Juana's Discourses
on Method." *Feminist Perspectives on Sor Juana Inés de la Cruz* Ed. Stepha-
nie Merrim. Detroit: Wayne State University Press, 1991. 124–41.
Arenal, Electa and Amanda Powell. "Introduction." *The Answer/La Respuesta*.
Ed. Electa Arenal and Amanda Powell. New York: Feminist Press, 2009. 1–37.
Benassy-Berling, Marie-Cécile. *Humanismo y religión en Sor Juana Inés de la
Cruz*. Trans. Laura López de Belair. Mexico: UNAM, 1983.
Bénassy-Berling, Marie-Cécile. *Sor Juana Inés de la Cruz: Une femme de letters
exceptionnelle, Mexique XVIIe Siècle*. Paris: L'Harmattan, 2010.
Bergmann, Emilie. "Optics and Varieties of the Visual in Luis de Góngora and
Sor Juana Inés de la Cruz." *Writing for the Eyes in the Spanish Golden Age*.
Ed. Frederick A. de Armas. Cranbury, NJ: Associated University Presses,
2004. 151–65.
———. "Sor Juana Inés de la Cruz: Dreaming in a Double Voice." *Women,
Culture and Politics in Latin America*. Ed. Janet Greenberg et al. Berkeley, CA:
Berkeley University Press, 1990. 151–72.
Bergmann, Emilie, and Stacey Schlau, eds. *Approaches to Teaching the Works
of Sor Juana Inés de la Cruz*. New York: Modern Language Association, 2007.
Buxó, José Pascual. *Sor Juana Inés de la Cruz: amor y conocimiento*. Mexico:
UNAM, 1996.
———. *Sor Juana Inés de la Cruz: lectura barroca de la poesia*. Mexico:
Renacimiento, 2006.
Findlen, Paula. "A Jesuit's Books in the New World: Athanasius Kircher and His
American Readers." *Athanasius Kircher: The Last Man Who Knew Everything*.
Ed. Paula Findlen. New York: Routledge, 2004. 329–64.
Fiol-Matta, Licia. "Visions of Gender: Sor Juana and the *First Dream*." *Nepantla*
4.2 (2003): 345–74.
Franco, Jean. *Plotting Women: Gender and Representation in Mexico*. New
York: Columbia University Press, 1989. Chap. 2.
Gaos, José. "El sueño de un sueño." *Historia Mexicana* 10.1 (1960): 54–71.
Gates, Eunice Joiner. "Reminiscences of Góngora in the Works of Sor Juana Inés
de la Cruz." *PMLA* 54.4 (1939): 1041–58.
Glantz, Margo. "The Construction of a Figure of Genius: Sor Juana Inés de la
Cruz." *Journal of Latin American Cultural Studies* 4.2 (1995): 175–89.
———. "Las finezas de Sor Juana: loa de *El Divino Narciso*." *Sor Juana Inés de
la Cruz: ¿Hagiografía o autobiografía?* Mexico: Grijalbo, 1995. 151–68.
———. "Prólogo." *Obra selecta*. Ed. Margo Glantz. Caracas: Biblioteca Aya-
cucho, 1994. ix–xc.
———. *Sor Juana: La comparación y la hipérbole*. Mexico: Conaculta, 2000.
———, ed. *Sor Juana Inés de la Cruz y sus contemporáneos*. Mexico: UNAM/
Centro de Estudios de la historia de México, 1998.

SELECTED BIBLIOGRAPHY 317

Hill, Ruth. *Sceptres and Sciences in the Spains*. Liverpool: Liverpool University Press, 2000. Chap. 1.

Johnson, Christopher. *Hyperboles: The Rhetoric of Excess in Baroque Literature and Thought*. Cambridge: Harvard University Press, 2010. Chaps. 7 and 8.

Kirk, Stephanie. "Gender and the Writing of Piety in New Spain." *American Literary History* 26.1 (2014): 6–27.

———. "Pain, Knowledge, and the Female Body in Sor Juana Inés de la Cruz." *Revista Hispánica Moderna* 61.1 (2008): 38–54.

———. *Sor Juana Ines de la Cruz and the Gender Politics of Culture in Colonial Mexico*. New York: Ashgate, 2016.

———. "Sor Margarida Ignácia's *Apologia a Favor do Reverendo P. António Vieyra*: An Eighteenth-Century Reply to Sor Juana Inés de la Cruz's *Carta Atenagórica*." *Colonial Latin American Review* 21.2 (2012): 267–91.

• Lavrin, Asunción. "Sor Juana Inés de la Cruz: autoridad y obediencia en su entorno religioso." *Revista Iberoamericana* 61.172–73 (1995): 605–22.

———. "Unlike Sor Juana? The Model Nun in the Religious Literature of Mexico." In *Feminist Perspectives on Sor Juana Inés de la Cruz*. Ed. Stephanie Merrim. Detroit, MI: Wayne State University Press, 1999. 61–85.

• Leonard, Irving. *Baroque Times in Old Mexico*. Ann Arbor: University of Michigan Press, 1959. Chap. 12.

Lopez Portillo, Carmen Beatriz, ed. *Sor Juana y su mundo: una mirada actual. Memorias del congreso internacional*. Mexico: UCSJ/UNESCO/Fondo de Cultura Económica, 1998.

Ludmer, Josefina. "Tricks of the Weak." In *Feminist Perspectives on Sor Juana Inés de la Cruz*. Ed. Stephanie Merrim. Detroit, MI: Wayne State University Press, 1991. pp. 86–93.

• Martínez-San Miguel, Yolanda. *Saberes americanos: subalternidad y epistemología en los escritos de Sor Juana*. Pittsburgh, PA: Instituto Internacional de Literatura Iberoamericana, 1999.

• Menéndez y Pelayo, Marcelino. *Antología de poetas Hispano-Americanos*. Vol. 1. Madrid: Real Academia Española, 1893.

Merrim, Stephanie. *Early Modern Women's Writing and Sor Juana Inés de la Cruz*. Nashville, TN: Vanderbilt University Press, 1999.

———, ed. *Feminist Perspectives on Sor Juana Inés de la Cruz*. Detroit: Wayne State University Press, 1999.

• ———. "Toward a Feminist Reading of Sor Juana Inés de la Cruz: Past, Present and Future Directions in Sor Juana Criticism." *Feminist Perspectives on Sor Juana Inés de la Cruz*. Ed. Stephanie Merrim. Detroit, MI: Wayne State University Press, 1999. 11–37.

More, Anna. "Sor Juana's Appetite: Body, Mind, and Vitality in 'First Dream.'" *The Cultural Politics of Blood, 1500–1900*. Ed. Kimberly Anne Coles, Ralph Bauer, Zita Nunes, and Carla L. Peterson. New York: Palgrave Macmillan, 2015. 127–45.

Myers, Kathleen Ann. *Neither Saints nor Sinners: Writing the Lives of Women in Spanish America*. New York: Oxford University Press, 2003. Chap. 4.

Paz, Octavio. *Sor Juana Inés de la Cruz o las trampas de la fe*. 3rd ed. Mexico: Fondo de Cultura Económica, 1983.

———. *Sor Juana: Her Life and Her World*. Trans. Margaret Sayers Peden. London: Faber & Faber, 1988.

• ———. *Sor Juana or, The Traps of Faith*. Trans. Margaret Sayers Peden. Cambridge: Belknap, Press, 1988.

Ortiz, Mario. "La musa y el melopeo: los diálogos transatlánticos entre Sor Juana Inés de la Cruz y Pietro Cerone." *Hispanic Review* 75.3 (2007): 243–64.

———. "Musical Settings of Sor Juana's Works and Music in Works of Sor Juana." *Approaches to Teaching Sor Juana Inés de la Cruz*. Ed. Emilie Bergmann and Stacey Schlau. New York: Modern Language Association, 2007. 238–46.

Perelmuter Pérez, Rosa. "*The Answer to Sor Filotea*: A Rhetorical Approach." *Approaches to Teaching Sor Juana Inés de la Cruz*. Ed. Emilie Bergmann and Stacey Schlau. New York: Modern Language Association, 2007. 186–92.

———. "La estructura retórica de la Respuesta a Sor Filotea." *Hispanic Review* 51.2 (1983): 147–58.

Pérez-Amador Adam, Alberto. *De finezas y libertad: acerca de la Carta Atenagórica de Sor Juana Inés de la Cruz y las ideas de Domingo de Báñez*. Mexico: Fondo de Cultura Ecónomica, 2011.

Poot Herrera, Sara, ed. *Sor Juana y su mundo. Una mirada actual*. Mexico: Universidad del Claustro de Sor Juana, 1995.

Rabin, Lisa. "Speaking to Silent Ladies: Images of Beauty and Politics in Poetic Portraits of Women from Petrarch to Sor Juana Inés de la Cruz." *MLN* 112.2 (March 1997): 147–65.

Ricard, Robert. "Antônio Vieira y Sor Juana Inés de la Cruz." *Revista de Indias* 43–44 (January–June 1951): 61–87.

Rivers, Elías L. "Sor Juana's Dream: In Search of a Scientific Vision." *Approaches to Teaching Sor Juana Inés de la Cruz*. Ed. Emilie Bergmann and Stacey Schlau. New York: Modern Language Association, 2007. 126–34.

Rodríguez Garrido, José Antonio. *La Carta Atenagórica de Sor Juana: textos inéditos de una polémica*. Mexico: UNAM, 2004.

Sabat de Rivers, Georgina. "A Feminist Rereading of Sor Juana's *Dream*." *Feminist Perspectives on Sor Juana Inés de la Cruz*. Ed. Stephanie Merrim. Detroit, MI: Wayne State University Press, 1991. 142–61.

———. "Introducción biográfica y crítica." *Inundación Castálida*. Madrid: Castalia, 1982. 9–86.

———. "Love in Some of Sor Juana's Sonnets." *Colonial Latin American Review* 4.2 (1995): 101–24.

———. *El "Sueño" de Sor Juana Inés de la Cruz: tradiciones literarias y originalidad*. London: Tamesis, 1977.

Sánchez Robayna, Andrés. *Para leer "Primero Sueño" de Sor Juana Inés de la Cruz*. Mexico: Fondo de Cultura Económica, 1991.

Schons, Dorothy. "Some Obscure Points in the Life of Sor Juana Inés de la Cruz." *Feminist Perspectives on Sor Juana Inés de la Cruz*. Ed. Stephanie Merrim. Detroit, MI: Wayne State University Press, 1991. 38–60.

Scott, Nina. "*La gran turba de las que merecieron nombres*: Sor Juana's Foremothers in *La Respuesta a Sor Filotea*." *Coded Encounters: Writing, Gender, and Ethnicity in Colonial Latin America*. Ed. Francisco Javier Cevallos-Candau, Jeffrey A. Cole, Nina M. Scott, and Nicomedes Suárez-Araúz. Amherst: University of Massachussetts Press, 1994. 206–23.

Soriano Vallès, Alejandro. *El Primero Sueño de Sor Juana Inés de la Cruz: bases tomistas*. Mexico: Universidad Nacional Autónoma de Mexico, 2000.

———. *Sor Juana Inés de la Cruz: Doncella del verbo*. Hermosillo, Sonora: Editorial Garabatos, 2010.

Tenorio, Martha Lilia. *Los villancicos de Sor Juana*. Mexico: El Colegio de Mexico, 1999.

General and Historical Context

Adorno, Rolena. *The Polemics of Possession in Spanish American Narrative*. New Haven, CT: Yale University Press, 2007.

Arenal, Electa, and Stacey Schlau. *Untold Sisters: Hispanic Nuns in Their Own Works*. Albuquerque: University of New Mexico Press, 1989.

Brading, D. A. *The First America: The Spanish Monarchy, Creole Patriots, and the Liberal State 1492–1867*. Cambridge: Cambridge University Press, 1991.

Calvo, Hortensia, and Beatriz Colombí. *Cartas de Lysi: La mecenas de Sor Juana Inés de la Cruz en correspondencia inédita*. Frankfurt am Main/México DF: Iberoamericana/Vervuert/Bonilla Artigas Editores, 2015.

Cañeque, Alejandro. *The King's Living Image: The Culture and Politics of Viceregal Power in Colonial Mexico*. New York: Routledge, 2004.

Cope, R. Douglas. *The Limits of Racial Domination: Plebeian Society in Colonial Mexico City, 1660–1720*. Madison: University of Wisconsin Press, 1994.

Elliott, J. H. *Empires of the Atlantic World: Britain and Spain in America 1492–1830*. New Haven, CT: Yale University Press, 2006.

———. *Spain and Its World, 1500–1700*. New Haven, CT: Yale University Press, 1989.

Kirk, Stephanie. *Convent Life in Colonial Mexico: A Tale of Two Communities*. Gainesville: University of Florida Press, 2007.

Lavrin, Asunción. *Brides of Christ: Conventual Life in Colonial Mexico*. Stanford, CA: Stanford University Press, 2008.

• Martínez, María Elena. *Genealogical Fictions:* Limpieza de Sangre, *Religion, and Gender in Colonial Mexico*. Stanford, CA: Stanford University Press, 2008.

More, Anna. *Baroque Sovereignty: Carlos de Sigüenza y Góngora and the Colonial Mexican Archive*. Philadelphia: University of Pennsylvania Press, 2013.

———. "Cosmopolitanism and Scientific Reason in New Spain: Sigüenza y Góngora and the Dispute over the 1680 Comet." *Science in the Spanish and Portuguese Empires, 1500–1800*. Ed. Daniela Bleichmar, Paula De Vos, Kristin Huffine, and Kevin Sheehan. Stanford, CA: Stanford University Press, 2009. 115–31.

• Ovid. *Metamorphoses*. Trans. Charles Martin. New York: Norton, 2004.

• *Provisiones, cédulas, capítulos de ordenanças, instruciones y cartas libradas y despachadas en diferentes tiempos por sus Magestades los Señores Reyes Católicos Don Fernando y Doña Ysabel*, Madrid: En la Imprenta Real, 1596.

Santa Cruz, Manuel Fernandez de. "Carta de sor Filotea de la Cruz." Unpublished edition by Jeremy Lawrance, 2002. http://faculty.arts.ubc.ca/jbmurray/teaching/files/span364_5.pdf (access date 11/25/2015).

• Teresa de Ávila, Saint. *The Life of Saint Teresa: Written by Herself*. Trans. John Dalton. London: Dolmon, 1851.

———. *La vida/Las moradas*. Madrid: Planeta, 1989.

Weber, Alison. *Teresa de Avila and the Rhetoric of Femininity*. Princeton, NJ: Princeton University Press, 1989.

Contemporary Influences

Anderson, Paul. *Hunger's Brides*. Toronto: Random House, 2004.

Bemberg, María Luisa. *Yo, la Peor de Todas*. 105 min. 1990. Film.

• Bergmann, Emilie. "Abjection and Ambiguity: Lesbian Desire in Bemberg's *Yo, la peor de todas*." *Hispanisms and Homosexualities*. Ed. Sylvia Molloy and Robert McKee Irwin. Durham, NC: Duke University Press. 229–47.

Gaspar de Alba, Alicia. *Sor Juana's Second Dream*. Albuquerque: University of New Mexico Press, 1999.

———. *[Un]framing the "Bad Woman": Sor Juana, Malinche, Coyolxauhqui, and Other Rebels with a Cause* Austin: University of Texas Press, 2014. Chaps. 1 and 7.

Hind, Emily. "The Sor Juana Archetype in Recent Works by Mexican Women Writers." *Hispanófila* 47.3 (2004): 89–103.

———. "Sor Juana, and Official Habit: Twentieth-Century Mexican Culture." *Approaches to Teaching Sor Juana Inés de la Cruz*. Ed. Emilie Bergmann and Stacey Schlau. New York: Modern Language Association, 2007. 247–55.

Mesa-Bains, Amalia. "The Latino Cabinet of Curiosities: A Postcolonial Reopening." *Museum and Curatorial Studies Review* 1.1 (2013): 27–52.

• Rodríguez, Jesusa. "Interview with Jesusa Rodríguez: On Sor Juana Inés de la Cruz (2010)." 35:44, 2010. hemisphericinstitute.org/hemi/es/modules/item/2227-interview-jesusa-sorjuana.

————. "*Jesusa en Almoloya (Pastorela Virtual)*." *Debate Feminista* 12 (Octubre 1995): 395–411.
————. "Jesusa Rodriguez: Sor Juana Striptease." 2007. Hemispheric Institute. hemisphericinstitute.org/hemi/en/enc07-performances/item/955-enc07-jesusa-rodriguez.
Santi, Enrico Mario. "Lecturas de restitución: Sor Juana y Octavio Paz." *Cuadernos del Lazarillo* 8 (Mayo–Agosto 1995): 37–41.